Best of Bridge
Home
Cooking

250 Easy
& Delicious Recipes

Robert
ROSE

For complete cataloguing information, see page 349.

Disclaimer
The recipes in this book have been carefully tested by our kitchen and our tasters. To the best of our knowledge, they are safe and nutritious for ordinary use and users. For those people with food or other allergies, or who have special food requirements or health issues, please read the suggested contents of each recipe carefully and determine whether or not they may create a problem for you. All recipes are used at the risk of the consumer.

We cannot be responsible for any hazards, loss or damage that may occur as a result of any recipe use.

For those with special needs, allergies, requirements or health problems, in the event of any doubt, please contact your medical adviser prior to the use of any recipe.

Design and Production: Joseph Gisini/PageWave Graphics Inc.
Editor: Sue Sumeraj
Proofreader: Kelly Jones
Indexer: Gillian Watts
Photographers: Colin Erricson and Mark T. Shapiro
Associate Photographer (for Colin): Matt Johannsson
Food Stylists: Kathryn Robertson, Michael Elliott and Kate Bush
Prop Stylist: Charlene Erricson

Cover image: Chicken and Vegetable Stew (page 129)

The publisher gratefully acknowledges the financial support of our publishing program by the Government of Canada through the Canada Book Fund.

Published by Robert Rose Inc.
120 Eglinton Avenue East, Suite 800, Toronto, Ontario, Canada M4P 1E2
Tel: (416) 322-6552 Fax: (416) 322-6936
www.robertrose.ca

Printed and bound in China

1 2 3 4 5 6 7 8 9 PPLS 23 22 21 20 19 18 17 16 15

CONTENTS

INTRODUCTION

THERE'S A REASON THE KITCHEN IS THE HEART OF THE HOME: THAT'S WHERE THE FOOD IS.

COOKING FOR AND FEEDING PEOPLE IS THE ULTIMATE COMFORT, CONNECTING PEOPLE IN A WAY NOTHING ELSE CAN. WE EAT TO SOCIALIZE, CELEBRATE AND CARE FOR EACH OTHER. FOOD BRINGS US TOGETHER, NOURISHING US NOT ONLY PHYSICALLY, BUT EMOTIONALLY AND CULTURALLY; IT BRINGS JOY, BUT ALSO THE SENSE OF WELL-BEING THAT COMES WITH A DAILY ROUTINE. AT HOME, THE DINNER TABLE HAS BECOME A GATHERING PLACE, WHERE FOOD ACTS AS A CATALYST FOR CONVERSATION, A PLACE TO DECOMPRESS AND COMPARE NOTES, TO UNPLUG AND RECONNECT.

THIS WAS THE INSPIRATION BEHIND *BEST OF BRIDGE HOME COOKING*: THE IDEA THAT OUR DAY-TO-DAY MEALS MAKE UP SUCH A BIG PART OF OUR LIVES AND CREATE OUR FOOD CULTURE. EVERYONE CAN RELATE TO HOME COOKING; GROWING UP, WE ESTABLISH A BASIC KNOWLEDGE OF INGREDIENTS AND GET TO KNOW OUR WAY AROUND THE KITCHEN, AND THE MORE WE COOK FROM SCRATCH, THE MORE OUR KIDS DEVELOP ESSENTIAL CULINARY SKILLS AND BUILD MEMORIES THAT WILL LAST A LIFETIME.

WE NEVER COOK ALONE — WE ALWAYS HAVE HISTORY AND INSPIRING FRIENDS AND RELATIVES BEHIND US. LIKE THE BEST MEALS, THIS BOOK WAS A COLLABORATIVE EFFORT: A GROUP OF COOKS IN THEIR OWN HOME KITCHENS, COMPILING SIMPLE RECIPES FOR MEALS WE HOPE WILL BECOME FAVORITES IN YOURS.

BREAKFAST, BREADS & MUFFINS

HOMEMADE GRANOLA

STORE IN A JAR ON THE COUNTERTOP
FOR A QUICK BREAKFAST OR SNACK.

4 CUPS	LARGE-FLAKE (OLD-FASHIONED) OATS	I L
I CUP	CHOPPED PECANS OR WALNUTS OR SLICED OR SLIVERED ALMONDS	250 ML
$\frac{1}{2}$ CUP	SHREDDED COCONUT	125 ML
$\frac{1}{4}$ CUP	SUNFLOWER OR SESAME SEEDS	60 ML
I TSP	GROUND CINNAMON	5 ML
$\frac{1}{4}$ TSP	SALT	I ML
$\frac{1}{3}$ CUP	PACKED BROWN SUGAR	75 ML
$\frac{1}{2}$ CUP	HONEY OR MAPLE SYRUP	125 ML
$\frac{1}{4}$ CUP	VEGETABLE OIL OR MELTED BUTTER	60 ML
$\frac{1}{2}$ CUP	DRIED CRANBERRIES, RAISINS OR SLIVERED APRICOTS	125 ML

PREHEAT OVEN TO 325°F (160°C). IN A LARGE BOWL, STIR TOGETHER OATS, NUTS, COCONUT, SEEDS, CINNAMON AND SALT. IN A SMALL BOWL, STIR TOGETHER BROWN SUGAR, HONEY AND OIL. POUR OVER THE OAT MIXTURE AND STIR WELL. SPREAD OUT ONTO A LARGE RIMMED BAKING SHEET AND BAKE FOR 30 MINUTES, STIRRING ONCE OR TWICE, UNTIL GOLDEN. STIR IN CRANBERRIES. LET COOL. MAKES 7 CUPS (1.75 L).

HOT MULTIGRAIN CEREAL

SLOW COOKER RECIPE

NOT ONLY ARE HOT MULTIGRAIN CEREALS DELICIOUS, THEY ARE ALSO HIGHLY NUTRITIOUS, PROVIDING A WIDE RANGE OF NUTRIENTS. YOUR SLOW COOKER TRANSFORMS THEM INTO AN EASY, NO-FUSS OPTION.

I CUP	MULTIGRAIN CEREAL	250 ML
$1/4$ TSP	SALT	I ML
4 CUPS	WATER	I L
2	ALL-PURPOSE APPLES, PEELED AND THICKLY SLICED	2
$1/4$ to $1/3$ CUP	RAISINS (OPTIONAL)	60 to 75 ML

GREASE THE STONEWARE OF A SMALL (MAXIMUM $3^1/_2$-QUART) SLOW COOKER. IN PREPARED STONEWARE, COMBINE CEREAL, SALT, WATER AND APPLES. COVER AND COOK ON LOW FOR 8 HOURS OR OVERNIGHT. JUST BEFORE SERVING, PLACE RAISINS (IF USING) IN A MICROWAVE-SAFE BOWL AND COVER WITH WATER. MICROWAVE FOR 20 SECONDS TO SOFTEN. ADD TO HOT CEREAL. STIR WELL AND SERVE. SERVES 6.

TIP: YOU CAN BUY MULTIGRAIN CEREALS PREPACKAGED, USUALLY IN 3-, 5- OR 7-GRAIN COMBINATIONS, OR YOU CAN MAKE YOUR OWN BY COMBINING YOUR FAVORITE GRAINS. STORE MULTIGRAIN CEREAL IN AN AIRTIGHT CONTAINER IN A COOL, DRY PLACE.

VARIATION: IF YOU PREFER, USE $1/2$ CUP (125 ML) EACH MULTIGRAIN CEREAL AND ROLLED OR STEEL-CUT OATS.

HOT OATMEAL

SLOW COOKER RECIPE

ROLLED OATS, OFTEN CALLED PORRIDGE WHEN COOKED, ARE PROBABLY THE MOST POPULAR BREAKFAST CEREAL. THEY COOK UP BEAUTIFULLY IN THE SLOW COOKER.

1¼ CUPS	ROLLED OATS	300 ML
½ TSP	SALT	2 ML
4 CUPS	WATER	1 L

GREASE THE STONEWARE OF A SMALL (MAXIMUM 3½-QUART) SLOW COOKER. IN PREPARED STONEWARE, COMBINE OATS, SALT AND WATER. COVER AND COOK ON LOW FOR 8 HOURS OR OVERNIGHT. STIR WELL AND SERVE. SERVES 6.

TIP: IF YOU CHOOSE TO HALVE THIS RECIPE, USE A 1½- TO 2-QUART SLOW COOKER.

YOU KNOW YOU'RE A TEACHER IF YOU CAN TELL IT'S A FULL MOON WITHOUT LOOKING OUTSIDE.

OATMEAL WITH APPLES AND CRANBERRIES

FAST-AND-EASY RECIPE

THE ADDITION OF APPLES AND DRIED CRANBERRIES MAKES OATMEAL EVEN MORE APPEALING AND NOURISHING.

1 1/3 CUPS	WATER OR APPLE JUICE	325 ML
PINCH	SALT (OPTIONAL)	PINCH
2/3 CUP	LARGE-FLAKE (OLD-FASHIONED) ROLLED OATS	150 ML
1	APPLE, PEELED AND CHOPPED	1
1/4 CUP	DRIED CRANBERRIES	60 ML
	MILK	
	CINNAMON SUGAR, HONEY OR MAPLE SYRUP	

IN A MEDIUM SAUCEPAN, BRING WATER TO A BOIL. SEASON WITH SALT (IF USING). STIR IN OATS, APPLE AND CRANBERRIES AND RETURN TO A BOIL, STIRRING CONSTANTLY. REDUCE HEAT TO LOW, PARTIALLY COVER AND SIMMER, STIRRING OCCASIONALLY, FOR 5 TO 7 MINUTES OR UNTIL OATS ARE TENDER. THIN WITH MILK TO DESIRED CONSISTENCY. SWEETEN TO TASTE. SERVES 2.

MICROWAVE METHOD: IN A LARGE 8-CUP (2 L) GLASS MEASURE OR CASSEROLE DISH, COMBINE WATER, SALT, OATS, APPLE AND CRANBERRIES. MICROWAVE, UNCOVERED, ON HIGH FOR 4 TO 6 MINUTES, STIRRING TWICE, UNTIL MIXTURE COMES TO A FULL ROLLING BOIL AND THICKENS. (WATCH CAREFULLY TO PREVENT MIXTURE FROM BOILING OVER.) THIN WITH MILK TO DESIRED CONSISTENCY. SWEETEN TO TASTE.

DUTCH BABY

1 TBSP	VEGETABLE OIL	15 ML
1 TBSP	BUTTER	15 ML
2	LARGE EGGS	2
1/2 CUP	ALL-PURPOSE FLOUR	125 ML
1/2 CUP	MILK	125 ML
PINCH	SALT	PINCH
	FRESH BERRIES	
	CONFECTIONERS' (ICING) SUGAR	
	LEMON WEDGES	

PLACE THE OIL AND BUTTER IN A 9- OR 10-INCH (23 OR 25 CM) OVENPROOF SKILLET. PUT THE SKILLET IN THE OVEN AND PREHEAT TO 425°F (220°C). IN A BOWL, USING A WHISK OR AN ELECTRIC MIXER, BEAT EGGS UNTIL FROTHY. BEAT IN FLOUR, MILK AND SALT AND BEAT UNTIL SMOOTH. (OR COMBINE EVERYTHING IN A BLENDER.) REMOVE THE PAN FROM THE OVEN AND POUR IN THE BATTER. BAKE FOR 15 TO 20 MINUTES OR UNTIL PUFFED AND GOLDEN. SERVE TOPPED WITH BERRIES, CONFECTIONERS' SUGAR AND A SQUEEZE OF LEMON. SERVES 4.

OVERNIGHT OVEN FRENCH TOAST

HERE'S A GREAT BREAKFAST DISH THAT CAN BE ASSEMBLED A DAY AHEAD. WHEN READY TO SERVE, ARRANGE THE TOASTS ON GREASED BAKING SHEETS AND POP IN THE OVEN WHILE YOU MAKE THE COFFEE AND FRY THE BACON.

4	LARGE EGGS	4
I CUP	MILK	250 ML
I TBSP	GRANULATED SUGAR	15 ML
I TSP	VANILLA EXTRACT	5 ML
12	SLICES DAY-OLD FRENCH BREAD, CUT $\frac{3}{4}$ INCH (2 CM) THICK	12
3 TBSP	MELTED BUTTER	45 ML

IN A BOWL, WHISK TOGETHER EGGS, MILK, SUGAR AND VANILLA. ARRANGE BREAD SLICES IN A SINGLE LAYER IN A 13- BY 9-INCH (33 BY 23 CM) BAKING DISH. POUR EGG MIXTURE OVER TOP. TURN SLICES OVER AND LET STAND UNTIL EGG MIXTURE IS ABSORBED. COVER AND REFRIGERATE UNTIL READY TO BAKE. (RECIPE CAN BE PREPARED UP TO THIS POINT THE NIGHT BEFORE.)

PREHEAT OVEN TO 425°F (220°C). GREASE A BAKING SHEET OR LINE IT WITH PARCHMENT PAPER. ARRANGE TOASTS IN A SINGLE LAYER ON PREPARED SHEET AND BRUSH TOPS WITH HALF OF MELTED BUTTER. BAKE FOR 10 MINUTES. TURN SLICES OVER; BRUSH TOPS WITH THE REMAINING MELTED BUTTER. BAKE FOR 8 MINUTES OR UNTIL PUFFED AND GOLDEN. SERVES 4.

EGG TOMATO MUFFIN MELT

THESE YUMMY EGGS ARE NOT JUST FOR BREAKFAST — THEY ALSO MAKE A GREAT SUPPER DISH WHEN YOU'RE LOOKING FOR SOMETHING FAST AND EASY.

	BUTTER	
4	THIN SLICES SMOKED HAM	4
I	LARGE TOMATO, CUT INTO 4 THICK SLICES	I
	SALT AND FRESHLY GROUND BLACK PEPPER	
4	LARGE EGGS	4
2	ENGLISH MUFFINS, SPLIT	2
4	THIN SLICES SHARP (OLD) CHEDDAR CHEESE	4

PREHEAT BROILER. IN A LARGE NONSTICK SKILLET, MELT 2 TSP (10 ML) BUTTER OVER MEDIUM HEAT AND COOK HAM SLICES FOR I MINUTE PER SIDE OR UNTIL LIGHTLY BROWNED. TRANSFER TO A PLATE AND KEEP WARM. ADD TOMATO SLICES TO SKILLET AND COOK FOR ABOUT 30 SECONDS PER SIDE OR UNTIL SOFTENED. SEASON TO TASTE WITH SALT AND PEPPER.

MEANWHILE, POACH, PAN-FRY OR SCRAMBLE EGGS AS DESIRED. TOAST ENGLISH MUFFINS; SPREAD WITH BUTTER, IF DESIRED. ARRANGE CUT SIDE UP ON BAKING SHEET. LAYER EACH MUFFIN HALF WITH I HAM SLICE, I TOMATO SLICE AND I EGG. TOP WITH SLICED CHEESE. BROIL FOR I TO 2 MINUTES OR UNTIL CHEESE IS MELTED. SERVE IMMEDIATELY. SERVES 2.

CREAMED EGGS WITH SMOKED HAM

SERVE THIS DISH WITH TOASTED BAGELS,
CREAM CHEESE AND PRESERVES.

8	LARGE EGGS	8
1/4 CUP	MILK	60 ML
1/4 TSP	SALT	1 ML
1/4 TSP	FRESHLY GROUND BLACK PEPPER	1 ML
1 TBSP	BUTTER	15 ML
1/2 CUP	SMOKED HAM, CUT INTO THIN STRIPS	125 ML
3	GREEN ONIONS, SLICED	3
1/4 CUP	LIGHT CREAM CHEESE, CUT INTO CUBES	60 ML
2 TBSP	CHOPPED FRESH PARSLEY	30 ML

IN A BOWL, BEAT EGGS, MILK, SALT AND PEPPER; SET
ASIDE. IN A LARGE NONSTICK SKILLET, MELT BUTTER OVER
MEDIUM HEAT. COOK HAM AND GREEN ONIONS, STIRRING,
FOR 2 TO 3 MINUTES OR UNTIL ONIONS ARE SOFTENED.
STIR IN CREAM CHEESE UNTIL MELTED AND SMOOTH. ADD
EGG MIXTURE AND COOK, STIRRING OFTEN, FOR ABOUT
4 MINUTES OR UNTIL EGGS ARE ALMOST SET BUT STILL
MOIST. SPRINKLE WITH PARSLEY AND SERVE. SERVES 4.

VARIATION
CREAMED EGGS WITH SMOKED SALMON: REPLACE HAM
WITH 2 OZ (60 G) SMOKED SALMON, CUT INTO STRIPS.
ADD SALMON WHEN EGGS ARE PARTIALLY COOKED
AND USE 1 TBSP (15 ML) CHOPPED FRESH DILL INSTEAD
OF PARSLEY.

LEEK, BACON AND GRUYÈRE STRATA

THIS APPEALING EGG DISH MAKES A WONDERFUL
BREAKFAST OR BRUNCH, OR SERVE IT ALONG
WITH A SALAD FOR A LIGHT SUPPER.

2 TBSP	BUTTER	30 ML
2	LEEKS, WHITE AND LIGHT GREEN PARTS ONLY, CLEANED (SEE TIP, OPPOSITE) AND CHOPPED	2
2	CLOVES GARLIC, FINELY CHOPPED	2
1	LARGE RED BELL PEPPER, DICED	1
10 CUPS	CUBED DAY-OLD ITALIAN BREAD (3/4-INCH/2 CM CUBES)	2.5 L
12	SLICES BACON, COOKED CRISP AND CRUMBLED	12
2 CUPS	SHREDDED GRUYÈRE OR CHEDDAR CHEESE	500 ML
8	LARGE EGGS	8
2 CUPS	MILK	500 ML
1/2 TSP	SALT	2 ML
1/4 TSP	FRESHLY GROUND BLACK PEPPER	1 ML
1/4 TSP	FRESHLY GRATED NUTMEG	1 ML

IN A LARGE NONSTICK SKILLET, MELT BUTTER OVER
MEDIUM HEAT. COOK LEEKS, GARLIC AND RED PEPPER,
STIRRING, FOR 5 MINUTES OR UNTIL SOFTENED. GREASE A
13- BY 9-INCH (33 BY 23 CM) BAKING DISH. LAYER HALF THE
BREAD CUBES IN BAKING DISH. TOP WITH HALF EACH OF
THE LEEK MIXTURE, BACON AND CHEESE. REPEAT LAYERS.
IN A BOWL, BEAT EGGS, MILK, SALT, PEPPER AND NUTMEG.

POUR EVENLY OVER BREAD MIXTURE. PRESS DOWN WITH A SPATULA TO HELP BREAD ABSORB EGG MIXTURE. COVER AND REFRIGERATE FOR AT LEAST 2 HOURS OR OVERNIGHT.

PREHEAT OVEN TO 350°F (180°C). UNCOVER STRATA AND BAKE FOR 40 TO 50 MINUTES OR UNTIL CENTER IS SET AND TOP IS PUFFED. LET STAND FOR 10 MINUTES BEFORE SERVING. SERVES 8.

TIP: TO CLEAN LEEKS, TRIM DARK GREEN TOPS. CUT DOWN CENTER ALMOST TO ROOT END AND CHOP. RINSE IN A SINK FULL OF COLD WATER TO REMOVE SAND; SCOOP UP LEEKS AND PLACE IN COLANDER TO DRAIN OR USE A SALAD SPINNER.

TIP: RECIPE CAN BE HALVED AND BAKED IN AN 8-INCH (20 CM) BAKING DISH FOR 30 TO 40 MINUTES.

SIGN ON GOLF COURSE:
PLEASE REFRAIN FROM PICKING UP LOST BALLS
UNTIL THEY HAVE FINISHED ROLLING.

BANANA NUT BREAD

HONEY GIVES THIS SIMPLE BREAD EXTRA
MOISTNESS THAT KEEPS IT FRESH FOR DAYS —
IF IT LASTS THAT LONG.

1 3/4 CUPS	ALL-PURPOSE FLOUR	425 ML
1 TSP	BAKING SODA	5 ML
1/4 TSP	SALT	1 ML
2	LARGE EGGS	2
1 CUP	MASHED RIPE BANANAS (ABOUT 3)	250 ML
1/3 CUP	VEGETABLE OIL	75 ML
1/2 CUP	LIQUID HONEY	125 ML
1/3 CUP	PACKED BROWN SUGAR	75 ML
1/2 CUP	CHOPPED WALNUTS	125 ML

PREHEAT OVEN TO 325°F (160°C). GREASE A 9- BY 5-INCH
(23 BY 12.5 CM) LOAF PAN. IN A BOWL, STIR TOGETHER
FLOUR, BAKING SODA AND SALT. IN ANOTHER BOWL,
BEAT EGGS. STIR IN BANANAS, OIL, HONEY AND BROWN
SUGAR. STIR DRY INGREDIENTS INTO BANANA MIXTURE
UNTIL COMBINED. FOLD IN WALNUTS. POUR BATTER INTO
PREPARED LOAF PAN. BAKE FOR 1 1/4 HOURS OR UNTIL CAKE
TESTER INSERTED IN CENTER COMES OUT CLEAN. LET PAN
COOL ON RACK FOR 15 MINUTES. RUN KNIFE AROUND EDGE;
TURN OUT LOAF AND LET COOL ON RACK. MAKES 1 LOAF.

TIP: LEFT WITH OVERRIPE BANANAS ON YOUR COUNTER
BUT HAVE NO TIME TO BAKE? SIMPLY FREEZE WHOLE
BANANAS WITH THE PEEL, THEN LEAVE AT ROOM
TEMPERATURE TO THAW.

CHEESE CORNBREAD

CUT THIS SAVORY CORNBREAD INTO SMALL SQUARES AND SERVE WITH A SALAD. OR CUT INTO 6 LARGE SQUARES AND SLICE IN HALF LENGTHWISE TO USE AS SANDWICH BASES. SPREAD WITH HERB CREAM CHEESE OR GOAT CHEESE, OR LAYER WITH YOUR FAVORITE COLD CUTS, SUCH AS SMOKED HAM OR TURKEY, TOPPED WITH TOMATO SLICES AND LETTUCE.

1 1/4 CUPS	ALL-PURPOSE FLOUR	300 ML
1 CUP	CORNMEAL	250 ML
2 TBSP	GRANULATED SUGAR	30 ML
1 TBSP	BAKING POWDER	15 ML
1/4 TSP	SALT	1 ML
3/4 CUP	SHREDDED CHEDDAR CHEESE	175 ML
2	LARGE EGGS	2
1 1/4 CUPS	MILK	300 ML
1/4 CUP	VEGETABLE OIL	60 ML

PREHEAT OVEN TO 375°F (190°C). GREASE A 13- BY 9-INCH (33 BY 23 CM) BAKING PAN. IN A BOWL, COMBINE FLOUR, CORNMEAL, SUGAR, BAKING POWDER AND SALT. STIR IN CHEESE. IN ANOTHER BOWL, BEAT EGGS WITH MILK AND OIL. POUR OVER FLOUR MIXTURE AND STIR UNTIL COMBINED. POUR BATTER INTO PREPARED BAKING PAN. BAKE FOR 25 TO 30 MINUTES OR UNTIL TOP SPRINGS BACK WHEN LIGHTLY TOUCHED IN CENTER. LET COOL ON RACK. CUT INTO SQUARES. SERVES 8.

VARIATION

JALAPEÑO CORNBREAD: ADD 1 DICED SMALL RED BELL PEPPER AND 2 TBSP (30 ML) MINCED SEEDED JALAPEÑO PEPPERS TO FLOUR MIXTURE ALONG WITH CHEESE.

CHEDDAR DROP BISCUITS

SERVE THESE WONDERFUL BISCUITS STRAIGHT
FROM THE OVEN. CONSIDER BAKING A DOUBLE BATCH
IF EXPECTING A HUNGRY CROWD.

2 CUPS	ALL-PURPOSE FLOUR	500 ML
1 TBSP	BAKING POWDER	15 ML
1/4 TSP	SALT	1 ML
1/3 CUP	BUTTER, AT ROOM TEMPERATURE, CUT INTO PIECES	75 ML
1 CUP	COARSELY SHREDDED SHARP (OLD) CHEDDAR CHEESE	250 ML
2 TBSP	CHOPPED FRESH CHIVES	30 ML
1 CUP	MILK	250 ML
	ADDITIONAL CHOPPED CHIVES	

PREHEAT OVEN TO 400°F (200°C). GREASE A BAKING
SHEET OR LINE IT WITH PARCHMENT PAPER. IN A LARGE
BOWL, COMBINE FLOUR, BAKING POWDER AND SALT. CUT
IN BUTTER USING A PASTRY BLENDER OR FORK TO MAKE
COARSE CRUMBS. ADD CHEDDAR CHEESE AND CHIVES.
STIR IN MILK TO MAKE A SOFT, STICKY DOUGH. DROP
12 HEAPING TABLESPOONFULS (15 ML) ONTO PREPARED
BAKING SHEET. SPRINKLE TOPS WITH CHOPPED CHIVES.
BAKE FOR 18 TO 20 MINUTES OR UNTIL EDGES ARE
GOLDEN. TRANSFER BISCUITS TO A RACK TO COOL.
MAKES 12 BISCUITS.

TIP: TO ASSEMBLE AHEAD, PLACE DRY INGREDIENTS
IN A BOWL. CUT IN BUTTER, ADD CHEESE, COVER AND
REFRIGERATE. WHILE OVEN IS PREHEATING, STIR IN THE
MILK AND CONTINUE WITH RECIPE.

BRAN MUFFINS

BRAN MUFFINS ARE NEVER OUT OF STYLE. NICELY MOISTENED WITH MOLASSES, THESE MUFFINS WILL BECOME A MORNING FAVORITE.

1 1/4 CUPS	WHOLE WHEAT FLOUR	300 ML
1 CUP	NATURAL BRAN	250 ML
1 TSP	BAKING SODA	5 ML
1/2 TSP	BAKING POWDER	2 ML
1/4 TSP	SALT	1 ML
2	LARGE EGGS	2
1 CUP	BUTTERMILK	250 ML
1/3 CUP	PACKED BROWN SUGAR	75 ML
1/4 CUP	VEGETABLE OIL	60 ML
1/4 CUP	LIGHT (FANCY) MOLASSES	60 ML
1/2 CUP	RAISINS OR CHOPPED DRIED APRICOTS	125 ML

PREHEAT OVEN TO 400°F (200°C). GREASE A 12-CUP MUFFIN PAN OR LINE THE CUPS WITH PAPER LINERS. IN A BOWL, COMBINE FLOUR, BRAN, BAKING SODA, BAKING POWDER AND SALT. IN ANOTHER BOWL, BEAT EGGS. ADD BUTTERMILK, BROWN SUGAR, OIL AND MOLASSES. STIR INTO FLOUR MIXTURE TO MAKE A SMOOTH BATTER; FOLD IN RAISINS. SPOON BATTER INTO PREPARED MUFFIN CUPS, FILLING THREE-QUARTERS FULL. BAKE FOR 20 TO 24 MINUTES OR UNTIL TOPS SPRING BACK WHEN LIGHTLY TOUCHED. LET COOL IN PAN FOR 10 MINUTES, THEN TRANSFER MUFFINS TO A WIRE RACK TO COOL. MAKES 12 MUFFINS.

LEMON BLUEBERRY MUFFINS

THESE YUMMY MUFFINS ARE EASY TO MAKE YEAR-ROUND WITH FROZEN BLUEBERRIES. THE SMALLER WILD BLUEBERRIES ARE THE IDEAL CHOICE.

1 3/4 CUPS	ALL-PURPOSE FLOUR	425 ML
2/3 CUP	GRANULATED SUGAR	150 ML
2 1/2 TSP	BAKING POWDER	12 ML
1/4 TSP	SALT	1 ML
2	LARGE EGGS	2
3/4 CUP	MILK	175 ML
1/3 CUP	BUTTER, MELTED	75 ML
2 TSP	GRATED LEMON ZEST	10 ML
1 CUP	FRESH OR FROZEN BLUEBERRIES	250 ML

PREHEAT OVEN TO 375°F (190°C). GREASE A 12-CUP MUFFIN PAN OR LINE THE CUPS WITH PAPER LINERS. IN A LARGE BOWL, COMBINE FLOUR, SUGAR, BAKING POWDER AND SALT. IN ANOTHER BOWL, BEAT EGGS. STIR IN MILK, MELTED BUTTER AND LEMON ZEST. STIR INTO FLOUR MIXTURE UNTIL JUST COMBINED. GENTLY FOLD IN BLUEBERRIES. SPOON BATTER INTO PREPARED MUFFIN CUPS, FILLING THREE-QUARTERS FULL. BAKE FOR 22 TO 25 MINUTES OR UNTIL LIGHTLY BROWNED AND TOPS SPRING BACK WHEN LIGHTLY TOUCHED. LET COOL IN PAN FOR 5 MINUTES, THEN TRANSFER MUFFINS TO A WIRE RACK TO COOL.

MAKES 12 MUFFINS.

MUESLI APPLESAUCE MUFFINS

WHOLESOME AND NUTRITIOUS, THESE TASTY
MUFFINS ARE GREAT FOR BREAKFAST OR AS A SNACK.

1 1/2 CUPS	WHOLE WHEAT FLOUR	375 ML
1 CUP	MUESLI WITH DRIED FRUITS AND NUTS	250 ML
2 TSP	BAKING POWDER	10 ML
1 1/2 TSP	GROUND CINNAMON	7 ML
1/2 TSP	BAKING SODA	2 ML
1/2 TSP	FRESHLY GRATED NUTMEG	2 ML
1	LARGE EGG	1
1 CUP	UNSWEETENED APPLESAUCE	250 ML
2/3 CUP	PACKED BROWN SUGAR	150 ML
1/2 CUP	VANILLA OR PLAIN YOGURT	125 ML
1/4 CUP	VEGETABLE OIL	60 ML
	ADDITIONAL MUESLI FOR TOPPING	

PREHEAT OVEN TO 375°F (190°C). GREASE A 12-CUP MUFFIN
PAN OR LINE THE CUPS WITH PAPER LINERS. IN A
LARGE BOWL, COMBINE FLOUR, MUESLI, BAKING POWDER,
CINNAMON, BAKING SODA AND NUTMEG. IN ANOTHER
BOWL, BEAT EGG. STIR IN APPLESAUCE, BROWN SUGAR,
YOGURT AND OIL. STIR INTO FLOUR MIXTURE UNTIL JUST
COMBINED. SPOON BATTER INTO PREPARED MUFFIN CUPS,
FILLING THREE-QUARTERS FULL. SPRINKLE TOPS WITH
ADDITIONAL MUESLI. BAKE FOR 20 TO 25 MINUTES OR
UNTIL TOPS SPRING BACK WHEN LIGHTLY TOUCHED. LET
COOL IN PAN FOR 5 MINUTES, THEN TRANSFER MUFFINS
TO A WIRE RACK TO COOL. MAKES 12 MUFFINS.

CARROT RAISIN MUFFINS

PACKED WITH NUTS, FRUITS AND CARROTS, THESE
SCRUMPTIOUS MUFFINS ARE PERFECT FOR BREAKFAST.
BUT THEY ARE JUST AS TASTY FOR AFTERNOON
SNACKS OR STOWED AWAY IN A LUNCH BOX.

2 CUPS	ALL-PURPOSE FLOUR	500 ML
3/4 CUP	GRANULATED SUGAR	175 ML
1 1/2 TSP	GROUND CINNAMON	7 ML
1 TSP	BAKING POWDER	5 ML
1 TSP	BAKING SODA	5 ML
1/2 TSP	FRESHLY GRATED NUTMEG	2 ML
1/4 TSP	SALT	1 ML
1 1/2 CUPS	GRATED CARROTS (ABOUT 3 MEDIUM)	375 ML
1 CUP	GRATED PEELED APPLES	250 ML
1/2 CUP	RAISINS	125 ML
1/2 CUP	SWEETENED SHREDDED COCONUT	125 ML
1/2 CUP	CHOPPED WALNUTS (OPTIONAL)	125 ML
2	LARGE EGGS	2
2/3 CUP	PLAIN YOGURT	150 ML
1/3 CUP	VEGETABLE OIL	75 ML

PREHEAT OVEN TO 375°F (190°C). GREASE 8 CUPS IN
EACH OF TWO 12-CUP MUFFIN PANS OR LINE THE CUPS
WITH PAPER LINERS. IN A LARGE BOWL, STIR TOGETHER
FLOUR, SUGAR, CINNAMON, BAKING POWDER, BAKING SODA,
NUTMEG AND SALT. STIR IN CARROTS, APPLES, RAISINS,
COCONUT AND WALNUTS (IF USING). IN ANOTHER BOWL,
BEAT EGGS; ADD YOGURT AND OIL. STIR INTO FLOUR
MIXTURE JUST UNTIL COMBINED. (BATTER WILL BE VERY
THICK.) SPOON BATTER INTO PREPARED MUFFIN CUPS,

FILLING ALMOST TO THE TOP. BAKE FOR 25 TO 30 MINUTES OR UNTIL TOPS SPRING BACK WHEN LIGHTLY TOUCHED. LET COOL IN PANS FOR 5 MINUTES, THEN TRANSFER MUFFINS TO A WIRE RACK TO COOL. MAKES 16 MUFFINS.

TIP: HAVE ONLY ONE MUFFIN PAN? PLACE MUFFIN PAPER LINERS IN 6-OZ (175 ML) GLASS CUSTARD CUPS OR SMALL RAMEKINS AND FILL WITH EXTRA BATTER. BAKE ALONGSIDE MUFFIN PAN.

SIGN ON A MUSIC STORE: OUT TO LUNCH.
BACH AT 1:30. OFFENBACH AT 2:00.

OATMEAL CRISP BARS

ENJOY YOUR MORNING OATS BAKED IN A BAR.
ACCOMPANY WITH A GLASS OF COLD MILK
FOR MORE NUTRIENTS.

$2/3$ CUP	BUTTER	150 ML
$2/3$ CUP	PACKED BROWN SUGAR	150 ML
$2\,2/3$ CUPS	LARGE-FLAKE (OLD-FASHIONED) ROLLED OATS	650 ML
1 TSP	GROUND CINNAMON	5 ML
PINCH	SALT	PINCH

PREHEAT OVEN TO 350°F (180°C). LINE A 13- BY 9-INCH
(33 BY 23 CM) BAKING PAN WITH FOIL AND GREASE THE
FOIL. IN A LARGE SAUCEPAN, MELT BUTTER OVER MEDIUM
HEAT. ADD BROWN SUGAR. COOK, STIRRING CONSTANTLY,
UNTIL SUGAR IS MELTED AND MIXTURE IS SMOOTH, ABOUT
1 MINUTE. STIR IN OATS, CINNAMON AND SALT, MIXING
UNTIL OATS ARE THOROUGHLY MOISTENED. PRESS EVENLY
INTO PREPARED PAN. BAKE UNTIL TOP IS GOLDEN, ABOUT
15 MINUTES. LET COOL COMPLETELY IN PAN ON RACK.
BREAK INTO IRREGULAR PIECES. MAKES ABOUT 24 PIECES.

TIP: USE COOKING SPRAY TO GREASE PANS. IT DOESN'T
BURN LIKE BUTTER DOES.

TIP: STORE CRISPS IN A TIGHTLY COVERED CONTAINER
WITH WAXED PAPER BETWEEN THE LAYERS TO PREVENT
THEM FROM GETTING SOFT. THEY ALSO FREEZE WELL FOR
UP TO 3 MONTHS.

VARIATION: DECREASE THE OATS TO $2\,1/3$ CUPS (575 ML)
AND ADD $1/3$ CUP (75 ML) TOASTED WHEAT GERM.

VARIATION: ADD $1/4$ CUP (60 ML) SESAME OR FLAX SEEDS.

SNACKS, SPREADS & DIPS

KETTLE CORN

MAKE THIS SALTY-SWEET CARNIVAL TREAT AT HOME — JUST BE SURE TO SHAKE IT!

1/4 CUP	VEGETABLE OIL	60 ML
1/2 CUP	POPCORN KERNELS	125 ML
1/4 CUP	GRANULATED SUGAR	60 ML
1 TSP	COARSE SALT	5 ML

LINE A BAKING SHEET OR LARGE ROASTING PAN WITH PARCHMENT PAPER. IN A LARGE POT WITH A TIGHT-FITTING LID, HEAT OIL OVER MEDIUM-HIGH HEAT. ADD POPCORN KERNELS AND SPRINKLE WITH SUGAR, STIRRING TO COAT. PLACE LID ON POT. ONCE KERNELS BEGIN TO POP, START SHAKING THE POT, RETURNING IT TO THE HEAT EVERY FEW SECONDS. SHAKE VIGOROUSLY UNTIL POPPING BEGINS TO SLOW, ABOUT 2 TO 3 MINUTES. REMOVE FROM HEAT IMMEDIATELY AND POUR ONTO PREPARED BAKING SHEET. SPRINKLE WITH SALT. SPREAD POPCORN APART SO THAT IT DOESN'T COOL IN CLUMPS. LET COOL. MAKES 10 CUPS (2.5 L).

SPICED NUTS

A DELICIOUS NIBBLE OR ADDITION TO A SALAD.

2 TBSP	OLIVE OIL OR MELTED BUTTER	30 ML
I	CLOVE GARLIC, PEELED AND FLATTENED SLIGHTLY WITH A FORK	I
2 CUPS	UNSALTED MIXED NUTS (SUCH AS PECANS, WALNUTS, CASHEWS AND ALMONDS)	500 ML
2 TSP	SEA SALT	IO ML
I TSP	CHILI POWDER	5 ML
$\frac{1}{2}$ TSP	GROUND CUMIN	2 ML
$\frac{1}{4}$ TSP	GROUND GINGER	I ML
$\frac{1}{4}$ TSP	GROUND CINNAMON	I ML

PREHEAT OVEN TO 325°F (160°C). POUR OIL INTO A SMALL BOWL AND ADD GARLIC, SWISHING IT AROUND. SET ASIDE FOR A FEW MINUTES, THEN REMOVE THE GARLIC. TOSS THE NUTS WITH THE OIL, SALT, CHILI POWDER, CUMIN, GINGER AND CINNAMON UNTIL WELL COATED. SPREAD OUT ON A RIMMED BAKING SHEET. BAKE FOR 20 TO 25 MINUTES, STIRRING ONCE OR TWICE, UNTIL GOLDEN. LET COOL ON THE SHEET. MAKES 2 CUPS (500 ML).

MIXED DOUBLES TENNIS IS OFTEN PLAYED BY ATHLETIC COUPLES WHO WANT TO BURN A FEW CALORIES WHILE ARGUING.

PICK-ME-UP BARS

THIS DENSE, SLIGHTLY CHEWY BAR IS A GREAT
BOOST IF YOU'RE EXPERIENCING AN AFTERNOON
LULL AND IS AN IDEAL AFTER-SCHOOL SNACK.

1 CUP	GRAHAM WAFER CRUMBS	250 ML
2/3 CUP	PACKED BROWN SUGAR	150 ML
1/2 CUP	WHOLE WHEAT FLOUR	125 ML
1/2 CUP	BUTTERSCOTCH CHIPS	125 ML
1/3 CUP	QUICK-COOKING ROLLED OATS	75 ML
1/3 CUP	SUNFLOWER SEEDS	75 ML
1 TSP	BAKING POWDER	5 ML
2	LARGE EGG WHITES	2
1 TBSP	VEGETABLE OIL	15 ML
1 1/2 TSP	VANILLA EXTRACT	7 ML

PREHEAT OVEN TO 350°F (180°C). GREASE AN 8-INCH
(20 CM) SQUARE METAL BAKING PAN. IN A BOWL,
COMBINE GRAHAM WAFER CRUMBS, BROWN SUGAR, FLOUR,
BUTTERSCOTCH CHIPS, OATS, SUNFLOWER SEEDS AND
BAKING POWDER. IN A SEPARATE BOWL, WHISK EGG
WHITES, OIL AND VANILLA UNTIL BLENDED. STIR INTO
DRY INGREDIENTS, MIXING WELL. PRESS EVENLY INTO
PREPARED PAN. BAKE UNTIL TOP IS GOLDEN, ABOUT
20 MINUTES. LET COOL COMPLETELY IN PAN ON RACK.
CUT INTO BARS. MAKES 18 TO 48 BARS.

VARIATION: YOU CAN REPLACE THE WHOLE WHEAT FLOUR
WITH ALL-PURPOSE FLOUR, BUT YOU'LL LOSE SOME OF
THE HEALTH BENEFITS, SUCH AS ADDED FIBER.

VARIATION: REPLACE THE SUNFLOWER SEEDS WITH A
MIXTURE OF SESAME AND FLAX SEEDS.

CRISPY CEREAL BARS

THESE NO-BAKE BARS ARE A GREAT WAY
FOR KIDS TO ENJOY THEIR BREAKFAST CEREAL. ADD
A GLASS OF MILK AND THEY'LL BE HAPPY CAMPERS.

1 CUP	QUICK-COOKING ROLLED OATS	250 ML
	NONSTICK COOKING SPRAY	
1/4 CUP	BUTTER	60 ML
8 OZ	MARSHMALLOWS (ABOUT 40 REGULAR SIZE)	250 G
1 TSP	VANILLA EXTRACT	5 ML
5 CUPS	CRISP RICE CEREAL	1.25 L
3/4 CUP	RAISINS	175 ML
1/3 CUP	SUNFLOWER SEEDS	75 ML
1/3 CUP	CHOPPED DRIED APRICOTS	75 ML
1/4 CUP	CHOPPED UNBLANCHED ALMONDS	60 ML

PREHEAT OVEN TO 350°F (180°C). SPRINKLE OATS EVENLY
IN A 13- BY 9-INCH (33 BY 23 CM) BAKING PAN. BAKE,
STIRRING OCCASIONALLY, UNTIL LIGHTLY TOASTED, ABOUT
10 MINUTES. TRANSFER TO A BOWL AND LET COOL FOR
15 MINUTES. SPRAY PAN LIGHTLY WITH NONSTICK COOKING
SPRAY. SET ASIDE. IN A LARGE SAUCEPAN, COMBINE
BUTTER AND MARSHMALLOWS. COOK OVER LOW HEAT,
STIRRING OFTEN, UNTIL MELTED AND SMOOTH. REMOVE
FROM HEAT. STIR IN VANILLA. STIR IN OATS, CEREAL,
RAISINS, SUNFLOWER SEEDS, APRICOTS AND ALMONDS,
MIXING WELL. USING AN OFFSET SPATULA OR THE BACK OF
A SPOON, PRESS MIXTURE EVENLY INTO PREPARED PAN.
LET COOL COMPLETELY, ABOUT 1 HOUR. CUT INTO BARS.
MAKES 20 TO 54 BARS.

FRUIT AND NUT SQUARES

HERE'S A HEALTHY VERSION OF AN OLD CLASSIC. IF YOU'RE WATCHING CALORIES, CUT THE SQUARES IN HALF INTO TRIANGLES.

1/2 CUP	BUTTER	125 ML
1 CUP	GRAHAM WAFER CRUMBS	250 ML
1/3 CUP	WHEAT GERM	75 ML
1	CAN (14 OZ OR 300 ML) LIGHT SWEETENED CONDENSED MILK	1
1 CUP	CHOPPED DRIED APRICOTS	250 ML
3/4 CUP	DRIED CRANBERRIES	175 ML
3/4 CUP	UNSWEETENED FLAKED COCONUT	175 ML
1/2 CUP	CHOPPED UNBLANCHED ALMONDS	125 ML
1/3 CUP	PUMPKIN SEEDS	75 ML

PREHEAT OVEN TO 350°F (180°C). PLACE BUTTER IN A 13- BY 9-INCH (33 BY 23 CM) METAL BAKING PAN AND MELT IN PREHEATED OVEN. REMOVE FROM OVEN AND TILT PAN TO COVER BOTTOM EVENLY WITH MELTED BUTTER. COMBINE GRAHAM WAFER CRUMBS AND WHEAT GERM. SPRINKLE EVENLY OVER BUTTER, PRESSING WITH AN OFFSET SPATULA OR THE BACK OF A SPOON TO MOISTEN. DRIZZLE SWEETENED CONDENSED MILK EVENLY OVER CRUMBS. SPRINKLE APRICOTS, CRANBERRIES, COCONUT, ALMONDS AND PUMPKIN SEEDS OVER TOP. PRESS IN LIGHTLY. BAKE UNTIL LIGHTLY BROWNED AROUND EDGES, 20 TO 25 MINUTES. LET COOL COMPLETELY IN PAN ON RACK. CUT INTO SQUARES. MAKES 24 SQUARES.

VARIATION: REPLACE THE DRIED CRANBERRIES WITH RAISINS, CHOPPED DRIED CHERRIES OR CHOPPED DRIED FIGS.

CHEDDAR JALAPEÑO TOASTS

GET A HEAD START ON YOUR PARTY PREPARATIONS WITH THESE TASTY APPETIZERS DESIGNED TO BE STORED IN THE FREEZER. WHEN FRIENDS ARRIVE, JUST POP THEM INTO A HOT OVEN.

8 OZ	SHARP (OLD) CHEDDAR CHEESE, SHREDDED	250 G
4 OZ	CREAM CHEESE, CUBED	125 G
2 TBSP	FINELY CHOPPED RED BELL PEPPER	30 ML
2 TBSP	MINCED SEEDED JALAPEÑO PEPPERS (OR 1 TBSP/15 ML MINCED PICKLED JALAPEÑO PEPPERS)	30 ML
2 TBSP	FINELY CHOPPED FRESH PARSLEY	30 ML
36	BAGUETTE SLICES, CUT $1/3$-INCH (8 MM) THICK	36

PREHEAT OVEN TO 375°F (190°C). IN A FOOD PROCESSOR, PURÉE CHEDDAR AND CREAM CHEESE UNTIL VERY SMOOTH. TRANSFER TO A BOWL; STIR IN RED PEPPER, JALAPEÑO PEPPERS AND PARSLEY. SPREAD BREAD SLICES WITH A GENEROUS TEASPOONFUL (5 ML) OF CHEESE MIXTURE; ARRANGE ON BAKING SHEETS. BAKE IN PREHEATED OVEN FOR 10 TO 12 MINUTES (UP TO 15 MINUTES, IF FROZEN), UNTIL TOPS ARE PUFFED AND EDGES TOASTED. SERVE WARM. MAKES 36 APPETIZERS.

TIP: TO FREEZE, SPREAD BREAD SLICES WITH CHEESE MIXTURE; ARRANGE IN A SINGLE LAYER ON BAKING SHEETS AND FREEZE. TRANSFER TO A RIGID CONTAINER, SEPARATING LAYERS WITH WAXED PAPER; FREEZE FOR UP TO 1 MONTH. NO NEED TO DEFROST BEFORE BAKING.

TIP: TO AVOID SKIN IRRITATION, WEAR RUBBER GLOVES WHEN HANDLING JALAPEÑO PEPPERS.

REFRIED NACHOS

FAST-AND-EASY RECIPE

A FAVORITE OF TEENAGERS, NACHOS ARE
ALSO A GREAT COMFORT FOOD DISH. IN THIS RECIPE,
THE DEGREE OF SPICE DEPENDS UPON THE HEAT
OF THE SALSA. IF YOU ARE HEAT-AVERSE, USE A MILD
SALSA; IF YOU ARE A HEAT-SEEKER, USE A SPICY ONE.

I	CAN (14 OZ/398 ML) REFRIED BEANS	I
I CUP	SALSA	250 ML
I	CAN (4$\frac{1}{2}$ OZ/127 ML) CHOPPED GREEN CHILES, DRAINED	I
2 CUPS	SHREDDED CHEDDAR OR MONTEREY JACK CHEESE	500 ML
	TORTILLA CHIPS OR TOSTADAS	

IN A SAUCEPAN OVER MEDIUM HEAT, BRING BEANS, SALSA
AND CHILES TO A BOIL. STIR IN CHEESE UNTIL MELTED.
SERVE WITH TORTILLA CHIPS OR TOSTADAS FOR DIPPING.
MAKES ABOUT 4 CUPS (I L).

TIP: TO JACK UP THE HEAT, ADD A FINELY CHOPPED
JALAPEÑO PEPPER ALONG WITH THE BEANS.

TIP: IF YOU LIKE A HINT OF SMOKE AS WELL AS HEAT, ADD
A FINELY CHOPPED CHIPOTLE PEPPER IN ADOBO SAUCE.

TIP
MICROWAVE METHOD: PLACE BEANS, SALSA AND CHILES
IN A MICROWAVE-SAFE DISH. MICROWAVE ON HIGH UNTIL
BUBBLING, ABOUT 4 MINUTES. STIR IN CHEESE AND
MICROWAVE UNTIL MELTED, ABOUT I$\frac{1}{2}$ MINUTES.

SLOW COOKER RECIPE

THANKS TO OUR DEAR FRIEND MARILYN LINTON, WRITER AND EDITOR EXTRAORDINAIRE, FOR THIS OH-SO-EASY "FONDUE." CREAMY AND DELICIOUS, IT IS A GREAT HIT WITH ADULTS AS WELL AS KIDS. GIVE EVERYONE THEIR OWN FONDUE FORK AND SERVE WITH THICK SLICES OF QUARTERED FRENCH BAGUETTE, CELERY STICKS OR SLICES OF GREEN PEPPER.

1	LARGE CAN (28 OZ/796 ML) TOMATOES, WITH JUICE	1
1 TSP	DRIED OREGANO	5 ML
1 TSP	SALT	5 ML
$\frac{1}{4}$ TSP	FRESHLY GROUND BLACK PEPPER	1 ML
3 CUPS	SHREDDED CHEDDAR CHEESE	750 ML

IN A FOOD PROCESSOR OR BLENDER, PROCESS TOMATOES UNTIL RELATIVELY SMOOTH. TRANSFER TO A SMALL (MAXIMUM 3$\frac{1}{2}$-QUART) SLOW COOKER. ADD OREGANO, SALT AND PEPPER AND COOK ON HIGH FOR 1 HOUR, UNTIL TOMATOES ARE HOT AND BUBBLY. ADD CHEESE IN HANDFULS, STIRRING TO COMBINE AFTER EACH ADDITION. REDUCE HEAT TO LOW AND SERVE, OR COVER AND KEEP ON LOW UNTIL READY TO SERVE. SERVES 6.

TIP: IF YOU CAN ONLY FIND A 35-OZ (980 ML) CAN OF TOMATOES, DRAIN OFF 1 CUP (250 ML) LIQUID BEFORE ADDING TO THE FOOD PROCESSOR.

GUACAMOLE

THERE ARE MANY VERSIONS OF THIS
POPULAR MEXICAN APPETIZER. HERE THE MASHED
AVOCADOS ARE ENHANCED BY GREEN ONIONS,
TOMATO AND JALAPEÑO PEPPER.

2	HASS AVOCADOS, PEELED	2
1	TOMATO, SEEDED AND DICED	1
1/3 CUP	COARSELY CHOPPED FRESH CILANTRO	75 ML
2	GREEN ONIONS, SLICED	2
1 to 2 TBSP	MINCED SEEDED JALAPEÑO PEPPERS	15 to 30 ML
1 TBSP	FRESHLY SQUEEZED LIME JUICE	15 ML
	SALT	
	TORTILLA CHIPS	

IN A BOWL, MASH AVOCADOS WITH A FORK. STIR IN
TOMATO, CILANTRO, GREEN ONIONS, JALAPEÑO PEPPER
AND LIME JUICE. SEASON TO TASTE WITH SALT. PLACE IN
A SERVING DISH AND ACCOMPANY WITH TORTILLA CHIPS.
MAKES 6 SERVINGS.

SIGN ON A DIVORCE LAWYER'S WALL:
SATISFACTION GUARANTEED OR YOUR HONEY BACK.

HUMMUS

YOU CAN BUY HUMMUS, THE CLASSIC SPREAD FROM THE MIDDLE EAST, IN SUPERMARKETS, BUT IT'S SO EASY TO MAKE AT HOME. SERVE IT AS A DIP WITH PITA WEDGES OR USE AS A SANDWICH SPREAD.

1	CAN (19 OZ/540 ML) CHICKPEAS, DRAINED AND RINSED	1
1/4 CUP	TAHINI	60 ML
2 to 3	CLOVES GARLIC, CHOPPED	2 to 3
1/4 CUP	OLIVE OIL	60 ML
1/4 CUP	FRESHLY SQUEEZED LEMON JUICE	60 ML
2 TBSP	WATER	30 ML
2 TBSP	FINELY CHOPPED FRESH PARSLEY	30 ML
	SALT AND FRESHLY GROUND BLACK PEPPER	

IN A FOOD PROCESSOR OR BLENDER, PURÉE CHICKPEAS, TAHINI, GARLIC, OLIVE OIL, LEMON JUICE AND WATER UNTIL SMOOTH. TRANSFER TO A BOWL; STIR IN PARSLEY AND SEASON TO TASTE WITH SALT AND PEPPER. MAKES A GENEROUS 2 CUPS (500 ML).

TIP: THIN HUMMUS, IF DESIRED, BY STIRRING IN ADDITIONAL WATER.

ZESTY CRAB SPREAD

SLOW COOKER RECIPE

SERVE THIS BUBBLING HOT, WITH CELERY
OR CARROT STICKS, OR SPREAD IT ON CRACKERS,
MELBA TOAST OR SLICED BAGUETTE. MAKE ENOUGH FOR
LEFTOVERS — IT REHEATS WELL AND IS A NICE TREAT
TO HAVE ON HAND FOR AFTER-SCHOOL SNACKS.

8 OZ	CREAM CHEESE, CUBED	250 G
1/4 CUP	TOMATO-BASED CHILI SAUCE	60 ML
1 TSP	DIJON MUSTARD	5 ML
2 TBSP	GRATED ONION	30 ML
1	CLOVE GARLIC, MINCED	1
	SALT AND FRESHLY GROUND BLACK PEPPER	
8 OZ	COOKED CRABMEAT, CHOPPED	250 G
1/2 TSP	MINCED FRESH CHILE PEPPER (OPTIONAL)	2 ML
	PAPRIKA	

IN A SMALL (MAXIMUM $3\frac{1}{2}$-QUART) SLOW COOKER,
COMBINE CREAM CHEESE, CHILI SAUCE, MUSTARD, ONION
AND GARLIC. SEASON TO TASTE WITH SALT AND PEPPER.
STIR WELL. COVER AND COOK ON HIGH FOR 1 HOUR. ADD
CRAB AND CHILE (IF USING). STIR WELL AND COOK ON HIGH
FOR 30 MINUTES, UNTIL HOT AND BUBBLY. SPRINKLE WITH
PAPRIKA TO TASTE AND SERVE. OR SET TO LOW OR WARM
UNTIL READY TO SERVE. SERVES 6.

TIP: LOOK FOR CANNED PASTEURIZED CRABMEAT IN THE
REFRIGERATED SECTION OF SUPERMARKETS. REGULAR
CANNED OR THAWED DRAINED FROZEN CRABMEAT WILL
ALSO WORK.

BLACK BEAN AND SALSA DIP

SLOW COOKER RECIPE

THIS TASTY CUBAN-INSPIRED DIP, WHICH CAN
BE MADE FROM INGREDIENTS YOU'RE LIKELY TO
HAVE ON HAND, IS NUTRITIOUS AND FLAVORFUL.

1	CAN (14 TO 19 OZ/398 TO 540 ML) BLACK BEANS, DRAINED AND RINSED	1
8 OZ	CREAM CHEESE, CUBED	250 G
1/2 CUP	SALSA	125 ML
1/4 CUP	SOUR CREAM	60 ML
1 TSP	CHILI POWDER	5 ML
1 TSP	GROUND CUMIN	5 ML
1 TSP	CRACKED BLACK PEPPERCORNS	5 ML
1	JALAPEÑO PEPPER, FINELY CHOPPED (OPTIONAL)	1
1	ROASTED RED BELL PEPPER (SEE TIPS, PAGE 149), FINELY CHOPPED (OPTIONAL)	1
	FINELY CHOPPED GREEN ONION (OPTIONAL)	
	FINELY CHOPPED CILANTRO (OPTIONAL)	

IN A SMALL TO MEDIUM (1 1/2- TO 3 1/2-QUART) SLOW
COOKER, COMBINE BEANS, CREAM CHEESE, SALSA, SOUR
CREAM, CHILI POWDER, CUMIN, PEPPERCORNS, JALAPEÑO
(IF USING) AND ROASTED PEPPER (IF USING). COVER AND
COOK ON HIGH FOR 1 HOUR. STIR AND COOK ON HIGH FOR
30 MINUTES, UNTIL MIXTURE IS HOT AND BUBBLY. SERVE
IMMEDIATELY OR SET TO LOW OR WARM UNTIL READY TO
SERVE. GARNISH WITH GREEN ONION AND/OR CILANTRO, IF
DESIRED. MAKES ABOUT 3 CUPS (750 ML).

ALWAYS POPULAR
LAYERED BEAN DIP

VARIATIONS OF THE POPULAR BEAN DIP ALWAYS
MAKE THE PARTY CIRCUIT. THIS UPDATED VERSION HAS
AN OREGANO-BEAN BASE, A CREAMY JALAPEÑO CHEESE
LAYER AND A VIBRANT FRESH TOPPING OF TOMATOES,
OLIVES AND CILANTRO. SERVE WITH TORTILLA CHIPS
OR PITA CRISPS (SEE TIP, OPPOSITE).

1	CAN (19 OZ/540 ML) RED KIDNEY BEANS OR BLACK BEANS, DRAINED AND RINSED	1
1	CLOVE GARLIC, MINCED	1
1 TSP	DRIED OREGANO	5 ML
1/2 TSP	GROUND CUMIN	2 ML
1 TBSP	WATER	15 ML
1 CUP	SHREDDED MONTEREY JACK OR CHEDDAR CHEESE	250 ML
3/4 CUP	SOUR CREAM	175 ML
1 TBSP	MINCED SEEDED FRESH OR PICKLED JALAPEÑO PEPPERS	15 ML
2	TOMATOES, SEEDED AND FINELY DICED	2
1	HASS AVOCADO, PEELED AND DICED (OPTIONAL)	1
2	GREEN ONIONS, SLICED	2
1/3 CUP	SLICED BLACK OLIVES	75 ML
1/3 CUP	CHOPPED FRESH CILANTRO OR PARSLEY	75 ML

IN A FOOD PROCESSOR, COMBINE BEANS, GARLIC,
OREGANO, CUMIN AND WATER; PROCESS UNTIL SMOOTH.
SPREAD IN AN 8-INCH (20 CM) SHALLOW ROUND SERVING
DISH OR PIE PLATE. IN A BOWL, COMBINE CHEESE, SOUR
CREAM AND JALAPEÑO PEPPERS. SPREAD OVER BEAN

LAYER. (CAN BE ASSEMBLED EARLIER IN DAY; COVER AND
REFRIGERATE.) JUST BEFORE SERVING, SPRINKLE WITH
TOMATOES, AVOCADO (IF USING), GREEN ONIONS, OLIVES
AND CILANTRO. SERVES 8.

TIP: FRESH CILANTRO LASTS ONLY A FEW DAYS IN THE
FRIDGE BEFORE IT DETERIORATES AND TURNS TASTELESS.
WASH CILANTRO WELL, SPIN DRY AND WRAP IN PAPER
TOWELS; STORE IN PLASTIC BAG IN THE FRIDGE. LEAVE
THE ROOTS ON — THEY KEEP THE LEAVES FRESH.

TIP
PITA CRISPS: SEPARATE THREE 7-INCH (18 CM) THIN PITAS
INTO ROUNDS AND CUT EACH INTO 8 WEDGES. PLACE IN A
SINGLE LAYER ON BAKING SHEETS; BAKE AT 350°F (180°C)
FOR 8 TO 10 MINUTES OR UNTIL CRISP AND LIGHTLY
TOASTED. LET COOL. STORE IN AN AIRTIGHT CONTAINER.
THE PITA CRISPS CAN BE MADE 1 DAY AHEAD OR LAYERED
IN A RIGID CONTAINER AND FROZEN FOR UP TO 2 WEEKS.

SIGN IN A COMPANY RECEPTION AREA:
WE SHOOT EVERY THIRD SALESMAN,
AND THE SECOND ONE JUST LEFT.

BASIL AND WHITE BEAN SPREAD

FAST-AND-EASY RECIPE

DON'T TELL AND NO ONE WILL EVER GUESS HOW EASY IT IS TO MAKE THIS DELICIOUS AND SOPHISTICATED SPREAD. SERVE WITH SLICED BAGUETTE OR CRACKERS.

1	CAN (19 OZ/540 ML) WHITE KIDNEY BEANS, DRAINED AND RINSED	1
2 CUPS	PACKED FLAT-LEAF (ITALIAN) PARSLEY LEAVES (SEE TIP, BELOW)	500 ML
2 TBSP	BASIL PESTO	30 ML
1 TBSP	MINCED GARLIC	15 ML
1 TBSP	FRESHLY SQUEEZED LEMON JUICE	15 ML
	SALT AND FRESHLY GROUND BLACK PEPPER	

IN A FOOD PROCESSOR, COMBINE BEANS, PARSLEY, BASIL PESTO, GARLIC AND LEMON JUICE. PROCESS UNTIL SMOOTH. SEASON TO TASTE WITH SALT AND BLACK PEPPER. MAKES ABOUT 3 CUPS (750 ML).

TIP: MAKE SURE YOU HAVE THOROUGHLY DRIED THE PARSLEY (PATTING BETWEEN LAYERS OF PAPER TOWEL) BEFORE ADDING TO THE FOOD PROCESSOR; OTHERWISE THE SPREAD MAY BE WATERY.

SOUPS

CHICKEN STOCK

IT'S EASY TO MAKE HOMEMADE STOCK INSTEAD OF RESORTING TO COMMERCIAL STOCK CUBES AND POWDERS, WHICH ARE LOADED WITH SALT.

3 LBS	CHICKEN BONES (SUCH AS NECK, BACKBONES AND WING TIPS)	1.5 KG
2	CARROTS, COARSELY CHOPPED	2
2	STALKS CELERY, INCLUDING LEAVES, CHOPPED	2
1	LARGE ONION, CHOPPED	1
1/2 TSP	DRIED THYME LEAVES	2 ML
1	BAY LEAF	1
	SALT AND FRESHLY GROUND BLACK PEPPER	

PLACE CHICKEN BONES IN A LARGE STOCKPOT. ADD WATER TO COVER (ABOUT 10 CUPS/2.5 L). ADD CARROTS, CELERY, ONION, THYME AND BAY LEAF. BRING TO A BOIL AND SKIM. SIMMER, COVERED, FOR 2 HOURS; STRAIN THROUGH A FINE SIEVE. SEASON TO TASTE WITH SALT AND PEPPER. MAKES ABOUT 8 CUPS (2 L).

SIGN IN A DO-IT-YOURSELF STORE: HUSBANDS CHOOSING COLORS MUST HAVE NOTE FROM WIVES.

HEARTY BEEF STOCK

SLOW COOKER RECIPE

3	ONIONS, QUARTERED	3
3	CARROTS, CUT INTO CHUNKS	3
3	STALKS CELERY	3
6	CLOVES GARLIC	6
2 TBSP	EXTRA VIRGIN OLIVE OIL OR MELTED BUTTER	30 ML
3 LBS	BEEF BONES	1.5 KG
4	SPRIGS FRESH PARSLEY	4
3	SPRIGS FRESH THYME	3
10	BLACK PEPPERCORNS	10
1/4 CUP	DRIED ALFALFA LEAVES (OPTIONAL)	60 ML
3 TBSP	RED WINE VINEGAR	45 ML
12 CUPS	FILTERED WATER	3 L

PREHEAT OVEN TO 375°F (190°C). PLACE ONIONS, CARROTS, CELERY AND GARLIC IN A ROASTING PAN AND TOSS WELL WITH OIL. ADD BONES AND TOSS AGAIN. ARRANGE IN A SINGLE LAYER (AS MUCH AS POSSIBLE) IN PAN AND ROAST UNTIL INGREDIENTS ARE BROWNING NICELY, ABOUT 1 HOUR. TRANSFER TO A LARGE (ABOUT 6-QUART) SLOW COOKER, ALONG WITH JUICES. ADD PARSLEY, THYME, PEPPERCORNS, ALFALFA LEAVES (IF USING), VINEGAR AND WATER. COVER AND COOK ON LOW FOR 12 HOURS OR ON HIGH FOR 6 HOURS, UNTIL STOCK IS BROWN AND FLAVORFUL. STRAIN THROUGH A SIEVE LINED WITH A DOUBLE LAYER OF CHEESECLOTH AND DISCARD SOLIDS. COOL SLIGHTLY. REFRIGERATE FOR UP TO 5 DAYS OR FREEZE IN PORTIONS IN AIRTIGHT CONTAINERS. MAKES ABOUT 12 CUPS (3 L).

CREAMY CAULIFLOWER SOUP

THIS SOUP REHEATS WELL, SO THERE IS
NO NEED TO BE CONCERNED ABOUT THE LARGER
QUANTITY IF YOU ARE SERVING FEWER PEOPLE.

2 TBSP	BUTTER	30 ML
1 CUP	FINELY CHOPPED ONION	250 ML
1 TSP	SALT	5 ML
	FRESHLY GROUND BLACK PEPPER	
2 CUPS	CHOPPED COOKED POTATOES	500 ML
4 CUPS	CAULIFLOWER FLORETS	1 L
6 CUPS	CHICKEN STOCK (PAGE 42) OR READY-TO-USE VEGETABLE OR CHICKEN BROTH	1.5 L
1/2 CUP	HEAVY OR WHIPPING (35%) CREAM	125 ML
2 TBSP	SUN-DRIED TOMATO PESTO	30 ML

IN A LARGE SAUCEPAN, MELT BUTTER OVER MEDIUM
HEAT. ADD ONION AND COOK, STIRRING, UNTIL SOFTENED,
ABOUT 3 MINUTES. ADD SALT AND SEASON TO TASTE
WITH BLACK PEPPER; COOK, STIRRING, FOR 1 MINUTE.
ADD POTATOES, CAULIFLOWER AND STOCK. BRING TO A
BOIL. REDUCE HEAT TO LOW. COVER AND COOK UNTIL
CAULIFLOWER IS TENDER AND FLAVORS ARE COMBINED,
ABOUT 15 MINUTES. USING A SLOTTED SPOON, TRANSFER
SOLIDS TO A FOOD PROCESSOR OR BLENDER. ADD 1/2 CUP
(125 ML) OF THE COOKING LIQUID AND PROCESS UNTIL
SMOOTH. (YOU CAN ALSO DO THIS IN THE SAUCEPAN,
USING A HANDHELD BLENDER.) RETURN MIXTURE TO
SAUCEPAN OVER LOW HEAT. ADD CREAM AND PESTO
AND HEAT GENTLY UNTIL MIXTURE ALMOST REACHES A
SIMMER. SERVE IMMEDIATELY. SERVES 6.

CLASSIC CREAM OF TOMATO SOUP

THIS SOUP, WHICH USES CANNED TOMATOES AS A BASE, IS DELICIOUS AND NOT MUCH MORE DIFFICULT TO MAKE THAN ITS PREPARED COUNTERPART.

1 TBSP	BUTTER	15 ML
1 CUP	DICED ONION	250 ML
PINCH	GROUND ALLSPICE	PINCH
PINCH	CAYENNE PEPPER	PINCH
1 TBSP	ALL-PURPOSE FLOUR	15 ML
2 CUPS	CHICKEN STOCK (PAGE 42) OR READY-TO-USE VEGETABLE OR CHICKEN BROTH	500 ML
1	CAN (28 OZ/796 ML) TOMATOES, COARSELY CHOPPED, WITH JUICE	1
1/2 CUP	HEAVY OR WHIPPING (35%) CREAM	125 ML
	SALT AND FRESHLY GROUND BLACK PEPPER	

IN A LARGE SAUCEPAN, MELT BUTTER OVER MEDIUM HEAT. ADD ONION AND COOK, STIRRING, UNTIL SOFTENED, ABOUT 3 MINUTES. STIR IN ALLSPICE AND CAYENNE. ADD FLOUR AND COOK, STIRRING, FOR 1 MINUTE. ADD STOCK AND TOMATOES. BRING TO A BOIL. REDUCE HEAT TO LOW AND SIMMER FOR 10 MINUTES. USING A SLOTTED SPOON, TRANSFER SOLIDS TO A FOOD PROCESSOR OR BLENDER. ADD 1/2 CUP (125 ML) OF THE COOKING LIQUID AND PROCESS UNTIL SMOOTH. RETURN MIXTURE TO SAUCEPAN OVER LOW HEAT. STIR IN CREAM AND HEAT THROUGH BUT DO NOT BOIL. SEASON TO TASTE WITH SALT AND BLACK PEPPER. LADLE INTO BOWLS AND SERVE IMMEDIATELY. SERVES 4.

TIP: GARNISH EACH SERVING WITH FINELY CHOPPED PARSLEY OR DILL.

CREAMY ONION SOUP WITH KALE

SLOW COOKER RECIPE

THERE IS NO CREAM IN THIS DELICIOUS SOUP — UNLESS YOU DECIDE TO DRIZZLE A BIT OVER INDIVIDUAL SERVINGS AS A FINISHING TOUCH. THE CREAMINESS IS ACHIEVED WITH THE ADDITION OF POTATOES, WHICH ARE PURÉED INTO THE SOUP, PROVIDING IT WITH A VELVETY TEXTURE.

1 TBSP	OLIVE OIL	15 ML
4	ONIONS, THINLY SLICED	4
2	CLOVES GARLIC, MINCED	2
4	WHOLE ALLSPICE	4
1	BAY LEAF	1
1 TSP	GRATED LEMON ZEST	5 ML
1/2 TSP	CRACKED BLACK PEPPERCORNS	2 ML
4 CUPS	READY-TO-USE VEGETABLE BROTH	1 L
3	POTATOES, PEELED AND DICED	3
1 TSP	PAPRIKA DISSOLVED IN 2 TBSP (30 ML) FRESHLY SQUEEZED LEMON JUICE (SEE TIP, OPPOSITE)	5 ML
4 CUPS	CHOPPED KALE	1 L

IN A SKILLET, HEAT OIL OVER MEDIUM HEAT. ADD ONIONS AND COOK, STIRRING, UNTIL SOFTENED, ABOUT 5 MINUTES. ADD GARLIC, ALLSPICE, BAY LEAF, LEMON ZEST AND PEPPERCORNS AND COOK, STIRRING, FOR 1 MINUTE. TRANSFER TO A MEDIUM TO LARGE (3$\frac{1}{2}$- TO 5-QUART) SLOW COOKER. STIR IN BROTH. (SOUP CAN BE COOLED, COVERED AND REFRIGERATED FOR UP TO 2 DAYS AT THIS POINT.)

ADD POTATOES AND STIR WELL. COVER AND COOK ON LOW FOR 8 HOURS OR ON HIGH FOR 4 HOURS, UNTIL POTATOES ARE TENDER. DISCARD ALLSPICE AND BAY LEAF. STIR IN PAPRIKA SOLUTION AND ADD KALE, IN BATCHES, STIRRING AFTER EACH TO SUBMERGE THE LEAVES IN THE LIQUID. COVER AND COOK ON HIGH FOR 20 MINUTES, UNTIL KALE IS TENDER. PURÉE USING AN IMMERSION BLENDER. (YOU CAN ALSO DO THIS IN BATCHES IN A FOOD PROCESSOR OR STAND BLENDER.) SERVE IMMEDIATELY. SERVES 6.

TIP: YOU CAN USE ANY KIND OF PAPRIKA IN THIS RECIPE: REGULAR, OR SWEET; HOT, WHICH PRODUCES A NICELY PEPPERY VERSION; OR SMOKED, WHICH ADDS A DELICIOUS NOTE OF SMOKINESS TO THE SOUP. IF YOU HAVE REGULAR PAPRIKA AND WOULD LIKE A BIT OF HEAT, DISSOLVE $1/4$ TSP (1 ML) CAYENNE PEPPER IN THE LEMON JUICE ALONG WITH THE PAPRIKA.

TIP: IF YOU CHOOSE TO HALVE THIS RECIPE, USE A SMALL (APPROX. 2-QUART) SLOW COOKER.

TIP: HATE SHEDDING TEARS WHEN CHOPPING ONIONS? TO MINIMIZE THE WEEPING PROBLEM, USE A RAZOR-SHARP KNIFE TO PREVENT LOSS OF JUICES, AND COVER THE CUT ONIONS WITH A PAPER TOWEL AS YOU CHOP THEM TO PREVENT THE VAPORS FROM RISING TO YOUR EYES.

WHY ISN'T "PHONETIC" SPELLED THE WAY IT SOUNDS?

CHEESE-SMOTHERED ONION SOUP

THIS SAVORY SOUP WILL WARM YOU UP ON COLD BLUSTERY DAYS. THE ASSERTIVE FLAVOR OF ONIONS MELLOWS AND SWEETENS WHEN COOKED UNTIL GOLDEN. THIS CLASSIC MAKES AN EASY TRANSITION FROM AN EVERYDAY DISH TO AN ENTERTAINMENT STANDOUT.

3 TBSP	BUTTER	45 ML
8 CUPS	THINLY SLICED SPANISH ONIONS (ABOUT 2 TO 3)	2 L
1/4 TSP	DRIED THYME	1 ML
1/4 TSP	FRESHLY GROUND BLACK PEPPER	1 ML
2 TBSP	ALL-PURPOSE FLOUR	30 ML
6 CUPS	HEARTY BEEF STOCK (PAGE 43) OR READY-TO-USE BEEF BROTH	1.5 L
1 TBSP	OLIVE OIL	15 ML
1	LARGE CLOVE GARLIC, MINCED	1
6	SLICES FRENCH BREAD, ABOUT 3/4-INCH (2 CM) THICK	6
2 CUPS	SHREDDED GRUYÈRE CHEESE	500 ML

IN A DUTCH OVEN OR LARGE HEAVY SAUCEPAN, MELT BUTTER OVER MEDIUM HEAT. ADD ONIONS, THYME AND PEPPER; COOK, STIRRING OFTEN, FOR 15 MINUTES OR UNTIL ONIONS ARE TENDER AND A RICH GOLDEN COLOR. BLEND IN FLOUR; STIR IN STOCK. BRING TO A BOIL, STIRRING, UNTIL THICKENED. REDUCE HEAT TO MEDIUM-LOW, COVER AND SIMMER FOR 15 MINUTES.

MEANWHILE, POSITION OVEN RACK 6 INCHES (15 CM) FROM BROILER; PREHEAT BROILER. IN A SMALL BOWL,

COMBINE OLIVE OIL AND GARLIC; LIGHTLY BRUSH OIL MIXTURE OVER BOTH SIDES OF BREAD. ARRANGE ON BAKING SHEET; PLACE UNDER BROILER AND TOAST ON BOTH SIDES.

PLACE TOASTS IN DEEP OVENPROOF SOUP BOWLS; SPRINKLE WITH HALF THE CHEESE. ARRANGE BOWLS IN A LARGE, SHALLOW BAKING PAN. LADLE HOT SOUP INTO BOWLS. SPRINKLE WITH THE REMAINING CHEESE. PLACE UNDER BROILER FOR 3 MINUTES OR UNTIL CHEESE MELTS AND IS LIGHTLY BROWNED. SERVE IMMEDIATELY. SERVES 6.

TIP: BUY FRENCH BREAD 3 TO 4 INCHES (7.5 TO 10 CM) IN DIAMETER. OR, IF USING A THIN BAGUETTE, USE 2 SLICES OF BREAD IN EACH BOWL.

TIP: THE ONION SOUP BASE CAN BE MADE AHEAD AND REFRIGERATED FOR UP TO 5 DAYS OR FROZEN FOR UP TO 3 MONTHS.

BUTTERNUT APPLE SOUP WITH SWISS CHEESE

SLOW COOKER RECIPE

TOPPED WITH MELTED CHEESE, THIS CREAMY AND DELICIOUS SOUP IS AN IDEAL ANTIDOTE TO A BLUSTERY DAY. SERVE IT AS A LIGHT MAIN COURSE, ACCOMPANIED BY A GREEN SALAD AND WHOLE-GRAIN BREAD OR AS A STARTER TO A MORE SUBSTANTIAL MEAL.

I TBSP	OLIVE OIL	15 ML
2	ONIONS, CHOPPED	2
4	CLOVES GARLIC, MINCED	4
2 TSP	DRIED ROSEMARY, CRUMBLED (OR I TBSP/15 ML CHOPPED FRESH ROSEMARY LEAVES)	10 ML
$\frac{1}{2}$ TSP	CRACKED BLACK PEPPERCORNS	2 ML
5 CUPS	CHICKEN STOCK (PAGE 42) OR READY-TO-USE VEGETABLE OR CHICKEN BROTH	1.25 L
I	BUTTERNUT SQUASH, PEELED, SEEDED AND CUT INTO I-INCH (2.5 CM) CUBES (ABOUT $2\frac{1}{2}$ LBS/1.25 KG)	I
2	TART APPLES (SUCH AS GRANNY SMITH), CORED, PEELED AND COARSELY CHOPPED	2
	SALT (OPTIONAL)	
I CUP	SHREDDED SWISS CHEESE	250 ML
$\frac{1}{2}$ CUP	FINELY CHOPPED WALNUTS (OPTIONAL)	125 ML

IN A SKILLET, HEAT OIL OVER MEDIUM HEAT FOR 30 SECONDS. ADD ONIONS AND COOK, STIRRING, UNTIL SOFTENED, ABOUT 3 MINUTES. ADD GARLIC, ROSEMARY AND PEPPERCORNS AND COOK, STIRRING, FOR I MINUTE. TRANSFER TO A LARGE (MINIMUM 5-QUART) SLOW COOKER.

ADD STOCK. (SOUP CAN BE COOLED, COVERED AND REFRIGERATED FOR UP TO 2 DAYS AT THIS POINT.)

STIR IN SQUASH AND APPLES. COVER AND COOK ON LOW FOR 8 HOURS OR ON HIGH FOR 4 HOURS, UNTIL SQUASH IS TENDER.

PREHEAT BROILER. WORKING IN BATCHES, PURÉE SOUP IN A FOOD PROCESSOR OR BLENDER. (YOU CAN ALSO DO THIS IN THE STONEWARE USING AN IMMERSION BLENDER.) SEASON TO TASTE WITH SALT (IF USING). LADLE SOUP INTO OVENPROOF BOWLS. SPRINKLE WITH CHEESE AND BROIL UNTIL CHEESE MELTS, ABOUT 2 MINUTES. (YOU CAN ALSO DO THIS IN A MICROWAVE OVEN, IN BATCHES, ON HIGH, ABOUT 1 MINUTE PER BATCH.) SPRINKLE WITH WALNUTS (IF USING). SERVES 6 TO 8.

IT'S NOT WHAT A TEENAGER KNOWS THAT BOTHERS HIS PARENTS; IT'S HOW HE FOUND OUT.

SAVORY CHEDDAR CHEESE SOUP

SLOW COOKER RECIPE

THIS IS ONE OF THOSE CLASSICS THAT ABSOLUTELY EVERYONE ADORES. SERVE IT WITH SLICED BAGUETTE, FLATBREAD OR EVEN CELERY STICKS AND WATCH IT DISAPPEAR RIGHT TO THE LAST DROP.

1 TBSP	BUTTER	15 ML
1	LEEK, WHITE PART WITH JUST A BIT OF GREEN, CLEANED (SEE TIP, PAGE 15) AND FINELY CHOPPED	1
2	CARROTS, FINELY CHOPPED	2
3	STALKS CELERY, PEELED AND FINELY CHOPPED	3
1 TSP	DRY MUSTARD	5 ML
1/2 TSP	SALT	2 ML
	FRESHLY GROUND BLACK PEPPER	
2 TBSP	ALL-PURPOSE FLOUR	30 ML
4 CUPS	HEARTY BEEF STOCK (PAGE 43) OR READY-TO-USE BEEF BROTH (SEE TIP, OPPOSITE)	1 L
1	BAY LEAF	1
1/4 CUP	HEAVY OR WHIPPING (35%) CREAM	60 ML
1 TBSP	WORCESTERSHIRE SAUCE	15 ML
3 CUPS	SHREDDED CHEDDAR CHEESE	750 ML
	HOT PEPPER SAUCE (OPTIONAL)	

IN A LARGE SKILLET, MELT BUTTER OVER MEDIUM HEAT. ADD LEEK, CARROTS AND CELERY. REDUCE HEAT TO LOW, COVER AND COOK UNTIL VEGETABLES ARE SOFT, ABOUT 10 MINUTES. STIR IN DRY MUSTARD, SALT, AND PEPPER TO TASTE. ADD FLOUR AND COOK, STIRRING, FOR 1 MINUTE.

ADD BROTH AND BAY LEAF AND COOK UNTIL SLIGHTLY THICKENED. (SOUP CAN BE COOLED, COVERED AND REFRIGERATED OVERNIGHT AT THIS POINT.)

TRANSFER SOUP TO A MEDIUM TO LARGE ($3\frac{1}{2}$- TO 5-QUART) SLOW COOKER. COVER AND COOK ON LOW FOR 6 HOURS OR ON HIGH FOR 3 HOURS. DISCARD BAY LEAF. IF DESIRED, TRANSFER SOLIDS PLUS 1 CUP (250 ML) LIQUID TO A FOOD PROCESSOR AND PROCESS UNTIL SMOOTH, THEN RETURN MIXTURE TO SLOW COOKER. ADD CREAM, WORCESTERSHIRE SAUCE AND CHEESE, COVER AND COOK ON HIGH FOR 15 MINUTES, UNTIL CHEESE IS MELTED AND MIXTURE IS BUBBLY. LADLE INTO INDIVIDUAL SERVING BOWLS AND PASS THE HOT PEPPER SAUCE, IF DESIRED.
SERVES 4 TO 6 AS A LIGHT MEAL OR 8 AS A STARTER.

TIP: SINCE IT'S IMPORTANT THAT THE BROTH FOR THIS SOUP BE TOP QUALITY, USE GOOD-QUALITY HOMEMADE STOCK OR ENHANCE STORE-BOUGHT BROTH. TO ENHANCE 4 CUPS (1 L) READY-TO-USE BROTH, POUR IT INTO A LARGE SAUCEPAN AND ADD 1 CARROT, COARSELY CHOPPED, $\frac{1}{2}$ TSP (2 ML) CELERY SEED, $\frac{1}{2}$ TSP (2 ML) CRACKED BLACK PEPPERCORNS, $\frac{1}{2}$ TSP (2 ML) DRIED THYME, 4 PARSLEY SPRIGS, 1 BAY LEAF AND $\frac{1}{2}$ CUP (125 ML) WHITE WINE. BRING TO A BOIL, THEN REDUCE HEAT TO LOW, COVER AND SIMMER FOR 30 MINUTES. STRAIN.

TIP: IF YOU CHOOSE TO HALVE THIS RECIPE, USE A 2- TO 3-QUART SLOW COOKER.

VARIATION: TO MAKE THIS SOUP VEGETARIAN, USE VEGETABLE BROTH AND VEGAN WORCESTERSHIRE SAUCE.

RED LENTIL AND CARROT SOUP WITH COCONUT

SLOW COOKER RECIPE

SERVE THIS MOUTH-WATERING, CREAMY SOUP AS A STARTER OR ADD AN INDIAN BREAD, SUCH AS NAAN, AND A GREEN SALAD FOR A DELICIOUS LIGHT MEAL.

1 TBSP	VEGETABLE OIL	15 ML
2	ONIONS, FINELY CHOPPED	2
4	CLOVES GARLIC, MINCED	4
2 TSP	GROUND TURMERIC	10 ML
2 TSP	CUMIN SEEDS, TOASTED AND GROUND (SEE TIP, OPPOSITE)	10 ML
1 TSP	SALT	5 ML
1/2 TSP	CRACKED BLACK PEPPERCORNS	2 ML
1	CAN (28 OZ/796 ML) TOMATOES, WITH JUICE	1
2	LARGE CARROTS, CUT IN HALF LENGTHWISE AND THINLY SLICED	2
2 CUPS	DRIED RED LENTILS, RINSED	500 ML
1 TBSP	FRESHLY SQUEEZED LEMON JUICE	15 ML
6 CUPS	CHICKEN STOCK (PAGE 42) OR READY-TO-USE VEGETABLE OR CHICKEN BROTH	1.5 L
1	CAN (14 OZ/398 ML) COCONUT MILK	1
1	LONG RED CHILE PEPPER (OR 2 THAI CHILES), FINELY CHOPPED	1
	THIN SLICES LEMON (OPTIONAL)	
	FINELY CHOPPED FRESH CILANTRO (OPTIONAL)	

CONTINUED ON PAGE 55...

54

Hot Multigrain Cereal (page 7)

Carrot Raisin Muffins (page 22)

Butternut Apple Soup with Swiss Cheese (page 50)

Kale and Brussels Sprout Slaw (page 76)

IN A LARGE SKILLET, HEAT OIL OVER MEDIUM HEAT FOR 30 SECONDS. ADD ONIONS AND COOK, STIRRING, UNTIL SOFTENED, ABOUT 3 MINUTES. ADD GARLIC, TURMERIC, TOASTED CUMIN, SALT AND PEPPERCORNS AND COOK, STIRRING, FOR I MINUTE. ADD TOMATOES AND BRING TO A BOIL, BREAKING UP WITH THE BACK OF A SPOON. TRANSFER TO A LARGE (MINIMUM 5-QUART) SLOW COOKER. (MIXTURE CAN BE COOLED, COVERED AND REFRIGERATED FOR UP TO 2 DAYS AT THIS POINT.)

STIR IN CARROTS, LENTILS, LEMON JUICE AND STOCK. COVER AND COOK ON LOW FOR 8 TO IO HOURS OR ON HIGH FOR 4 TO 5 HOURS, UNTIL LENTILS ARE TENDER AND MIXTURE IS BUBBLY. STIR IN COCONUT MILK AND CHILE PEPPER AND COOK ON HIGH FOR 20 TO 30 MINUTES, UNTIL HEATED THROUGH. WHEN READY TO SERVE, LADLE INTO BOWLS AND TOP WITH LEMON SLICES AND CILANTRO (IF USING). SERVES 8 TO IO AS A STARTER OR 4 TO 6 AS A MAIN COURSE.

TIP: TO TOAST CUMIN SEEDS, PLACE SEEDS IN A DRY SKILLET OVER MEDIUM HEAT AND COOK, STIRRING, UNTIL FRAGRANT, ABOUT 3 MINUTES. IMMEDIATELY TRANSFER TO A MORTAR OR A SPICE GRINDER AND GRIND. IF YOU PREFER TO USE GROUND CUMIN, SUBSTITUTE HALF THE QUANTITY CALLED FOR.

TIP: IF YOU DON'T HAVE FRESH CHILE PEPPERS, STIR IN YOUR FAVORITE HOT PEPPER SAUCE, TO TASTE, JUST BEFORE SERVING.

MEDITERRANEAN LENTIL SOUP WITH SPINACH

SLOW COOKER RECIPE

SERVE THIS DELICIOUS SOUP, DELICATELY FLAVORED WITH LEMON AND CUMIN, AS A STARTER OR ADD A GREEN SALAD AND WARM COUNTRY-STYLE BREAD FOR A REFRESHING AND NUTRITIOUS LIGHT MEAL.

I TBSP	VEGETABLE OIL	15 ML
2	ONIONS, CHOPPED	2
2	STALKS CELERY, CHOPPED	2
2	LARGE CARROTS, CHOPPED	2
I	CLOVE GARLIC, MINCED	I
I TSP	CUMIN SEEDS, TOASTED AND GROUND (SEE TIP, PAGE 55)	5 ML
I TSP	GRATED LEMON ZEST	5 ML
6 CUPS	CHICKEN STOCK (PAGE 42) OR READY-TO-USE VEGETABLE OR CHICKEN BROTH	1.5 L
I	POTATO, PEELED AND GRATED	I
I CUP	DRIED GREEN OR BROWN LENTILS, RINSED	250 ML
2 TBSP	FRESHLY SQUEEZED LEMON JUICE	30 ML
1/2 TSP	CAYENNE PEPPER (OPTIONAL; SEE TIP, OPPOSITE)	2 ML
I LB	SPINACH LEAVES	500 G

IN A SKILLET, HEAT OIL OVER MEDIUM HEAT FOR 30 SECONDS. ADD ONIONS, CELERY AND CARROTS AND COOK, STIRRING, UNTIL CARROTS ARE SOFTENED, ABOUT 7 MINUTES. ADD GARLIC, TOASTED CUMIN AND LEMON ZEST AND COOK, STIRRING, FOR I MINUTE. TRANSFER TO

A LARGE (MINIMUM 5-QUART) SLOW COOKER. ADD STOCK.
(SOUP CAN BE COOLED, COVERED AND REFRIGERATED FOR
UP TO 2 DAYS AT THIS POINT.)

STIR IN POTATO AND LENTILS. COVER AND COOK ON
LOW FOR 8 TO 10 HOURS OR ON HIGH FOR 4 TO 6 HOURS,
UNTIL VEGETABLES ARE TENDER. ADD LEMON JUICE
AND CAYENNE (IF USING) AND STIR. ADD SPINACH. COVER
AND COOK ON HIGH FOR 20 MINUTES, UNTIL SPINACH IS
COOKED AND MIXTURE IS HOT AND BUBBLY. SERVES 6
TO 8.

TIP: IF YOU'RE USING CAYENNE PEPPER, DISSOLVE IT IN
THE LEMON JUICE BEFORE ADDING TO THE SLOW COOKER.

WHY DO HUSBANDS OFTEN TALK IN THEIR SLEEP?
IT'S THE ONLY CHANCE THEY GET.

SOUTH AMERICAN BLACK BEAN SOUP

SLOW COOKER RECIPE

THE FLAVOR OF THIS SOUP ACTUALLY IMPROVES IF IT IS ALLOWED TO SIT OVERNIGHT AND THEN REHEATED. GARNISH WITH FINELY CHOPPED CILANTRO, SOUR CREAM OR SALSA.

6	SLICES BACON, CHOPPED	6
2	ONIONS, FINELY CHOPPED	2
2	STALKS CELERY, FINELY CHOPPED	2
2	CARROTS, FINELY CHOPPED	2
2	CLOVES GARLIC, MINCED	2
2 TBSP	CUMIN SEEDS, TOASTED AND GROUND (SEE TIP, PAGE 55)	30 ML
1 TBSP	DRIED OREGANO LEAVES	15 ML
1 TSP	DRIED THYME LEAVES	5 ML
1 TSP	SALT	5 ML
1 TSP	CRACKED BLACK PEPPERCORNS	5 ML
2 TBSP	TOMATO PASTE	30 ML
6 CUPS	CHICKEN STOCK (PAGE 42) OR READY-TO-USE CHICKEN BROTH	1.5 L
4 CUPS	COOKED DRIED OR CANNED BLACK BEANS, DRAINED AND RINSED (SEE TIP, OPPOSITE)	1 L
1/3 CUP	FRESHLY SQUEEZED LIME JUICE	75 ML
1/4 TSP	CAYENNE PEPPER	1 ML
1	JALAPEÑO PEPPER, CHOPPED (OPTIONAL)	1

IN A SKILLET, COOK BACON OVER MEDIUM-HIGH HEAT UNTIL CRISP. DRAIN THOROUGHLY ON PAPER TOWEL. COVER AND REFRIGERATE UNTIL READY TO USE. DRAIN ALL BUT 1 TBSP (15 ML) FAT FROM PAN. REDUCE HEAT TO MEDIUM.

ADD ONIONS, CELERY AND CARROTS AND COOK, STIRRING, UNTIL VEGETABLES ARE SOFTENED, ABOUT 7 MINUTES. ADD GARLIC, TOASTED CUMIN, OREGANO, THYME, SALT AND PEPPERCORNS AND COOK, STIRRING, FOR 1 MINUTE. ADD TOMATO PASTE AND STIR TO COMBINE THOROUGHLY. TRANSFER TO A LARGE (MINIMUM 5-QUART) SLOW COOKER. STIR IN STOCK. (SOUP CAN BE COOLED, COVERED AND REFRIGERATED FOR UP TO 2 DAYS AT THIS POINT.)

ADD BEANS AND RESERVED BACON AND STIR WELL. COVER AND COOK ON LOW FOR 8 TO 10 HOURS OR ON HIGH FOR 4 TO 6 HOURS, UNTIL VEGETABLES ARE TENDER. STIR IN LIME JUICE, CAYENNE AND JALAPEÑO (IF USING). COVER AND COOK ON HIGH FOR 10 MINUTES, UNTIL HEATED THROUGH. WORKING IN BATCHES, PURÉE SOUP IN A FOOD PROCESSOR OR BLENDER. (YOU CAN ALSO DO THIS IN THE STONEWARE USING AN IMMERSION BLENDER.) SPOON INTO BOWLS AND GARNISH. SERVES 4 TO 6 AS A MAIN COURSE OR 6 TO 8 AS A STARTER.

TIP: YOU CAN USE COOKED DRIED BEANS OR CANNED BEANS INTERCHANGEABLY. ONE CUP (250 ML) DRIED BEANS, COOKED, IS ABOUT 2 CUPS (500 ML) CANNED BEANS.

VEGETABLE MINESTRONE WITH SUN-DRIED TOMATO PESTO

MAKE A DOUBLE BATCH OF THIS HEARTY VEGETABLE SOUP EACH FALL WHEN VEGETABLES ARE AT THEIR PRIME. PACK IT INTO CONTAINERS AND PUT IN THE FREEZER FOR EASY MIDWEEK MEALS ON CHILLY DAYS. ANY COMBINATION OF VEGETABLES CAN BE USED, DEPENDING ON WHAT'S IN YOUR FRIDGE.

1 TBSP	OLIVE OIL	15 ML
2	LARGE ONIONS, CHOPPED	2
3	CLOVES GARLIC, FINELY CHOPPED	3
2	CARROTS, CHOPPED	2
2	STALKS CELERY, CHOPPED	2
10 CUPS	CHICKEN STOCK (PAGE 42) OR READY-TO-USE VEGETABLE OR CHICKEN BROTH (APPROX.)	2.5 L
2 CUPS	SHREDDED CABBAGE	500 ML
2 CUPS	SMALL CAULIFLOWER FLORETS	500 ML
1/3 CUP	SHORT FINE NOODLES OR OTHER SMALL-SHAPED PASTA, SUCH AS SHELLS	75 ML
1 CUP	FROZEN PEAS	250 ML
1	CAN (19 OZ/540 ML) ROMANO OR NAVY BEANS, DRAINED AND RINSED	1
3/4 CUP	SUN-DRIED TOMATO PESTO	175 ML
	FRESHLY GRATED PARMESAN CHEESE (OPTIONAL)	

IN A DUTCH OVEN OR LARGE STOCKPOT, HEAT OIL OVER MEDIUM HEAT. ADD ONIONS, GARLIC, CARROTS AND CELERY; COOK, STIRRING OCCASIONALLY, FOR 10 MINUTES OR UNTIL SOFTENED. ADD STOCK AND CABBAGE; BRING TO A BOIL

OVER HIGH HEAT. REDUCE HEAT, COVER AND SIMMER FOR
20 MINUTES OR JUST UNTIL VEGETABLES ARE TENDER.
STIR IN CAULIFLOWER AND PASTA; SIMMER, COVERED,
FOR 8 MINUTES OR JUST UNTIL PASTA IS TENDER. STIR
IN PEAS AND BEANS; COOK FOR 2 MINUTES. LADLE INTO
BOWLS. SWIRL A GENEROUS TABLESPOON (15 ML) OF
PESTO INTO EACH. SPRINKLE WITH PARMESAN, IF DESIRED.
SOUP THICKENS SLIGHTLY AS IT COOLS; ADD MORE
STOCK, IF NECESSARY. SERVES 8.

TIP: SERVE WITH ADDITIONAL PARMESAN CHEESE AT THE
TABLE. REFRIGERATE SOUP FOR UP TO 5 DAYS OR FREEZE
IN AIRTIGHT CONTAINERS FOR UP TO 3 MONTHS.

*HAVE YOU EVER HAD ONE OF THOSE DAYS WHEN YOU'RE
HOLDING A STICK AND EVERYBODY LOOKS LIKE A PIÑATA?*

ITALIAN-STYLE GREEN PEA SOUP

SLOW COOKER RECIPE

THIS IS A PERFECT SOUP FOR THOSE WHO ARE FEELING UNDER THE WEATHER — MILD, FLAVORFUL AND VERY RESTORATIVE.

I TBSP	OLIVE OIL	15 ML
2	ONIONS, FINELY CHOPPED	2
4	CLOVES GARLIC, MINCED	4
I TSP	DRIED THYME	5 ML
1/2 TSP	SALT	2 ML
1/2 TSP	CRACKED BLACK PEPPERCORNS	2 ML
2	BAY LEAVES	2
1/2 CUP	SHORT-GRAIN WHITE OR BROWN RICE (SUCH AS ARBORIO)	125 ML
6 CUPS	READY-TO-USE VEGETABLE BROTH, DIVIDED	1.5 L
2 CUPS	GREEN PEAS, THAWED IF FROZEN	500 ML
1/2 CUP	FRESHLY GRATED PARMESAN CHEESE OR VEGAN ALTERNATIVE	125 ML
1/4 CUP	FINELY CHOPPED FRESH PARSLEY	60 ML
I TBSP	BUTTER (OPTIONAL)	15 ML

IN A SKILLET, HEAT OIL OVER MEDIUM HEAT. ADD ONIONS AND COOK, STIRRING, UNTIL SOFTENED, ABOUT 3 MINUTES. ADD GARLIC, THYME, SALT, PEPPERCORNS AND BAY LEAVES AND COOK, STIRRING, FOR I MINUTE. ADD RICE AND 2 CUPS (500 ML) BROTH AND BRING TO A BOIL. BOIL RAPIDLY FOR 2 MINUTES. TRANSFER TO A MEDIUM TO LARGE (4- TO 5-QUART) SLOW COOKER. (SOUP CAN BE COOLED, COVERED AND REFRIGERATED FOR UP TO 2 DAYS AT THIS POINT.)

ADD THE REMAINING BROTH AND STIR WELL. COVER AND COOK ON LOW FOR 6 HOURS OR ON HIGH FOR 3 HOURS, UNTIL RICE IS TENDER. STIR IN PEAS, PARMESAN, PARSLEY, AND BUTTER (IF USING). STIR WELL. COVER AND COOK ON HIGH FOR 15 MINUTES, UNTIL PEAS ARE TENDER. DISCARD BAY LEAVES. SERVES 6 TO 8.

TIP: USING A RICE THAT IS HIGH IN STARCH, SUCH AS ARBORIO, IMBUES THIS SOUP WITH A CREAMY FINISH. IF YOU PREFER A MORE NUTRITIOUS OPTION, USE SHORT-GRAIN BROWN RICE, WHICH IS STARCHIER THAN LONGER-GRAIN VARIETIES.

TIP: TO MAKE THIS SOUP VEGAN, OMIT THE BUTTER AND DRIZZLE THE SOUP WITH EXTRA VIRGIN OLIVE OIL AFTER IT IS LADLED INTO BOWLS.

TIP: IF YOU CHOOSE TO HALVE THIS RECIPE, USE A SMALL (ABOUT 2-QUART) SLOW COOKER.

HE WHO HESITATES IS ... UM ...

CLAM CHOWDER

THICK AND CREAMY, LADEN WITH CHUNKS OF
POTATOES AND FEATURING THE SMOKY FLAVOR
OF BACON, THIS RESTAURANT FAVORITE IS EASY
TO RECREATE IN YOUR HOME KITCHEN.

4	SLICES BACON, CHOPPED	4
1	CAN (5 OZ/142 G) CLAMS, DRAINED, JUICE RESERVED	1
1	SMALL ONION, FINELY CHOPPED	1
1	STALK CELERY, FINELY DICED	1
1	CLOVE GARLIC, FINELY CHOPPED	1
1	BAY LEAF	1
1½ CUPS	CUBED PEELED POTATOES (½-INCH/ 1 CM CUBES)	375 ML
1 CUP	FISH STOCK OR READY-TO-USE CHICKEN BROTH	250 ML
2 CUPS	MILK	500 ML
3 TBSP	ALL-PURPOSE FLOUR	45 ML
2 TBSP	FINELY CHOPPED FRESH PARSLEY	30 ML
	SALT AND FRESHLY GROUND BLACK PEPPER	

IN A LARGE SAUCEPAN, COOK BACON OVER MEDIUM HEAT,
STIRRING, FOR 4 MINUTES OR UNTIL CRISP. REMOVE;
BLOT WITH PAPER TOWELS AND SET ASIDE. ADD DRAINED
CLAMS, ONION, CELERY, GARLIC AND BAY LEAF; COOK,
STIRRING OFTEN, FOR 3 MINUTES OR UNTIL VEGETABLES
ARE SOFTENED. STIR IN RESERVED CLAM JUICE, POTATOES
AND STOCK; BRING TO A BOIL. REDUCE HEAT TO MEDIUM-
LOW, COVER AND SIMMER FOR 15 MINUTES OR UNTIL
VEGETABLES ARE TENDER. IN A BOWL, BLEND FLOUR WITH

1/3 CUP (75 ML) MILK TO MAKE A SMOOTH PASTE. STIR IN THE REMAINING MILK. ADD TO SAUCEPAN; BRING TO A BOIL OVER MEDIUM-HIGH HEAT, STIRRING OFTEN, UNTIL MIXTURE THICKENS. STIR IN BACON BITS AND PARSLEY; SEASON WITH SALT, IF NEEDED, AND PEPPER TO TASTE. REMOVE BAY LEAF BEFORE SERVING. SERVES 4.

VARIATION

FISH CHOWDER: OMIT CANNED CLAMS. INCREASE FISH STOCK TO 2 CUPS (500 ML). ADD 12 OZ (375 G) CUBED FISH, SUCH AS COD, HADDOCK OR BLUEFISH, AT END OF COOKING ALONG WITH BACON BITS. SIMMER FOR 5 MINUTES OR UNTIL FISH FLAKES. ADD MORE STOCK, IF NECESSARY, TO THIN SOUP TO DESIRED CONSISTENCY.

PUMPKIN SOUP WITH SHRIMP AND LIME

SLOW COOKER RECIPE

THIS SOUP, WHICH IS DELICIOUS HOT OR COLD, HAS ITS ORIGINS IN BOTH FRENCH PROVINCIAL AND LATIN AMERICAN CUISINE. IF PUMPKIN IS UNAVAILABLE, SUBSTITUTE ANY ORANGE-FLESHED SQUASH, SUCH AS ACORN OR BUTTERNUT.

6 CUPS	CUBED PEELED PIE PUMPKIN (2-INCH/ 5 CM CUBES)	1.25 L
3	LEEKS, WHITE PART ONLY, CLEANED (SEE TIP, PAGE 15) AND COARSELY CHOPPED	3
4 CUPS	CHICKEN STOCK (PAGE 42) OR READY-TO-USE CHICKEN OR VEGETABLE BROTH	1 L
1 TSP	SALT	5 ML
1/4 TSP	FRESHLY GROUND BLACK PEPPER	1 ML
	GRATED ZEST AND JUICE OF 1 LIME	
PINCH	CAYENNE PEPPER	PINCH
1 CUP	HEAVY OR WHIPPING (35%) CREAM	250 ML
8 OZ	COOKED SALAD SHRIMP (OR TWO 3 3/4-OZ/106 G CANS SHRIMP, DRAINED AND RINSED)	250 G
6 to 8	CHERRY TOMATOES, HALVED	6 to 8
2 TBSP	TOASTED PUMPKIN SEEDS (OPTIONAL)	30 ML
	FINELY CHOPPED FRESH CHIVES OR CILANTRO	

IN A LARGE (MINIMUM 5-QUART) SLOW COOKER, COMBINE PUMPKIN, LEEKS, STOCK, SALT AND PEPPER. COVER AND COOK ON LOW FOR 8 TO 10 HOURS OR ON HIGH FOR 4 TO 6 HOURS, UNTIL PUMPKIN IS TENDER. WORKING

IN BATCHES, PURÉE SOUP IN A FOOD PROCESSOR OR BLENDER. (YOU CAN ALSO DO THIS IN THE STONEWARE USING AN IMMERSION BLENDER.) IF SERVING HOT, RETURN SOUP TO SLOW COOKER, ADD LIME ZEST AND JUICE, CAYENNE, CREAM AND SHRIMP AND COOK ON HIGH FOR 20 MINUTES, OR UNTIL SHRIMP ARE HEATED THROUGH. IF SERVING COLD, COMBINE INGREDIENTS IN A LARGE BOWL AND CHILL THOROUGHLY. WHEN READY TO SERVE, LADLE SOUP INTO INDIVIDUAL BOWLS AND GARNISH WITH CHERRY TOMATOES, PUMPKIN SEEDS (IF USING) AND CHIVES. SERVES 6 TO 8.

TIP: IF USING PUMPKIN SEEDS, PAN-FRY IN A DRY, HOT SKILLET OVER MEDIUM HEAT UNTIL THEY ARE LIGHTLY BROWNED AND PUFFED. WHEN PURCHASING PUMPKIN SEEDS, TASTE FIRST, AS THEY TEND TO GO RANCID QUICKLY. STORE IN THE FREEZER UNTIL READY TO USE.

HE HAD A PHOTOGRAPHIC MEMORY
THAT WAS NEVER DEVELOPED.

CHICKEN NOODLE SOUP

OFTEN CALLED "JEWISH PENICILLIN,"
CHICKEN SOUP IS THE PERFECT ANTIDOTE TO
AN ONCOMING COLD. BUT THERE'S MORE TO ITS
RESTORATIVE POWERS: RICH AND DELICIOUS, IT CAN
BANISH THE WINTER BLUES AND MAKE YOU FEEL
JUST PLAIN GOOD ANY DAY OF THE YEAR.

3 LBS	WHOLE CHICKEN OR CHICKEN PIECES, SUCH AS LEGS AND BREASTS	1.5 KG
10 CUPS	WATER (APPROX.)	2.5 L
1	LARGE ONION, FINELY CHOPPED	1
3	CARROTS, CHOPPED	3
2	STALKS CELERY, INCLUDING LEAVES, CHOPPED	2
2 TBSP	CHOPPED FRESH PARSLEY	30 ML
$\frac{1}{2}$ TSP	DRIED THYME	2 ML
2 TSP	SALT	10 ML
$\frac{1}{4}$ TSP	FRESHLY GROUND BLACK PEPPER	1 ML
1	BAY LEAF	1
2 CUPS	MEDIUM OR BROAD EGG NOODLES	500 ML
1 CUP	FINELY DICED ZUCCHINI OR SMALL CAULIFLOWER FLORETS	250 ML
2 TBSP	CHOPPED FRESH DILL OR PARSLEY	30 ML

RINSE CHICKEN; REMOVE AS MUCH SKIN AND EXCESS FAT
AS POSSIBLE. PLACE IN A LARGE STOCKPOT; ADD WATER
TO COVER. BRING TO A BOIL OVER HIGH HEAT; USING A
SLOTTED SPOON, SKIM OFF FOAM AS IT RISES TO THE
SURFACE. ADD ONION, CARROTS, CELERY, PARSLEY, THYME,
SALT, PEPPER AND BAY LEAF. REDUCE HEAT TO MEDIUM-
LOW; COVER AND SIMMER FOR ABOUT $1\frac{1}{4}$ HOURS OR UNTIL

CHICKEN IS TENDER. REMOVE CHICKEN WITH SLOTTED SPOON AND PLACE IN A LARGE BOWL; LET COOL SLIGHTLY. PULL CHICKEN MEAT OFF THE BONES, DISCARDING SKIN AND BONES. CUT MEAT INTO BITE-SIZE PIECES. RESERVE 2 CUPS (500 ML) FOR SOUP. (USE REMAINDER FOR CASSEROLES AND SANDWICHES.) SKIM FAT FROM SURFACE OF SOUP; BRING TO A BOIL. ADD CUBED CHICKEN, NOODLES, ZUCCHINI AND DILL; COOK FOR 10 MINUTES OR UNTIL NOODLES AND VEGETABLES ARE TENDER. REMOVE BAY LEAF. ADJUST SEASONING WITH SALT AND PEPPER TO TASTE. SERVES 8.

TIP: YOU DON'T HAVE TO SLAVE OVER THE STOVE TO MAKE THIS SOUL-SATISFYING SOUP. ADDING THE CHICKEN AND THE VEGETABLES TO THE POT AT THE SAME TIME STREAMLINES THE PROCESS AND DOES AWAY WITH THE CHORE OF MAKING STOCK FIRST. THE RESULTS ARE EVERY BIT AS PLEASING.

A NOISE WOKE ME UP THIS MORNING.
IT WAS THE CRACK OF DAWN.

OLD-FASHIONED SCOTCH BROTH

THIS HEARTY MEAL-IN-A-BOWL IS THE PERFECT
DISH FOR COLD WINTER WEEKENDS. SERVE STEAMING
MUGS AFTER A BRISK WALK OR A DAY ON THE SLOPES.
TO ENHANCE THE EXPERIENCE, MAKE IT IN YOUR SLOW
COOKER SO IT'S READY WHEN YOU COME THROUGH
THE DOOR. ADD A TOSSED SALAD AND WHOLE-GRAIN
BREAD FOR A GREAT LIGHT MEAL.

1 to 2 TBSP	OLIVE OIL	15 to 30 ML
1 LB	BONELESS LAMB SHOULDER OR STEWING BEEF, TRIMMED OF FAT AND DICED	500 G
3	LEEKS, WHITE AND LIGHT GREEN PARTS ONLY, CLEANED (SEE TIP, PAGE 15) AND THINLY SLICED	3
4	STALKS CELERY, DICED	4
4	CARROTS, DICED	4
2	PARSNIPS, DICED	2
2 TSP	DRIED THYME, CRUMBLED	10 ML
1/2 TSP	CRACKED BLACK PEPPERCORNS	2 ML
1	BAY LEAF	1
1 1/4 CUPS	WHOLE (HULLED) BARLEY, DRAINED AND RINSED	300 ML
8 CUPS	HEARTY BEEF STOCK (PAGE 43) OR READY-TO-USE BEEF BROTH	2 L
2 CUPS	WATER	500 ML
1 1/2 CUPS	GREEN PEAS, THAWED IF FROZEN	375 ML
1/2 CUP	FINELY CHOPPED FRESH PARSLEY	125 ML

IN A LARGE SAUCEPAN, STOCKPOT OR DUTCH OVEN,
HEAT 1 TBSP (15 ML) OIL OVER MEDIUM-HIGH HEAT FOR
30 SECONDS. ADD LAMB, IN BATCHES, AND COOK, STIRRING,

UNTIL BROWNED, ABOUT I MINUTE PER BATCH. TRANSFER TO A PLATE AS COMPLETED. REDUCE HEAT TO MEDIUM. ADD MORE OIL TO POT, IF NECESSARY. ADD LEEKS, CELERY, CARROTS AND PARSNIPS AND COOK, STIRRING, UNTIL VEGETABLES ARE SOFTENED, ABOUT 7 MINUTES. ADD THYME, PEPPERCORNS AND BAY LEAF AND COOK, STIRRING, FOR I MINUTE. ADD BARLEY AND TOSS UNTIL WELL COATED WITH MIXTURE. ADD STOCK, WATER AND RESERVED LAMB AND BRING TO A BOIL. REDUCE HEAT TO LOW. COVER AND SIMMER UNTIL BARLEY IS TENDER, ABOUT I HOUR. ADD GREEN PEAS AND COOK UNTIL TENDER, ABOUT 5 MINUTES. DISCARD BAY LEAF. SERVE HOT, LIBERALLY GARNISHED WITH PARSLEY. MAKES 8 MAIN-COURSE SERVINGS.

TIP

SLOW COOKER METHOD: START BY PREPARING THE RECIPE AS DESCRIBED, REDUCING THE WATER TO I CUP (250 ML). AFTER ADDING THE STOCK, WATER AND RESERVED LAMB AND BRINGING TO A BOIL, TRANSFER SOUP TO SLOW COOKER STONEWARE. COVER AND COOK ON LOW FOR 8 HOURS OR ON HIGH FOR 4 HOURS, UNTIL BARLEY IS TENDER. ADD GREEN PEAS. COVER AND COOK ON HIGH FOR IO MINUTES, UNTIL TENDER. GARNISH WITH PARSLEY.

CREAM OF MUSHROOM SOUP

2 TBSP	BUTTER	30 ML
1	LARGE ONION, FINELY CHOPPED	1
2	CLOVES GARLIC, FINELY CHOPPED	2
8 OZ	ASSORTED MUSHROOMS, SUCH AS SHIITAKE AND CREMINI, SLICED	250 G
1½ TSP	CHOPPED FRESH THYME LEAVES (OR ½ TSP/2 ML DRIED THYME)	7 ML
2 TBSP	ALL-PURPOSE FLOUR	30 ML
4 CUPS	CHICKEN STOCK (PAGE 42) OR READY-TO-USE CHICKEN BROTH	1 L
½ TSP	SALT	2 ML
¼ TSP	FRESHLY GROUND BLACK PEPPER	1 ML
1 CUP	TABLE (18%) CREAM	250 ML
¼ CUP	MEDIUM-DRY SHERRY (OPTIONAL)	60 ML
2 TBSP	CHOPPED FRESH CHIVES OR PARSLEY	30 ML

IN A DUTCH OVEN OR LARGE SAUCEPAN, HEAT BUTTER OVER MEDIUM-HIGH HEAT. COOK ONION AND GARLIC, STIRRING, FOR 2 MINUTES, UNTIL SOFTENED. STIR IN MUSHROOMS AND THYME; COOK, STIRRING OFTEN, FOR 5 MINUTES OR UNTIL MUSHROOMS ARE TENDER. BLEND IN FLOUR; STIR IN STOCK, SALT AND PEPPER. BRING TO A BOIL OVER HIGH HEAT. REDUCE HEAT TO MEDIUM-LOW, COVER AND SIMMER FOR 25 MINUTES. LET COOL SLIGHTLY. IN A FOOD PROCESSOR OR BLENDER, PURÉE SOUP IN BATCHES. RETURN TO SAUCEPAN. PLACE OVER MEDIUM HEAT; STIR IN CREAM AND SHERRY (IF USING). ADJUST SEASONING WITH SALT AND PEPPER TO TASTE. HEAT UNTIL PIPING HOT. LADLE INTO HEATED BOWLS AND SPRINKLE WITH CHIVES. SERVES 6.

SALADS

CREAMY COLESLAW

A FAMILY BARBECUE AND PICNIC CALLS FOR A GENEROUS BOWL OF OLD-FASHIONED CABBAGE SLAW WITH A CREAMY MAYONNAISE-MUSTARD DRESSING.

8 CUPS	FINELY SHREDDED GREEN CABBAGE	2 L
5	GREEN ONIONS, SLICED	5
2	CARROTS, SHREDDED	2
2 TBSP	CHOPPED FRESH PARSLEY	30 ML
1/2 CUP	LIGHT MAYONNAISE	125 ML
2 TBSP	LIQUID HONEY	30 ML
2 TBSP	CIDER VINEGAR	30 ML
1 TBSP	DIJON MUSTARD	15 ML
1/2 TSP	CELERY SEEDS (OPTIONAL)	2 ML
1/2 TSP	SALT	2 ML
1/4 TSP	FRESHLY GROUND BLACK PEPPER	1 ML

IN A SERVING BOWL, COMBINE CABBAGE, GREEN ONIONS, CARROTS AND PARSLEY. IN ANOTHER BOWL, STIR TOGETHER MAYONNAISE, HONEY, VINEGAR, MUSTARD, CELERY SEEDS (IF USING), SALT AND PEPPER. POUR OVER CABBAGE MIXTURE; TOSS TO COAT WELL. REFRIGERATE UNTIL READY TO SERVE. SERVES 6.

VARIATION

WALDORF COLESLAW: SUBSTITUTE 2 CHOPPED LARGE STALKS CELERY FOR THE CARROTS, AND ADD 2 DICED APPLES AND 3/4 CUP (175 ML) COARSELY CHOPPED WALNUTS.

ASIAN SLAW

A DIFFERENT WAY TO DRESS UP A BAG OF COLESLAW.

DRESSING

I TSP	GRATED GINGERROOT	5 ML
2 TBSP	PACKED BROWN SUGAR	30 ML
1/4 CUP	VEGETABLE OIL	60 ML
3 TBSP	SOY SAUCE	45 ML
3 TBSP	RICE VINEGAR	45 ML
I TSP	SESAME OIL	5 ML

SALAD

I	BAG COLESLAW MIX	I
I	SMALL RED BELL PEPPER, THINLY SLICED	I
3	GREEN ONIONS, CHOPPED	3
1/3 CUP	CHOPPED FRESH CILANTRO	75 ML
1/4 CUP	CHOPPED PEANUTS OR SLICED ALMONDS	60 ML

DRESSING: IN A SMALL BOWL OR JAR, WHISK OR SHAKE TOGETHER GINGER, BROWN SUGAR, VEGETABLE OIL, SOY SAUCE, RICE VINEGAR AND SESAME OIL.

SALAD: IN A LARGE BOWL, COMBINE COLESLAW, RED PEPPER, GREEN ONIONS AND CILANTRO. ADD DRESSING AND TOSS TO COAT. SERVE SPRINKLED WITH PEANUTS. SERVES 6.

KALE AND BRUSSELS SPROUT SLAW

DRESSING

1/4 CUP	OLIVE OIL	60 ML
2 TBSP	FRESHLY SQUEEZED LEMON JUICE	30 ML
2 TBSP	CIDER VINEGAR	30 ML
1 TBSP	GRAINY OR DIJON MUSTARD	15 ML
1 TBSP	LIQUID HONEY	15 ML

SALAD

5 CUPS	LOOSELY PACKED KALE	1.25 L
8	LARGE BRUSSELS SPROUTS, ENDS TRIMMED	8
1	SMALL APPLE, DICED	1
1/3 CUP	CRUMBLED FETA CHEESE	75 ML
1/3 CUP	CHOPPED PECANS, TOASTED (SEE TIP, BELOW)	75 ML

DRESSING: IN A SMALL BOWL OR JAR, WHISK OR SHAKE TOGETHER OIL, LEMON JUICE, VINEGAR, MUSTARD AND HONEY.

SALAD: PULL THE KALE LEAVES OFF THE STALKS AND DISCARD THE STALKS. STACK AND THINLY SLICE THE LEAVES. HALVE THE BRUSSELS SPROUTS LENGTHWISE AND THINLY SLICE. IN A LARGE BOWL, COMBINE KALE, BRUSSELS SPROUTS, APPLE AND FETA. DRIZZLE WITH DRESSING AND TOSS TO COMBINE. SERVE SPRINKLED WITH PECANS. SERVES 6.

TIP: TOAST PECANS IN A SMALL DRY SKILLET OVER MEDIUM HEAT, SHAKING THE PAN OFTEN, UNTIL PALE GOLDEN AND FRAGRANT. LET COOL BEFORE ADDING TO YOUR SALAD.

CLASSIC GREEK SALAD

GREEK'S SIGNATURE SALAD SINGS WHEN YOU USE THE RIPEST TOMATOES AND REALLY GOOD OLIVE OIL, ALONG WITH IMPORTED GREEK FETA AND OREGANO.

2	RIPE TOMATOES, HALVED LENGTHWISE AND CUT INTO WEDGES	2
1	SMALL VIDALIA OR RED ONION, HALVED AND CUT INTO WEDGES	1
1/2	ENGLISH CUCUMBER, QUARTERED LENGTHWISE AND CUT INTO THICK SLICES	1/2
1	RED BELL PEPPER, CUT INTO CUBES	1
1	YELLOW OR GREEN BELL PEPPER, CUT INTO CUBES	1
1/4 CUP	OLIVE OIL	60 ML
2 TBSP	FRESHLY SQUEEZED LEMON JUICE	30 ML
1 TSP	DRIED OREGANO	5 ML
1/4 TSP	SALT	1 ML
	FRESHLY GROUND BLACK PEPPER	
2 TBSP	CHOPPED FRESH FLAT-LEAF (ITALIAN) PARSLEY	30 ML
4 OZ	FETA CHEESE, CUBED	125 G
12	KALAMATA OLIVES	12

IN A SALAD BOWL, COMBINE TOMATOES, ONION, CUCUMBER AND PEPPERS. IN A SEPARATE BOWL, WHISK TOGETHER OIL, LEMON JUICE, OREGANO, SALT, AND PEPPER TO TASTE. POUR DRESSING OVER VEGETABLES AND GENTLY TOSS. SPRINKLE WITH PARSLEY AND GARNISH WITH FETA AND OLIVES. SERVE IMMEDIATELY. SERVES 4.

TIP: USE THE FINEST EXTRA VIRGIN OLIVE OIL FOR BEST FLAVOR. EXPERIMENT WITH OILS FROM DIFFERENT COUNTRIES.

CAESAR SALAD

THE KING OF TOSSED SALADS WAS NAMED AFTER
A TIJUANA RESTAURATEUR BY THE NAME OF CAESAR
CARDINI. HERE, MAYONNAISE GIVES THIS CLASSIC SALAD
AN EVEN CREAMIER TEXTURE THAN THE ORIGINAL.

GARLIC CROUTONS

4 CUPS	CUBED CRUSTY BREAD ($\frac{1}{2}$-INCH/I CM CUBES)	I L
2 TBSP	OLIVE OIL	30 ML
I	CLOVE GARLIC, MINCED	I
2 TBSP	FRESHLY GRATED PARMESAN CHEESE	30 ML

SALAD

$\frac{1}{3}$ CUP	OLIVE OIL	75 ML
2 TBSP	LIGHT MAYONNAISE	30 ML
2 TBSP	FRESHLY SQUEEZED LEMON JUICE	30 ML
2 TBSP	WATER	30 ML
I TSP	DIJON MUSTARD	5 ML
2	CLOVES GARLIC, MINCED	2
3	ANCHOVY FILLETS, CHOPPED, OR I TBSP (I5 ML) ANCHOVY PASTE	3
$\frac{1}{4}$ TSP	FRESHLY GROUND BLACK PEPPER	I ML
I	LARGE HEAD ROMAINE LETTUCE, TORN INTO BITE-SIZE PIECES (ABOUT I2 CUPS/3 L)	I
6	SLICES BACON, COOKED CRISP AND CRUMBLED (OPTIONAL)	6
$\frac{1}{3}$ CUP	FRESHLY GRATED PARMESAN CHEESE	75 ML
	SALT	

GARLIC CROUTONS: PREHEAT OVEN TO 375°F (190°C).

PLACE BREAD CUBES IN A BOWL. COMBINE OIL AND GARLIC;

DRIZZLE OVER BREAD CUBES AND TOSS. SPRINKLE WITH

PARMESAN AND TOSS AGAIN. ARRANGE IN A SINGLE LAYER ON A RIMMED BAKING SHEET. BAKE, STIRRING ONCE, FOR ABOUT 10 MINUTES OR UNTIL GOLDEN.

SALAD: IN A FOOD PROCESSOR, COMBINE OIL, MAYONNAISE, LEMON JUICE, WATER, MUSTARD, GARLIC, ANCHOVY FILLETS AND PEPPER; PROCESS UNTIL SMOOTH AND CREAMY. ARRANGE LETTUCE IN SALAD BOWL; POUR DRESSING OVER AND TOSS LIGHTLY. ADD CROUTONS; SPRINKLE WITH CRUMBLED BACON (IF USING) AND PARMESAN CHEESE. TOSS AGAIN. TASTE AND SEASON WITH SALT AND PEPPER, IF NEEDED. SERVE IMMEDIATELY. SERVES 6.

TIP: MAKE SURE SALAD GREENS ARE WASHED AND DRIED THOROUGHLY, PREFERABLY IN A SALAD SPINNER, FOR BEST RESULTS.

TIP: HOMEMADE CROUTONS MAKE A DEFINITE FLAVOR DIFFERENCE, BUT 3 CUPS (750 ML) STORE-BOUGHT CROUTONS WORK IN A PINCH.

WITH ANYTHING NEW IT'S ALWAYS
A GOOD IDEA TO START AT THE BOTTOM,
EXCEPT WHEN YOU'RE LEARNING TO SWIM.

CARROT, ORANGE AND ONION SALAD

IF YOUR TASTE BUDS ARE TIRED AND LOOKING FOR A LIFT, TRY THIS DELICIOUS AND UNUSUAL SALAD.

2 CUPS	SLICED CARROTS, COOKED UNTIL TENDER-CRISP AND PLUNGED INTO ICE WATER	500 ML
1	CAN (10 OZ/284 ML) MANDARIN ORANGE SEGMENTS IN SYRUP, DRAINED, SYRUP RESERVED	1
1/2 CUP	THINLY SLICED RED ONION	125 ML
1 TBSP	FRESHLY SQUEEZED LEMON JUICE	15 ML
1 TBSP	ORANGE MARMALADE	15 ML
1 TBSP	MAPLE SYRUP OR LIQUID HONEY	15 ML
	SALT AND FRESHLY GROUND BLACK PEPPER	

IN A SERVING BOWL, COMBINE CARROTS, ORANGES AND ONION. IN A SMALL BOWL, COMBINE LEMON JUICE, MARMALADE, MAPLE SYRUP AND 2 TBSP (30 ML) RESERVED SYRUP FROM ORANGES. MIX WELL. POUR OVER CARROT MIXTURE AND TOSS TO COMBINE. SEASON TO TASTE WITH SALT AND BLACK PEPPER. SERVES 4.

TIP: GARNISH EACH SERVING WITH FINELY CHOPPED FRESH PARSLEY.

BEST-EVER POTATO SALAD

IF ANYTHING SIGNALS THE ARRIVAL OF SUMMER DAYS AND BACKYARD BARBECUES, IT'S A POTATO SALAD.

6	NEW POTATOES (ABOUT 2 LBS/1 KG)	6
2 TBSP	RED WINE VINEGAR	30 ML
1 TBSP	DIJON MUSTARD	15 ML
1	CLOVE GARLIC, MINCED	1
4	GREEN ONIONS, SLICED	4
2	STALKS CELERY, DICED	2
1/4 CUP	CHOPPED FRESH PARSLEY OR DILL	60 ML
1/2 CUP	LIGHT MAYONNAISE	125 ML
1/4 CUP	SOUR CREAM OR PLAIN YOGURT	60 ML
1/2 TSP	SALT	2 ML
	FRESHLY GROUND BLACK PEPPER	

IN A MEDIUM SAUCEPAN OF BOILING SALTED WATER, COOK WHOLE POTATOES FOR 20 TO 25 MINUTES, UNTIL JUST TENDER. DRAIN; WHEN COOL ENOUGH TO HANDLE, PEEL AND CUT INTO 1/2-INCH (1 CM) CUBES. PLACE IN A SERVING BOWL. IN A SMALL BOWL, STIR TOGETHER VINEGAR, MUSTARD AND GARLIC; POUR OVER WARM POTATOES AND TOSS GENTLY. LET COOL TO ROOM TEMPERATURE. STIR IN GREEN ONIONS, CELERY AND PARSLEY. IN A BOWL, COMBINE MAYONNAISE, SOUR CREAM, SALT AND PEPPER TO TASTE. FOLD INTO POTATO MIXTURE UNTIL EVENLY COATED. REFRIGERATE UNTIL SERVING TIME. SERVES 6.

VARIATION: ADD 3 CHOPPED HARD-COOKED EGGS (SEE TIP, PAGE 82) AND 3/4 CUP (175 ML) FROZEN PEAS, RINSED UNDER HOT WATER AND DRAINED WELL.

MEDITERRANEAN POTATO SALAD

HERE'S A VARIATION OF SALADE NIÇOISE, A FAMOUS PROVENÇAL DISH THAT MAKES A PARTICULARLY ENJOYABLE LIGHT MEAL. USE THIS RECIPE TO MAKE A MINIMALIST VERSION, THEN ADD WHATEVER EXTRAS YOU HAVE ON HAND.

1	CAN (6 OZ/170 G) OLIVE OIL-PACKED TUNA (PREFERABLY ITALIAN), DRAINED	1
2 CUPS	SLICED COOKED POTATOES	500 ML
1/4 CUP	CHOPPED GREEN ONION	60 ML
1 TBSP	DRAINED CAPERS	15 ML
3/4 CUP	OIL AND VINEGAR DRESSING	175 ML
1	BAG (10 OZ/300 G) WASHED SALAD GREENS OR 4 CUPS (1 L) TORN LETTUCE, WASHED AND DRIED	1
2	HARD-COOKED EGGS (SEE TIP, BELOW), QUARTERED OR THINLY SLICED (OPTIONAL)	2

IN A BOWL, COMBINE TUNA, POTATOES, ONION AND CAPERS. ADD DRESSING AND TOSS TO COMBINE. ARRANGE SALAD GREENS IN A SHALLOW SERVING DISH OR DEEP PLATTER. SPOON TUNA MIXTURE OVER TOP. GARNISH WITH EGGS (IF USING). SERVES 4.

TIP: TO HARD-COOK EGGS, PLACE EGGS IN A SAUCEPAN AND ADD COLD WATER TO COVER. BRING TO A BOIL AND COOK VIGOROUSLY FOR 2 MINUTES. REMOVE FROM HEAT AND LET STAND FOR 15 MINUTES. DRAIN AND IMMEDIATELY PLUNGE EGGS INTO A BOWL OF COLD WATER. REFRIGERATE UNTIL READY TO USE.

SCANDINAVIAN PASTA SALAD

THIS SALAD IS VERY TASTY YET SO EASY
TO MAKE THAT IT IS SURE TO BECOME A STAPLE
AT YOUR HOUSE. IT IS ALSO A GREAT DISH TO
CONTRIBUTE TO A POTLUCK. TRICOLORED PASTA ADDS
VISUAL INTEREST AND CREATES THE IMPRESSION
OF EFFORT, BUT THE SALAD TASTES JUST AS
DELICIOUS MADE WITH PLAIN MACARONI.

2 CUPS	ROTINI OR FUSILLI PASTA, PREFERABLY TRICOLOR	500 ML
1/2 CUP	MAYONNAISE	125 ML
1/2 CUP	SOUR CREAM	125 ML
1 TBSP	DIJON MUSTARD	15 ML
1/2 TSP	SALT	2 ML
	FRESHLY GROUND BLACK PEPPER	
8 OZ	SHREDDED SMOKED DELI HAM, SUCH AS BLACK FOREST HAM OR DICED COOKED HAM	250 G
1	ROASTED RED BELL PEPPER (SEE TIPS, PAGE 149), FINELY CHOPPED	1
2	HARD-COOKED EGGS (SEE TIP, OPPOSITE), THINLY SLICED	2
	FRESH DILL OR PARSLEY SPRIGS (OPTIONAL)	

IN A POT OF BOILING SALTED WATER, COOK PASTA
UNTIL AL DENTE, ABOUT 8 MINUTES. DRAIN AND RINSE
UNDER COLD RUNNING WATER. IN A SERVING BOWL, MIX
TOGETHER MAYONNAISE, SOUR CREAM, DIJON MUSTARD,
SALT, AND BLACK PEPPER TO TASTE. ADD COOKED PASTA,
HAM AND ROASTED PEPPER. TOSS TO COMBINE. CHILL
THOROUGHLY. GARNISH WITH SLICED EGG AND DILL (IF
USING) JUST BEFORE SERVING. SERVES 4.

ITALIAN PASTA SALAD

PASTA SALADS ARE ALWAYS A HIT, BRIGHTENING UP A BUFFET, BACKYARD BARBECUE OR YOUR DINNER TABLE.

SALAD

8 OZ	PASTA (SUCH AS FUSILLI OR PENNE)	250 G
4 OZ	PROVOLONE CHEESE, CUT INTO SMALL CUBES	125 G
1 CUP	CHERRY TOMATOES, HALVED OR QUARTERED, IF LARGE	250 ML
1/3 CUP	FINELY CHOPPED RED ONIONS	75 ML
1/2	LARGE RED BELL PEPPER, CUT INTO THIN 1 1/2-INCH (4 CM) STRIPS	1/2
1/2	LARGE GREEN BELL PEPPER, CUT INTO THIN 1 1/2-INCH (4 CM) STRIPS	1/2
1/3 CUP	KALAMATA OLIVES (OPTIONAL)	75 ML
1/3 CUP	FINELY CHOPPED FRESH PARSLEY	75 ML

DRESSING

1/4 CUP	OLIVE OIL	60 ML
2 TBSP	RED WINE VINEGAR	30 ML
1 TBSP	DIJON MUSTARD	15 ML
1	LARGE CLOVE GARLIC, MINCED	1
1 TSP	DRIED BASIL	5 ML
1 TSP	DRIED OREGANO	5 ML
1/2 TSP	SALT	2 ML
1/4 TSP	FRESHLY GROUND BLACK PEPPER	1 ML

SALAD: COOK PASTA IN A LARGE POT OF BOILING SALTED WATER UNTIL TENDER BUT STILL FIRM. DRAIN; RINSE UNDER COLD WATER AND DRAIN WELL. IN A LARGE SERVING BOWL, COMBINE PASTA, CHEESE CUBES, TOMATOES, ONIONS, RED PEPPER, OLIVES (IF USING) AND PARSLEY.

DRESSING: IN A BOWL, COMBINE OIL, VINEGAR, MUSTARD, GARLIC, BASIL, OREGANO, SALT AND PEPPER.

POUR DRESSING OVER PASTA MIXTURE; TOSS UNTIL WELL COATED. LET STAND AT ROOM TEMPERATURE FOR UP TO 30 MINUTES, ALLOWING FLAVORS TO BLEND. REFRIGERATE IF MAKING AHEAD. SERVES 6.

TIP: DRIED BASIL AND OREGANO CAN BE REPLACED WITH I TBSP (15 ML) EACH CHOPPED FRESH. (AS A GENERAL RULE, WHEN SUBSTITUTING FRESH FOR DRIED HERBS USE THREE TIMES THE AMOUNT OF FRESH FOR THE DRIED.)

VARIATION: YOU CAN ALSO ADD 4 OZ (125 G) PEPPERONI, SALAMI OR HAM, CUT INTO THIN I-INCH (2.5 CM) STRIPS.

ANYBODY CAN WIN UNLESS THERE HAPPENS TO BE A SECOND ENTRY.

MARINATED LENTIL SALAD

GREAT BESIDE ROASTED MEATS OR ON
ITS OWN FOR A PACKED LUNCH, THIS SALAD
HAS BOLD FLAVORS AND KEEPS WELL.

1 CUP	DRIED GREEN, BLUE OR BROWN LENTILS	250 ML
2	LARGE CARROTS, FINELY DICED	2
1	CLOVE GARLIC, FINELY GRATED OR MINCED	1
$1/2$ TSP	GROUND CUMIN	2 ML
$1/8$ TSP	GROUND CORIANDER	0.5 ML
$1/4$ TSP	SALT	1 ML
	FRESHLY GROUND BLACK PEPPER	
$1/4$ CUP	OLIVE OIL	60 ML
2 TBSP	WHITE WINE VINEGAR	30 ML
1 CUP	CRUMBLED FETA CHEESE	250 ML
1	BUNCH FRESH PARSLEY, LEAVES ROUGHLY CHOPPED	1

PLACE LENTILS IN A MEDIUM SAUCEPAN AND COVER WITH
ABOUT 1 INCH (2.5 CM) OF WATER. BRING TO A BOIL OVER
HIGH HEAT. REDUCE HEAT AND SIMMER UNTIL LENTILS
ARE NEARLY TENDER, ABOUT 25 MINUTES. ADD CARROTS
AND COOK FOR 5 MINUTES (CARROTS SHOULD STILL BE
CRISP). DRAIN WELL AND TRANSFER TO A BOWL. WHILE
THE LENTILS ARE STILL WARM, STIR IN GARLIC, CUMIN,
CORIANDER, SALT, PEPPER TO TASTE, OIL AND VINEGAR.
LET COOL COMPLETELY. ADD FETA AND PARSLEY. COVER
AND REFRIGERATE FOR AT LEAST 30 MINUTES TO BLEND
THE FLAVORS OR STORE IN AN AIRTIGHT CONTAINER
IN THE REFRIGERATOR FOR UP TO 3 DAYS. SERVES 6.

TUSCAN BEAN SALAD

FAST-AND-EASY RECIPE

SERVED WITH HOT CRUSTY BREAD, THIS DELECTABLE SALAD IS A MEAL IN ITSELF. WHEN CHILLED, IT IS A GREAT ADDITION TO A PICNIC BASKET.

1	CAN (6 OZ/170 G) OLIVE OIL-PACKED TUNA (PREFERABLY ITALIAN), DRAINED	1
1	CAN (19 OZ/540 ML) WHITE KIDNEY BEANS, DRAINED AND RINSED	1
4	GREEN ONIONS, WHITE PARTS FINELY CHOPPED	4
1 TBSP	SUN-DRIED TOMATO PESTO	15 ML
1/2 CUP	OIL AND VINEGAR DRESSING	125 ML
	SALT AND FRESHLY GROUND BLACK PEPPER	

IN A BOWL, COMBINE TUNA, BEANS, WHITE PARTS OF GREEN ONIONS AND PESTO. POUR IN DRESSING AND TOSS WELL. SEASON TO TASTE WITH SALT AND BLACK PEPPER. SERVE IMMEDIATELY OR REFRIGERATE FOR AT LEAST 2 HOURS. SERVES 4.

TIP: IF YOU DON'T HAVE SUN-DRIED TOMATO PESTO, USE 1 TBSP (15 ML) DIJON MUSTARD OR BASIL PESTO INSTEAD.

VARIATION
SALAMI AND WHITE BEAN SALAD: SUBSTITUTE 4 OZ (125 G) DICED SALAMI FOR THE TUNA.

VARIATION
BRUSCHETTA WITH BEANS: LIGHTLY BRUSH 6 TO 8 SLICES OF COUNTRY-STYLE BREAD WITH OLIVE OIL ON BOTH SIDES AND TOAST UNDER THE BROILER, TURNING ONCE. SPOON THE BEAN SALAD EVENLY OVER THE BREAD AND SERVE.

SOUTHWESTERN BEAN AND BARLEY SALAD WITH ROASTED PEPPERS

INGREDIENTS TRADITIONALLY ASSOCIATED WITH THE AMERICAN SOUTHWEST — BEANS, CORN AND PEPPERS — COMBINE WITH HEARTY BARLEY TO PRODUCE THIS DELICIOUSLY ROBUST SALAD.

DRESSING

3 TBSP	RED WINE VINEGAR	45 ML
1/2 TSP	SALT	2 ML
	FRESHLY GROUND BLACK PEPPER	
1/2	CLOVE GARLIC, FINELY GRATED OR PRESSED	1/2
1/2 CUP	EXTRA VIRGIN OLIVE OIL	125 ML

SALAD

3 CUPS	COOKED WHOLE (HULLED) BARLEY, COOLED	750 ML
1	CAN (14 TO 19 OZ/398 TO 540 ML) RED KIDNEY BEANS, DRAINED AND RINSED	1
2 CUPS	COOKED CORN KERNELS	500 ML
2	ROASTED POBLANO PEPPERS, FINELY CHOPPED (SEE TIP, OPPOSITE)	2
2	WHOLE SUN-DRIED TOMATOES, PACKED IN OLIVE OIL, FINELY CHOPPED	2
1	SMALL RED ONION, FINELY CHOPPED	1
1/4 CUP	FINELY CHOPPED FRESH PARSLEY	60 ML

DRESSING: IN A SMALL BOWL, COMBINE VINEGAR, SALT AND PEPPER TO TASTE, STIRRING UNTIL SALT DISSOLVES. STIR IN GARLIC. GRADUALLY WHISK IN OLIVE OIL. SET ASIDE.

SALAD: IN A SERVING BOWL, COMBINE BARLEY, KIDNEY BEANS, CORN, ROASTED PEPPERS, SUN-DRIED TOMATOES

AND ONION. ADD DRESSING AND TOSS WELL. GARNISH WITH PARSLEY. CHILL UNTIL READY TO SERVE. MAKES 8 SIDE SERVINGS.

TIP: POBLANO PEPPERS ARE A MILD CHILE PEPPER. IF YOU ARE A HEAT SEEKER, YOU MIGHT WANT TO ADD AN EXTRA PEPPER, OR EVEN A MINCED SEEDED JALAPEÑO PEPPER FOR SOME REAL PUNCH. THE SUGGESTED QUANTITY PRODUCES A MILD RESULT, WHICH MOST PEOPLE WILL ENJOY. IF YOU'RE HEAT AVERSE, USE BELL PEPPERS INSTEAD. TO ROAST PEPPERS, SEE TIP, PAGE 149.

VARIATION: SUBSTITUTE AN EQUAL QUANTITY OF COOKED WHEAT, SPELT OR KAMUT BERRIES OR FARRO FOR THE BARLEY.

TIME IS WHAT KEEPS EVERYTHING
FROM HAPPENING AT ONCE.

TABBOULEH

THIS LEBANESE SALAD IS A GOOD EXAMPLE OF THE VIBRANT COMFORT FOODS FROM THE MEDITERRANEAN THAT HAVE BECOME SO POPULAR IN RECENT YEARS.

3/4 CUP	FINE BULGUR	175 ML
2 CUPS	FINELY CHOPPED FRESH FLAT-LEAF (ITALIAN) PARSLEY	500 ML
4	GREEN ONIONS, FINELY CHOPPED	4
1/4 CUP	FINELY CHOPPED FRESH MINT (OPTIONAL)	60 ML
1/4 CUP	OLIVE OIL	60 ML
1/4 CUP	FRESHLY SQUEEZED LEMON JUICE	60 ML
1 TSP	SALT	5 ML
1/2 TSP	PAPRIKA	2 ML
1/4 TSP	FRESHLY GROUND BLACK PEPPER	1 ML
2	TOMATOES, SEEDED AND DICED	2

PLACE BULGUR IN A BOWL; ADD COLD WATER TO COVER. LET STAND FOR 30 MINUTES. DRAIN IN A FINE SIEVE. USING THE BACK OF A SPOON, OR WITH YOUR HANDS, SQUEEZE OUT AS MUCH WATER AS POSSIBLE. IN A SERVING BOWL, COMBINE SOFTENED BULGUR, PARSLEY, GREEN ONIONS AND MINT (IF USING). IN A SMALL BOWL, STIR TOGETHER OIL, LEMON JUICE, SALT, PAPRIKA AND PEPPER. POUR OVER BULGUR MIXTURE; TOSS WELL. COVER AND REFRIGERATE UNTIL SERVING TIME. JUST BEFORE SERVING, SPRINKLE WITH TOMATOES. SERVES 8.

TIP: THIS SALAD KEEPS WELL FOR SEVERAL DAYS. IT'S BETTER TO ADD THE TOMATOES AS A GARNISH JUST BEFORE SERVING TO PREVENT THE SALAD FROM BECOMING SOGGY.

RICE SALAD NIÇOISE

THIS REFRESHING SALAD WITH A MEDITERRANEAN SPIN
IS A PERFECT DINNER SOLUTION FOR THOSE SUMMER
DAYS WHEN IT'S TOO HOT TO COOK AND YOU CAN'T
BEAR THE THOUGHT OF A HEAVY MEAL. JUST COOK THE
RICE IN A RICE COOKER, RINSE AND DRAIN. PREPARE
THE RECIPE AND CHILL OVERNIGHT. THE SALAD
IS READY TO EAT WHENEVER YOU ARE.

2 CUPS	COOKED BROWN AND WILD RICE MIXTURE, RINSED IN COLD WATER AND DRAINED	500 ML
1	CAN (6 OZ/170 G) OLIVE OIL-PACKED TUNA (PREFERABLY ITALIAN), DRAINED	1
2	ROASTED RED BELL PEPPERS (SEE TIPS, PAGE 149), CHOPPED	2
1/2 CUP	CHOPPED DRAINED MARINATED ARTICHOKE HEARTS	125 ML
1/2 CUP	PITTED BLACK OLIVES, SLICED	125 ML
1/2 CUP	PITTED GREEN OLIVES, SLICED	125 ML
	CHOPPED HOT PICKLED PEPPERS (OPTIONAL)	
2 TBSP	RED WINE VINEGAR	30 ML
1/2 TSP	SALT	2 ML
1/4 TSP	FRESHLY GROUND BLACK PEPPER	1 ML
1/4 CUP	EXTRA VIRGIN OLIVE OIL	60 ML

IN A SERVING BOWL, COMBINE RICE, TUNA, RED PEPPERS,
ARTICHOKE HEARTS, BLACK AND GREEN OLIVES AND
HOT PEPPERS (IF USING). IN A SMALL BOWL, COMBINE
VINEGAR, SALT AND BLACK PEPPER, STIRRING UNTIL SALT
DISSOLVES. GRADUALLY WHISK IN OLIVE OIL. ADD TO RICE
MIXTURE AND TOSS WELL. CHILL THOROUGHLY. SERVES 4.

QUINOA SALAD WITH MINT AND FETA

FRESH AND SPRINGY, PACKED WITH FRESH HERBS AND A SIMPLE LEMONY DRESSING, THIS SALAD IS A QUINOA TAKE ON TABBOULEH.

1 CUP	QUINOA, RINSED	250 ML
2 CUPS	WATER	500 ML
1/4 CUP	FRESHLY SQUEEZED LEMON JUICE	60 ML
2 TBSP	OLIVE OIL	30 ML
1 TSP	DIJON MUSTARD	5 ML
	SALT AND FRESHLY GROUND BLACK PEPPER	
1/2	CUCUMBER, DICED	1/2
2 CUPS	LOOSELY PACKED FRESH PARSLEY LEAVES, FINELY CHOPPED	500 ML
1 CUP	LOOSELY PACKED FRESH MINT LEAVES, FINELY CHOPPED	250 ML
1/2 CUP	CRUMBLED FETA CHEESE	125 ML

IN A MEDIUM SAUCEPAN, COMBINE QUINOA AND WATER. BRING TO A BOIL OVER HIGH HEAT. REDUCE HEAT TO MEDIUM-LOW, COVER AND SIMMER FOR 15 MINUTES OR UNTIL WATER IS ABSORBED. REMOVE FROM HEAT AND TRANSFER TO A LARGE BOWL TO COOL.

MEANWHILE, IN A SMALL BOWL OR JAR, WHISK OR SHAKE TOGETHER LEMON JUICE, OIL AND MUSTARD. SEASON TO TASTE WITH SALT AND PEPPER.

ADD CUCUMBER, PARSLEY, MINT AND FETA TO THE QUINOA. ADD DRESSING AND TOSS TO COAT. SERVES 6.

CHICKEN SALAD AMANDINE

THIS OLD-FASHIONED RECIPE IS A GREAT WAY TO USE UP LEFTOVER CHICKEN. IT MAKES A DELICIOUS LUNCH OR A LIGHT ONE-COURSE DINNER. THE QUANTITY OF DRESSING MAY SEEM SUBSTANTIAL FOR THE AMOUNT OF CHICKEN, BUT IT ALSO DRESSES THE SALAD GREENS.

1/4 CUP	MAYONNAISE	60 ML
2 TBSP	OLIVE OIL	30 ML
2 TBSP	FRESHLY SQUEEZED LEMON JUICE	30 ML
1/2 TSP	SALT	2 ML
	FRESHLY GROUND BLACK PEPPER	
4 CUPS	CUBED COOKED CHICKEN (1/2-INCH/1 CM CUBES)	1 L
1/2 CUP	FINELY CHOPPED CELERY	125 ML
2 TBSP	FINELY CHOPPED RED OR GREEN ONION	30 ML
1	BAG (10 OZ/300 G) SALAD GREENS, SUCH AS HEARTS OF ROMAINE (OR 4 CUPS/1 L TORN LETTUCE)	1
2 TBSP	TOASTED SLIVERED OR SLICED ALMONDS (SEE TIP, BELOW)	30 ML

IN A BOWL, COMBINE MAYONNAISE, OLIVE OIL, LEMON JUICE, SALT, AND BLACK PEPPER TO TASTE. IN A SEPARATE BOWL, COMBINE CHICKEN, CELERY AND ONION. ADD MAYONNAISE MIXTURE. TOSS TO COMBINE. SPREAD SALAD GREENS OVER A DEEP PLATTER. SPOON CHICKEN MIXTURE ON TOP. GARNISH WITH ALMONDS AND SERVE IMMEDIATELY. SERVES 4.

TIP: TO TOAST ALMONDS, IN A DRY NONSTICK SKILLET OVER MEDIUM HEAT, STIR ALMONDS CONSTANTLY UNTIL GOLDEN BROWN, 3 TO 4 MINUTES. IMMEDIATELY TRANSFER TO A SMALL BOWL TO PREVENT BURNING.

COBB SALAD

DRESSING

1/3 CUP	OLIVE OIL	75 ML
2 TBSP	RED WINE VINEGAR	30 ML
2 TSP	WHOLE-SEED MUSTARD	10 ML
1/2 TSP	DRIED TARRAGON	2 ML
1/2 TSP	SALT	2 ML
1/4 TSP	FRESHLY GROUND BLACK PEPPER	1 ML

SALAD

8 CUPS	BABY SALAD GREENS	2 L
1 1/2 CUPS	DICED COOKED CHICKEN	375 ML
2	RIPE BUT FIRM TOMATOES, SEEDED AND DICED	2
1	HASS AVOCADO, PEELED AND CUT INTO SLICES	1
2	HARD-COOKED EGGS, SLICED (SEE TIP, PAGE 82)	2
6	SLICES BACON, COOKED CRISP AND CRUMBLED	6
3/4 CUP	CRUMBLED BLUE CHEESE	175 ML
2 TBSP	CHOPPED FRESH CHIVES	30 ML

DRESSING: IN A BOWL, WHISK TOGETHER OLIVE OIL, VINEGAR, MUSTARD, TARRAGON, SALT AND PEPPER.

SALAD: PLACE LETTUCE IN A LARGE, WIDE, SHALLOW SALAD OR SERVING BOWL. POUR HALF THE DRESSING OVER GREENS AND TOSS TO COAT WELL. LAYER WITH CHICKEN, TOMATO, AVOCADO, EGG, BACON BITS AND BLUE CHEESE. SPRINKLE WITH CHIVES AND DRIZZLE WITH THE REMAINING DRESSING. SERVE IMMEDIATELY. SERVES 4.

SANDWICHES, LUNCHES & LIGHT SUPPERS

EGG SALAD ON A KAISER

FAST-AND-EASY RECIPE

THIS VERSATILE EGG SALAD IS GREAT ON A KAISER OR TUCKED INTO PITA POCKETS WITH SHREDDED LETTUCE OR SPROUTS AND TOMATO WEDGES.

2 TBSP	CREAM CHEESE, SOFTENED	30 ML
2 TBSP	PLAIN YOGURT	30 ML
1 TSP	DIJON MUSTARD	5 ML
1/4 TSP	SALT	1 ML
1/4 TSP	FRESHLY GROUND BLACK PEPPER	1 ML
3	HARD-COOKED EGGS, FINELY CHOPPED (SEE TIP, PAGE 82)	3
1	SMALL GREEN ONION, FINELY CHOPPED	1
2	WHOLE WHEAT KAISER ROLLS, SPLIT	2
	LEAF OR ROMAINE LETTUCE	
6	THIN SLICES TOMATO	6

IN A BOWL, COMBINE CREAM CHEESE, YOGURT, MUSTARD, SALT AND PEPPER. STIR IN EGGS AND GREEN ONION. (THE EGG SALAD CAN BE COVERED AND REFRIGERATED FOR UP TO 2 DAYS AT THIS POINT.)

SPREAD EGG SALAD OVER TOP HALVES OF ROLLS. ARRANGE LETTUCE AND TOMATO SLICES ON BOTTOM HALVES; SANDWICH TOGETHER. MAKES 2 SANDWICHES.

VARIATION

EGG SALAD TORTILLA SPIRALS: SPREAD EGG SALAD ON TWO 9-INCH (23 CM) FLOUR TORTILLAS, LEAVING A 1-INCH (2.5 CM) BORDER. LAYER WITH LETTUCE. FOLD BOTTOM OVER FILLING, THEN SIDES; ROLL UP TIGHTLY. WRAP IN PLASTIC WRAP AND REFRIGERATE OVERNIGHT.

CURRIED CHICKEN SALAD SANDWICHES

THESE CHICKEN SALAD SANDWICHES HAVE ADDED PIZZAZZ WITH APPLES AND A HINT OF CURRY.

1/3 CUP	LIGHT MAYONNAISE	75 ML
2 TBSP	MANGO CHUTNEY	30 ML
1 TSP	MILD CURRY PASTE (OR TO TASTE)	5 ML
1 1/2 CUPS	FINELY DICED COOKED CHICKEN	375 ML
1/2 CUP	FINELY DICED APPLE (UNPEELED)	125 ML
3 TBSP	GOLDEN RAISINS OR DRIED CRANBERRIES	45 ML
2 TBSP	FINELY CHOPPED GREEN ONIONS	30 ML
	SALT	
4	SLICES THICK-CUT WHOLE-GRAIN BREAD	4
	ADDITIONAL LIGHT MAYONNAISE	
	RED LEAF OR BOSTON LETTUCE	

IN A BOWL, BLEND MAYONNAISE WITH CHUTNEY AND CURRY PASTE. STIR IN CHICKEN, APPLE, RAISINS AND GREEN ONIONS; SEASON TO TASTE WITH SALT. SPREAD BREAD SLICES WITH ADDITIONAL MAYONNAISE. SPREAD 2 BREAD SLICES GENEROUSLY WITH CHICKEN MIXTURE; TOP WITH LETTUCE AND THE REMAINING BREAD. CUT IN HALF. MAKES 2 SANDWICHES.

VARIATION

MANGO CHICKEN SALAD SANDWICHES: REPLACE THE APPLE WITH DICED FRESH MANGO. ADD 1/4 CUP (60 ML) CHOPPED FRESH CILANTRO.

SUMPTUOUS CHICKEN SANDWICH WITH BRIE

FAST-AND-EASY RECIPE

THIS SANDWICH IS SO SPECTACULAR THAT NO ONE WILL BELIEVE HOW EASY IT IS TO MAKE.

2 TBSP	MAYONNAISE	30 ML
2 TBSP	SUN-DRIED TOMATO PESTO	30 ML
1 TSP	DIJON MUSTARD	5 ML
1/4 TSP	SALT	1 ML
	FRESHLY GROUND BLACK PEPPER	
2 CUPS	CUBED COOKED CHICKEN (1/2-INCH/ 1 CM CUBES)	500 ML
4	ONION OR KAISER BUNS, HALVED	4
8 OZ	BRIE CHEESE, THINLY SLICED	250 G
	LETTUCE (OPTIONAL)	
	SLICED TOMATO (OPTIONAL)	

PREHEAT BROILER. IN A BOWL, COMBINE MAYONNAISE, PESTO, MUSTARD, SALT, AND BLACK PEPPER TO TASTE. STIR UNTIL BLENDED. ADD CHICKEN AND TOSS TO COMBINE. SPREAD BOTTOM HALVES OF BUNS WITH EQUAL PORTIONS OF CHICKEN MIXTURE. LAY CHEESE SLICES ACROSS TOP HALVES. PLACE TOPS ON A BAKING SHEET AND BROIL UNTIL CHEESE IS JUST BEGINNING TO MELT AND RUN OVER THE SIDES OF THE BUN, ABOUT 2 MINUTES. GARNISH WITH LETTUCE AND TOMATOES, IF DESIRED. UNITE WITH BOTTOMS, CUT IN HALF AND SERVE.

SERVES 4.

PROVENÇAL TUNA BAGUETTE

PACKED IN A COOLER, THIS SANDWICH IS
A FAVORITE PICNIC STAPLE. IT ALSO DOES EXTRA
DUTY AS AN EASY MAKE-AHEAD TIDBIT FOR
A TASTING PLATTER OR CANAPÉ TRAY.

1	CAN (6 OZ/170 G) FLAKED WHITE TUNA, DRAINED		1
2 TBSP	EACH FINELY CHOPPED RED OR GREEN ONION, CELERY, PARSLEY, ROASTED RED BELL PEPPER (SEE TIPS, PAGE 149) AND/OR PITTED BLACK OLIVES	30 ML	
2 TBSP	MAYONNAISE	30 ML	
1 TBSP	FRESHLY SQUEEZED LEMON JUICE	15 ML	
1 TBSP	OLIVE OIL	15 ML	
1/2 TSP	SALT	2 ML	
	FRESHLY GROUND BLACK PEPPER		
1	BAGUETTE, HERO LOAF OR 4 CRUSTY ROLLS, SPLIT LENGTHWISE		1

IN A BOWL, COMBINE TUNA, VEGETABLES, MAYONNAISE, LEMON JUICE, OLIVE OIL, SALT, AND BLACK PEPPER TO TASTE. MIX WELL. SPREAD MIXTURE EVENLY OVER BOTTOM HALF OF BAGUETTE. COVER WITH THE TOP PORTION AND CUT IN HALF. PRESS DOWN FIRMLY ON EACH PIECE, THEN WRAP TIGHTLY IN PLASTIC WRAP. PLACE IN A PAN AND COVER WITH A HEAVY WEIGHT (SUCH AS A FOIL-WRAPPED BRICK). REFRIGERATE FOR 4 HOURS OR OVERNIGHT.

TO SERVE AS A SANDWICH, CUT EACH BAGUETTE PIECE IN HALF. TO SERVE AS A CANAPÉ, CUT EACH PIECE INTO 4 OR 5 SLICES. SERVES 4 AS A SANDWICH OR 8 TO 10 AS A CANAPÉ.

TUNA CHEDDAR MELT

*WHEN YOU'RE TOO BUSY TO COOK DINNER,
RELY ON THIS SIMPLE, SATISFYING SANDWICH
INSTEAD OF ORDERING TAKEOUT.*

1	CAN (6 OZ/170 G) FLAKED WHITE TUNA, DRAINED	1
1/4 CUP	LIGHT MAYONNAISE	60 ML
1/4 CUP	FINELY CHOPPED CELERY	60 ML
1	GREEN ONION, FINELY CHOPPED	1
1 TSP	FRESHLY SQUEEZED LEMON JUICE	5 ML
4	SLICES WHOLE-GRAIN BREAD	4
8	THIN TOMATO SLICES	8
	SALT AND FRESHLY GROUND BLACK PEPPER	
4	SLICES CHEDDAR CHEESE	4

PREHEAT BROILER. IN A BOWL, COMBINE TUNA, MAYONNAISE, CELERY, GREEN ONION AND LEMON JUICE. SPREAD BREAD SLICES WITH TUNA MIXTURE. LAYER WITH TOMATO SLICES; SEASON WITH SALT AND PEPPER. TOP WITH CHEDDAR CHEESE SLICES. ARRANGE ON A BAKING SHEET; PLACE UNDER BROILER FOR ABOUT 3 MINUTES OR UNTIL CHEESE IS MELTED. SERVE IMMEDIATELY. MAKES 4 OPEN-FACE SANDWICHES.

TOMATO RAREBIT

FAST-AND-EASY RECIPE

*HERE'S A DELICIOUS SOLUTION TO WHAT
TO DO WITH LEFTOVER CANNED TOMATOES.
DOUBLE OR TRIPLE THE QUANTITY, AS DESIRED.*

1 CUP	DRAINED CANNED TOMATOES, COARSELY CHOPPED	250 ML
1 TSP	WORCESTERSHIRE SAUCE	5 ML
1 TSP	DIJON MUSTARD	5 ML
1 CUP	SHREDDED CHEDDAR CHEESE	250 ML
	SALT AND FRESHLY GROUND BLACK PEPPER	
2	SLICES (OR MORE) TOAST	2

IN A SMALL SAUCEPAN OVER MEDIUM HEAT, COMBINE TOMATOES, WORCESTERSHIRE SAUCE AND DIJON MUSTARD. BRING TO A BOIL. REDUCE HEAT TO LOW. ADD CHEESE AND COOK, STIRRING, UNTIL MELTED. SEASON TO TASTE WITH SALT AND BLACK PEPPER. SPOON OVER WARM TOAST AND SERVE. SERVES 2.

*AN ALARM CLOCK IS A DEVICE FOR
WAKING CHILDLESS HOUSEHOLDS.*

BEEFY PIZZA SUBS

WHY ORDER OUT WHEN IT'S SO EASY TO PREPARE THESE PIZZA-STYLE SANDWICHES AT HOME?

1 TBSP	OLIVE OIL	15 ML
2 CUPS	SLICED MUSHROOMS	500 ML
1	GREEN BELL PEPPER, CUT INTO THIN STRIPS	1
1	ONION, CUT INTO THIN WEDGES	1
1	LARGE CLOVE GARLIC, FINELY CHOPPED	1
1 TSP	DRIED BASIL OR OREGANO	5 ML
1/4 TSP	HOT PEPPER FLAKES	1 ML
1 1/2 CUPS	THINLY SLICED COOKED FLANK STEAK OR 6 OZ (175 G) DELI ROAST BEEF, CUT INTO STRIPS	375 ML
3/4 CUP	PIZZA SAUCE OR TOMATO PASTA SAUCE	175 ML
	SALT AND FRESHLY GROUND BLACK PEPPER	
4	CRUSTY ROLLS	4
6 OZ	THINLY SLICED MILD PROVOLONE OR MOZZARELLA CHEESE	175 G

PREHEAT BROILER. IN A LARGE NONSTICK SKILLET, HEAT OIL OVER MEDIUM-HIGH HEAT. ADD MUSHROOMS, GREEN PEPPER, ONION, GARLIC, BASIL AND HOT PEPPER FLAKES; COOK, STIRRING, FOR 5 MINUTES OR UNTIL SOFTENED. STIR IN BEEF AND PIZZA SAUCE; COOK UNTIL HEATED THROUGH. REMOVE FROM HEAT; SEASON TO TASTE WITH SALT AND PEPPER. CUT ROLLS ALONG ONE SIDE AND OPEN LIKE A BOOK; LAYER WITH CHEESE SLICES. ARRANGE ON A BAKING SHEET; PLACE UNDER BROILER FOR 1 MINUTE OR UNTIL CHEESE MELTS. WATCH CAREFULLY. SPOON BEEF MIXTURE INTO ROLLS AND SERVE IMMEDIATELY. SERVES 4.

PANINI WITH PROSCIUTTO AND PROVOLONE

FAST-AND-EASY RECIPE

LIKE ALL GOOD THINGS ITALIAN, THESE WONDERFUL PRESSED SANDWICHES CAN BE MADE WITH A VARIETY OF FILLINGS. HERE'S ONE DELICIOUS COMBINATION.

4	PANINI, CIABATTA OR CRUSTY BUNS, SPLIT IN HALF LENGTHWISE	4
	DIJON, WHOLE-SEED OR HONEY MUSTARD (OPTIONAL)	
8	THIN SLICES PROVOLONE OR FONTINA CHEESE	8
8	SLICES PROSCIUTTO OR SMOKED HAM	8
8	OIL-PACKED SUN-DRIED TOMATO HALVES, BLOTTED DRY AND CUT INTO THIN STRIPS	8
1½ CUPS	LIGHTLY PACKED FRESH BABY SPINACH	375 ML

PREHEAT PANINI GRILL TO MEDIUM AND PREHEAT OVEN TO 200°F (100°C). PLACE BUNS ON WORK SURFACE, CUT SIDE UP. THINLY SPREAD WITH MUSTARD (IF USING). LAYER EACH HALF WITH A SLICE OF CHEESE AND PROSCIUTTO. LAYER BOTTOM HALVES WITH SUN-DRIED TOMATOES AND SPINACH. COVER WITH TOP HALVES AND PRESS LIGHTLY TO PACK. PLACE 2 SANDWICHES IN GRILL, CLOSE THE TOP PLATE AND COOK FOR 2 MINUTES. ROTATE SANDWICHES TO CREATE CROSSED GRILL MARKS AND COOK FOR 1 TO 2 MINUTES OR UNTIL CHEESE IS MELTED AND BUNS ARE GOLDEN BROWN AND CRUSTY. PLACE COOKED PANINI ON A BAKING SHEET AND KEEP WARM IN PREHEATED OVEN WHILE GRILLING THE REMAINING SANDWICHES. CUT SANDWICHES IN HALF AND SERVE. SERVES 4.

HOT SAUSAGE SANDWICHES

SLOW COOKER RECIPE

THESE ITALIAN-INSPIRED SANDWICHES MAKE A GREAT WEEKNIGHT MEAL THAT'S A BIG HIT WITH BOTH KIDS AND ADULTS. IF YOU LIKE YOUR SANDWICHES SPICY, GARNISH THEM WITH ROASTED BANANA PEPPERS. ALL THIS NEEDS IS A TOSSED SALAD TO COMPLETE THE MEAL.

1 TBSP	OLIVE OIL	15 ML
1 LB	ITALIAN SAUSAGE (BULK OR CASINGS REMOVED)	500 G
1	ONION, FINELY CHOPPED	1
2	STALKS CELERY, DICED	2
1	CARROT, DICED	1
2 TSP	DRIED OREGANO	10 ML
1/2 TSP	SALT	2 ML
1/2 TSP	CRACKED BLACK PEPPERCORNS	2 ML
1	2-INCH (5 CM) CINNAMON STICK	1
1/2 CUP	DRY WHITE WINE (OPTIONAL)	125 ML
1	CAN (28 OZ/796 ML) DICED TOMATOES, DRAINED	1
1	FRENCH BAGUETTE, CUT INTO 4 PIECES AND SPLIT HORIZONTALLY	1
1 CUP	SHREDDED MOZZARELLA CHEESE	250 ML
	ROASTED BANANA PEPPERS (OPTIONAL)	

IN A SKILLET, HEAT OIL OVER MEDIUM-HIGH HEAT. ADD SAUSAGE, ONION, CELERY AND CARROT AND COOK, STIRRING, UNTIL SAUSAGE IS NO LONGER PINK, ABOUT 7 MINUTES. ADD OREGANO, SALT, PEPPERCORNS AND CINNAMON STICK AND COOK, STIRRING, FOR 1 MINUTE. ADD

WINE (IF USING), BRING TO A BOIL AND BOIL, SCRAPING UP BROWN BITS FROM BOTTOM OF PAN, FOR 2 MINUTES. STIR IN TOMATOES. (MIXTURE CAN BE COOLED, COVERED AND REFRIGERATED FOR UP TO 2 DAYS AT THIS POINT.)

TRANSFER TO A MEDIUM TO LARGE ($3\frac{1}{2}$- TO 5-QUART) SLOW COOKER. COVER AND COOK ON LOW FOR 6 TO 8 HOURS OR ON HIGH FOR 3 TO 4 HOURS, UNTIL HOT AND BUBBLY.

WHEN READY TO SERVE, PREHEAT BROILER. PLACE TOP HALVES OF BAGUETTE ON BAKING SHEET AND SPRINKLE LIBERALLY WITH MOZZARELLA. PLACE UNDER BROILER UNTIL CHEESE MELTS AND BEGINS TO BROWN. PLACE I BOTTOM HALF OF BAGUETTE ON EACH PLATE. SPOON SAUSAGE MIXTURE OVER, GARNISH WITH HOT PEPPERS (IF USING) AND TOP WITH GRILLED CHEESE HALF. SERVES 4.

TIP: IF YOU CHOOSE TO HALVE THIS RECIPE, USE A SMALL ($1\frac{1}{2}$- TO 3-QUART) SLOW COOKER.

OLD SOUTH PULLED PORK ON A BUN

SLOW COOKER RECIPE

PULLED PORK IS A BELOVED SLOW-COOKED BARBECUE SPECIALTY FROM NORTH CAROLINA. THE SHREDDED MEAT HOLDS ON TO SAUCE BETTER THAN SLICED MEAT WOULD. IT'S A GREAT DISH FOR WEEKENDS IN THE COUNTRY, FRIDAY NIGHT DINNERS OR EVENINGS WHEN YOU HAVE A HOUSE FULL OF TEENAGE BOYS WHO CAN'T GET ENOUGH OF THE RICH, SMOKY SAUCE.

I TBSP	VEGETABLE OIL	15 ML
2	ONIONS, FINELY CHOPPED	2
6	CLOVES GARLIC, MINCED	6
I TBSP	CHILI POWDER	15 ML
I TSP	CRACKED BLACK PEPPERCORNS	5 ML
I CUP	TOMATO-BASED CHILI SAUCE	250 ML
1/4 CUP	PACKED BROWN SUGAR	60 ML
1/4 CUP	CIDER VINEGAR	60 ML
I TBSP	WORCESTERSHIRE SAUCE	15 ML
I TSP	LIQUID SMOKE (SEE TIP, OPPOSITE)	5 ML
3 LB	TRIMMED BONELESS PORK SHOULDER OR BLADE (BUTT) ROAST, PATTED DRY	1.5 KG
	KAISER OR ONION BUNS, HALVED AND WARMED	

IN A SKILLET, HEAT OIL OVER MEDIUM HEAT. ADD ONIONS AND COOK, STIRRING, UNTIL SOFTENED, ABOUT 3 MINUTES. ADD GARLIC, CHILI POWDER AND PEPPERCORNS AND COOK, STIRRING, FOR I MINUTE. ADD CHILI SAUCE, BROWN SUGAR, VINEGAR, WORCESTERSHIRE SAUCE AND LIQUID SMOKE. STIR TO COMBINE AND BRING TO A BOIL.

(SAUCE CAN BE COOLED, COVERED AND REFRIGERATED OVERNIGHT AT THIS POINT.)

PLACE PORK IN A MEDIUM (ABOUT 4-QUART) SLOW COOKER AND POUR SAUCE OVER. COVER AND COOK ON LOW FOR 10 HOURS OR ON HIGH FOR 5 HOURS, UNTIL PORK IS FALLING APART. TRANSFER PORK TO A CUTTING BOARD AND PULL THE MEAT APART IN SHREDS, USING TWO FORKS. RETURN TO SAUCE AND KEEP WARM. WHEN READY TO SERVE, SPOON SHREDDED PORK AND SAUCE OVER WARM BUNS. SERVES 6 TO 8.

TIP: LOOK FOR LIQUID SMOKE IN WELL-STOCKED SUPERMARKETS. IT GIVES A WONDERFULLY SMOKY FLAVOR TO THIS DISH. IF YOU CAN'T FIND IT, SUBSTITUTE 1 TSP (5 ML) SMOKED PAPRIKA.

A WOMAN'S "I'LL BE READY IN FIVE MINUTES" IS THE SAME AS A MAN'S "I'LL BE HOME IN FIVE MINUTES."

TURKEY SLOPPY JOES

HERE'S A KID-FRIENDLY MEAL THAT IS IDEAL FOR BUSY EVENINGS. OPEN A BAG OF MIXED SALAD GREENS, ADD SOME CHOPPED GREEN ONION AND TOSS WITH A SIMPLE DRESSING FOR A NUTRITIOUS AND SATISFYING MEAL.

1 CUP	TOMATO-BASED CHILI SAUCE	250 ML
1 TBSP	DIJON MUSTARD	15 ML
1 TBSP	WORCESTERSHIRE SAUCE	15 ML
1 TBSP	VEGETABLE OIL	15 ML
1 LB	LEAN GROUND TURKEY OR CHICKEN	500 G
1 CUP	FINELY CHOPPED ONION	250 ML
1 TBSP	MINCED GARLIC	15 ML
1/2 TSP	SALT	2 ML
	FRESHLY GROUND BLACK PEPPER	
4 OZ	CREAM CHEESE (OPTIONAL)	125 G
	TOASTED ONION OR HAMBURGER BUNS	

IN A BOWL, COMBINE CHILI SAUCE, MUSTARD AND WORCESTERSHIRE SAUCE. SET ASIDE. IN A SKILLET, HEAT OIL OVER MEDIUM HEAT. ADD TURKEY AND ONION AND COOK, STIRRING AND BREAKING UP TURKEY UNTIL NO LONGER PINK INSIDE AND ONION IS SOFTENED, ABOUT 5 MINUTES. ADD GARLIC, SALT, AND BLACK PEPPER TO TASTE. COOK, STIRRING, FOR 1 MINUTE. STIR IN RESERVED SAUCE AND BRING TO BOIL. REDUCE HEAT TO LOW. ADD CREAM CHEESE, IF USING. SIMMER FOR 10 MINUTES OR UNTIL CHEESE IS MELTED AND FLAVORS ARE COMBINED. SPOON OVER TOASTED BUNS. SERVES 4.

TIP: ADD THE CREAM CHEESE IF YOU PREFER A MORE MELLOW MIXTURE OR IF YOU NEED TO STRETCH THE RECIPE TO FEED AN EXTRA PERSON.

Hot Sausage Sandwiches (page 104)

Old South Pulled Pork on a Bun (page 106)

Chicken Tacos (page 118)

Chicken and Vegetable Stew (page 129)

TERRIFIC CHICKEN BURGERS

LAYER THESE PATTIES IN A TOASTED ONION BUN
FOR AN EASY BURGER SUPPER, OR ACCOMPANY THEM
WITH STIR-FRIED RICE AND VEGETABLES.

1	LARGE EGG	1
1/2 CUP	FINE DRY BREAD CRUMBS	125 ML
1/3 CUP	FINELY CHOPPED GREEN ONIONS	75 ML
1 TSP	GROUND CORIANDER	5 ML
1 TSP	GRATED LEMON ZEST	5 ML
1/2 TSP	SALT	2 ML
1/4 TSP	FRESHLY GROUND BLACK PEPPER	1 ML
1 LB	GROUND CHICKEN OR TURKEY	500 G
1 TBSP	VEGETABLE OIL	15 ML

IN A BOWL, BEAT EGG; STIR IN BREAD CRUMBS, GREEN
ONIONS, CORIANDER, LEMON ZEST, SALT AND PEPPER; MIX
IN CHICKEN. WITH WET HANDS, SHAPE INTO FOUR 3/4-INCH
(2 CM) THICK PATTIES. IN A LARGE NONSTICK SKILLET,
HEAT OIL OVER MEDIUM HEAT; COOK PATTIES FOR 5 TO
6 MINUTES ON EACH SIDE OR UNTIL GOLDEN BROWN
ON OUTSIDE AND NO LONGER PINK IN CENTER. MAKES
4 BURGERS.

MAMA'S ITALIAN CHEESEBURGERS

IF BURGERS ARE STARTING TO BECOME MUNDANE, PUT SHREDDED CHEESE RIGHT IN THE GROUND MEAT MIXTURE FOR MOIST BURGERS WITH A TWIST. MAMA WOULD BE PLEASED.

1/4 CUP	TOMATO PASTA SAUCE	60 ML
1/4 CUP	GRATED OR MINCED ONION	60 ML
1	CLOVE GARLIC, MINCED	1
1/4 TSP	DRIED BASIL OR OREGANO	1 ML
1/4 TSP	SALT	1 ML
1/4 TSP	FRESHLY GROUND BLACK PEPPER	1 ML
3/4 CUP	SHREDDED MOZZARELLA CHEESE	175 ML
1/3 CUP	DRY SEASONED BREAD CRUMBS	75 ML
1 LB	LEAN GROUND BEEF	500 G
4	HAMBURGER BUNS, SPLIT AND TOASTED	4

PREHEAT GREASED BARBECUE GRILL TO MEDIUM-HIGH. IN A BOWL, COMBINE TOMATO PASTA SAUCE, ONION, GARLIC, BASIL, SALT AND PEPPER. STIR IN CHEESE AND BREAD CRUMBS; MIX IN BEEF. SHAPE INTO FOUR 3/4-INCH (2 CM) THICK PATTIES. GRILL, TURNING ONCE, FOR 6 TO 7 MINUTES ON EACH SIDE OR UNTIL NO LONGER PINK IN CENTER. SERVE IN BUNS. MAKES 4 BURGERS.

TIP: FOR AN EASY VEGETABLE TOPPING, CUT BELL PEPPERS AND A LARGE RED ONION INTO ROUNDS, BRUSH LIGHTLY WITH OLIVE OIL AND GRILL ALONGSIDE BURGERS.

SALMON BURGERS

FAST-AND-EASY RECIPE

HERE'S A YUMMY FISH-BASED BURGER. TO SERVE MORE, SIMPLY DOUBLE OR TRIPLE THE RECIPE.

1	CAN (7 1/2 OZ/213 G) SALMON, DRAINED	1
1	LARGE EGG, BEATEN	1
1/2 CUP	FINE DRY BREAD CRUMBS, DIVIDED	125 ML
1 TSP	DRIED ITALIAN SEASONING	5 ML
1/4 TSP	SALT	1 ML
	FRESHLY GROUND BLACK PEPPER	
2 TBSP	VEGETABLE OIL	30 ML
2	ONION OR WHOLE WHEAT BUNS, SPLIT AND TOASTED	2
	TARTAR SAUCE (SEE TIP, BELOW)	

IN A BOWL, COMBINE SALMON, EGG, 1/4 CUP (60 ML) BREAD CRUMBS, ITALIAN SEASONING, SALT, AND BLACK PEPPER TO TASTE. MIX WELL. FORM MIXTURE INTO 2 PATTIES, ABOUT 1/2 INCH (1 CM) THICK. SPREAD THE REMAINING BREAD CRUMBS ON A PLATE. DIP EACH PATTY INTO CRUMBS, COVERING BOTH SIDES. IN A NONSTICK SKILLET, HEAT OIL OVER MEDIUM HEAT. ADD PATTIES AND COOK, TURNING ONCE, UNTIL HOT AND GOLDEN, ABOUT 3 MINUTES PER SIDE. SERVE ON WARM BUNS SLATHERED WITH TARTAR SAUCE AND ADD YOUR FAVORITE TOPPINGS. SERVES 2.

TIP: BOTTLED TARTAR SAUCE WORKS WELL WITH THESE BURGERS, BUT IF YOU DON'T HAVE ANY ON HAND, SIMPLY COMBINE 1/2 CUP (125 ML) MAYONNAISE AND 2 TBSP (30 ML) SWEET GREEN PICKLE RELISH.

HOISIN PORK LETTUCE WRAPS

BOTTLED HOISIN SAUCE MAKES LETTUCE WRAPS EASY. INSTRUCT EVERYONE TO FILL THEIR OWN LEAVES, WRAP AND EAT.

I TSP	VEGETABLE OIL	5 ML
I	SMALL RED BELL PEPPER, FINELY CHOPPED	I
I LB	LEAN GROUND PORK	500 G
2	CLOVES GARLIC, CRUSHED	2
2 TSP	GRATED GINGERROOT	IO ML
1/3 CUP	CHOPPED FRESH CILANTRO	75 ML
1/3 CUP	HOISIN SAUCE	75 ML
I TBSP	SOY SAUCE	I5 ML
I	HEAD BUTTER OR LEAF LETTUCE, SEPARATED INTO LEAVES	I
	ADDITIONAL CHOPPED FRESH CILANTRO	

IN A LARGE SKILLET, HEAT OIL OVER MEDIUM-HIGH HEAT. ADD RED PEPPER AND PORK; COOK, BREAKING PORK UP WITH A SPOON, UNTIL PORK IS NO LONGER PINK. ADD GARLIC, GINGER AND CILANTRO; COOK, STIRRING, FOR I MINUTE. STIR IN HOISIN SAUCE AND SOY SAUCE; COOK UNTIL HEATED THROUGH. SERVE WITH LETTUCE LEAVES AND ADDITIONAL CILANTRO. SERVES 4 TO 6.

CHICKEN CAESAR WRAPS

2	BONELESS SKINLESS CHICKEN BREASTS	2
2 TSP	OLIVE OIL	10 ML
1	SMALL CLOVE GARLIC, MINCED	1
1/2 CUP	LIGHT MAYONNAISE	125 ML
1 TBSP	FRESHLY SQUEEZED LEMON JUICE	15 ML
1 TSP	DIJON MUSTARD	5 ML
6	SLICES BACON, COOKED CRISP AND CRUMBLED	6
1/4 CUP	OIL-PACKED SUN-DRIED TOMATOES, CHOPPED (OPTIONAL)	60 ML
2 TBSP	FRESHLY GRATED PARMESAN CHEESE	30 ML
	FRESHLY GROUND BLACK PEPPER	
6	9-INCH (23 CM) FLOUR TORTILLAS	6
6 CUPS	SHREDDED ROMAINE LETTUCE	1.5 L

SLICE CHICKEN BREASTS HORIZONTALLY INTO TWO THIN PIECES EACH. IN A NONSTICK SKILLET, HEAT OIL OVER MEDIUM-HIGH HEAT. COOK CHICKEN FOR 3 MINUTES PER SIDE OR UNTIL NO LONGER PINK INSIDE. TRANSFER TO A CUTTING BOARD AND CUT INTO THIN STRIPS. IN A BOWL, COMBINE GARLIC, MAYONNAISE, LEMON JUICE AND MUSTARD. ADD BACON, SUN-DRIED TOMATOES (IF USING) AND PARMESAN CHEESE. SEASON TO TASTE WITH PEPPER. THINLY SPREAD MAYONNAISE MIXTURE OVER EACH TORTILLA, LEAVING A 1-INCH (2.5 CM) BORDER. ON BOTTOM HALF OF EACH TORTILLA, LAYER WITH SOME OF THE CHICKEN STRIPS AND 1 CUP (250 ML) ROMAINE. FOLD 1 INCH (2.5 CM) OF THE RIGHT AND LEFT SIDES OF TORTILLA OVER FILLING; STARTING FROM BOTTOM, ROLL TORTILLAS AROUND FILLING. SERVE IMMEDIATELY. MAKES 6 WRAPS.

GREEK CHICKEN PITAS

1 LB	BONELESS SKINLESS CHICKEN BREASTS, CUT INTO VERY THIN STRIPS	500 G
1 TBSP	FRESHLY SQUEEZED LEMON JUICE	15 ML
1	LARGE CLOVE GARLIC, FINELY CHOPPED	1
3/4 TSP	DRIED OREGANO	3 ML
1/4 TSP	SALT	1 ML
1/4 TSP	FRESHLY GROUND BLACK PEPPER	1 ML
2 TSP	OLIVE OIL	10 ML
1	SMALL RED ONION, HALVED LENGTHWISE AND THINLY SLICED	1
1	RED OR GREEN BELL PEPPER, CUT INTO THIN 2-INCH (5 CM) STRIPS	1
4	7-INCH (18 CM) PITAS, HALVED TO FORM POCKETS	4
3/4 CUP	TZATZIKI	175 ML
4 CUPS	SHREDDED ROMAINE LETTUCE	1 L
2	TOMATOES, CUT INTO WEDGES	2

IN A BOWL, COMBINE CHICKEN, LEMON JUICE, GARLIC, OREGANO, SALT AND PEPPER; MARINATE AT ROOM TEMPERATURE FOR 10 MINUTES. IN A LARGE NONSTICK SKILLET, HEAT OIL OVER MEDIUM-HIGH HEAT; COOK CHICKEN, STIRRING, FOR 5 MINUTES OR UNTIL NO LONGER PINK. ADD ONION AND BELL PEPPER; COOK, STIRRING, FOR 2 MINUTES OR UNTIL VEGETABLES ARE SOFTENED. WRAP PITAS IN PAPER TOWELS; MICROWAVE ON MEDIUM (50%) FOR 1 1/2 MINUTES OR UNTIL WARM. SPOON CHICKEN MIXTURE INTO PITA HALVES; TOP WITH A GENEROUS SPOONFUL OF TZATZIKI SAUCE, SHREDDED LETTUCE AND TOMATO WEDGES. MAKES 4 PITAS.

FALAFEL IN PITA

FAST-AND-EASY RECIPE

THESE TASTY TREATS ARE A GIFT FROM THE MIDDLE EAST, WHERE THEY ARE EATEN THE WAY HAMBURGERS ARE IN NORTH AMERICA. LIBERALLY GARNISHED, THEY MAKE A GREAT LUNCH OR LIGHT DINNER.

1	CAN (19 OZ/540 ML) CHICKPEAS, DRAINED AND RINSED	1
1/2 CUP	SLICED GREEN ONION	125 ML
2 TBSP	FRESHLY SQUEEZED LEMON JUICE	30 ML
1 TBSP	MINCED GARLIC	15 ML
1 to 2 TSP	CURRY POWDER	5 to 10 ML
1	LARGE EGG	1
2 TBSP	VEGETABLE OIL	30 ML
1/2 CUP	ALL-PURPOSE FLOUR	125 ML
4	PITA BREADS	4
	CHOPPED PEELED CUCUMBER, TOMATO, SHREDDED LETTUCE, PLAIN YOGURT	

IN A FOOD PROCESSOR, COMBINE CHICKPEAS, ONION, LEMON JUICE, GARLIC, AND CURRY POWDER TO TASTE. PROCESS UNTIL BLENDED BUT CHICKPEAS RETAIN THEIR TEXTURE. USING YOUR HANDS, SHAPE INTO 4 LARGE PATTIES. IN A SHALLOW BOWL, LIGHTLY BEAT EGG. IN A SKILLET, HEAT OIL OVER MEDIUM HEAT. DIP EACH PATTY INTO THE EGG, THEN INTO THE FLOUR, COATING BOTH SIDES WELL. FRY UNTIL GOLDEN AND HEATED THROUGH, ABOUT 2 MINUTES PER SIDE. FILL EACH PITA BREAD WITH A FALAFEL AND GARNISH WITH CUCUMBER, TOMATO, LETTUCE AND YOGURT, AS DESIRED. SERVES 4.

TACO PITAS

WALK RIGHT ON BY THE PREPACKAGED TACO
MIXES AND SHELLS IN SUPERMARKETS. ONCE THE
MEAT IS BROWNED, IT TAKES NO TIME TO ADD
THE BEANS AND SEASONINGS TO MAKE THIS
TASTY FILLING, SERVED IN PITAS.

8 OZ	LEAN GROUND BEEF	250 G
I	SMALL ONION, FINELY CHOPPED	I
I	LARGE CLOVE GARLIC, FINELY CHOPPED	I
2 TSP	CHILI POWDER	10 ML
2 TSP	ALL-PURPOSE FLOUR	10 ML
1/2 TSP	DRIED OREGANO	2 ML
1/2 TSP	GROUND CUMIN	2 ML
PINCH	CAYENNE PEPPER	PINCH
1/2 CUP	HEARTY BEEF STOCK (PAGE 43) OR READY-TO-USE BEEF BROTH	125 ML
I	CAN (19 OZ/540 ML) PINTO, BLACK OR RED KIDNEY BEANS, DRAINED AND RINSED	I
4	7-INCH (18 CM) PITAS, HALVED TO FORM POCKETS, WARMED (SEE TIP, OPPOSITE)	4
	SALSA, SHREDDED LETTUCE, TOMATO WEDGES, BELL PEPPER STRIPS, SHREDDED MOZZARELLA OR CHEDDAR CHEESE	

IN A LARGE NONSTICK SKILLET OVER MEDIUM-HIGH
HEAT, COOK BEEF, BREAKING UP WITH THE BACK OF A
WOODEN SPOON, FOR 4 MINUTES OR UNTIL NO LONGER
PINK. REDUCE HEAT TO MEDIUM. ADD ONION, GARLIC,
CHILI POWDER, FLOUR, OREGANO, CUMIN AND CAYENNE
PEPPER. COOK, STIRRING OFTEN, FOR 5 MINUTES OR UNTIL
ONIONS ARE SOFTENED. POUR IN STOCK; COOK, STIRRING,

UNTIL SLIGHTLY THICKENED. STIR IN BEANS; COOK FOR 2 MINUTES OR UNTIL HEATED THROUGH. SPOON $\frac{1}{4}$ CUP (60 ML) BEAN MIXTURE INTO EACH PITA POCKET; TOP WITH SALSA, LETTUCE, TOMATO, PEPPERS AND CHEESE. SERVES 4.

TIP: TO WARM PITAS, WRAP THEM IN FOIL AND PLACE IN A 350°F (180°C) OVEN FOR 15 TO 20 MINUTES. OR WRAP 4 AT A TIME IN PAPER TOWELS AND MICROWAVE ON HIGH FOR 1 TO $1\frac{1}{2}$ MINUTES.

VARIATION
SLOPPY JOE PITAS: INCREASE BEEF TO 1 LB (500 G). OMIT THE BEANS AND ADD A $7\frac{1}{2}$-OZ (213 ML) CAN OF TOMATO SAUCE; COOK FOR 3 MINUTES OR UNTIL SAUCE IS SLIGHTLY THICKENED.

IT'S LONELY AT THE TOP, BUT YOU EAT BETTER.

CHICKEN TACOS

KIDS LOVE THIS TACTILE DISH, AND ADULTS ENJOY ITS TEX-MEX FLAVORS AND EASE OF PREPARATION.

1 TBSP	VEGETABLE OIL	15 ML
8 OZ	SKINLESS BONELESS CHICKEN BREASTS, CUT INTO $1/2$-INCH (1 CM) CUBES	250 G
1/2 TSP	CHILI POWDER	2 ML
	FRESHLY GROUND BLACK PEPPER	
1 CUP	DRAINED CANNED OR THAWED FROZEN CORN KERNELS	250 ML
1	ROASTED RED BELL PEPPER (SEE TIPS, PAGE 149), FINELY CHOPPED	1
1	CAN (14 OZ/398 ML) REFRIED BEANS	1
1 CUP	SHREDDED TEX-MEX CHEESE MIX OR MONTEREY JACK CHEESE	250 ML
12	TACO SHELLS	12
	SALSA, SHREDDED LETTUCE, CHOPPED TOMATO, FINELY CHOPPED RED OR GREEN ONION, CUBED AVOCADO, SOUR CREAM	

IN A SKILLET, HEAT OIL OVER MEDIUM HEAT. ADD CHICKEN AND COOK, STIRRING, UNTIL LIGHTLY BROWNED AND NO LONGER PINK INSIDE, ABOUT 5 MINUTES. SPRINKLE WITH CHILI POWDER, AND BLACK PEPPER TO TASTE. COOK, STIRRING, FOR 1 MINUTE. ADD CORN, RED PEPPER AND BEANS AND BRING TO A BOIL. REDUCE HEAT TO LOW AND SIMMER FOR 2 TO 3 MINUTES. ADD CHEESE AND STIR UNTIL MELTED. WARM TACO SHELLS ACCORDING TO PACKAGE DIRECTIONS. FILL WITH BEAN MIXTURE AND GARNISH WITH ANY COMBINATION OF SALSA, LETTUCE, TOMATO, ONION, AVOCADO AND/OR SOUR CREAM.

SERVES 4.

AMAZING CHICKEN ENCHILADAS

INSTEAD OF TURNING CHICKEN LEFTOVERS
INTO COLD SANDWICHES, WHIP UP THIS FAST-FIX
DINNER WITH LOADS OF FAMILY APPEAL.

4 OZ	CREAM CHEESE	125 G
1/2 CUP	PLAIN YOGURT OR SOUR CREAM	125 ML
2 CUPS	COOKED CHICKEN, CUT INTO THIN STRIPS	500 ML
3	GREEN ONIONS, SLICED	3
2	TOMATOES, SEEDED AND DICED	2
1/4 CUP	CHOPPED FRESH CILANTRO OR PARSLEY	60 ML
6	9-INCH (23 CM) FLOUR TORTILLAS	6
1 1/2 CUPS	MILD OR MEDIUM SALSA	375 ML
1 CUP	SHREDDED CHEDDAR OR MONTEREY JACK CHEESE	250 ML

PREHEAT OVEN TO 350°F (180°C). GREASE A 13- BY 9-INCH
(33 BY 23 CM) BAKING DISH. PLACE CREAM CHEESE IN A
LARGE BOWL; MICROWAVE ON MEDIUM (50%) FOR 1 MINUTE
TO SOFTEN. STIR WELL. STIR IN YOGURT, CHICKEN, GREEN
ONIONS, TOMATOES AND CILANTRO. SPREAD ABOUT
1/2 CUP (125 ML) CHICKEN MIXTURE DOWN CENTER OF EACH
TORTILLA AND ROLL UP. ARRANGE TORTILLAS IN A SINGLE
LAYER, SEAM SIDE DOWN, IN PREPARED BAKING DISH.
SPREAD EACH TORTILLA WITH SALSA AND SPRINKLE WITH
CHEESE. BAKE FOR 30 TO 35 MINUTES OR UNTIL HEATED
THROUGH. SPRINKLE WITH EXTRA CHOPPED CILANTRO, IF
DESIRED. MAKES 6 ENCHILADAS.

TIP: YOU CAN ASSEMBLE THIS DISH A DAY AHEAD OF
BAKING; JUST TOP WITH SALSA AND CHEESE PRIOR TO
POPPING IN THE OVEN.

CHICKEN FAJITAS

THIS QUICK AND EASY MAIN DISH IS IDEAL FOR
AN IMPROMPTU DINNER. SET OUT BOWLS OF THE
GARNISHES AND LET EVERYONE HELP THEMSELVES.

1 LB	BONELESS SKINLESS CHICKEN BREASTS OR BONELESS TURKEY BREAST, CUT INTO THIN SLICES	500 G
1 TBSP	FRESHLY SQUEEZED LIME JUICE	15 ML
1	CLOVE GARLIC, FINELY CHOPPED	1
1 TSP	DRIED OREGANO	5 ML
1/2 TSP	GROUND CUMIN	2 ML
1/2 TSP	GROUND CORIANDER	2 ML
1/2 TSP	SALT	2 ML
PINCH	CAYENNE PEPPER	PINCH
2 TBSP	OLIVE OIL	30 ML
1	RED ONION, THINLY SLICED	1
1	SMALL RED BELL PEPPER, CUT INTO THIN 2-INCH (5 CM) STRIPS	1
1	SMALL GREEN BELL PEPPER, CUT INTO THIN 2-INCH (5 CM) STRIPS	1
6	9-INCH (23 CM) FLOUR TORTILLAS, WARMED (SEE TIP, OPPOSITE)	6
	SALSA, SOUR CREAM, SHREDDED LETTUCE, SHREDDED CHEDDAR CHEESE	

IN A BOWL, TOSS CHICKEN WITH LIME JUICE, GARLIC,
OREGANO, CUMIN, CORIANDER, SALT AND CAYENNE PEPPER.
MARINATE FOR 15 MINUTES AT ROOM TEMPERATURE, OR
LONGER IN THE REFRIGERATOR. IN A LARGE NONSTICK
SKILLET, HEAT 1 TBSP (15 ML) OIL OVER HIGH HEAT; COOK
CHICKEN FOR 2 TO 3 MINUTES PER SIDE OR UNTIL
LIGHTLY BROWNED AND NO LONGER PINK IN CENTER.

TRANSFER TO PLATE; KEEP WARM. ADD THE REMAINING OIL TO SKILLET; COOK ONION AND PEPPERS, STIRRING, FOR 3 MINUTES OR UNTIL TENDER-CRISP. REMOVE FROM HEAT. TOSS CHICKEN WITH ONION-PEPPER MIXTURE. SPOON CHICKEN MIXTURE DOWN CENTER OF EACH TORTILLA; ADD A SMALL SPOONFUL OF SALSA AND SOUR CREAM, IF DESIRED, AND SPRINKLE WITH SHREDDED LETTUCE AND CHEESE. ROLL UP. MAKES 6 FAJITAS.

TIP: CHICKEN CAN ALSO BE BARBECUED. MARINATE AS DIRECTED AND BRUSH WITH 1 TBSP (15 ML) OIL; GRILL OVER MEDIUM HEAT FOR 3 MINUTES PER SIDE OR UNTIL NO LONGER PINK.

TIP: TO WARM TORTILLAS, WRAP THEM IN FOIL AND PLACE IN A 350°F (180°C) OVEN FOR 15 TO 20 MINUTES. OR GRILL TORTILLAS OVER MEDIUM HEAT FOR 30 TO 60 SECONDS PER SIDE.

CONFESSION IS GOOD FOR YOUR SOUL
BUT BAD FOR YOUR CAREER.

CHEESE AND SALSA QUESADILLAS

FAST-AND-EASY RECIPE

HERE'S A MODERN RENDITION OF GRILLED CHEESE: THIN FLOUR TORTILLAS REPLACE SLICED BREAD, MOZZARELLA SUBSTITUTES FOR PROCESSED CHEESE AND CHUNKY SALSA STANDS IN FOR THE KETCHUP. THE BEANS MAKE A WHOLESOME ADDITION.

1/2 CUP	SALSA	125 ML
4	9-INCH (23 CM) FLOUR TORTILLAS	4
1 CUP	RINSED DRAINED CANNED BLACK OR PINTO BEANS	250 ML
1 CUP	SHREDDED MOZZARELLA, MONTEREY JACK OR CHEDDAR CHEESE	250 ML
	ADDITIONAL SALSA	

SPREAD 2 TBSP (30 ML) SALSA ON HALF OF EACH TORTILLA. SPRINKLE WITH 1/4 CUP (60 ML) EACH OF THE BEANS AND THE CHEESE. FOLD TORTILLAS OVER AND PRESS DOWN LIGHTLY. IN A LARGE NONSTICK SKILLET OVER MEDIUM HEAT, COOK TORTILLAS, 2 AT A TIME, PRESSING DOWN LIGHTLY WITH THE BACK OF A METAL SPATULA, FOR ABOUT 2 MINUTES PER SIDE, UNTIL LIGHTLY TOASTED AND CHEESE IS MELTED. (OR PLACE DIRECTLY ON BARBECUE GRILL OVER MEDIUM HEAT UNTIL LIGHTLY TOASTED ON BOTH SIDES.) CUT INTO WEDGES AND SERVE WARM WITH ADDITIONAL SALSA, IF DESIRED. MAKES 4 QUESADILLAS.

TIP: SERVE THESE WARM CHEESY WEDGES WITH SOUP FOR AN EASY DINNER. THEY'RE ALSO GREAT AS A SNACK THAT BOTH KIDS AND GROWN-UPS APPLAUD.

POTATO PANCAKES WITH SMOKED SALMON

POTATO PANCAKES, ALSO KNOWN AS LATKES,
ARE ONE OF THE WORLD'S GREAT COMFORT FOODS.
TOPPED WITH SMOKED SALMON AND A DOLLOP OF
SOUR CREAM, THEY MAKE AN EXQUISITE LIGHT MEAL.

1	CAN (19 OZ/540 ML) WHOLE WHITE POTATOES, DRAINED (OR 2 MEDIUM POTATOES, COOKED AND PEELED)	1
1/2 CUP	FINELY CHOPPED ONION	125 ML
1	LARGE EGG, BEATEN	1
1 TBSP	ALL-PURPOSE FLOUR	15 ML
1/2 TSP	SALT	2 ML
	FRESHLY GROUND BLACK PEPPER	
2 TBSP	VEGETABLE OIL (APPROX.)	30 ML
4	SLICES SMOKED SALMON, THAWED IF FROZEN	4
	SOUR CREAM	

PREHEAT OVEN TO 250°F (120°C). SHRED POTATOES
ON COARSE GRATER AND FINELY CHOP ANY LEFTOVER
BITS. IN A BOWL, COMBINE POTATOES, ONION, EGG,
FLOUR, SALT, AND BLACK PEPPER TO TASTE. MIX WELL.
SHAPE INTO 4 SMALL, THIN PANCAKES. IN A NONSTICK
SKILLET, HEAT OIL OVER MEDIUM HEAT. FRY PANCAKES,
IN BATCHES, TURNING ONCE, UNTIL GOLDEN, ABOUT
3 MINUTES PER SIDE. ADD MORE OIL AS REQUIRED. KEEP
COOKED PANCAKES WARM IN PREHEATED OVEN. TO
SERVE, PLACE 2 PANCAKES ON EACH PLATE. TOP EACH
PANCAKE WITH A PIECE OF SALMON AND A DOLLOP OF
SOUR CREAM. SERVES 2.

OLIVE-STUDDED STRATA WITH TOMATOES

SLOW COOKER RECIPE

SERVED WITH SALAD, THIS BREAD-BASED DISH MAKES A DELICIOUS MEAL, FROM BRUNCH TO DINNER.

1/4 CUP	BUTTER, SOFTENED (APPROX.)	60 ML
3	1-INCH (2.5 CM) THICK SLICES OLIVE BREAD (SEE TIPS, OPPOSITE)	3
1/4 CUP	FRESH THYME OR FINELY CHOPPED FRESH PARSLEY	60 ML
2 TBSP	FINELY CHOPPED RECONSTITUTED SUN-DRIED TOMATOES	30 ML
3	LARGE EGGS	3
2	LARGE EGG YOLKS	2
1 CUP	EVAPORATED MILK	250 ML
1 TSP	SALT	5 ML
1 TSP	CRACKED BLACK PEPPERCORNS	5 ML
1	CAN (28 OZ/796 ML) DICED TOMATOES, WITH ALL BUT 1/2 CUP (125 ML) JUICE	1
2 CUPS	SHREDDED FONTINA CHEESE, DIVIDED	500 ML

BUTTER THE BREAD ON BOTH SIDES AND CUT INTO 1-INCH (2.5 CM) CUBES. PLACE IN A LARGE MIXING BOWL (SEE TIP, OPPOSITE). ADD THYME AND SUN-DRIED TOMATOES AND TOSS WELL. IN A SEPARATE BOWL, WHISK EGGS, EGG YOLKS, MILK, SALT AND PEPPERCORNS UNTIL BLENDED. WHISK IN TOMATOES AND THE APPROPRIATE AMOUNT OF JUICE, THEN STIR IN 1 1/2 CUPS (375 ML) FONTINA (COVER THE REMAINING CHEESE AND REFRIGERATE UNTIL READY TO USE). POUR OVER BREAD MIXTURE, STIRRING UNTIL WELL COATED. COVER WITH PLASTIC WRAP AND, USING YOUR HANDS, PUSH THE BREAD DOWN SO IT IS

SUBMERGED IN THE LIQUID. REFRIGERATE FOR AT LEAST 2 HOURS OR OVERNIGHT, PUSHING THE BREAD DOWN INTO THE LIQUID ONCE OR TWICE, IF POSSIBLE.

TRANSFER BREAD MIXTURE TO A LIGHTLY GREASED 8-CUP (2 L) BAKING OR SOUFFLÉ DISH. COVER WITH FOIL, LEAVING ROOM FOR THE STRATA TO EXPAND, AND SECURE WITH A STRING. PLACE DISH IN A LARGE (MINIMUM 5-QUART) OVAL SLOW COOKER AND POUR IN ENOUGH BOILING WATER TO REACH 1 INCH (2.5 CM) UP THE SIDES OF THE DISH. COVER AND COOK ON HIGH FOR 3 TO 4 HOURS, UNTIL PUDDING IS PUFFED.

PREHEAT BROILER. REMOVE FOIL AND SPRINKLE THE REMAINING FONTINA OVER TOP OF PUDDING. PLACE UNDER BROILER UNTIL MELTED AND NICELY BROWNED. SERVES 8.

TIP: IF YOU CAN'T FIND OLIVE BREAD, USE COUNTRY-STYLE BREAD AND ADD 1/4 CUP (60 ML) CHOPPED PITTED BLACK OLIVES ALONG WITH THE SUN-DRIED TOMATOES. REDUCE THE QUANTITY OF SALT TO 1/2 TSP (2 ML).

TIP: FOR BEST RESULTS, USE SLIGHTLY STALE BREAD. IF YOUR BREAD IS VERY FRESH, THE STRATA IS LIKELY TO BE A BIT SOGGY. THE DENSER YOUR BREAD (USUALLY A POSITIVE), THE MORE VOLUME YOU'LL HAVE. YOU MAY FIND YOU HAVE JUST SLIGHTLY TOO MUCH TO FIT IN YOUR DISH. IN THIS CASE, DISCARD THE EXCESS.

TIP: IT'S BEST TO SOAK THE BREAD MIXTURE IN A LARGE MIXING BOWL BECAUSE THE BREAD CONDENSES AS IT ABSORBS THE LIQUID AND IS MORE LIKELY TO FIT INTO THE BAKING DISH WHEN TRANSFERRED.

SAVORY MUSHROOM AND BRIE TART

THIS COMBINATION OF FLAVORFUL MUSHROOMS, TOMATOES, LIGHT CRISPY PASTRY AND OOZING HOT BRIE IS SUBLIME.

1	SHEET FROZEN PUFF PASTRY, THAWED (ABOUT 6 OZ/175 G)	1
1 TBSP	VEGETABLE OIL	15 ML
8 OZ	SLICED MUSHROOMS	250 G
1/4 TSP	SALT	1 ML
	FRESHLY GROUND BLACK PEPPER	
1 TBSP	FRESHLY SQUEEZED LEMON JUICE	15 ML
2 TBSP	BASIL PESTO	30 ML
12	CHERRY OR GRAPE TOMATOES, HALVED	12
6 OZ	BRIE CHEESE, WITH RIND, THINLY SLICED	175 G

PREHEAT OVEN TO 400°F (200°C). ON A LIGHTLY FLOURED BOARD, ROLL PASTRY INTO A 12- BY 9-INCH (30 BY 23 CM) RECTANGLE. FOLD EDGES OVER TO FORM A 1/2-INCH (1 CM) BORDER. CAREFULLY TRANSFER TO A BAKING SHEET. IN A SKILLET, HEAT OIL OVER MEDIUM HEAT. ADD MUSHROOMS AND COOK, STIRRING, UNTIL THEY BEGIN TO BROWN AND TO LOSE THEIR LIQUID, ABOUT 7 MINUTES. SEASON WITH SALT, AND BLACK PEPPER TO TASTE. STIR IN LEMON JUICE. REMOVE SKILLET FROM HEAT AND SET ASIDE. SPREAD PESTO EVENLY OVER PASTRY, LEAVING A 1/2-INCH (1 CM) BORDER. SPREAD MUSHROOMS EVENLY OVER TOP. ARRANGE TOMATO HALVES EVENLY OVER MUSHROOMS. LAY CHEESE SLICES EVENLY OVER TOP. BAKE UNTIL CHEESE IS MELTED AND CRUST IS BROWNED, 10 TO 15 MINUTES. SERVES 4 TO 6.

ONE-POT DINNERS

EASY CURRIED FISH STEW

GINGERROOT ADDS SPARKLING FLAVOR TO THIS LOW-CAL STEW. SERVE STEAMING BOWLS WITH CHUNKS OF CRUSTY WHOLE-GRAIN BREAD. IT'S A COMPLETE MEAL!

1 TBSP	VEGETABLE OIL	15 ML
1	SMALL ONION, FINELY CHOPPED	1
1 TBSP	MINCED GINGERROOT	15 ML
2 TSP	MILD CURRY PASTE (OR TO TASTE)	10 ML
2 CUPS	DICED PEELED POTATOES	500 ML
1 1/2 CUPS	THINLY SLICED CARROTS	375 ML
2 1/4 CUPS	FISH STOCK OR READY-TO-USE CHICKEN BROTH	550 ML
1 TBSP	CORNSTARCH	15 ML
	SALT AND FRESHLY GROUND BLACK PEPPER	
1 1/2 CUPS	SNOW PEAS, ENDS TRIMMED, HALVED	375 ML
1 LB	FISH FILLETS, CUT INTO CHUNKS	500 G

IN A LARGE SAUCEPAN, HEAT OIL OVER MEDIUM HEAT. COOK ONION, GINGER AND CURRY PASTE, STIRRING, FOR 2 MINUTES OR UNTIL SOFTENED. ADD POTATOES, CARROTS AND STOCK. BRING TO A BOIL; REDUCE HEAT, COVER AND SIMMER FOR 10 TO 12 MINUTES OR UNTIL VEGETABLES ARE JUST TENDER. IN A BOWL, BLEND CORNSTARCH WITH 2 TBSP (30 ML) WATER. ADD TO STEW AND COOK, STIRRING, UNTIL THICKENED. SEASON TO TASTE WITH SALT AND PEPPER. STIR IN SNOW PEAS AND FISH; COVER AND COOK FOR 2 TO 3 MINUTES OR UNTIL SNOW PEAS ARE TENDER-CRISP AND FISH IS OPAQUE. LADLE INTO BOWLS AND SERVE. SERVES 4.

CHICKEN AND VEGETABLE STEW

EVEN IF YOU DON'T HAVE A LOT OF TIME TO
SPEND IN THE KITCHEN, YOU CAN RUSTLE UP A
GREAT-TASTING STEW USING BONELESS CHICKEN
THIGHS AND CONVENIENT FROZEN VEGETABLES.
SERVE OVER NOODLES.

I TBSP	BUTTER	15 ML
I	LARGE ONION, CHOPPED	I
2	CLOVES GARLIC, FINELY CHOPPED	2
I TSP	DRIED ITALIAN HERBS OR FINES HERBES	5 ML
I LB	BONELESS SKINLESS CHICKEN THIGHS (ABOUT 8), CUT INTO I-INCH (2.5 CM) CUBES	500 G
3 TBSP	ALL-PURPOSE FLOUR	45 ML
2 CUPS	CHICKEN STOCK (PAGE 42) OR READY-TO-USE CHICKEN BROTH	500 ML
I	PACKAGE (I LB/500 G) FROZEN MIXED VEGETABLES	I
	SALT AND FRESHLY GROUND BLACK PEPPER	

IN A DUTCH OVEN OR LARGE SAUCEPAN, MELT BUTTER
OVER MEDIUM HEAT. ADD ONION, GARLIC AND ITALIAN
HERBS; COOK, STIRRING, FOR 4 MINUTES OR UNTIL ONIONS
ARE LIGHTLY BROWNED. IN A BOWL, TOSS CHICKEN WITH
FLOUR UNTIL WELL-COATED. ADD TO PAN ALONG WITH
ANY REMAINING FLOUR; STIR IN STOCK. BRING TO A BOIL
AND COOK, STIRRING, UNTIL SAUCE THICKENS. REDUCE
HEAT, COVER AND SIMMER, STIRRING OCCASIONALLY, FOR
20 MINUTES. ADD FROZEN VEGETABLES; RETURN TO A
BOIL. SEASON TO TASTE WITH SALT AND PEPPER. REDUCE
HEAT, COVER AND SIMMER FOR 10 MINUTES OR UNTIL
CHICKEN AND VEGETABLES ARE TENDER. SERVES 4.

SPANISH-STYLE FISH STEW

SLOW COOKER RECIPE

ENLIVENED BY KALE AND SPICY CHORIZO, THIS EASY STEW HAS THE IMPACT OF A SPECIAL-OCCASION DISH. IT'S GOOD ON ITS OWN, BUT IF YOU WANT TO KICK IT UP A NOTCH, TOP IT WITH AïOLI-BRUSHED CROSTINI (SEE TIP, OPPOSITE).

1 TBSP	OLIVE OIL	15 ML
1 LB	SOFT CHORIZO SAUSAGE (BULK OR CASINGS REMOVED)	500 G
2	ONIONS, THINLY SLICED ON THE VERTICAL	2
2	STALKS CELERY, DICED	2
4	CLOVES GARLIC, MINCED	4
1 TSP	SALT	5 ML
1 TSP	CRACKED BLACK PEPPERCORNS	5 ML
2	BAY LEAVES	2
1 CUP	DRY WHITE WINE	250 ML
4 CUPS	FISH STOCK OR 2 CUPS (500 ML) EACH BOTTLED CLAM JUICE AND WATER	1 L
2	POTATOES, PEELED AND SHREDDED	2
1 TSP	SMOKED PAPRIKA	5 ML
4 CUPS	COARSELY CHOPPED KALE	1 L
1½ LBS	FIRM WHITE FISH FILLETS, SUCH AS PACIFIC HALIBUT, TURBOT OR HADDOCK, CUT INTO BITE-SIZE PIECES	750 G

IN A SKILLET, HEAT OIL OVER MEDIUM HEAT. ADD CHORIZO, ONIONS AND CELERY AND COOK, STIRRING, UNTIL MEAT IS COOKED, ABOUT 7 MINUTES. ADD GARLIC, SALT, PEPPERCORNS AND BAY LEAVES AND COOK, STIRRING, FOR 1 MINUTE. ADD WINE, BRING TO A BOIL AND BOIL

FOR 2 MINUTES. TRANSFER TO A MEDIUM TO LARGE ($3\frac{1}{2}$- TO 5-QUART) SLOW COOKER. (MIXTURE CAN BE COOLED, COVERED AND REFRIGERATED FOR UP TO 2 DAYS AT THIS POINT.)

ADD STOCK AND POTATOES. COVER AND COOK ON LOW FOR 6 HOURS OR ON HIGH FOR 3 HOURS, UNTIL POTATOES ARE TENDER. STIR IN PAPRIKA AND KALE. COVER AND COOK ON HIGH FOR 15 MINUTES. STIR IN FISH. COVER AND COOK ON HIGH ABOUT 7 MINUTES, UNTIL COOKED THROUGH. DISCARD BAY LEAVES. SERVES 6.

TIP: CHORIZO COMES IN VARIOUS DEGREES OF SPICINESS. USE THE ONE THAT SUITS YOUR TASTE.

TIP: IF YOU PREFER, SUBSTITUTE AN EXTRA CUP (250 ML) OF WATER PLUS 1 TBSP (15 ML) LEMON JUICE FOR THE WHITE WINE.

TIP: IF YOU CHOOSE TO HALVE THIS RECIPE, USE A SMALL (2- TO 3-QUART) SLOW COOKER.

TIP

AÏOLI-BRUSHED CROSTINI: PREHEAT BROILER. BRUSH BAGUETTE SLICES WITH OLIVE OIL ON BOTH SIDES, PLACE ON A BAKING SHEET AND TOAST UNDER BROILER UNTIL LIGHTLY BROWNED, TURNING ONCE. WATCH CLOSELY. YOU CAN USE PREPARED AÏOLI OR MAKE A QUICK VERSION OF YOUR OWN BY COMBINING $\frac{1}{4}$ CUP (60 ML) MAYONNAISE WITH 2 TSP (10 ML) FINELY MINCED GARLIC. BRUSH OVER CROSTINI JUST BEFORE SERVING.

CHICKEN STEW WITH DUMPLINGS

THE ULTIMATE ONE-POT COMFORT FOOD.

STEW

1 TBSP	VEGETABLE OIL	15 ML
6 to 8	BONE-IN SKINLESS CHICKEN THIGHS	6 to 8
1 TBSP	BUTTER	15 ML
1	ONION, FINELY CHOPPED	1
1 TSP	DRIED THYME	5 ML
3 TBSP	ALL-PURPOSE FLOUR	45 ML
4 CUPS	CHICKEN STOCK (PAGE 42) OR READY-TO-USE CHICKEN BROTH	1 L
1	CARROT, FINELY CHOPPED	1
1/2 CUP	FROZEN GREEN PEAS	125 ML
1/3 CUP	HEAVY OR WHIPPING (35%) CREAM	75 ML

DUMPLINGS

1 1/3 CUPS	ALL-PURPOSE FLOUR	325 ML
1 1/2 TSP	BAKING POWDER	7 ML
1/4 TSP	SALT	1 ML
1 CUP	HEAVY OR WHIPPING (35%) CREAM	250 ML

STEW: IN A WIDE, HEAVY POT, HEAT OIL OVER MEDIUM-HIGH HEAT. ADD CHICKEN AND BROWN ON ALL SIDES. TRANSFER CHICKEN TO A PLATE. ADD BUTTER, ONION AND THYME TO THE POT AND COOK, STIRRING, UNTIL SOFTENED. ADD FLOUR AND STIR TO COAT. ADD STOCK, RETURN CHICKEN TO THE POT AND BRING TO A SIMMER. REDUCE HEAT TO MEDIUM-LOW, COVER AND SIMMER FOR 20 MINUTES. STIR IN CARROT, PEAS AND CREAM.

DUMPLINGS: MEANWHILE, IN A MEDIUM BOWL, STIR TOGETHER FLOUR, BAKING POWDER AND SALT. STIR IN CREAM. DROP DOUGH BY SPOONFULS ONTO THE SIMMERING STEW, SPACING THEM ABOUT 1 INCH (2.5 CM) APART. COVER AND SIMMER UNTIL DUMPLINGS HAVE DOUBLED IN SIZE, ABOUT 15 MINUTES. SERVES 4 TO 6.

THE BEST WAY TO SERVE CABBAGE
IS TO SOMEONE ELSE.

CLASSIC BEEF STEW

SLOW COOKER RECIPE

THERE'S NOTHING FANCY ABOUT BEEF STEW — JUST BASIC MEAT AND VEGETABLES — BUT THE HOUSE ALWAYS SMELLS SO GOOD WHILE IT'S COOKING.

I TBSP	OIL	15 ML
2 LBS	STEWING BEEF, CUT INTO I-INCH (2.5 CM) CUBES AND PATTED DRY	I KG
2	ONIONS, FINELY CHOPPED	2
4	STALKS CELERY, THINLY SLICED	4
2	LARGE CARROTS, DICED	2
2	CLOVES GARLIC, MINCED	2
I TSP	DRIED THYME	5 ML
I TSP	SALT	5 ML
1/2 TSP	CRACKED BLACK PEPPERCORNS	2 ML
2	BAY LEAVES	2
1/4 CUP	ALL-PURPOSE FLOUR	60 ML
2 CUPS	HEARTY BEEF STOCK (PAGE 43) OR READY-TO-USE BEEF BROTH	500 ML
1/2 CUP	DRY RED WINE OR WATER	125 ML
	FINELY CHOPPED FRESH PARSLEY LEAVES	

IN A SKILLET, HEAT OIL OVER MEDIUM-HIGH HEAT. ADD BEEF, IN BATCHES, AND BROWN, ABOUT 4 MINUTES PER BATCH. USING A SLOTTED SPOON, TRANSFER TO A MEDIUM TO LARGE (3 1/2- TO 5-QUART) SLOW COOKER. REDUCE HEAT UNDER SKILLET TO MEDIUM. ADD ONIONS, CELERY AND CARROTS AND COOK, STIRRING, UNTIL VEGETABLES ARE SOFTENED, ABOUT 7 MINUTES. ADD GARLIC, THYME, SALT, PEPPERCORNS AND BAY LEAVES AND COOK, STIRRING, FOR I MINUTE. ADD FLOUR AND

COOK, STIRRING, FOR I MINUTE. ADD STOCK AND WINE AND COOK, STIRRING, UNTIL THICKENED. TRANSFER TO SLOW COOKER AND STIR WELL. COVER AND COOK ON LOW FOR 8 HOURS OR ON HIGH FOR 4 HOURS, UNTIL BEEF IS VERY TENDER. DISCARD BAY LEAVES. JUST BEFORE SERVING, GARNISH LIBERALLY WITH PARSLEY. SERVES 6.

TIP: IF YOU CHOOSE TO HALVE THIS RECIPE, USE A SMALL (2- TO 3-QUART) SLOW COOKER.

VARIATION

CLASSIC BEEF STEW WITH MADEIRA MUSHROOMS: IN A SKILLET, MELT 2 TBSP (30 ML) BUTTER OVER MEDIUM-HIGH HEAT. ADD 12 OZ (375 G) SLICED BUTTON MUSHROOMS AND SAUTÉ UNTIL MUSHROOMS RELEASE THEIR LIQUID, ABOUT 7 MINUTES. SEASON TO TASTE, THEN SPRINKLE WITH I TBSP (15 ML) ALL-PURPOSE FLOUR. COOK, STIRRING, FOR I MINUTE. ADD $1/4$ CUP (60 ML) MADEIRA OR PORT WINE AND STIR UNTIL THICKENED. JUST BEFORE SERVING, STIR INTO STEW, THEN GARNISH WITH PARSLEY.

VARIATION

BEEF STEW WITH ROASTED GARLIC: MASH 6 CLOVES ROASTED GARLIC AND STIR INTO STEW BEFORE GARNISHING WITH PARSLEY. AN EASY WAY TO ROAST THIS AMOUNT OF GARLIC IS TO PEEL THE CLOVES, REMOVE THE PITH (THE CENTER PART THAT OFTEN SPROUTS), THEN PLACE THE CLOVES ON A PIECE OF FOIL. DRIZZLE ABOUT $1/2$ TSP (2 ML) OLIVE OIL OVER THE GARLIC, THEN FOLD UP THE FOIL TO MAKE A TIGHT PACKET. BAKE IN 400°F (200°C) OVEN FOR 20 MINUTES.

IRISH STEW

SLOW COOKER RECIPE

THIS HEARTY AND DELICIOUS STEW IS AN
OLD FAVORITE THAT REALLY CAN'T BE IMPROVED
UPON. ALL IT NEEDS IS A GREEN VEGETABLE SUCH
AS STRING BEANS OR BROCCOLI, CRUSTY ROLLS OR A
LOAF OF COUNTRY-STYLE BREAD, AND A BIG GLASS
OF GUINNESS OR A ROBUST RED WINE.

1/4 CUP	ALL-PURPOSE FLOUR	60 ML
1 TSP	SALT	5 ML
1/2 TSP	CRACKED BLACK PEPPERCORNS	2 ML
2 LBS	STEWING LAMB, CUT INTO 1-INCH (2.5 CM) CUBES	1 KG
1/4 CUP	VEGETABLE OIL	60 ML
3	ONIONS, FINELY CHOPPED	3
2	LARGE CARROTS, DICED	2
1 TSP	DRIED THYME	5 ML
2 TBSP	TOMATO PASTE	30 ML
1 CUP	HEARTY BEEF STOCK (PAGE 43) OR READY-TO-USE BEEF BROTH	250 ML
4	POTATOES, PEELED AND CUT INTO 1/2-INCH (1 CM) CUBES	4
1 1/2 CUPS	GREEN PEAS	375 ML
1 TBSP	WORCESTERSHIRE SAUCE	15 ML

ON A PLATE, COMBINE FLOUR, SALT AND PEPPERCORNS.
LIGHTLY COAT LAMB WITH MIXTURE, SHAKING OFF THE
EXCESS. SET ANY REMAINING FLOUR MIXTURE ASIDE. IN
A SKILLET, HEAT OIL OVER MEDIUM-HIGH HEAT. ADD LAMB,
IN BATCHES, AND BROWN, ABOUT 4 MINUTES PER BATCH.
TRANSFER TO A LARGE (ABOUT 5-QUART) SLOW COOKER.

REDUCE HEAT UNDER THE SKILLET TO MEDIUM. DRAIN ALL BUT 1 TBSP (15 ML) FAT FROM PAN. ADD ONIONS AND CARROTS TO PAN AND COOK, STIRRING, UNTIL SOFTENED, ABOUT 7 MINUTES. ADD THYME AND RESERVED FLOUR MIXTURE AND COOK, STIRRING, FOR 1 MINUTE. STIR IN TOMATO PASTE AND STOCK AND BRING TO A BOIL. PLACE POTATOES IN SLOW COOKER. ADD ONION MIXTURE AND STIR TO COMBINE. COVER AND COOK ON LOW FOR 8 HOURS OR ON HIGH FOR 4 HOURS, UNTIL MIXTURE IS BUBBLY AND LAMB IS TENDER. STIR IN PEAS AND WORCESTERSHIRE SAUCE. COVER AND COOK ON HIGH FOR 15 TO 20 MINUTES. SERVES 6 TO 8.

TIP: IF YOU CHOOSE TO HALVE THIS RECIPE, USE A SMALL (2- TO $3\frac{1}{2}$-QUART) SLOW COOKER.

IF THERE WERE NO GOLF BALLS,
HOW WOULD WE MEASURE HAIL?

VERY VEGGIE CHILI

HERE'S A TASTY VEGETARIAN CHILI THAT USES CHILI POWDER AND TOMATO SAUCE SPIKED WITH HOT PEPPERS TO QUICKLY ACHIEVE AN AUTHENTIC CHILI FLAVOR. SERVE IT THE OLD-FASHIONED WAY — WITH TOAST — AND TOP WITH A DOLLOP OF SOUR CREAM, IF DESIRED.

1 TBSP	VEGETABLE OIL	15 ML
1 CUP	FINELY CHOPPED ONION	250 ML
2	ZUCCHINI, CUT INTO $1/2$-INCH (1 CM) CUBES (ABOUT 1 LB/500 G)	2
1 TBSP	MINCED GARLIC	15 ML
1 TBSP	CHILI POWDER	15 ML
1	CAN (12 OZ/341 ML) CORN KERNELS, DRAINED (OR $1 1/2$ CUPS/375 ML FROZEN CORN KERNELS, THAWED)	1
1	CAN (19 OZ/540 ML) RED KIDNEY BEANS, DRAINED AND RINSED	1
2 CUPS	SPICY TOMATO SAUCE, SUCH AS ARRABBIATA	500 ML

IN A LARGE SAUCEPAN, HEAT OIL OVER MEDIUM HEAT. ADD ONION AND ZUCCHINI AND COOK, STIRRING OCCASIONALLY, UNTIL ZUCCHINI IS TENDER, ABOUT 8 MINUTES. ADD GARLIC AND CHILI POWDER AND COOK, STIRRING, FOR 1 MINUTE. ADD CORN, KIDNEY BEANS AND TOMATO SAUCE. BRING TO A BOIL. REDUCE HEAT TO LOW AND SIMMER FOR 10 MINUTES TO COMBINE FLAVORS. SERVES 4.

VARIATION

SQUASH AND BLACK BEAN CHILI: SUBSTITUTE 3 CUPS (750 ML) DICED BUTTERNUT SQUASH FOR THE ZUCCHINI AND 1 CAN (19 OZ/540 ML) BLACK BEANS FOR THE KIDNEY BEANS.

CHICKEN AND BLACK BEAN CHILI

THIS TASTY CHILI IS LIGHTER THAN ONE MADE
WITH BEEF. SERVE IT WITH HOT CRUSTY BREAD
AND A STEAMED GREEN VEGETABLE.

1 TBSP	VEGETABLE OIL	15 ML
1 LB	SKINLESS BONELESS CHICKEN BREASTS, CUT INTO 1/2-INCH (1 CM) CUBES	500 G
1 TBSP	MINCED GARLIC	15 ML
1 TBSP	CHILI POWDER	15 ML
1 TSP	CUMIN SEEDS, CRUSHED	5 ML
1 1/2 CUPS	SPICY TOMATO SAUCE, SUCH AS ARRABBIATA	375 ML
1	CAN (19 OZ/540 ML) BLACK BEANS, DRAINED AND RINSED	1
1 TBSP	FRESHLY SQUEEZED LEMON OR LIME JUICE	15 ML

IN A LARGE SAUCEPAN, HEAT OIL OVER MEDIUM HEAT.
ADD CHICKEN AND COOK, STIRRING, UNTIL IT BEGINS
TO BROWN AND IS NO LONGER PINK INSIDE, ABOUT
3 MINUTES. ADD GARLIC, CHILI POWDER AND CUMIN SEEDS
AND COOK, STIRRING, FOR 1 MINUTE. ADD TOMATO SAUCE,
BEANS AND LEMON JUICE. STIR TO COMBINE. REDUCE
HEAT TO LOW AND SIMMER FOR 10 MINUTES TO ALLOW
FLAVORS TO COMBINE. SERVES 4.

VARIATION

CHICKEN, SAUSAGE AND BLACK BEAN CHILI: STIR IN 4 OZ
(125 G) KIELBASA, CUT INTO 1/2-INCH (1 CM) SLICES AND
QUARTERED, ALONG WITH THE TOMATO SAUCE.

TURKEY CHILI WITH BLACK-EYED PEAS

SLOW COOKER RECIPE

SERVE THIS DELICIOUS CHILI (OR ALMOST ANY CHILI) WITH AN AVOCADO TOPPING (SEE TIP, OPPOSITE).

I TBSP	VEGETABLE OIL	15 ML
2	ONIONS, FINELY CHOPPED	2
3	CLOVES GARLIC, MINCED	3
2 TSP	DRIED OREGANO	IO ML
2 TSP	GROUND CORIANDER	IO ML
2 TSP	GROUND CUMIN	IO ML
I TSP	CRACKED BLACK PEPPERCORNS	5 ML
	SALT	
I	CAN (28 OZ/796 ML) TOMATOES, WITH JUICE, COARSELY CHOPPED	I
2 CUPS	CHICKEN STOCK (PAGE 42) OR READY-TO-USE CHICKEN BROTH	500 ML
2 LBS	SKINLESS BONELESS TURKEY BREAST OR THIGHS, CUT INTO I-INCH (2.5 CM) CUBES	I KG
3 CUPS	COOKED BLACK-EYED PEAS (SEE TIP, OPPOSITE)	750 ML
2	GREEN BELL PEPPERS, CUT INTO THIN STRIPS	2
2	JALAPEÑO PEPPERS, FINELY CHOPPED	2
2 TBSP	CHILI POWDER	30 ML
	AVOCADO TOPPING (SEE TIP, OPPOSITE), SHREDDED MONTEREY JACK CHEESE, SOUR CREAM, FINELY CHOPPED RED ONION, FINELY CHOPPED CILANTRO LEAVES	

IN A LARGE SAUCEPAN, HEAT OIL OVER MEDIUM HEAT.

ADD ONIONS AND GARLIC AND COOK, STIRRING, UNTIL

SOFTENED, ABOUT 3 MINUTES. ADD OREGANO, CORIANDER, CUMIN, PEPPERCORNS, AND SALT TO TASTE, AND COOK, STIRRING, FOR I MINUTE. ADD TOMATOES AND STOCK AND BRING TO A BOIL. (MIXTURE CAN BE COOLED, COVERED AND REFRIGERATED FOR UP TO 2 DAYS AT THIS POINT.)

TRANSFER MIXTURE TO A LARGE (ABOUT 5-QUART) SLOW COOKER. ADD TURKEY AND PEAS AND STIR TO COMBINE. COVER AND COOK ON LOW FOR 6 TO 8 HOURS OR ON HIGH FOR 3 TO 4 HOURS, UNTIL TURKEY IS NO LONGER PINK INSIDE. STIR IN BELL PEPPERS, JALAPEÑO PEPPERS AND CHILI POWDER. COVER AND COOK FOR 20 TO 25 MINUTES, UNTIL PEPPERS ARE TENDER. SPOON INTO INDIVIDUAL BOWLS AND GARNISH AS DESIRED. SERVES 6 TO 8.

TIP: FOR THIS AMOUNT OF BLACK-EYED PEAS, USE 1½ CANS (EACH 14 TO 19 OZ/398 TO 540 ML), DRAINED AND RINSED, OR SOAK AND COOK ¾ CUP (175 ML) DRIED BLACK-EYED PEAS.

TIP: IF YOU CHOOSE TO HALVE THIS RECIPE, USE A SMALL (2½- TO 3½-QUART) SLOW COOKER.

TIP

AVOCADO TOPPING: IN A BOWL, COMBINE I AVOCADO, CUT INTO ½-INCH (I CM) CUBES, I TBSP (I5 ML) FRESHLY SQUEEZED LIME JUICE AND 2 TBSP (30 ML) EACH FINELY CHOPPED RED ONION AND FRESH CILANTRO. MIX WELL. SEASON TO TASTE WITH SALT AND FRESHLY GROUND BLACK PEPPER.

CHILI CON CARNE PRONTO

HERE'S A TASTY OLD-FASHIONED CHILI THAT IS QUICK AND EASY TO MAKE. SERVE WITH HOT BUTTERED TOAST.

1 TBSP	VEGETABLE OIL	15 ML
1 LB	LEAN GROUND BEEF	500 G
1 CUP	FINELY CHOPPED ONION	250 ML
1 TBSP	MINCED GARLIC	15 ML
1 TBSP	CHILI POWDER	15 ML
1/2 TSP	CELERY SEED	2 ML
2 CUPS	SPICY TOMATO SAUCE, SUCH AS ARRABBIATA	500 ML
1	CAN (19 OZ/540 ML) KIDNEY BEANS, DRAINED AND RINSED	1

IN A LARGE SAUCEPAN, HEAT OIL OVER MEDIUM-HIGH HEAT. ADD BEEF AND ONION AND COOK, BREAKING UP MEAT WITH A SPOON, UNTIL BEEF IS NO LONGER PINK INSIDE, ABOUT 5 MINUTES. ADD GARLIC, CHILI POWDER AND CELERY SEED AND COOK, STIRRING, FOR 1 MINUTE. ADD TOMATO SAUCE AND BEANS. BRING TO A BOIL. REDUCE HEAT TO LOW AND SIMMER UNTIL BEANS ARE HEATED THROUGH AND FLAVORS ARE COMBINED, ABOUT 10 MINUTES. SERVES 4.

VARIATION: ADD 1/2 CUP (125 ML) FINELY CHOPPED BELL PEPPER WITH THE GARLIC.

VARIATION: FOR A SPICIER VERSION, ADD 1 FINELY CHOPPED JALAPEÑO PEPPER OR, IF YOU PREFER A BIT OF SMOKE, 1 FINELY CHOPPED CHIPOTLE PEPPER IN ADOBO SAUCE WITH THE GARLIC.

AMAZING CHILI

1½ LBS	LEAN GROUND BEEF	750 G
2	ONIONS, CHOPPED	2
3	CLOVES GARLIC, FINELY CHOPPED	3
2	STALKS CELERY, CHOPPED	2
1	LARGE GREEN BELL PEPPER, CHOPPED	1
2 TBSP	CHILI POWDER	30 ML
1½ TSP	DRIED OREGANO	7 ML
1½ TSP	GROUND CUMIN	7 ML
¾ TSP	SALT	3 ML
½ TSP	HOT PEPPER FLAKES (OR TO TASTE)	2 ML
1	CAN (28 OZ/796 ML) TOMATOES, WITH JUICE, CHOPPED	1
1 CUP	HEARTY BEEF STOCK (PAGE 43) OR READY-TO-USE BEEF BROTH	250 ML
1	CAN (19 OZ/540 ML) PINTO OR RED KIDNEY BEANS, DRAINED AND RINSED	1
¼ CUP	CHOPPED FRESH PARSLEY OR CILANTRO	60 ML

IN A DUTCH OVEN OR LARGE SAUCEPAN, COOK BEEF OVER MEDIUM-HIGH HEAT, BREAKING UP WITH A WOODEN SPOON, FOR ABOUT 7 MINUTES OR UNTIL NO LONGER PINK. DRAIN OFF ANY FAT. REDUCE HEAT TO MEDIUM. ADD ONIONS, GARLIC, CELERY, GREEN PEPPER, CHILI POWDER, OREGANO, CUMIN, SALT AND HOT PEPPER FLAKES; COOK, STIRRING OFTEN, FOR 5 MINUTES OR UNTIL VEGETABLES ARE SOFTENED. STIR IN TOMATOES AND STOCK. BRING TO A BOIL; REDUCE HEAT, COVER AND SIMMER, STIRRING OCCASIONALLY, FOR 1 HOUR. ADD BEANS AND PARSLEY; COVER AND SIMMER FOR 10 MINUTES. SERVES 6 TO 8.

MOLASSES BAKED BEANS

HERE'S AN OLD-TIME FAVORITE THAT STIRS
MEMORIES OF THE PIONEER SPIRIT. THIS RUSTIC DISH
IS A WINTER STANDBY AND WONDERFUL WHEN
SERVED WITH HOME-BAKED BREAD.

1 LB	DRIED GREAT NORTHERN OR WHITE PEA BEANS, RINSED AND PICKED OVER (ABOUT 2$\frac{1}{4}$ CUPS/550 ML)	500 G
14 CUPS	COLD WATER, DIVIDED	3.5 L
6	SLICES LEAN SMOKY BACON, CHOPPED	6
1	LARGE ONION, CHOPPED	1
3	CLOVES GARLIC, FINELY CHOPPED	3
1	CAN (7$\frac{1}{2}$ OZ/213 ML) TOMATO SAUCE	1
$\frac{1}{3}$ CUP	LIGHT (FANCY) MOLASSES	75 ML
$\frac{1}{4}$ CUP	PACKED BROWN SUGAR	60 ML
2 TBSP	BALSAMIC VINEGAR	30 ML
2 TSP	DRY MUSTARD	10 ML
1 TSP	SALT	5 ML
$\frac{1}{4}$ TSP	FRESHLY GROUND BLACK PEPPER	1 ML

IN A DUTCH OVEN OR LARGE SAUCEPAN, COMBINE BEANS
AND 6 CUPS (1.5 L) COLD WATER. BRING TO A BOIL OVER
HIGH HEAT; BOIL FOR 2 MINUTES. REMOVE FROM HEAT,
COVER AND LET STAND FOR 1 HOUR.

DRAIN BEANS AND COVER WITH THE REMAINING COLD
WATER. BRING TO A BOIL; REDUCE HEAT, COVER AND
SIMMER FOR 30 TO 40 MINUTES OR UNTIL BEANS ARE
JUST TENDER BUT STILL HOLD THEIR SHAPE. DRAIN,
RESERVING 2 CUPS (500 ML) COOKING LIQUID. PLACE
BEANS IN A 12-CUP (3 L) CASSEROLE DISH OR BEAN POT.

PREHEAT OVEN TO 300°F (150°C). IN A SAUCEPAN, COOK BACON OVER MEDIUM HEAT, STIRRING OFTEN, FOR 5 MINUTES OR UNTIL CRISP. DRAIN ALL BUT 2 TBSP (30 ML) FAT FROM PAN. ADD ONION AND GARLIC; COOK, STIRRING, FOR 3 MINUTES OR UNTIL SOFTENED. ADD 2 CUPS (500 ML) RESERVED BEAN-COOKING LIQUID, TOMATO SAUCE, MOLASSES, BROWN SUGAR, BALSAMIC VINEGAR, MUSTARD, SALT AND PEPPER. STIR INTO BEANS. COVER AND BAKE FOR 2½ TO 3 HOURS OR UNTIL MOST OF LIQUID HAS BEEN ABSORBED. SERVES 8.

VARIATION: FOR A VEGETARIAN VERSION, OMIT BACON AND COOK ONIONS AND GARLIC IN 2 TBSP (30 ML) VEGETABLE OIL.

A WOMAN ENJOYS A MAN OF STRONG WILL — AS LONG AS IT'S MADE OUT TO HER.

SPINACH RISOTTO

ALTHOUGH IT NEEDS TO BAKE FOR 30 MINUTES, THIS METHOD FOR COOKING RISOTTO ELIMINATES THE TEDIOUS TASK OF STIRRING THE LIQUID UNTIL IT IS ABSORBED. ADD CRUSTY ROLLS AND A CRISP GREEN SALAD FOR A TASTY MEAL.

2 TBSP	BUTTER	30 ML
I CUP	FINELY CHOPPED ONION	250 ML
I CUP	ARBORIO RICE	250 ML
I TBSP	MINCED GARLIC	15 ML
I	PACKAGE (IO OZ/300 G) FROZEN SPINACH, PARTIALLY THAWED (SEE TIP, OPPOSITE)	I
3 CUPS	READY-TO-USE VEGETABLE BROTH	750 ML
3 TBSP	PREPARED SUN-DRIED TOMATO PESTO	45 ML
	FRESHLY GRATED PARMESAN CHEESE	

PREHEAT OVEN TO 400°F (200°C). IN A SAUCEPAN WITH AN OVENPROOF HANDLE (SEE TIP, OPPOSITE), MELT BUTTER OVER MEDIUM HEAT. ADD ONION AND COOK UNTIL SOFTENED, ABOUT 3 MINUTES. ADD RICE AND GARLIC; COOK, STIRRING, UNTIL THE GRAINS OF RICE ARE COATED WITH BUTTER, ABOUT I MINUTE. ADD SPINACH AND COOK, BREAKING UP WITH A SPOON, UNTIL THOROUGHLY INTEGRATED INTO THE RICE, ABOUT 2 MINUTES. STIR IN BROTH AND PESTO. BRING TO A BOIL. TRANSFER SAUCEPAN TO OVEN AND BAKE, STIRRING PARTWAY THROUGH, UNTIL RICE HAS ABSORBED THE LIQUID, ABOUT 30 MINUTES. REMOVE FROM OVEN AND SPRINKLE PARMESAN OVER TOP. SERVE IMMEDIATELY. SERVES 4.

TIP: TO PARTIALLY THAW THE SPINACH FOR THIS RECIPE, PLACE THE PACKAGE IN A MICROWAVE AND HEAT ON HIGH FOR 3 MINUTES. IT CAN EASILY BE SEPARATED USING A FORK BUT WILL STILL HAVE SOME ICE CRYSTALS. DO NOT DRAIN BEFORE ADDING TO RICE.

TIP: IF YOU DON'T HAVE A SAUCEPAN WITH AN OVENPROOF HANDLE, TRANSFER THE MIXTURE TO A DEEP 6-CUP (1.5 L) BAKING DISH AFTER ADDING THE BROTH AND PESTO AND BRINGING THE MIXTURE TO A BOIL.

VARIATION: SPRINKLE 2 TBSP (30 ML) TOASTED PINE NUTS OVER THE RISOTTO JUST BEFORE SERVING. TO TOAST PINE NUTS, COOK, STIRRING, IN A DRY SKILLET OVER MEDIUM HEAT. BROWN FOR 3 TO 5 MINUTES. REMOVE FROM HEAT AND TRANSFER TO A COOL BOWL.

NOTICE IN CHURCH BULLETIN: FOR THOSE OF YOU
WHO HAVE CHILDREN AND DON'T KNOW IT,
WE HAVE A NURSERY DOWNSTAIRS.

SAUSAGE AND RED PEPPER RISOTTO

ALTHOUGH THIS RECIPE HAS A FAIRLY LONG COOKING TIME, IT IS ACTUALLY CONVENIENT AS IT ELIMINATES THE CONSTANT STIRRING USUALLY ASSOCIATED WITH COOKING RISOTTO. ADD SALAD AND CRUSTY ROLLS FOR A SATISFYING FAMILY MEAL.

1 TBSP	VEGETABLE OIL	15 ML
1 LB	MILD OR HOT ITALIAN SAUSAGE (BULK OR CASINGS REMOVED)	500 G
1 CUP	FINELY CHOPPED ONION	250 ML
1 TBSP	MINCED GARLIC	15 ML
1/2 TSP	SALT	2 ML
	FRESHLY GROUND BLACK PEPPER	
1 1/2 CUPS	ARBORIO RICE (SEE TIP, OPPOSITE)	375 ML
3 CUPS	CHICKEN STOCK (PAGE 42) OR READY-TO-USE CHICKEN BROTH	750 ML
1/2 CUP	WHITE WINE OR WATER	125 ML
2	ROASTED RED BELL PEPPERS (SEE TIPS, OPPOSITE), CHOPPED	2
	FRESHLY GRATED PARMESAN CHEESE (OPTIONAL)	

PREHEAT OVEN TO 350°F (180°C). IN A SAUCEPAN WITH AN OVENPROOF HANDLE (SEE TIP, PAGE 147), HEAT OIL OVER MEDIUM HEAT. ADD SAUSAGE AND COOK, BREAKING UP WITH A WOODEN SPOON, UNTIL LIGHTLY BROWNED AND NO LONGER PINK INSIDE, ABOUT 5 MINUTES. USING A SLOTTED SPOON, TRANSFER TO A BOWL AND KEEP WARM. DRAIN OFF ALL BUT 1 TBSP (15 ML) FAT. ADD ONION TO PAN AND COOK, STIRRING, UNTIL SOFTENED, ABOUT 3 MINUTES. ADD GARLIC, SALT, AND BLACK PEPPER TO

TASTE. COOK, STIRRING, FOR 1 MINUTE. ADD RICE AND COOK, STIRRING, UNTIL ALL THE GRAINS ARE COATED WITH OIL. ADD STOCK AND WINE. BRING TO A BOIL. STIR IN ROASTED PEPPERS AND RESERVED SAUSAGE MEAT. TRANSFER SAUCEPAN TO OVEN AND BAKE, STIRRING PARTWAY THROUGH COOKING, UNTIL RICE HAS ABSORBED LIQUID, ABOUT 30 MINUTES. TOP EACH SERVING WITH PARMESAN, IF DESIRED. SERVES 4 TO 6.

TIP: BE SURE TO USE SHORT-GRAIN ARBORIO RICE WHEN MAKING RISOTTO, AS ITS HIGH-STARCH CONTENT IS ESSENTIAL TO PRODUCE THE NECESSARY CREAMINESS.

TIP: FOR BEST RESULTS, STIR THE RISOTTO PARTWAY THROUGH COOKING. THIS PREVENTS THE GRAINS ON TOP FROM DRYING OUT.

TIP: TO ROAST PEPPERS: PREHEAT OVEN TO 400°F (200°C). PLACE PEPPERS ON A BAKING SHEET AND ROAST, TURNING TWO TO THREE TIMES, UNTIL THE SKIN ON ALL SIDES IS BLACKENED, ABOUT 25 MINUTES. TRANSFER PEPPERS TO A HEATPROOF BOWL. COVER WITH A PLATE AND LET STAND UNTIL COOL. USING A SHARP KNIFE, LIFT OFF SKINS. DISCARD SKINS AND CHOP OR SLICE PEPPERS.

TIP: IF YOU DON'T HAVE TIME TO ROAST YOUR OWN PEPPERS, USE BOTTLED ROASTED RED PEPPERS.

SPANISH VEGETABLE PAELLA

TRADITIONAL PAELLA IS MADE IN A WIDE SHALLOW PAN, BUT TODAY'S NONSTICK SKILLET MAKES A VERY GOOD SUBSTITUTE AND REDUCES THE AMOUNT OF OIL NEEDED FOR THIS DISH.

4 CUPS	ASSORTED PREPARED VEGETABLES (SEE TIP, OPPOSITE)	1 L
3½ CUPS	CHICKEN STOCK (PAGE 42) OR READY-TO-USE CHICKEN OR VEGETABLE BROTH	875 ML
¼ TSP	SAFFRON THREADS, CRUSHED	1 ML
PINCH	HOT PEPPER FLAKES	PINCH
	SALT	
2 TBSP	OLIVE OIL	30 ML
4	GREEN ONIONS, CHOPPED	4
3	LARGE CLOVES GARLIC, FINELY CHOPPED	3
1½ CUPS	SHORT-GRAIN WHITE RICE, SUCH AS ARBORIO	375 ML

PREHEAT OVEN TO 375°F (190°C). COOK VEGETABLES (EXCEPT PEPPERS AND ZUCCHINI) IN A SAUCEPAN OF BOILING, LIGHTLY SALTED WATER FOR 1 MINUTE. RINSE UNDER COLD WATER TO CHILL; DRAIN WELL. IN THE SAME SAUCEPAN, BRING STOCK TO A BOIL. ADD SAFFRON AND HOT PEPPER FLAKES; SEASON TO TASTE WITH SALT. KEEP WARM. IN A LARGE NONSTICK SKILLET, HEAT OIL OVER MEDIUM-HIGH HEAT. ADD GREEN ONIONS AND GARLIC; COOK, STIRRING, FOR 1 MINUTE. ADD VEGETABLES TO SKILLET; COOK, STIRRING OFTEN, FOR 4 MINUTES OR UNTIL LIGHTLY BROWNED. STIR IN RICE AND HOT STOCK MIXTURE. REDUCE HEAT SO RICE COOKS AT A GENTLE BOIL:

COOK, UNCOVERED, WITHOUT STIRRING, FOR 10 MINUTES OR UNTIL MOST OF THE LIQUID IS ABSORBED. COVER SKILLET WITH LID OR FOIL. (IF SKILLET HANDLE IS NOT OVENPROOF, WRAP IN DOUBLE LAYER OF FOIL.) BAKE FOR 15 MINUTES OR UNTIL ALL LIQUID IS ABSORBED AND RICE IS TENDER. REMOVE; LET STAND, COVERED, FOR 5 MINUTES BEFORE SERVING. SERVES 4.

TIP: TRY A VARIETY OF DIFFERENT VEGETABLES, INCLUDING BITE-SIZE PIECES OF BROCCOLI, CAULIFLOWER, ASPARAGUS, GREEN BEANS, BELL PEPPERS AND ZUCCHINI.

"VIRUS" IS A LATIN WORD USED BY DOCTORS.
IT MEANS: "YOUR GUESS IS AS GOOD AS MINE."

SKILLET SHRIMP AND RICE CREOLE

THIS CLASSIC SOUTHERN SPECIALTY TAKES ONLY 30 MINUTES TO COOK.

1 TBSP	VEGETABLE OIL	15 ML
1	LARGE ONION, CHOPPED	1
2	CLOVES GARLIC, FINELY CHOPPED	2
2	STALKS CELERY, CHOPPED	2
1/2 TSP	DRIED THYME LEAVES	2 ML
1	BAY LEAF	1
1 CUP	LONG-GRAIN WHITE RICE	250 ML
1	RED BELL PEPPER, DICED	1
1	CAN (14 OZ/398 ML) TOMATOES, WITH JUICE, CHOPPED	1
1 CUP	FISH STOCK OR READY-TO-USE CHICKEN BROTH	250 ML
1/2 TSP	SALT	2 ML
PINCH	CAYENNE PEPPER	PINCH
2	SMALL ZUCCHINI, HALVED LENGTHWISE AND THINLY SLICED	2
1 LB	LARGE RAW SHRIMP, PEELED AND DEVEINED, WITH TAILS LEFT ON	500 G

IN A LARGE NONSTICK SKILLET, HEAT OIL OVER MEDIUM HEAT. COOK ONION, GARLIC, CELERY, THYME AND BAY LEAF, STIRRING, FOR 5 MINUTES OR UNTIL SOFTENED. STIR IN RICE AND RED PEPPER; COOK FOR 2 MINUTES. ADD TOMATOES, STOCK, SALT AND A GENEROUS PINCH CAYENNE PEPPER. BRING TO A BOIL; REDUCE HEAT, COVER AND SIMMER FOR 15 MINUTES. STIR IN ZUCCHINI; BURY SHRIMP IN RICE. COVER AND COOK FOR 8 MINUTES OR UNTIL ZUCCHINI ARE TENDER AND SHRIMP ARE PINK AND FIRM. SERVES 4.

ONE-POT PASTA

FAST-AND-EASY RECIPE

EVERYTHING — INCLUDING THE PASTA — IS COOKED IN ONE POT! SUBSTITUTE SHREDDED LEFTOVER CHICKEN AND A MINCED GARLIC CLOVE FOR THE HAM IF YOU WISH, OR USE WHATEVER YOU HAVE ON HAND!

I LB	ROTINI OR FUSILLI PASTA	500 G
I LB	SLICED MUSHROOMS	500 G
4 OZ	DICED HAM	125 G
I CUP	FROZEN PEAS	250 ML
1/2 TSP	DRIED THYME	2 ML
	SALT AND FRESHLY GROUND BLACK PEPPER	
3 CUPS	WATER	750 ML
1/4 CUP	GRATED PARMESAN CHEESE	60 ML
1/2 CUP	HEAVY OR WHIPPING (35%) CREAM, OR HALF-AND-HALF (10%) CREAM	125 ML

PLACE THE PASTA IN A LARGE SAUCEPAN OR DUTCH OVEN. ADD MUSHROOMS, HAM, PEAS, THYME, SALT AND PEPPER. POUR IN WATER AND BRING TO A BOIL OVER HIGH HEAT. REDUCE HEAT TO MEDIUM-LOW, COVER, LEAVING LID AJAR, AND SIMMER, STIRRING ONCE OR TWICE, FOR 8 TO 10 MINUTES OR UNTIL PASTA IS AL DENTE AND THE LIQUID IS REDUCED TO A FEW TABLESPOONS (45 TO 60 ML). STIR IN CHEESE AND CREAM. SERVES 4 TO 6.

SAUSAGE PIE WITH POLENTA CRUST

SLOW COOKER RECIPE

THIS DELICIOUS ONE-DISH DINNER COULDN'T BE EASIER. SERVE WITH A CRISP GREEN SALAD FOR A COMPLETE AND NUTRITIOUS MEAL. AND, IF YOU'RE FEELING FESTIVE, OPEN A BOTTLE OF CHIANTI.

2 LBS	HOT OR MILD ITALIAN SAUSAGE (BULK OR CASINGS REMOVED)	I KG
4	STALKS CELERY, THINLY SLICED	4
I TSP	DRIED OREGANO	5 ML
I	CAN (28 OZ/796 ML) TOMATOES, WITH JUICE, COARSELY CHOPPED	I

POLENTA CRUST

3 CUPS	CHICKEN STOCK (PAGE 42), READY-TO-USE CHICKEN BROTH OR WATER	750 ML
I TBSP	BUTTER	15 ML
I TSP	SALT	5 ML
1/2 TSP	CRACKED BLACK PEPPERCORNS	2 ML
I CUP	CORNMEAL	250 ML
1/2 CUP	FRESHLY GRATED PARMESAN CHEESE	125 ML
1/4 CUP	FINELY CHOPPED FLAT-LEAF (ITALIAN) PARSLEY LEAVES	60 ML

IN A SKILLET OVER MEDIUM-HIGH HEAT, COOK SAUSAGES, BREAKING UP WITH A SPOON, UNTIL MEAT IS NO LONGER PINK. USING A SLOTTED SPOON, TRANSFER TO A MEDIUM (ABOUT 4-QUART) SLOW COOKER. DRAIN OFF LIQUID. REDUCE HEAT UNDER SKILLET TO MEDIUM. ADD CELERY AND COOK, STIRRING, UNTIL SOFT, ABOUT 4 MINUTES. ADD OREGANO

AND COOK, STIRRING, FOR 1 MINUTE. ADD TOMATOES AND BRING TO A BOIL. TRANSFER MIXTURE TO SLOW COOKER. (COOLED COOKED SAUSAGE AND TOMATO MIXTURES CAN BE REFRIGERATED SEPARATELY OVERNIGHT AT THIS POINT.)

POLENTA CRUST: IN A LARGE HEAVY-BOTTOMED SAUCEPAN, BRING STOCK TO A BOIL. STIR IN BUTTER, SALT AND PEPPERCORNS. REDUCE HEAT TO LOW. GRADUALLY ADD CORNMEAL IN A THIN STREAM, STIRRING CONSTANTLY, UNTIL ALL CORNMEAL IS ABSORBED. COOK FOR 2 OR 3 MINUTES, STIRRING EVERY MINUTE OR SO, UNTIL MIXTURE BUBBLES ACTIVELY. STIR IN PARMESAN AND PARSLEY AND REMOVE FROM HEAT. SPOON POLENTA OVER SAUSAGE MIXTURE AND, USING A SPATULA, SMOOTH IT OUT TO MAKE AN EVEN CRUST. COVER AND COOK ON LOW FOR 6 HOURS OR ON HIGH FOR 3 HOURS, UNTIL HOT AND BUBBLY. SERVES 6 TO 8.

SYNONYM: A WORD YOU USE WHEN YOU CAN'T SPELL THE OTHER ONE.

SHEPHERD'S PIE

MUSHROOMS ADD DEPTH OF FLAVOR TO THIS
DISH AND HELP CUT DOWN ON THE AMOUNT OF
MEAT USED. IF YOUR CHILDREN DON'T LIKE THE SIGHT
OF MUSHROOMS IN THEIR FAVORITE SUPPER DISH,
FINELY CHOP THEM IN A FOOD PROCESSOR — THEY'LL
NEVER KNOW THE DIFFERENCE.

MASHED POTATO TOPPING

6	POTATOES, PEELED AND CUBED (ABOUT 2 LBS/1 KG)	6
3/4 CUP	MILK OR BUTTERMILK	175 ML
	SALT AND FRESHLY GROUND BLACK PEPPER	

MEAT LAYER

1 LB	LEAN GROUND BEEF OR VEAL	500 G
8 OZ	MUSHROOMS, SLICED OR CHOPPED	250 G
1	ONION, FINELY CHOPPED	1
2	CLOVES GARLIC, FINELY CHOPPED	2
1/2 TSP	DRIED THYME	2 ML
1/2 TSP	DRIED MARJORAM	2 ML
3 TBSP	ALL-PURPOSE FLOUR	45 ML
1 1/2 CUPS	HEARTY BEEF STOCK (PAGE 43) OR READY-TO-USE BEEF BROTH	375 ML
2 TBSP	TOMATO PASTE	30 ML
2 TSP	WORCESTERSHIRE SAUCE	10 ML
	SALT AND FRESHLY GROUND BLACK PEPPER	
1	CAN (12 OZ/341 ML) CORN KERNELS, DRAINED	1

BREAD CRUMB TOPPING

2 TBSP	FINE DRY BREAD CRUMBS	30 ML
2 TBSP	FRESHLY GRATED PARMESAN CHEESE	30 ML
1/4 TSP	PAPRIKA	1 ML

MASHED POTATO TOPPING: IN A LARGE SAUCEPAN OF BOILING SALTED WATER, COOK POTATOES UNTIL TENDER. DRAIN AND MASH USING A POTATO MASHER OR HAND-HELD ELECTRIC MIXER; BEAT IN MILK UNTIL SMOOTH. SEASON TO TASTE WITH SALT AND PEPPER.

MEAT LAYER: IN A LARGE NONSTICK SKILLET, COOK BEEF OVER MEDIUM-HIGH HEAT, BREAKING UP WITH A WOODEN SPOON, FOR 5 MINUTES OR UNTIL NO LONGER PINK. REDUCE HEAT TO MEDIUM. ADD MUSHROOMS, ONION, GARLIC, THYME AND MARJORAM; COOK, STIRRING OFTEN, FOR 5 MINUTES OR UNTIL SOFTENED. SPRINKLE WITH FLOUR; STIR IN STOCK, TOMATO PASTE AND WORCESTERSHIRE SAUCE. BRING TO A BOIL; REDUCE HEAT AND SIMMER, COVERED, FOR 8 MINUTES. SEASON WITH SALT, IF NEEDED, AND PEPPER TO TASTE. SPREAD MEAT MIXTURE IN A 10-CUP (2.5 L) SHALLOW BAKING DISH; LAYER WITH CORN. PLACE SMALL SPOONFULS OF MASHED POTATOES OVER CORN AND SPREAD EVENLY. (THE RECIPE CAN BE PREPARED UP TO THIS POINT EARLIER IN THE DAY OR THE DAY BEFORE, THEN COVERED AND REFRIGERATED.)

BREAD CRUMB TOPPING: PREHEAT OVEN TO 375°F (190°C). IN A SMALL BOWL, COMBINE BREAD CRUMBS, PARMESAN AND PAPRIKA; SPRINKLE OVER TOP OF SHEPHERD'S PIE. BAKE IN PREHEATED OVEN FOR 25 TO 30 MINUTES (40 MINUTES, IF REFRIGERATED) OR UNTIL FILLING IS BUBBLY. SERVES 6.

LENTIL SHEPHERD'S PIE

HERE'S A FLAVORFUL RENDITION OF AN OLD FAVORITE, IN WHICH LENTILS ARE SUBSTITUTED FOR THE TRADITIONAL MEAT. SERVE WITH A TOSSED SALAD FOR A NUTRITIOUS AND SATISFYING MEAL.

TOPPING

2 CUPS	CUBED COOKED POTATOES	500 ML
1/2 CUP	MILK	125 ML
1 CUP	SHREDDED ITALIAN FOUR-CHEESE MIX	250 ML
1/2 CUP	DRY BREAD CRUMBS	125 ML
4	GREEN ONIONS (WHITE PART ONLY), COARSELY CHOPPED	4
1 TBSP	BUTTER, SOFTENED	15 ML
1/2 TSP	SALT	2 ML
	FRESHLY GROUND BLACK PEPPER	

FILLING

1 TBSP	VEGETABLE OIL	15 ML
2 CUPS	DICED ONION	500 ML
1 CUP	DICED CELERY	250 ML
1	CAN (28 OZ/796 ML) TOMATOES, DRAINED AND COARSELY CHOPPED	1
1	CAN (19 OZ/540 ML) LENTILS, DRAINED AND RINSED	1
2 TBSP	BASIL PESTO	30 ML
2 TBSP	SHREDDED ITALIAN FOUR-CHEESE MIX	30 ML

PREHEAT OVEN TO 350°F (180°C). LIGHTLY GREASE AN 8-CUP (2 L) BAKING DISH.

TOPPING: IN A FOOD PROCESSOR, COMBINE POTATOES AND MILK. PULSE SEVERAL TIMES TO COMBINE. ADD

CHEESE, BREAD CRUMBS, ONIONS, BUTTER, SALT, AND
BLACK PEPPER TO TASTE. PROCESS UNTIL BLENDED
BUT POTATOES ARE STILL A BIT LUMPY (SEE TIP, BELOW).
SET ASIDE.

FILLING: IN A SKILLET, HEAT OIL OVER MEDIUM HEAT. ADD
ONION AND CELERY AND COOK, STIRRING, UNTIL CELERY
IS SOFTENED, ABOUT 8 MINUTES. ADD TOMATOES AND
LENTILS. BRING TO A BOIL. STIR IN PESTO AND POUR
INTO PREPARED BAKING DISH. SPREAD RESERVED POTATO
MIXTURE EVENLY OVER LENTIL MIXTURE. SPRINKLE WITH
SHREDDED CHEESE. BAKE IN PREHEATED OVEN UNTIL
TOP IS BROWNED AND MIXTURE IS BUBBLING, ABOUT
25 MINUTES. SERVES 4.

TIP: USE SHREDDED CHEDDAR CHEESE INSTEAD OF THE
ITALIAN FOUR-CHEESE MIXTURE, IF YOU PREFER.

TIP: SUBSTITUTE $\frac{1}{2}$ CUP (125 ML) LOOSELY PACKED
PARSLEY LEAVES FOR THE GREEN ONIONS, IF YOU PREFER.

TIP: BE CAREFUL NOT TO OVERPROCESS THE POTATO
MIXTURE OR THE TOPPING WILL BE MUSHY. SMALL LUMPS
OF POTATO SHOULD REMAIN.

BROCCOLI- AND CHEESE-STUFFED POTATOES

*THESE DELICIOUS BAKED POTATOES ARE GREAT
TO PACK ALONG TO WORK IF YOU HAVE THE USE
OF A MICROWAVE FOR REHEATING.*

4	LARGE BAKING POTATOES (EACH 10 OZ/300 G)	4
3 CUPS	SMALL BROCCOLI FLORETS AND CHOPPED PEELED STEMS	750 ML
1/2 CUP	SOUR CREAM, PLAIN YOGURT OR BUTTERMILK (APPROX.)	125 ML
2	GREEN ONIONS, SLICED	2
1 1/3 CUPS	SHREDDED CHEDDAR OR GRUYÈRE CHEESE, DIVIDED	325 ML
	SALT AND CAYENNE PEPPER	

PREHEAT OVEN TO 400°F (200°C). SCRUB POTATOES
WELL AND PIERCE SKINS WITH A FORK IN SEVERAL
PLACES TO ALLOW STEAM TO ESCAPE. BAKE FOR 1 HOUR
OR UNTIL POTATOES GIVE SLIGHTLY WHEN SQUEEZED.
(ALTERNATIVELY, ARRANGE POTATOES IN THE MICROWAVE
IN A CIRCLE 1 INCH (2.5 CM) APART ON A PAPER TOWEL.
MICROWAVE ON HIGH FOR 10 TO 12 MINUTES, TURNING
HALFWAY THROUGH, UNTIL POTATOES ARE JUST TENDER
WHEN PIERCED.)

IN A SAUCEPAN, COOK OR STEAM BROCCOLI UNTIL
JUST TENDER-CRISP. (ALTERNATIVELY, PLACE IN COVERED
CASSEROLE WITH 2 TBSP (30 ML) WATER AND MICROWAVE
ON HIGH FOR 2 TO 2 1/2 MINUTES.) DRAIN WELL.

CUT A THIN SLICE FROM TOPS OF WARM POTATOES.
SCOOP OUT POTATO, LEAVING A 1/4-INCH (0.5 CM) SHELL,

BEING CAREFUL NOT TO TEAR THE SKINS. IN A BOWL, MASH POTATO WITH POTATO MASHER OR FORK; BEAT IN ENOUGH SOUR CREAM UNTIL SMOOTH. ADD BROCCOLI, GREEN ONIONS AND 1 CUP (250 ML) CHEESE. SEASON TO TASTE WITH SALT AND CAYENNE. SPOON FILLING INTO POTATO SHELLS, MOUNDING THE TOPS. ARRANGE IN A 13- BY 9-INCH (33 BY 23 CM) BAKING DISH; SPRINKLE WITH THE REMAINING CHEESE. BAKE FOR 15 MINUTES OR UNTIL CHEESE MELTS. (ALTERNATIVELY, PLACE ON A LARGE SERVING PLATE AND MICROWAVE ON MEDIUM-HIGH (70%) FOR 4 TO 6 MINUTES OR UNTIL HEATED THROUGH AND CHEESE MELTS.) SERVES 4.

TIP: CHEDDAR AND BROCCOLI ARE A CLASSIC COMBO, BUT GET ADVENTUROUS WITH WHATEVER CHEESE AND VEGETABLES ARE IN THE FRIDGE. ANOTHER FAVORITE IS MOZZARELLA CHEESE, LIGHTLY SAUTÉED MUSHROOMS AND FINELY CHOPPED RED PEPPERS SEASONED WITH BASIL.

CATS AND TEENAGERS DO NOT IMPROVE ANYONE'S FURNITURE.

BEEF-STUFFED SPUDS

MAKE THESE AHEAD FOR THOSE NIGHTS
WHEN EVERYONE IS ON A DIFFERENT SCHEDULE.
THE POTATOES NEED ONLY A QUICK REHEAT IN THE
MICROWAVE AS EACH PERSON WALKS THROUGH
THE DOOR, FOR AN INSTANT SUPPER.

4	LARGE BAKING POTATOES (EACH 10 OZ/300 G)	4
8 OZ	LEAN GROUND BEEF OR VEAL	250 G
1/3 CUP	FINELY CHOPPED ONIONS	75 ML
1	CLOVE GARLIC, FINELY CHOPPED	1
1 TSP	WORCESTERSHIRE SAUCE	5 ML
	SALT AND FRESHLY GROUND BLACK PEPPER	
1/2 CUP	SOUR CREAM, PLAIN YOGURT OR BUTTERMILK (APPROX.)	125 ML
1 CUP	SHREDDED CHEDDAR CHEESE, DIVIDED	250 ML
2 TBSP	CHOPPED FRESH PARSLEY	30 ML

PREHEAT OVEN TO 400°F (200°C). SCRUB POTATOES
WELL AND PIERCE SKINS WITH A FORK IN SEVERAL
PLACES TO ALLOW STEAM TO ESCAPE. BAKE FOR 1 HOUR
OR UNTIL POTATOES GIVE SLIGHTLY WHEN SQUEEZED.
(ALTERNATIVELY, ARRANGE POTATOES IN THE MICROWAVE
IN A CIRCLE 1 INCH (2.5 CM) APART ON A PAPER TOWEL.
MICROWAVE ON HIGH FOR 10 TO 12 MINUTES, TURNING
HALFWAY THROUGH, UNTIL POTATOES ARE JUST TENDER
WHEN PIERCED.)

CONTINUED ON PAGE 163...

Spanish Vegetable Paella (page 150)

Shepherd's Pie (page 156)

Beans, Beef and Biscuits (page 174)

Creamy Tuna Pasta Bake (page 188)

IN A LARGE NONSTICK SKILLET OVER MEDIUM-HIGH HEAT, COOK BEEF, BREAKING UP WITH A WOODEN SPOON, FOR 4 MINUTES OR UNTIL NO LONGER PINK. DRAIN OFF ANY FAT. REDUCE HEAT TO MEDIUM. ADD ONIONS, GARLIC AND WORCESTERSHIRE SAUCE; SEASON WITH SALT AND PEPPER. COOK, STIRRING OFTEN, FOR 4 MINUTES OR UNTIL ONIONS ARE SOFTENED.

CUT WARM POTATOES IN HALF LENGTHWISE. CAREFULLY SCOOP OUT EACH POTATO, LEAVING A $\frac{1}{4}$-INCH (0.5 CM) SHELL; SET SHELLS ASIDE. IN A BOWL, MASH POTATOES WITH POTATO MASHER OR FORK; BEAT IN ENOUGH SOUR CREAM UNTIL SMOOTH. STIR IN BEEF MIXTURE, HALF THE CHEESE AND ALL THE PARSLEY; SEASON TO TASTE WITH SALT AND PEPPER. SPOON INTO POTATO SHELLS; TOP WITH THE REMAINING CHEESE. ARRANGE IN A 13- BY 9-INCH (33 BY 23 CM) SHALLOW DISH. BAKE FOR 15 MINUTES OR UNTIL CHEESE IS MELTED. (ALTERNATIVELY, PLACE ON A LARGE SERVING PLATE; MICROWAVE ON MEDIUM-HIGH (70%) FOR 4 TO 6 MINUTES OR UNTIL HEATED THROUGH AND CHEESE MELTS.) SERVES 4.

MUSSELS MARINARA

HERE'S THE PERFECT SIMPLE MEAL: A BOWLFUL OF THESE PLUMP MUSSELS SERVED WITH CRUSTY BREAD TO DIP INTO THE GARLICKY TOMATO BROTH.

2 LBS	MUSSELS	1 KG
1 TBSP	OLIVE OIL	15 ML
1	SMALL ONION, CHOPPED	1
3	CLOVES GARLIC, MINCED	3
1/2 TSP	SALT	2 ML
PINCH	HOT PEPPER FLAKES	PINCH
4	RIPE TOMATOES, SEEDED AND CHOPPED	4
1/2 CUP	DRY WHITE WINE	125 ML
2 TBSP	CHOPPED FRESH PARSLEY	30 ML

SCRUB MUSSELS UNDER COLD WATER; REMOVE ANY BEARDS. DISCARD ANY MUSSELS THAT DO NOT CLOSE WHEN TAPPED. IN A LARGE SAUCEPAN, HEAT OIL OVER MEDIUM HEAT; COOK ONION, GARLIC, SALT AND HOT PEPPER FLAKES, STIRRING, FOR 2 MINUTES OR UNTIL SOFTENED. ADD TOMATOES AND WINE; COVER AND COOK FOR 10 MINUTES OR UNTIL SAUCE-LIKE. ADD MUSSELS; INCREASE HEAT TO MEDIUM-HIGH. COVER AND STEAM FOR 4 TO 5 MINUTES OR UNTIL SHELLS OPEN. DISCARD ANY MUSSELS THAT DO NOT OPEN. TO SERVE, SPOON MUSSELS IN THEIR SHELLS ALONG WITH SAUCE INTO SERVING BOWLS. SPRINKLE WITH PARSLEY. SERVES 2.

TIP: TO REMOVE THE MUSSEL'S BEARD (A CLUMP OF STRING-LIKE MATERIAL THAT CLINGS TO THE SHELL), TUG IT OFF WITH YOUR FINGERS.

CREAMY CORN AND SHRIMP

QUICK, EASY AND DELICIOUS, THIS VERSATILE CASSEROLE IS GREAT FOR DINNER OR AS PART OF A BUFFET. SERVE WITH FLUFFY WHITE RICE OR PASTA, ACCOMPANIED BY A SIMPLE GREEN SALAD TOSSED IN A VINAIGRETTE DRESSING.

I LB	COOKED PEELED SHRIMP, THAWED IF FROZEN, TAILS REMOVED	500 G
2 TBSP	FRESHLY SQUEEZED LEMON JUICE	30 ML
I TSP	PAPRIKA	5 ML
1/4 TSP	FRESHLY GROUND BLACK PEPPER	I ML
I	CAN (19 OZ/540 ML) CORN KERNELS, DRAINED (OR 2 CUPS/500 ML COOKED CORN KERNELS)	I
I CUP	ALFREDO SAUCE	250 ML
I	ROASTED RED BELL PEPPER (SEE TIPS, PAGE 149), CHOPPED	I
1/2 CUP	FINELY CHOPPED RED OR GREEN ONION	125 ML

PREHEAT OVEN TO 400°F (200°C). GREASE A 6-CUP (1.5 L) BAKING DISH. IN A BOWL, COMBINE SHRIMP, LEMON JUICE, PAPRIKA AND BLACK PEPPER. SET ASIDE. IN PREPARED BAKING DISH, COMBINE CORN, ALFREDO SAUCE, ROASTED PEPPER AND ONION. ADD SHRIMP AND TOSS TO COMBINE. BAKE IN PREHEATED OVEN UNTIL HOT AND BUBBLING, ABOUT 15 MINUTES. SERVES 4.

CHICKEN ENCHILADA CASSEROLE

	NONSTICK COOKING SPRAY	
8	SMALL CORN TORTILLAS (OR 4 LARGE FLOUR TORTILLAS), CUT INTO STRIPS	8
3 CUPS	CHOPPED OR SHREDDED COOKED CHICKEN	750 ML
1½ CUPS	SHREDDED CHEDDAR CHEESE	375 ML
1½ CUPS	SHREDDED MOZZARELLA CHEESE	375 ML
½ CUP	SOUR CREAM	125 ML
1	CAN (4½ OZ/127 ML) CHOPPED GREEN CHILES	1
1 TBSP	CHILI POWDER	15 ML
1½ CUPS	MEDIUM SALSA	375 ML
1 CUP	FRESH, FROZEN OR DRAINED CANNED CORN KERNELS	250 ML
1	CAN (14 OZ/398 ML) BLACK BEANS, DRAINED AND RINSED	1
1	AVOCADO, DICED	1
1	TOMATO, DICED	1

PREHEAT OVEN TO 350°F (180°C). SPRAY A 13- BY 9-INCH (33 BY 23 CM) BAKING DISH WITH NONSTICK COOKING SPRAY AND LINE THE BOTTOM WITH HALF OF THE TORTILLA STRIPS. IN A LARGE BOWL, COMBINE CHICKEN, HALF THE CHEDDAR, HALF THE MOZZARELLA, SOUR CREAM AND CHILES. STIR THE CHILI POWDER INTO THE SALSA AND SPREAD HALF OVER THE TORTILLAS, FOLLOWED BY HALF THE CORN, HALF THE BEANS AND HALF THE CHICKEN MIXTURE. REPEAT LAYERS. TOP WITH REMAINING CHEESE. BAKE FOR 45 TO 50 MINUTES OR UNTIL CHEESE IS MELTED AND GOLDEN. LET STAND FOR 10 MINUTES, THEN TOP WITH AVOCADO AND TOMATO. SERVES 6.

TRAY-BAKED CHICKEN DINNER

A WHOLE MEAL — CHICKEN, POTATO AND VEGGIES — WITH ONLY ONE TRAY TO WASH.

2	CLOVES GARLIC, MINCED	2
1 TSP	DRIED THYME	5 ML
	SALT AND FRESHLY GROUND BLACK PEPPER	
1/4 CUP	OLIVE OIL	60 ML
	JUICE OF 1 LEMON	
1 LB	NEW POTATOES, HALVED	500 G
1	RED ONION, CUT INTO WEDGES	1
2	RED BELL PEPPERS, COARSELY CHOPPED	2
8	BONELESS SKINLESS CHICKEN THIGHS	8
2 CUPS	GRAPE OR CHERRY TOMATOES	500 ML

PREHEAT OVEN TO 400°F (200°C). IN A SMALL BOWL, COMBINE GARLIC, THYME, SALT AND PEPPER TO TASTE, OIL AND LEMON JUICE. TOSS CHICKEN IN HALF THE OIL MIXTURE AND SET ASIDE. SPREAD POTATOES, ONION AND PEPPERS IN A SINGLE LAYER ON A RIMMED BAKING SHEET OR A LARGE ROASTING PAN AND DRIZZLE WITH THE REMAINING OIL MIXTURE, TOSSING WITH YOUR HANDS TO COAT. ARRANGE CHICKEN ON TOP. BAKE FOR 20 MINUTES. SPRINKLE TOMATOES OVER TOP. BAKE FOR 30 MINUTES OR UNTIL POTATOES ARE TENDER AND JUICES RUN CLEAR WHEN CHICKEN IS PIERCED. SERVES 4 TO 6.

ITALIAN SAUSAGES BRAISED WITH POTATOES

THIS RUSTIC DISH IS PERFECT WITH A GLASS OF RED WINE ON A WIND-DOWN FRIDAY NIGHT. DO GIVE THE FENNEL A TRY; WHEN RAW, THIS VEGETABLE HAS AN ASSERTIVE ANISE TASTE. HOWEVER, WHEN COOKED, IT'S MUCH MORE MELLOW AND INVITING.

I LB	MILD OR HOT ITALIAN SAUSAGES	500 G
2 TBSP	WATER (APPROX.)	30 ML
I TBSP	OLIVE OIL	15 ML
I	LARGE ONION, HALVED LENGTHWISE, SLICED	I
I	FENNEL BULB, TRIMMED, CORED AND CUT INTO STRIPS	I
2	CLOVES GARLIC, FINELY CHOPPED	2
I TSP	DRIED OREGANO	5 ML
4	POTATOES, PEELED AND CUBED (ABOUT I½ LBS/750 G)	4
I	CAN (14 OZ/398 ML) TOMATOES, WITH JUICE, CHOPPED	I
½ CUP	HEARTY BEEF STOCK (PAGE 43) OR READY-TO-USE BEEF BROTH	125 ML
½ TSP	SALT	2 ML
¼ TSP	FRESHLY GROUND BLACK PEPPER	I ML
2 TBSP	CHOPPED FRESH PARSLEY	30 ML

WITH A FORK, PRICK SAUSAGES ALL OVER. PLACE IN A LARGE NONSTICK SKILLET OVER MEDIUM-HIGH HEAT. ADD WATER AND COOK, TURNING OFTEN AND ADDING MORE WATER AS NEEDED (TO PREVENT SAUSAGES FROM STICKING), FOR 10 TO 12 MINUTES OR UNTIL BROWNED AND NO LONGER PINK IN CENTER. TRANSFER TO A CUTTING

BOARD. LET COOL SLIGHTLY; CUT INTO SLICES. DRAIN FAT FROM SKILLET; ADD OIL, ONION, FENNEL, GARLIC AND OREGANO. COOK, STIRRING, FOR 3 MINUTES OR UNTIL SOFTENED. ADD POTATOES, TOMATOES, STOCK, SALT AND PEPPER; BRING TO A BOIL. REDUCE HEAT, COVER AND COOK FOR 15 MINUTES OR UNTIL POTATOES ARE ALMOST TENDER. RETURN SAUSAGE TO PAN; COVER AND COOK FOR 8 MINUTES OR UNTIL POTATOES ARE TENDER. SPRINKLE WITH PARSLEY. SERVES 4.

VARIATION: INSTEAD OF FENNEL, USE ABOUT 3 CUPS (750 ML) SHREDDED CABBAGE.

I EARN A SEVEN-FIGURE SALARY. UNFORTUNATELY, THERE'S A DECIMAL POINT INVOLVED.

BISTRO LENTILS WITH SMOKED SAUSAGE

IT'S FRIDAY NIGHT. YOU'VE WORKED HARD ALL WEEK. DON'T EVEN BOTHER SETTING THE TABLE. HERE'S A SUPPER DISH THAT'S EASY TO BALANCE ON YOUR LAP WHILE YOU RELAX IN FRONT OF THE TV. AS A BONUS, THIS DISH GOES GREAT WITH A COLD BEER.

3½ CUPS	CHICKEN STOCK (PAGE 42) OR READY-TO-USE CHICKEN OR VEGETABLE BROTH (APPROX.)	875 ML
1½ CUPS	DRIED LENTILS, RINSED (SEE TIP, OPPOSITE)	375 ML
½ TSP	DRIED THYME	2 ML
2 TBSP	OLIVE OIL	30 ML
1 CUP	FINELY CHOPPED RED ONIONS	250 ML
3	CLOVES GARLIC, FINELY CHOPPED	3
2	CARROTS, DICED	2
1 CUP	DICED FENNEL OR CELERY	250 ML
1	RED BELL PEPPER, FINELY CHOPPED	1
2 TBSP	BALSAMIC VINEGAR	30 ML
8 OZ	SMOKED SAUSAGE, SUCH AS KIELBASA, CUT INTO ½-INCH (1 CM) CHUNKS	250 G
	FRESHLY GROUND BLACK PEPPER	
¼ CUP	CHOPPED FRESH PARSLEY	60 ML

IN A LARGE SAUCEPAN, BRING STOCK TO A BOIL OVER HIGH HEAT. ADD LENTILS AND THYME; REDUCE HEAT TO MEDIUM-LOW, COVER AND SIMMER FOR 25 TO 30 MINUTES OR UNTIL LENTILS ARE JUST TENDER BUT STILL HOLD THEIR SHAPE.

MEANWHILE, HEAT OIL IN A LARGE NONSTICK SKILLET OVER MEDIUM HEAT. ADD ONIONS, GARLIC, CARROTS AND FENNEL; COOK, STIRRING OFTEN, FOR 8 MINUTES. ADD RED PEPPER; COOK, STIRRING, FOR 2 MINUTES OR UNTIL VEGETABLES ARE JUST TENDER. STIR IN VINEGAR; REMOVE FROM HEAT. ADD VEGETABLES AND SMOKED SAUSAGE TO LENTILS IN SAUCEPAN; SEASON TO TASTE WITH PEPPER. COVER AND COOK FOR 5 TO 8 MINUTES OR UNTIL SAUSAGE IS HEATED THROUGH. (ADD MORE STOCK OR WATER, IF NECESSARY, TO PREVENT LENTILS FROM STICKING.) STIR IN PARSLEY. SERVE WARM OR AT ROOM TEMPERATURE. SERVES 6.

TIP: SMALL GREEN LAIRD LENTILS HOLD THEIR SHAPE IN COOKING AND ARE THE PREFERRED CHOICE FOR THIS RECIPE.

TIP: ANY KIND OF SMOKED SAUSAGE OR HAM WORKS WELL IN THIS RECIPE.

BEEF AND BROCCOLI WITH RICE STICK NOODLES

HERE'S A TASTY STIR-FRY THAT USES DRIED
RICE NOODLES, WHICH DON'T NEED TO BE COOKED.
JUST COVER WITH BOILING WATER UNTIL THEY
SOFTEN TO THE DESIRED CONSISTENCY.

8 OZ	THICK RICE NOODLES	250 G
2 TBSP	VEGETABLE OIL, DIVIDED	30 ML
3 CUPS	BROCCOLI FLORETS	750 ML
6 TBSP	SOY SAUCE	90 ML
2 TBSP	VODKA, READY-TO-USE BEEF BROTH OR WATER	30 ML
I TBSP	MINCED GARLIC	15 ML
I TBSP	MINCED GINGERROOT	15 ML
I TBSP	CORNSTARCH, DISSOLVED IN 2 TBSP (30 ML) WATER	15 ML
I TSP	GRANULATED SUGAR	5 ML
	FRESHLY GROUND BLACK PEPPER	
12 OZ	THINLY SLICED SIRLOIN STEAK OR STIR-FRY STRIPS (SEE TIP, OPPOSITE)	375 G
I TSP	SESAME OIL	5 ML

SOAK RICE NOODLES IN A BOWL OF BOILING WATER FOR
10 MINUTES. DRAIN AND TOSS WITH I TBSP (15 ML) OF THE
VEGETABLE OIL. SET ASIDE. IN A POT OF BOILING SALTED
WATER, COOK BROCCOLI FLORETS FOR 3 MINUTES. DRAIN
AND SET ASIDE.

MEANWHILE, IN A BOWL, COMBINE SOY SAUCE, VODKA,
GARLIC, GINGER, CORNSTARCH MIXTURE, SUGAR, AND BLACK
PEPPER TO TASTE. SET ASIDE. IN A WOK OR NONSTICK
SKILLET, HEAT THE REMAINING OIL OVER MEDIUM HEAT.

ADD BEEF AND COOK, STIRRING, UNTIL COOKED THROUGH, ABOUT 4 MINUTES. ADD RESERVED SOY SAUCE MIXTURE AND COOK, STIRRING, UNTIL BEEF IS WELL COATED AND MIXTURE THICKENS, ABOUT 2 MINUTES. ADD BROCCOLI AND COOK, STIRRING, FOR I MINUTE. STIR IN RESERVED NOODLES AND COOK UNTIL HEATED THROUGH AND WELL COATED WITH SAUCE, ABOUT 2 MINUTES. SPRINKLE WITH SESAME OIL AND SERVE IMMEDIATELY. SERVES 4.

TIP: SLICED BEEF FOR STIR-FRIES IS WIDELY AVAILABLE IN SUPERMARKETS. IT CAN BE PURCHASED FRESH OR FROZEN. IF FROZEN, THAW BEFORE USING IN THIS RECIPE.

VARIATION: ADD 2 TBSP (30 ML) CHOPPED, DRAINED WATER CHESTNUTS ALONG WITH THE BROCCOLI.

VARIATION: GARNISH WITH I TBSP (15 ML) TOASTED SESAME SEEDS OR I FRESH RED CHILE PEPPER, THINLY SLICED.

VARIATION: ADD A GARNISH OF FINELY CHOPPED GREEN ONION.

NOTICE IN CHURCH BULLETIN: THE PASTOR WOULD APPRECIATE IT IF THE LADIES OF THE CONGREGATION WOULD LEND HIM THEIR ELECTRIC GIRDLES FOR THE PANCAKE BREAKFAST.

BEANS, BEEF AND BISCUITS

TOPPED WITH HOT BISCUITS, THIS HEARTY DISH LOOKS AS GOOD AS IT TASTES.

1 TBSP	VEGETABLE OIL	15 ML
1 LB	LEAN GROUND BEEF	500 G
1 CUP	FINELY CHOPPED ONION	250 ML
1/2 CUP	FINELY CHOPPED CELERY	125 ML
2 CUPS	SPICY TOMATO SAUCE (SUCH AS ARRABBIATA)	500 ML
2	CANS (EACH 14 OZ/398 ML) BAKED BEANS IN TOMATO SAUCE	2
1 TBSP	WORCESTERSHIRE SAUCE	15 ML
1	CAN (8 OZ/250 G) COUNTRY-STYLE BISCUIT DOUGH	1

PREHEAT OVEN TO 375°F (190°C). LIGHTLY GREASE AN 8-CUP (2 L) BAKING DISH. IN A SKILLET, HEAT OIL OVER MEDIUM HEAT. ADD BEEF, ONION AND CELERY AND COOK, BREAKING UP MEAT WITH A SPOON, UNTIL BEEF IS NO LONGER PINK AND VEGETABLES ARE SOFTENED, ABOUT 7 MINUTES. ADD TOMATO SAUCE, BAKED BEANS AND WORCESTERSHIRE SAUCE AND BRING TO A BOIL. REDUCE HEAT TO LOW AND SIMMER FOR 2 MINUTES. POUR INTO PREPARED DISH. SEPARATE DOUGH INTO INDIVIDUAL BISCUITS. ARRANGE EVENLY OVER TOP OF BEAN MIXTURE (THERE WILL BE SPACES IN BETWEEN). BAKE IN PREHEATED OVEN UNTIL BISCUITS ARE PUFFED AND BROWN, 10 TO 12 MINUTES. SERVE IMMEDIATELY. SERVES 6.

TIP: PLACING THE BISCUITS ON A HOT FILLING PREVENTS THEM FROM BECOMING MUSHY ON THE BOTTOM DURING BAKING.

PIZZA, PASTA & NOODLES

BIG-BATCH TOMATO SAUCE

KEEP THIS INDISPENSABLE SAUCE HANDY IN THE FREEZER TO USE AS A BASE FOR YOUR FAMILY'S FAVORITE PASTA DISHES.

2 TBSP	OLIVE OIL	30 ML
1	ONION, FINELY CHOPPED	1
2	CARROTS, FINELY CHOPPED	2
1	STALK CELERY, INCLUDING LEAVES, FINELY CHOPPED	1
4	CLOVES GARLIC, FINELY CHOPPED	4
1 TBSP	DRIED BASIL	15 ML
1 1/2 TSP	DRIED OREGANO	7 ML
1 TSP	SALT	5 ML
1 TSP	GRANULATED SUGAR	5 ML
1/2 TSP	FRESHLY GROUND BLACK PEPPER	2 ML
1	BAY LEAF	1
2	CANS (EACH 28 OZ/796 ML) TOMATOES, WITH JUICE, CHOPPED	2
1	CAN (5 1/2 OZ/156 ML) TOMATO PASTE	1
1/4 CUP	FINELY CHOPPED FRESH PARSLEY	60 ML

IN A DUTCH OVEN OR LARGE SAUCEPAN, HEAT OIL OVER MEDIUM-HIGH HEAT. ADD ONION, CARROTS, CELERY, GARLIC, BASIL, OREGANO, SALT, SUGAR, PEPPER AND BAY LEAF; COOK, STIRRING OFTEN, FOR 5 MINUTES OR UNTIL VEGETABLES ARE SOFTENED. STIR IN TOMATOES, TOMATO PASTE AND 1 TOMATO-PASTE CAN OF WATER. BRING TO A BOIL; REDUCE HEAT AND SIMMER, PARTIALLY COVERED, FOR 35 TO 40 MINUTES, STIRRING OCCASIONALLY, UNTIL SLIGHTLY THICKENED. REMOVE BAY LEAF; STIR IN PARSLEY.

LET COOL; PACK INTO CONTAINERS AND REFRIGERATE OR FREEZE. MAKES ABOUT 7 CUPS (1.75 L).

TIP: IN SUMMER, INSTEAD OF CANNED TOMATOES, MAKE THIS SAUCE WITH 5 LBS (2.5 KG) OF FRESH RIPE TOMATOES, PREFERABLY PLUM (ROMA). TO PREPARE, REMOVE TOMATO CORES; CUT AN X IN THE BOTTOM OF EACH TOMATO. PLUNGE IN BOILING WATER FOR 30 SECONDS TO LOOSEN SKINS. CHILL IN COLD WATER; DRAIN. SLIP OFF SKINS; CUT TOMATOES IN HALF CROSSWISE AND SQUEEZE OUT SEEDS. CHOP FINELY.

TIP: INSTEAD OF DRIED BASIL AND OREGANO, REPLACE DRIED HERBS WITH $1/3$ CUP (75 ML) CHOPPED FRESH BASIL; ADD TOWARD END OF COOKING.

TIP: TO SAVE TIME, CHOP VEGETABLES IN THE FOOD PROCESSOR.

MEN PREFER YOUNGER WOMEN
BECAUSE THEY TELL SHORTER STORIES.

177

EASY BOLOGNESE SAUCE

GONE ARE THE DAYS WHEN MAKING BOLOGNESE SAUCE WAS A TIME-CONSUMING AFFAIR. THIS DELICIOUS SAUCE, WHICH DEPENDS UPON GOOD PREPARED TOMATO SAUCE TO JUMP-START THE COOKING PROCESS, IS READY AS SOON AS THE PASTA IS COOKED. SERVE WITH SALAD FOR A GREAT WEEKNIGHT MEAL.

1 TBSP	VEGETABLE OIL	15 ML
1 LB	LEAN GROUND BEEF	500 G
1 CUP	FINELY CHOPPED ONION	250 ML
1 TBSP	MINCED GARLIC	15 ML
	FRESHLY GROUND BLACK PEPPER	
2 CUPS	TOMATO SAUCE	500 ML

IN A SKILLET, HEAT OIL OVER MEDIUM-HIGH HEAT. ADD BEEF AND ONION. BROWN, BREAKING UP MEAT, UNTIL BEEF IS NO LONGER PINK INSIDE, ABOUT 5 MINUTES. DRAIN OFF ALL BUT 1 TBSP (15 ML) FAT. REDUCE HEAT TO MEDIUM. ADD GARLIC, AND BLACK PEPPER TO TASTE. COOK, STIRRING, FOR 1 MINUTE. STIR IN TOMATO SAUCE. REDUCE HEAT TO LOW AND SIMMER FOR 10 MINUTES. MAKES ABOUT 4 CUPS (1 L).

VARIATION: FOR A RICHER RESULT, ADD 1 CUP (250 ML) DRY RED WINE AFTER THE GARLIC AND BLACK PEPPER HAVE COOKED FOR A MINUTE. BRING TO A BOIL AND COOK UNTIL SLIGHTLY REDUCED, 3 TO 4 MINUTES, THEN CONTINUE WITH THE RECIPE.

VARIATION: ADD $\frac{1}{4}$ CUP (60 ML) HEAVY OR WHIPPING (35%) CREAM AFTER SIMMERING TOMATO SAUCE. COOK UNTIL HEATED THROUGH.

PIZZA WITH RED PEPPERS AND GOAT CHEESE

HERE'S A DELICIOUS PIZZA WITH SOPHISTICATED INGREDIENTS THAT COULDN'T BE EASIER.

1	10-INCH (25 CM) PIZZA CRUST OR PREPARED PIZZA DOUGH (SEE TIP, BELOW)	1
1 TBSP	OLIVE OIL	15 ML
1/4 CUP	PREPARED SUN-DRIED TOMATO PESTO	60 ML
1 1/2 CUPS	FINELY SHREDDED MOZZARELLA CHEESE	375 ML
4 OZ	PROSCIUTTO OR THINLY SLICED SMOKED HAM	125 G
2	ROASTED RED BELL PEPPERS (SEE TIPS, PAGE 149), CHOPPED	2
4 OZ	SOFT GOAT CHEESE, CRUMBLED	125 G

PREHEAT OVEN TO 400°F (200°C). PLACE CRUST ON A LIGHTLY GREASED BAKING SHEET. BRUSH WITH OIL AND PESTO. SPRINKLE MOZZARELLA EVENLY OVER TOP. TEAR PROSCIUTTO INTO THIN STRIPS AND ARRANGE EVENLY OVER CHEESE. SPRINKLE RED PEPPER THEN GOAT CHEESE EVENLY OVER PROSCIUTTO. BAKE UNTIL CRUST IS GOLDEN AND CHEESE IS MELTED, 10 TO 15 MINUTES. SERVES 4 TO 6.

TIP: WHEN USING PREPARED PIZZA DOUGH, READ THE PACKAGE INSTRUCTIONS AND ADJUST THIS METHOD ACCORDINGLY.

TIP: WATCH CAREFULLY TO ENSURE THE EDGES OF THE CRUST DON'T BURN.

VARIATION: SPRINKLE WITH SLICED BLACK OLIVES AND/OR SLICED RED ONION BEFORE BAKING.

ALL-DRESSED PIZZA

"LET'S ORDER PIZZA!" THE NEXT TIME YOU HEAR THIS REQUEST FROM YOUR KIDS, ASSEMBLE THE INGREDIENTS HERE AND GET THEM COOKING. WHY ORDER OUT WHEN MAKING PIZZA AT HOME USING STORE-BOUGHT BREAD BASES AND SAUCES IS SUCH A BREEZE? IT'S MORE ECONOMICAL, TOO.

1 TBSP	VEGETABLE OR OLIVE OIL	15 ML
1	SMALL ONION, THINLY SLICED	1
1	CLOVE GARLIC, FINELY CHOPPED	1
1 CUP	SLICED MUSHROOMS	250 ML
1	SMALL GREEN OR RED BELL PEPPER, CUT INTO THIN STRIPS	1
1/2 TSP	DRIED BASIL	2 ML
1/2 TSP	DRIED OREGANO	2 ML
1	12-INCH (30 CM) PREBAKED PIZZA BASE OR 9- BY 12-INCH (23 BY 30 CM) FOCACCIA	1
1/2 CUP	PIZZA SAUCE (APPROX.)	125 ML
2 CUPS	SHREDDED CHEESE, SUCH AS MOZZARELLA, FONTINA OR PROVOLONE	500 ML

PREHEAT OVEN TO 400°F (200°C). IN A LARGE NONSTICK SKILLET, HEAT OIL OVER MEDIUM-HIGH HEAT. ADD ONION, GARLIC, MUSHROOMS, PEPPER, BASIL AND OREGANO; COOK, STIRRING, FOR 4 MINUTES OR UNTIL SOFTENED. ARRANGE PIZZA BASE ON A BAKING SHEET; SPREAD WITH PIZZA SAUCE. TOP WITH VEGETABLES AND SHREDDED CHEESE. BAKE FOR 20 TO 25 MINUTES OR UNTIL CHEESE IS MELTED AND CRUST IS GOLDEN. SERVES 4.

MAC AND CHEESE
WITH TOMATOES

WARM, CREAMY AND DELICIOUS, MACARONI AND CHEESE
IS A FAVORITE COMFORT FOOD. THIS EASY VERSION USES
CHEDDAR CHEESE SOUP TO ACHIEVE ITS FLAVORFUL
CREAMINESS AND CANNED TOMATOES FOR
A SLIGHTLY PIQUANT TOUCH.

12 OZ	ELBOW MACARONI	375 G
1/2 CUP	DRY BREAD CRUMBS	125 ML
2 TBSP	MELTED BUTTER	30 ML
1	CAN (28 OZ/796 ML) TOMATOES, COARSELY CHOPPED, WITH JUICE	1
1	CAN (10 OZ/284 ML) CONDENSED CHEDDAR CHEESE SOUP	1
2 CUPS	SHREDDED CHEDDAR CHEESE	500 ML
1 TSP	SALT	5 ML
	FRESHLY GROUND BLACK PEPPER	

PREHEAT OVEN TO 350°F (180°C). LIGHTLY GREASE AN
8-CUP (2 L) BAKING DISH. COOK MACARONI IN A POT
OF BOILING SALTED WATER UNTIL AL DENTE, ABOUT
8 MINUTES. DRAIN. IN A BOWL, COMBINE BREAD CRUMBS
AND MELTED BUTTER. SET ASIDE. IN A LARGE BOWL,
COMBINE TOMATOES, CHEDDAR CHEESE SOUP, CHEDDAR
CHEESE, SALT, AND BLACK PEPPER TO TASTE. ADD HOT
MACARONI AND STIR WELL. TRANSFER MIXTURE TO
PREPARED BAKING DISH. SPREAD BREAD CRUMB MIXTURE
EVENLY OVER TOP. BAKE UNTIL CRUMBS ARE GOLDEN AND
MIXTURE IS BUBBLING, ABOUT 25 MINUTES. SERVES 6.

BEST-EVER MACARONI AND CHEESE

AS POPULAR TODAY AS IN THE 1950S, CLASSIC MACARONI AND CHEESE HAS A LOT GOING FOR IT. IT'S NOT HARD TO MAKE, SO WHY OPEN UP A BOX OF THE PREPACKAGED STUFF WHEN YOU CAN CREATE THE REAL THING?

3 TBSP	BUTTER	45 ML
1/4 CUP	ALL-PURPOSE FLOUR	60 ML
1	BAY LEAF	1
3 CUPS	MILK	750 ML
1 TBSP	DIJON MUSTARD	15 ML
2 CUPS	SHREDDED CHEDDAR CHEESE, PREFERABLY AGED (ABOUT 8 OZ/250 G)	500 ML
	SALT AND CAYENNE PEPPER	
2 CUPS	ELBOW MACARONI	500 ML
1 TBSP	BUTTER, MELTED	15 ML
1 CUP	SOFT FRESH BREAD CRUMBS	250 ML

PREHEAT OVEN TO 375°F (190°C). GREASE AN 8-CUP (2 L) DEEP CASSEROLE DISH. IN A LARGE SAUCEPAN, MELT BUTTER OVER MEDIUM HEAT. BLEND IN FLOUR AND ADD BAY LEAF; COOK, STIRRING, FOR 30 SECONDS. POUR IN 1 CUP (250 ML) MILK, WHISKING CONSTANTLY, UNTIL MIXTURE COMES TO A BOIL AND IS VERY THICK. POUR IN THE REMAINING MILK IN A SLOW STREAM, WHISKING CONSTANTLY, UNTIL SAUCE COMES TO A FULL BOIL AND IS SMOOTH. WHISK IN MUSTARD. REDUCE HEAT TO LOW; STIR IN CHEESE UNTIL MELTED. REMOVE BAY LEAF; SEASON TO TASTE WITH SALT AND CAYENNE. REMOVE FROM HEAT.

MEANWHILE, IN A LARGE POT OF BOILING SALTED WATER, COOK MACARONI FOR 8 MINUTES OR UNTIL JUST TENDER. (DO NOT OVERCOOK; PASTA CONTINUES TO COOK IN SAUCE.) DRAIN WELL. STIR INTO CHEESE SAUCE UNTIL WELL COATED. SPOON INTO PREPARED CASSEROLE DISH. IN A BOWL, TOSS 1 TBSP (15 ML) MELTED BUTTER WITH BREAD CRUMBS; SPRINKLE OVER TOP. BAKE FOR 25 MINUTES OR UNTIL BUBBLY AND TOP IS LIGHTLY BROWNED. SERVES 4 TO 6.

TIP: CAN'T FIGURE OUT THE VOLUME OF A CASSEROLE DISH? LOOK FOR THE MEASUREMENTS ON THE BOTTOM OF DISH OR MEASURE BY POURING IN ENOUGH WATER TO FILL COMPLETELY.

I'VE BEEN HIDING FROM EXERCISE.
I'M IN THE FITNESS PROTECTION PROGRAM.

CANNELLONI WITH TOMATO EGGPLANT SAUCE

SLOW COOKER RECIPE

HERE'S A GREAT RECIPE FOR CANNELLONI THAT IS REMARKABLY EASY TO MAKE. OVEN-READY PASTA IS FILLED WITH RICOTTA AND BABY SPINACH AND BATHED IN A TOMATO EGGPLANT SAUCE. ADD SOME CRUSTY BREAD AND A SALAD OF ROASTED PEPPERS OR CRISP GREENS FOR A TERRIFIC MEAL.

SAUCE

1	EGGPLANT, PEELED, CUT INTO 2-INCH (5 CM) CUBES, AND DRAINED OF EXCESS MOISTURE (SEE TIP, OPPOSITE)	1
2 TBSP	OLIVE OIL	30 ML
2	CLOVES GARLIC, MINCED	2
1/2 TSP	CRACKED BLACK PEPPERCORNS	2 ML
3 CUPS	TOMATO SAUCE	750 ML

FILLING

2 CUPS	RICOTTA CHEESE	500 ML
1/2 CUP	FRESHLY GRATED PARMESAN CHEESE	125 ML
1 1/2 CUPS	CHOPPED BABY SPINACH	375 ML
1 TSP	FRESHLY GRATED NUTMEG	5 ML
1	LARGE EGG, BEATEN	1
1/4 TSP	SALT	1 ML
1/4 TSP	FRESHLY GROUND BLACK PEPPER	1 ML
24	OVEN-READY CANNELLONI SHELLS	24

SAUCE: IN A SKILLET, HEAT OIL OVER MEDIUM HEAT. ADD EGGPLANT, IN BATCHES, AND COOK, STIRRING, UNTIL IT BEGINS TO BROWN, ADDING MORE OIL IF NECESSARY. RETURN ALL EGGPLANT TO PAN. ADD GARLIC AND

PEPPERCORNS AND COOK, STIRRING, FOR 1 MINUTE. ADD
TOMATO SAUCE, STIR WELL AND BRING TO A BOIL. REMOVE
FROM HEAT AND SET ASIDE.

FILLING: IN A BOWL, COMBINE RICOTTA, PARMESAN,
SPINACH, NUTMEG, EGG, SALT AND PEPPER. USING YOUR
FINGERS, FILL PASTA SHELLS WITH MIXTURE AND PLACE
FILLED SHELLS SIDE BY SIDE IN A MEDIUM TO LARGE
(4- TO 5-QUART) SLOW COOKER, THEN ON TOP OF EACH
OTHER WHEN BOTTOM LAYER IS COMPLETE. POUR SAUCE
OVER SHELLS. (CANNELLONI CAN BE COOLED, COVERED
AND REFRIGERATED FOR UP TO 2 DAYS AT THIS POINT.)
COVER AND COOK ON LOW FOR 6 HOURS OR ON HIGH FOR
3 HOURS, UNTIL HOT AND BUBBLY. SERVES 8.

TIP: ALTHOUGH EGGPLANT IS DELICIOUS WHEN PROPERLY
COOKED, SOME VARIETIES TEND TO BE BITTER. SINCE
THE BITTERNESS IS CONCENTRATED UNDER THE SKIN,
PEEL EGGPLANT BEFORE USE. SPRINKLING THE PIECES
WITH SALT AND LEAVING THEM TO "SWEAT" FOR AN HOUR
OR TWO ALSO DRAWS OUT THE BITTER JUICE. IF TIME
IS SHORT, BLANCH THE PIECES FOR A MINUTE OR TWO
IN HEAVILY SALTED WATER. IN EITHER CASE, RINSE
THOROUGHLY IN FRESH COLD WATER AND, USING YOUR
HANDS, SQUEEZE OUT THE EXCESS MOISTURE. PAT DRY
WITH PAPER TOWELS AND IT'S READY FOR COOKING.

TIP: OVEN-READY CANNELLONI IS A GREAT TIME SAVER AND
COOKS TO PERFECTION IN THE SLOW COOKER.

TIP: IF YOU CHOOSE TO HALVE THIS RECIPE, USE A SMALL
(2- TO 3-QUART) SLOW COOKER.

BEEFY MACARONI

NO NEED TO BUY PRICEY PACKAGED DINNER MIXES WHEN IT'S EASY TO CREATE YOUR OWN.

I LB	LEAN GROUND BEEF, CHICKEN OR TURKEY	500 G
I	SMALL ONION, CHOPPED	I
2	CLOVES GARLIC, FINELY CHOPPED	2
I TSP	DRIED BASIL OR OREGANO	5 ML
I 1/2 CUPS	TOMATO PASTA SAUCE (SEE TIP, BELOW)	375 ML
I 1/2 CUPS	HEARTY BEEF STOCK (PAGE 43), CHICKEN STOCK (PAGE 42) OR READY-TO-USE BEEF OR CHICKEN BROTH (APPROX.)	375 ML
I CUP	ELBOW MACARONI	250 ML
2	ZUCCHINI, CUT INTO 1/2-INCH (I CM) CUBES	2

IN A LARGE NONSTICK SKILLET OVER MEDIUM-HIGH HEAT, COOK BEEF, BREAKING UP WITH A WOODEN SPOON, FOR 5 MINUTES OR UNTIL NO LONGER PINK. ADD ONION, GARLIC AND BASIL; COOK, STIRRING, FOR 2 MINUTES. ADD TOMATO PASTA SAUCE AND STOCK; BRING TO A BOIL. STIR IN PASTA; REDUCE HEAT, COVER AND COOK FOR 2 MINUTES. STIR IN ZUCCHINI; COOK, COVERED, STIRRING OCCASIONALLY, ADDING MORE STOCK IF NEEDED, FOR 5 TO 7 MINUTES OR UNTIL PASTA AND ZUCCHINI ARE TENDER. SERVES 4.

TIP: USE YOUR OWN HOMEMADE TOMATO SAUCE (TRY BIG-BATCH TOMATO SAUCE, PAGE 176) OR RELY ON ONE OF THE MANY PASTA SAUCES AVAILABLE IN SUPERMARKETS TO CUT DOWN ON PREPARATION TIME.

SPINACH TORTELLINI BAKE

ALTHOUGH MOST PASTA IS TRADITIONALLY
SERVED AS A FIRST COURSE IN ITALY, BAKED PASTA
HAS ALWAYS BEEN A MAIN COURSE.

1	PACKAGE (16 OZ/500 G) CHEESE-FILLED TORTELLINI	1
2½ CUPS	TOMATO SAUCE (APPROX.)	625 ML
2 CUPS	BABY SPINACH	500 ML
2 CUPS	SHREDDED MOZZARELLA CHEESE	500 ML
2 TBSP	FRESHLY GRATED PARMESAN CHEESE	30 ML

PREHEAT OVEN TO 400°F (200°C). GREASE A BAKING DISH.
COOK TORTELLINI ACCORDING TO PACKAGE DIRECTIONS.
DRAIN. SPREAD ABOUT ½ CUP (125 ML) TOMATO SAUCE
OVER BOTTOM OF PREPARED BAKING DISH. TOP WITH HALF
EACH OF THE HOT TORTELLINI AND SPINACH. SPRINKLE
WITH HALF THE MOZZARELLA AND HALF OF THE REMAINING
SAUCE. REPEAT LAYERS. SPRINKLE WITH PARMESAN. BAKE
UNTIL CHEESE IS MELTED AND MIXTURE IS HOT AND
BUBBLING, ABOUT 20 MINUTES. SERVES 4.

VARIATION: SPRINKLE WITH 2 TBSP (30 ML) TOASTED PINE
NUTS BEFORE SERVING.

CREAMY TUNA PASTA BAKE

THIS MODERN RENDITION OF A TUNA CASSEROLE
INCLUDES A NUTRITIONAL BOOST OF BROCCOLI
IN A CREAMY BASIL SAUCE.

2 TBSP	BUTTER	30 ML
6	GREEN ONIONS, CHOPPED	6
3	CLOVES GARLIC, FINELY CHOPPED	3
4 CUPS	SLICED MUSHROOMS	1 L
$1/2$ TSP	SALT	2 ML
$1/2$ TSP	FRESHLY GROUND BLACK PEPPER	2 ML
$1/3$ CUP	ALL-PURPOSE FLOUR	75 ML
2 CUPS	LIGHT (5%) CREAM OR MILK	500 ML
$1 1/2$ CUPS	CHICKEN STOCK (PAGE 42) OR READY-TO-USE CHICKEN BROTH	375 ML
3	TOMATOES, SEEDED AND DICED	3
$2/3$ CUP	FRESHLY GRATED PARMESAN CHEESE	150 ML
$1/2$ CUP	CHOPPED FRESH BASIL	125 ML
12 OZ	PENNE	375 G
4 CUPS	BROCCOLI FLORETS AND CHOPPED PEELED STEMS	1 L
2	CANS (EACH 6 OZ/170 G) SOLID WHITE TUNA, DRAINED AND FLAKED	2
$1 1/2$ CUPS	SOFT FRESH BREAD CRUMBS	375 ML
1 CUP	SHREDDED ASIAGO OR MOZZARELLA CHEESE	250 ML

PREHEAT OVEN TO 350°F (180°C). GREASE A 13- BY 9-INCH
(33 BY 23 CM) BAKING DISH. IN A DUTCH OVEN OR LARGE
SAUCEPAN, MELT BUTTER OVER MEDIUM-HIGH HEAT.
COOK GREEN ONIONS, GARLIC, MUSHROOMS, SALT AND
PEPPER, STIRRING OCCASIONALLY, FOR 5 MINUTES OR

UNTIL SOFTENED. IN A BOWL, WHISK FLOUR WITH $\frac{1}{2}$ CUP (125 ML) CREAM UNTIL SMOOTH; ADD THE REMAINING CREAM. ADD TO PAN ALONG WITH STOCK. BRING TO A BOIL, STIRRING, FOR 3 MINUTES OR UNTIL SAUCE THICKENS. REMOVE FROM HEAT. STIR IN TOMATOES, PARMESAN AND BASIL. (CAN BE PREPARED TO THIS POINT, COVERED AND REFRIGERATED FOR UP TO 1 DAY.)

IN A LARGE POT OF BOILING SALTED WATER, COOK PASTA FOR 7 MINUTES OR UNTIL ALMOST TENDER. ADD BROCCOLI; COOK FOR 2 MINUTES OR UNTIL BROCCOLI IS BRIGHT GREEN AND CRISP, AND PASTA IS JUST TENDER. DRAIN; CHILL UNDER COLD WATER. DRAIN WELL AND RETURN TO POT. STIR IN TUNA AND SAUCE. SPREAD IN BAKING DISH. (CASSEROLE CAN BE PREPARED TO THIS POINT; COVER AND REFRIGERATE FOR UP TO 4 HOURS BEFORE SERVING. INCREASE BAKING TIME BY 15 MINUTES.)

IN A BOWL, COMBINE BREAD CRUMBS AND ASIAGO CHEESE; SPRINKLE OVER TOP. BAKE FOR 40 TO 45 MINUTES OR UNTIL GOLDEN AND CENTER IS PIPING HOT. SERVES 8.

TIP: IF FRESH BASIL IS UNAVAILABLE, SUBSTITUTE 2 TSP (10 ML) DRIED BASIL AND COOK WITH ONIONS.

TIP: ASSEMBLE THE DISH NO MORE THAN 4 HOURS AHEAD TO PREVENT PASTA FROM SOAKING UP THE SAUCE.

VARIATION: FOR A VEGETARIAN VERSION, OMIT TUNA AND SUBSTITUTE 1 CAN (19 OZ/540 ML) KIDNEY BEANS, DRAINED AND RINSED.

PENNE WITH TUNA AND PEPPERS

FAST-AND-EASY RECIPE

HERE'S A SPEEDIER VERSION OF A MARCELLA HAZAN RECIPE.

12 OZ	PENNE	375 G
4 TBSP	OLIVE OIL (PREFERABLY EXTRA VIRGIN), DIVIDED	60 ML
1 TBSP	MINCED GARLIC	15 ML
2	DRAINED BOTTLED ROASTED RED BELL PEPPERS, CUT INTO STRIPS	2
2 TBSP	FINELY CHOPPED FRESH PARSLEY	30 ML
2 TBSP	DRAINED CAPERS	30 ML
1	CAN (6 OZ/170 G) OLIVE OIL-PACKED TUNA (PREFERABLY ITALIAN), DRAINED	1
	FRESHLY GROUND BLACK PEPPER	
1/4 CUP	TOASTED CROUTONS OR 2 TBSP (30 ML) COARSE DRY BREAD CRUMBS	60 ML
	ADDITIONAL OLIVE OIL	

COOK PENNE IN A POT OF BOILING SALTED WATER UNTIL AL DENTE, ABOUT 8 MINUTES. DRAIN. IN A WARM SERVING BOWL, COMBINE HOT PENNE WITH 2 TBSP (30 ML) OLIVE OIL. KEEP WARM. MEANWHILE, IN A SMALL SAUCEPAN OVER LOW HEAT, HEAT THE REMAINING OLIVE OIL. ADD GARLIC AND COOK, STIRRING OCCASIONALLY, UNTIL LIGHT GOLDEN, ABOUT 3 MINUTES. ADD RED PEPPER STRIPS AND STIR UNTIL WELL COATED WITH OIL. ADD PARSLEY AND CAPERS. STIR WELL AND REMOVE FROM HEAT. STIR IN TUNA AND BLACK PEPPER TO TASTE. SPREAD SAUCE ATTRACTIVELY OVER TOP OF WARM PENNE. SPRINKLE WITH CROUTONS. DRIZZLE WITH OLIVE OIL AND SERVE. SERVES 4.

LINGUINE WITH CLAM SAUCE

2 TBSP	OLIVE OIL	30 ML
1	ONION, CHOPPED	1
3	LARGE CLOVES GARLIC, FINELY CHOPPED	3
1/4 TSP	HOT PEPPER FLAKES (OR TO TASTE)	1 ML
2	CANS (EACH 5 OZ/142 G) BABY CLAMS, DRAINED, JUICE RESERVED	2
1/2 CUP	DRY WHITE WINE	125 ML
2 CUPS	CHOPPED SEEDED FRESH PLUM (ROMA) TOMATOES	500 ML
1/2 CUP	HEAVY OR WHIPPING (35%) CREAM	125 ML
1/4 CUP	CHOPPED FRESH PARSLEY	60 ML
	SALT AND FRESHLY GROUND BLACK PEPPER	
12 OZ	LINGUINE, SPAGHETTI OR FETTUCCINE	375 G

IN A LARGE SKILLET, HEAT OIL OVER MEDIUM-HIGH HEAT. COOK ONION, GARLIC AND HOT PEPPER FLAKES, STIRRING, FOR 2 MINUTES. ADD CLAMS AND COOK, STIRRING, FOR 2 MINUTES. ADD WINE; COOK FOR 1 MINUTE OR UNTIL SLIGHTLY REDUCED. STIR IN TOMATOES AND 1/2 CUP (125 ML) OF THE RESERVED CLAM JUICE. REDUCE HEAT TO MEDIUM AND COOK, STIRRING OCCASIONALLY, FOR 5 MINUTES OR UNTIL SAUCE-LIKE. ADD CREAM AND PARSLEY. SEASON TO TASTE WITH SALT AND PEPPER. COOK FOR 1 MINUTE OR UNTIL HEATED THROUGH.

MEANWHILE, COOK PASTA IN A LARGE POT OF BOILING SALTED WATER UNTIL TENDER BUT FIRM. DRAIN WELL. RETURN TO POT AND ADD CLAM SAUCE; TOSS TO COAT PASTA IN THE SAUCE. SERVE IMMEDIATELY. SERVES 4.

SPAGHETTI CARBONARA

WITH A FEW BASIC INGREDIENTS ON HAND, YOU CAN WHIP UP THIS GREAT-TASTING DISH IN ABOUT THE SAME TIME IT TAKES TO COOK THE PASTA.

6	SLICES BACON, CHOPPED	6
2	CLOVES GARLIC, FINELY CHOPPED	2
2 TBSP	CHOPPED FRESH PARSLEY	30 ML
4	LARGE EGGS	4
1/2 CUP	FRESHLY GRATED PARMESAN CHEESE	125 ML
1/2 TSP	SALT	2 ML
	FRESHLY GROUND BLACK PEPPER	
12 OZ	SPAGHETTI OR LINGUINE	375 G

IN A LARGE NONSTICK SKILLET, COOK BACON OVER MEDIUM HEAT, STIRRING, FOR 5 MINUTES OR UNTIL CRISP. DRAIN FAT IN SKILLET. ADD GARLIC AND COOK, STIRRING, FOR 30 SECONDS OR UNTIL FRAGRANT. ADD PARSLEY AND RESERVE. IN A BOWL, BEAT EGGS WITH PARMESAN CHEESE, SALT AND PEPPER.

MEANWHILE, IN A LARGE POT OF BOILING SALTED WATER, COOK PASTA UNTIL TENDER BUT FIRM. DRAIN WELL AND RETURN TO POT. IMMEDIATELY POUR EGG AND BACON MIXTURES OVER HOT PASTA AND TOSS UNTIL WELL COATED AND EGGS ARE SET. SERVE IMMEDIATELY. SERVES 4.

TIP: PARMESAN LOSES ITS WONDERFUL AROMATIC FLAVOR AND MOISTURE IF GRATED AHEAD. CHOOSE A WEDGE IN A CHEESE SHOP AND HAVE IT GRATED FOR YOU. FREEZE IN AN AIRTIGHT CONTAINER. OR BETTER STILL, GRATE THE CHEESE AS YOU NEED IT.

KIDS' FAVORITE SPAGHETTI PIE

8 OZ	MILD OR HOT ITALIAN SAUSAGES (BULK OR CASINGS REMOVED) OR LEAN GROUND BEEF	250 G
2 CUPS	SLICED MUSHROOMS	500 ML
1	SMALL ONION, CHOPPED	1
1	LARGE CLOVE GARLIC, FINELY CHOPPED	1
1 1/2 TSP	DRIED OREGANO	7 ML
2 CUPS	TOMATO PASTA SAUCE	500 ML
2 CUPS	SMALL BROCCOLI FLORETS	500 ML
3 CUPS	COOKED SPAGHETTI OR OTHER STRING PASTA (6 OZ/175 G UNCOOKED)	750 ML
1 1/2 CUPS	SHREDDED MOZZARELLA CHEESE	375 ML

PREHEAT OVEN TO 350°F (180°C). GREASE A 9- OR 10-INCH (23 OR 25 CM) GLASS PIE PLATE. IN A MEDIUM SAUCEPAN OVER MEDIUM-HIGH HEAT, COOK SAUSAGE MEAT, BREAKING IT UP WITH A SPOON, FOR 4 MINUTES OR UNTIL NO LONGER PINK. DRAIN IN SIEVE TO REMOVE ANY FAT. RETURN TO SAUCEPAN. ADD MUSHROOMS, ONION, GARLIC AND OREGANO; COOK, STIRRING, FOR 3 MINUTES OR UNTIL VEGETABLES ARE SOFTENED. ADD TOMATO PASTA SAUCE; COVER AND SIMMER FOR 10 MINUTES. RINSE BROCCOLI; PLACE IN A COVERED CASSEROLE DISH. MICROWAVE ON HIGH FOR 2 TO 2 1/2 MINUTES OR UNTIL BRIGHT GREEN AND ALMOST TENDER. RINSE UNDER COLD WATER TO CHILL; DRAIN. ARRANGE SPAGHETTI IN PIE PLATE. SPREAD WITH MEAT SAUCE; TOP WITH BROCCOLI AND SPRINKLE WITH CHEESE. BAKE FOR 25 TO 30 MINUTES OR UNTIL CHEESE IS MELTED. CUT INTO WEDGES AND SERVE. SERVES 4.

CLASSIC LASAGNA

SLOW COOKER RECIPE

LASAGNA IS THE ULTIMATE COMFORT FOOD, A WONDERFULLY SOOTHING COMBINATION OF SOFT NOODLES AND WARM CHEESE BLENDED WITH A ROBUST TOMATO SAUCE.

2 TBSP	OLIVE OIL	30 ML
I LB	LEAN GROUND BEEF	500 G
8 OZ	ITALIAN SAUSAGE, REMOVED FROM CASINGS	250 G
2	ONIONS, FINELY CHOPPED	2
2	STALKS CELERY, DICED	2
I	CARROT, DICED	I
4	CLOVES GARLIC, MINCED	4
I TBSP	DRIED ITALIAN SEASONING	15 ML
I TSP	SALT	5 ML
I TSP	CRACKED BLACK PEPPERCORNS	5 ML
I CUP	DRY RED WINE	250 ML
I	CAN (28 OZ/796 ML) TOMATOES, WITH JUICE, COARSELY CHOPPED	I
2 CUPS	RICOTTA CHEESE	500 ML
I	LARGE EGG YOLK	I
$\frac{1}{2}$ TSP	FRESHLY GRATED NUTMEG	2 ML
12	OVEN-READY LASAGNA NOODLES	12
2 CUPS	SHREDDED MOZZARELLA	500 ML
$\frac{1}{2}$ CUP	FINELY GRATED PARMESAN CHEESE	125 ML

LIGHTLY GREASE THE STONEWARE OF A LARGE (ABOUT 5-QUART) OVAL SLOW COOKER. IN A LARGE SKILLET, HEAT OIL OVER MEDIUM-HIGH HEAT. ADD GROUND BEEF, SAUSAGE, ONIONS, CELERY AND CARROT AND COOK,

STIRRING, UNTIL MEAT IS NO LONGER PINK, ABOUT
10 MINUTES. ADD GARLIC, ITALIAN SEASONING, SALT
AND PEPPERCORNS AND COOK, STIRRING, FOR 1 MINUTE.
ADD WINE, BRING TO A BOIL AND BOIL, STIRRING AND
SCRAPING UP BROWN BITS FROM BOTTOM OF PAN, FOR
2 MINUTES. ADD TOMATOES AND BRING TO A BOIL. REDUCE
HEAT AND SIMMER FOR 5 MINUTES TO MELD FLAVORS.
REMOVE FROM HEAT AND SET ASIDE. IN A BOWL, COMBINE
RICOTTA, EGG YOLK AND NUTMEG. USING YOUR HANDS,
MIX WELL AND SET ASIDE.

SPREAD ONE-QUARTER OF MEAT SAUCE OVER BOTTOM
OF PREPARED STONEWARE. COVER WITH 4 NOODLES,
BREAKING TO FIT WHERE NECESSARY. SPREAD WITH
A THIN LAYER OF MEAT SAUCE, HALF THE RICOTTA
MIXTURE AND ONE-THIRD EACH OF THE MOZZARELLA AND
PARMESAN. REPEAT. ARRANGE FINAL LAYER OF NOODLES
OVER CHEESES. POUR THE REMAINING SAUCE OVER TOP
AND SPRINKLE WITH THE REMAINING MOZZARELLA AND
PARMESAN. PLACE A CLEAN TEA TOWEL, FOLDED IN HALF
(SO YOU WILL HAVE 2 LAYERS), OVER TOP OF STONEWARE
TO ABSORB MOISTURE. COVER AND COOK ON LOW FOR
5 TO 6 HOURS OR ON HIGH FOR $2\frac{1}{4}$ TO 3 HOURS, UNTIL
HOT AND BUBBLY. SERVES 6 TO 8.

TIP: COOKING TIMES VARY SUBSTANTIALLY AMONG SLOW
COOKERS, AND LASAGNA SEEMS PARTICULARLY SENSITIVE
TO OVERCOOKING IN THE SLOW COOKER. BEGIN CHECKING
THIS RECIPE AFTER THE FOOD HAS COOKED FOR 5 HOURS
ON LOW OR $2\frac{1}{4}$ HOURS ON HIGH.

MUSHROOM AND ARTICHOKE LASAGNA

SLOW COOKER RECIPE

THE UNUSUAL COMBINATION OF FLAVORS IN THIS LASAGNA IS REMINISCENT OF A PROVENÇAL GRATIN. IN ADDITION TO ADDING FLAVOR AND COLOR, THE BABY SPINACH IS A GREAT TIMESAVER, AS IT DOESN'T REQUIRE PRECOOKING.

2 TBSP	BUTTER	30 ML
1	ONION, FINELY CHOPPED	1
1 LB	MUSHROOMS, TRIMMED AND SLICED	500 G
4	CLOVES GARLIC, MINCED	4
3½ CUPS	QUARTERED ARTICHOKE HEARTS (SEE TIP, OPPOSITE)	875 ML
¾ CUP	DRY WHITE WINE OR READY-TO-USE VEGETABLE BROTH	175 ML
12	OVEN-READY LASAGNA NOODLES	12
2½ CUPS	RICOTTA CHEESE	625 ML
2 CUPS	BABY SPINACH	500 ML
2½ CUPS	SHREDDED MOZZARELLA CHEESE	625 ML
½ CUP	FRESHLY GRATED PARMESAN CHEESE	125 ML

GREASE THE STONEWARE OF A LARGE (MINIMUM 5-QUART) OVAL SLOW COOKER. IN A SKILLET, MELT BUTTER OVER MEDIUM HEAT. ADD ONION AND COOK, STIRRING, UNTIL SOFTENED, ABOUT 3 MINUTES. ADD MUSHROOMS AND GARLIC AND COOK, STIRRING, UNTIL MUSHROOMS BEGIN TO RELEASE THEIR LIQUID. STIR IN ARTICHOKES AND WINE AND BRING TO A BOIL. COOK, STIRRING, UNTIL LIQUID REDUCES SLIGHTLY, FOR 1 TO 2 MINUTES. SET ASIDE.

COVER BOTTOM OF SLOW COOKER STONEWARE WITH 4 NOODLES, BREAKING TO FIT WHERE NECESSARY. SPREAD WITH HALF THE RICOTTA, HALF THE MUSHROOM MIXTURE, HALF THE SPINACH AND ONE-THIRD EACH OF THE MOZZARELLA AND PARMESAN. REPEAT LAYERS. ARRANGE FINAL LAYER OF NOODLES OVER CHEESES. POUR ANY LIQUID REMAINING FROM MUSHROOM MIXTURE OVER NOODLES (SEE TIP, BELOW). SPRINKLE WITH THE REMAINING MOZZARELLA AND PARMESAN. (LASAGNA CAN BE COOLED, COVERED AND REFRIGERATED OVERNIGHT AT THIS POINT.)

COVER AND COOK ON LOW FOR 6 HOURS OR ON HIGH FOR 3 HOURS, UNTIL HOT AND BUBBLY. SERVES 6 TO 8.

TIP: IF USING CANNED ARTICHOKE HEARTS, CHOOSE THOSE THAT ARE PACKED IN WATER AND DRAIN BEFORE USING. IF USING FROZEN, THAW FIRST.

TIP: UNLIKE MANY RECIPES FOR LASAGNA, THIS ONE IS NOT TERRIBLY SAUCY. AS A RESULT, THE NOODLES ON THE TOP LAYER TEND TO DRY OUT. LEAVE A SMALL AMOUNT OF THE COOKING LIQUID FROM THE MUSHROOM MIXTURE BEHIND IN THE PAN AS YOU ADD THE MUSHROOM MIXTURE TO THE SLOW COOKER. POUR THAT OVER THE TOP LAYER OF NOODLES, PARTICULARLY AROUND THE EDGES, WHERE THEY ARE MOST LIKELY TO DRY OUT. IF IT STILL SEEMS DRY, DRIZZLE WITH A LITTLE VEGETABLE BROTH, WATER OR EXTRA VIRGIN OLIVE OIL.

SINGAPORE NOODLES

THIS POPULAR NOODLE DISH IS EASY TO CREATE IN YOUR HOME KITCHEN.

6 OZ	RICE VERMICELLI	175 G
3 TBSP	SOY SAUCE	45 ML
2 TSP	MILD CURRY PASTE (OR TO TASTE)	10 ML
2 TBSP	VEGETABLE OIL, DIVIDED	30 ML
1	RED OR GREEN BELL PEPPER, CUT INTO THIN STRIPS	1
5	GREEN ONIONS, SLICED	5
2	LARGE CLOVES GARLIC, MINCED	2
3 CUPS	BEAN SPROUTS, RINSED AND DRIED	750 ML
12 OZ	COOKED PEELED BABY SHRIMP	375 G

PLACE VERMICELLI IN A BOWL AND COVER WITH BOILING WATER. LET SOAK FOR 3 MINUTES TO SOFTEN. DRAIN; CHILL UNDER COLD WATER AND DRAIN WELL. CUT NOODLES USING SCISSORS INTO 3-INCH (7.5 CM) LENGTHS; SET ASIDE. IN A SMALL BOWL, COMBINE SOY SAUCE AND CURRY PASTE; SET ASIDE. HEAT A WOK OR LARGE NONSTICK SKILLET OVER HIGH HEAT UNTIL VERY HOT; ADD 1 TBSP (15 ML) OIL, TILTING WOK TO COAT SIDES. STIR-FRY PEPPER STRIPS, GREEN ONIONS AND GARLIC FOR 1 MINUTE. ADD BEAN SPROUTS AND SHRIMP; STIR-FRY FOR 1 TO 2 MINUTES OR UNTIL VEGETABLES ARE TENDER-CRISP. TRANSFER TO A BOWL. ADD THE REMAINING OIL TO WOK; WHEN VERY HOT, ADD NOODLES AND SOY SAUCE MIXTURE. STIR-FRY FOR 1 MINUTE OR UNTIL HEATED THROUGH. RETURN VEGETABLE-SHRIMP MIXTURE TO WOK AND STIR-FRY FOR 1 MINUTE MORE. SERVE IMMEDIATELY. SERVES 4.

Classic Lasagna (page 194)

Peas and Greens (page 214)

Poached Eggs on Spicy Lentils (page 222)

Shrimp in Tomato Sauce with Feta (page 241)

COLD SESAME NOODLES

FAST-AND-EASY RECIPE

THE DRESSING CAN BE MADE IN LESS TIME THAN IT TAKES THE NOODLES TO COOK! FEEL FREE TO ADD COOKED SHRIMP, CHICKEN OR VEGGIES.

12 OZ	DRY THIN OR MEDIUM ASIAN EGG NOODLES OR SPAGHETTI	375 G
2	CLOVES GARLIC, MINCED	2
1 TBSP	GRATED GINGERROOT	15 ML
2 TBSP	PACKED BROWN SUGAR	30 ML
3 TBSP	SESAME OIL	45 ML
3 TBSP	SOY SAUCE	45 ML
2 TBSP	RICE VINEGAR	30 ML
1 TSP	CHILI SAUCE	5 ML
2 to 3	GREEN ONIONS, THINLY SLICED	2 to 3
1/4 CUP	SESAME SEEDS, TOASTED	60 ML

IN A LARGE POT OF BOILING WATER, COOK NOODLES ACCORDING TO PACKAGE DIRECTIONS UNTIL AL DENTE. DRAIN AND RUN UNDER COLD WATER TO COOL. IN A LARGE BOWL, STIR TOGETHER GARLIC, GINGER, BROWN SUGAR, OIL, SOY SAUCE, VINEGAR AND CHILI SAUCE. ADD NOODLES AND TOSS TO COMBINE. SERVE TOPPED WITH GREEN ONIONS AND SESAME SEEDS. SERVES 4 TO 6.

PAD THAI

PAD THAI IS THE MOST POPULAR DISH IN THAILAND, AND ITS ADDICTIVE APPEAL HAS SPREAD FAR BEYOND THAT COUNTRY'S BORDERS.

8 OZ	WIDE RICE STICK NOODLES	250 G
1/3 CUP	CHILI SAUCE OR KETCHUP	75 ML
1/4 CUP	FISH SAUCE (NAM PLA)	60 ML
3 TBSP	FRESHLY SQUEEZED LIME JUICE	45 ML
1 TBSP	PACKED BROWN SUGAR	15 ML
1 TSP	ASIAN CHILI SAUCE (OR TO TASTE)	5 ML
2 TBSP	VEGETABLE OIL, DIVIDED	30 ML
8 OZ	MEDIUM SHRIMP, PEELED AND DEVEINED	250 G
8 OZ	BONELESS SKINLESS CHICKEN BREASTS, CUT INTO THIN STRIPS	250 G
3	CLOVES GARLIC, MINCED	3
2	LARGE EGGS, LIGHTLY BEATEN	2
2 CUPS	BEAN SPROUTS	500 ML
5	GREEN ONIONS, SLICED	5
1/2 CUP	COARSELY CHOPPED FRESH CILANTRO	125 ML
1/3 CUP	COARSELY CHOPPED ROASTED PEANUTS	75 ML
	LIME WEDGES	

PLACE NOODLES IN A LARGE BOWL. ADD HOT WATER TO COVER. LET STAND FOR 15 MINUTES OR UNTIL SOFTENED. DRAIN. IN A BOWL, COMBINE CHILI SAUCE, FISH SAUCE, LIME JUICE, BROWN SUGAR AND ASIAN CHILI SAUCE. IN A LARGE WOK OR NONSTICK SKILLET, HEAT 1 TBSP (15 ML) OIL OVER MEDIUM-HIGH HEAT. COOK SHRIMP AND CHICKEN, STIRRING, FOR 3 MINUTES OR UNTIL CHICKEN IS COOKED THROUGH AND SHRIMP ARE PINK. ADD TO CHILI SAUCE MIXTURE

AND TOSS. ADD THE REMAINING OIL TO THE SKILLET. COOK GARLIC, STIRRING, FOR 15 SECONDS OR UNTIL FRAGRANT. ADD EGGS; COOK, STIRRING CONSTANTLY, FOR 30 SECONDS OR UNTIL SOFT-SCRAMBLED. ADD SPROUTS AND GREEN ONIONS; COOK, STIRRING, FOR 1 MINUTE. ADD NOODLES AND SHRIMP MIXTURE; COOK, STIRRING, FOR 2 MINUTES OR UNTIL HEATED THROUGH. TRANSFER TO A PLATTER; SPRINKLE WITH CILANTRO AND PEANUTS. GARNISH WITH LIME WEDGES. SERVES 6.

TIP: FISH SAUCE (ALSO CALLED NAM PLA) IS AN IMPORTANT FLAVORING INGREDIENT IN THIS DISH. LOOK FOR IT IN THE ASIAN FOODS SECTION OF MOST LARGE SUPERMARKETS OR IN ASIAN MARKETS.

MARY HAD A LITTLE LAMB ...
WITH A NICE MINT SAUCE.

CREAMY PEANUT NOODLES

A DIFFERENT WAY TO DRESS YOUR NOODLES – AND PERFECTLY PORTABLE FOR A PARTY OR LUNCH AT WORK.

DRESSING

1/3 CUP	PEANUT BUTTER	75 ML
1/4 CUP	WARM WATER	60 ML
2 TBSP	SOY SAUCE	30 ML
2 TBSP	FRESHLY SQUEEZED LIME JUICE	30 ML
1 TBSP	LIQUID HONEY	15 ML
1 TSP	SRIRACHA OR CHILI SAUCE	5 ML

SALAD

12 OZ	DRY THIN ASIAN EGG NOODLES OR SPAGHETTI	375 G
2	GREEN ONIONS, THINLY SLICED	2
1	SMALL RED BELL PEPPER, THINLY SLICED	1
1	CARROT, CUT INTO MATCHSTICKS	1
1 CUP	SNOW OR SUGAR SNAP PEA PODS	250 ML
1/4 CUP	CHOPPED PEANUTS	60 ML

DRESSING: IN A SMALL BOWL OR JAR, STIR OR SHAKE TOGETHER PEANUT BUTTER, WATER, SOY SAUCE, LIME JUICE, HONEY AND SRIRACHA.

SALAD: IN A LARGE POT OF BOILING SALTED WATER, COOK NOODLES ACCORDING TO PACKAGE DIRECTIONS UNTIL AL DENTE. DRAIN AND RUN UNDER COLD WATER TO COOL. IN A LARGE BOWL, COMBINE NOODLES, GREEN ONIONS, RED PEPPER, CARROT AND PEA PODS. DRIZZLE WITH DRESSING AND TOSS TO COAT. SERVE SPRINKLED WITH PEANUTS.

SERVES 4.

MEATLESS MAINS

TOMATO GRATIN

2	LARGE POTATOES, COOKED UNTIL FORK-TENDER, PEELED AND THINLY SLICED	2
1 TBSP	VEGETABLE OIL	15 ML
2 CUPS	FINELY CHOPPED ONION	500 ML
1 TBSP	MINCED GARLIC	15 ML
1 TSP	DRIED ITALIAN SEASONING	5 ML
1 TSP	SALT	5 ML
	FRESHLY GROUND BLACK PEPPER	
1	CAN (28 OZ/796 ML) TOMATOES, DRAINED AND COARSELY CHOPPED	1
1/4 CUP	SLICED BLACK OLIVES	60 ML
1 CUP	SHREDDED ITALIAN FOUR-CHEESE MIX	250 ML

PREHEAT OVEN TO 375°F (190°C). LIGHTLY GREASE A 6-CUP (1.5 L) SHALLOW BAKING DISH. IN A SKILLET, HEAT OIL OVER MEDIUM HEAT. ADD ONION AND COOK, STIRRING, UNTIL SOFTENED, ABOUT 3 MINUTES. ADD GARLIC, DRIED ITALIAN SEASONING, SALT, AND BLACK PEPPER TO TASTE AND COOK, STIRRING, FOR 1 MINUTE. ADD TOMATOES AND BRING TO A BOIL. REDUCE HEAT TO LOW AND SIMMER FOR 5 MINUTES. LADLE ONE-THIRD OF THE TOMATO MIXTURE INTO PREPARED DISH. ARRANGE POTATOES IN A SINGLE LAYER OVER THE TOP. SPRINKLE EVENLY WITH OLIVES AND COVER WITH THE REMAINING SAUCE. SPRINKLE CHEESE EVENLY OVER TOP. BAKE UNTIL CHEESE IS GOLDEN AND TOMATOES ARE BUBBLING AND HOT, ABOUT 30 MINUTES. SERVES 4.

TIP: SUBSTITUTE SHREDDED CHEDDAR CHEESE FOR THE ITALIAN FOUR-CHEESE MIX, IF DESIRED.

RATATOUILLE

THIS CLASSIC FRENCH VEGETABLE STEW
MAKES THE BEST OF A GOOD HARVEST.

I TBSP	VEGETABLE OIL (APPROX.)	15 ML
I	PURPLE ONION, COARSELY CHOPPED	I
4	CLOVES GARLIC, CRUSHED	4
I	SMALL EGGPLANT, CUT INTO BITE-SIZE PIECES	I
I	RED, YELLOW OR ORANGE BELL PEPPER, CHOPPED	I
I	ZUCCHINI, CUT INTO BITE-SIZE PIECES	I
3	RIPE TOMATOES, COARSELY CHOPPED	3
2 TBSP	TOMATO PASTE	30 ML
I TSP	DRIED OREGANO OR DRIED ITALIAN SEASONING	5 ML
	SALT AND FRESHLY GROUND BLACK PEPPER	

IN A LARGE SKILLET, HEAT OIL OVER MEDIUM-HIGH HEAT. ADD ONION AND COOK, STIRRING, UNTIL SOFTENED. ADD GARLIC AND EGGPLANT; COOK, STIRRING, UNTIL SOFTENED, ADDING MORE OIL IF NECESSARY. ADD RED PEPPER AND ZUCCHINI; COOK, STIRRING UNTIL VEGETABLES ARE SOFT AND STARTING TO TURN GOLDEN AT THE EDGES. ADD TOMATOES, TOMATO PASTE, OREGANO, AND SALT AND PEPPER TO TASTE; COOK, STIRRING, UNTIL THICKENED.

SERVES 6.

VEGETABLE FRIED RICE

USE THIS RECIPE AS A GUIDE TO CREATE YOUR OWN VERSIONS OF FRIED RICE, DEPENDING ON WHAT TYPE OF VEGGIES YOU HAVE IN THE FRIDGE. WITH RICE COOKED AHEAD, IT TAKES NO TIME TO PREPARE THIS QUICK SUPPER DISH.

I TBSP	VEGETABLE OIL	15 ML
3	GREEN ONIONS, CHOPPED	3
I½ TSP	MINCED GINGERROOT	7 ML
I	CLOVE GARLIC, MINCED	I
3 CUPS	COLD COOKED RICE	750 ML
I CUP	FROZEN PEAS	250 ML
½	RED BELL PEPPER, CUT INTO THIN STRIPS, I½ INCHES (4 CM) LONG	½
2 TBSP	SOY SAUCE	30 ML
I TSP	MILD CURRY PASTE (OPTIONAL)	5 ML
2 CUPS	BEAN SPROUTS	500 ML

IN A LARGE NONSTICK SKILLET, HEAT OIL OVER HIGH HEAT. ADD GREEN ONIONS, GINGER AND GARLIC; COOK, STIRRING, FOR 15 SECONDS OR UNTIL FRAGRANT. ADD RICE, PEAS AND PEPPER; COOK, STIRRING OFTEN, FOR 5 TO 7 MINUTES OR UNTIL RICE IS HEATED THROUGH AND VEGETABLES ARE TENDER. IN A SMALL BOWL, COMBINE SOY SAUCE AND CURRY PASTE (IF USING); STIR INTO RICE MIXTURE ALONG WITH BEAN SPROUTS. COOK, STIRRING, FOR I TO 2 MINUTES OR UNTIL HEATED THROUGH. SERVE IMMEDIATELY. SERVES 4.

VARIATION: INSTEAD OF PEAS, TRY BLANCHED DICED CARROTS, SNOW PEAS CUT INTO I-INCH (2.5 CM) PIECES,

1 ZUCCHINI, HALVED LENGTHWISE AND SLICED, OR SMALL BROCCOLI FLORETS.

VARIATION

CHICKEN OR PORK FRIED RICE: CUT 8 OZ (250 G) CHICKEN BREASTS OR LEAN BONELESS PORK LOIN INTO THIN STRIPS. IN A SKILLET, HEAT 1 TBSP (15 ML) OIL OVER MEDIUM-HIGH HEAT; COOK MEAT, STIRRING, FOR 5 MINUTES OR UNTIL NO LONGER PINK. REMOVE; KEEP WARM. CONTINUE WITH RECIPE AS DIRECTED. RETURN MEAT TO SKILLET WITH BEAN SPROUTS.

CARBON. DON'T DATE WITHOUT IT.

RED BEANS AND GREENS

SLOW COOKER RECIPE

FEW MEALS COULD BE MORE HEALTHFUL THAN THIS DELICIOUS COMBINATION OF HOT LEAFY GREENS OVER FLAVORFUL BEANS.

2 CUPS	DRIED KIDNEY BEANS	500 ML
I TBSP	VEGETABLE OIL	15 ML
2	ONIONS, FINELY CHOPPED	2
2	STALKS CELERY, FINELY CHOPPED	2
4	CLOVES GARLIC, MINCED	4
I TSP	DRIED OREGANO	5 ML
I TSP	SALT	5 ML
1/2 TSP	CRACKED BLACK PEPPERCORNS	2 ML
1/2 TSP	DRIED THYME	2 ML
1/4 TSP	GROUND ALLSPICE (OR 6 WHOLE ALLSPICE, TIED IN A PIECE OF CHEESECLOTH)	I ML
2	BAY LEAVES	2
4 CUPS	READY-TO-USE VEGETABLE BROTH, DIVIDED	I L
I TSP	SMOKED PAPRIKA, DISSOLVED IN I TBSP (15 ML) BOILING WATER (OPTIONAL)	5 ML

GREENS

8 CUPS	GREENS, STEMS REMOVED, CHOPPED	2 L
	BUTTER OR OLIVE OIL	
I TBSP	BALSAMIC VINEGAR	15 ML
	SALT AND FRESHLY GROUND BLACK PEPPER	

IN A POT, COMBINE BEANS AND WATER. COVER AND BRING TO A BOIL. BOIL FOR 3 MINUTES. TURN OFF HEAT AND SOAK FOR I HOUR. DRAIN AND RINSE THOROUGHLY UNDER COLD WATER. SET ASIDE. IN A SKILLET, HEAT OIL

OVER MEDIUM HEAT. ADD ONIONS AND CELERY AND COOK, STIRRING, UNTIL SOFTENED, ABOUT 5 MINUTES. ADD GARLIC, OREGANO, SALT, PEPPERCORNS, THYME, ALLSPICE AND BAY LEAVES AND COOK, STIRRING, FOR 1 MINUTE. ADD 2 CUPS (500 ML) BROTH AND STIR WELL. TRANSFER TO A LARGE (ABOUT 5-QUART) SLOW COOKER. (MIXTURE CAN BE COOLED, COVERED AND REFRIGERATED FOR UP TO 2 DAYS AT THIS POINT.)

ADD THE REMAINING BROTH AND SOAKED BEANS TO SLOW COOKER. COVER AND COOK ON LOW FOR 8 TO 10 HOURS OR ON HIGH FOR 4 TO 5 HOURS, UNTIL BEANS ARE TENDER. DISCARD BAY LEAVES, AND ALLSPICE IN CHEESECLOTH (IF USING). STIR IN SMOKED PAPRIKA SOLUTION (IF USING).

GREENS: STEAM GREENS UNTIL TENDER, ABOUT 10 MINUTES FOR COLLARDS. TOSS WITH BUTTER AND BALSAMIC VINEGAR. SEASON TO TASTE WITH SALT AND PEPPER. ADD TO BEANS AND STIR TO COMBINE. SERVE IMMEDIATELY. SERVES 8.

TIP: TRY COLLARD GREENS OR OTHER DARK LEAFY GREENS, SUCH AS KALE.

TIP: IF HALVING THIS RECIPE, BE SURE TO USE A SMALL TO MEDIUM (2- TO 3½-QUART) SLOW COOKER.

TIP: IF YOU'RE COOKING FOR A SMALLER GROUP, MAKE THE FULL QUANTITY OF BEANS, SPOON OFF WHAT IS NEEDED, AND SERVE WITH THE APPROPRIATE QUANTITY OF COOKED GREENS. REFRIGERATE OR FREEZE THE LEFTOVER BEANS FOR ANOTHER MEAL.

MEXICAN RICE AND BEANS

THE COMBINATION OF RICE AND BEANS IS A
FAVORITE COMFORT FOOD IN MANY CULTURES. THIS
VERSION MAKES A TASTY VEGETARIAN DISH TO SERVE
WITH A TOSSED SALAD FOR A LIGHT SUPPER.

1 TBSP	VEGETABLE OIL	15 ML
1	ONION, CHOPPED	1
2	CLOVES GARLIC, MINCED	2
1	GREEN BELL PEPPER, FINELY CHOPPED	1
1 to 2	JALAPEÑO PEPPERS, SEEDED AND MINCED (OPTIONAL)	1 to 2
1 TBSP	CHILI POWDER	15 ML
1 TSP	DRIED OREGANO	5 ML
2	TOMATOES, SEEDED AND DICED	2
2 CUPS	READY-TO-USE VEGETABLE BROTH	500 ML
1 CUP	LONG-GRAIN WHITE RICE	250 ML
1	CAN (19 OZ/540 ML) BLACK BEANS OR KIDNEY BEANS, DRAINED AND RINSED	1
1/4 CUP	CHOPPED FRESH CILANTRO (OPTIONAL)	60 ML

IN A LARGE SAUCEPAN, HEAT OIL OVER MEDIUM HEAT.
COOK ONION, GARLIC, GREEN PEPPER, JALAPEÑO PEPPERS
(IF USING), CHILI POWDER AND OREGANO, STIRRING, FOR
5 MINUTES OR UNTIL SOFTENED. ADD TOMATOES; COOK
FOR 3 MINUTES OR UNTIL SAUCE-LIKE. ADD BROTH AND
BRING TO A BOIL. STIR IN RICE AND BLACK BEANS. REDUCE
HEAT TO LOW; COVER AND COOK FOR 20 MINUTES OR
UNTIL RICE IS TENDER. STIR IN CILANTRO (IF USING).
SERVES 6.

TIP: TO AVOID SKIN IRRITATION, WEAR RUBBER GLOVES
WHEN HANDLING JALAPEÑO PEPPERS.

ZESTY BLACK BEAN PIE

CRUST

30	CHEESE-FLAVORED CRACKERS, SUCH AS RITZ (ABOUT HALF AN 8-OZ/250 G BOX)	30
1/4 CUP	BUTTER, MELTED	60 ML

FILLING

1 TBSP	VEGETABLE OIL	15 ML
1 CUP	DICED ONION	250 ML
1 TSP	MINCED GARLIC	5 ML
1 TSP	GROUND CUMIN	5 ML
1	CAN (19 OZ/540 ML) BLACK BEANS, DRAINED AND RINSED	1
1 1/2 CUPS	CORN KERNELS, THAWED IF FROZEN	375 ML
1 CUP	TOMATO SALSA	250 ML
4 OZ	CREAM CHEESE, CUT INTO 1/2-INCH (1 CM) CUBES AND SOFTENED	125 G

CRUST: PREHEAT OVEN TO 350°F (180°C). IN A FOOD PROCESSOR, PULSE CRACKERS UNTIL THEY RESEMBLE COARSE CRUMBS. IN A BOWL, COMBINE CRACKER CRUMBS AND BUTTER. PRESS INTO A 9-INCH (23 CM) PIE PLATE. BAKE UNTIL GOLDEN, ABOUT 8 MINUTES.

FILLING: MEANWHILE, IN A SKILLET, HEAT OIL OVER MEDIUM HEAT. ADD ONION AND COOK, STIRRING, UNTIL SOFTENED, ABOUT 3 MINUTES. ADD GARLIC AND CUMIN AND COOK, STIRRING, FOR 1 MINUTE. STIR IN BEANS, CORN AND SALSA. BRING TO A BOIL. ADD CREAM CHEESE AND COOK, STIRRING, UNTIL CHEESE IS MELTED AND MIXTURE HOLDS TOGETHER, ABOUT 2 MINUTES. REMOVE FROM HEAT. SPREAD MIXTURE EVENLY OVER COOKED CRUST. BAKE FOR 10 MINUTES TO COMBINE FLAVORS. SERVES 4.

ENCHILADAS IN SALSA VERDE

THIS TASTY VARIATION OF A CLASSIC
MEXICAN DISH HAS AN APPEALING COMBINATION OF
INGREDIENTS AND FLAVORS. SERVE WITH A SIMPLE
AVOCADO AND ONION SALAD FOR A MEAL WITH
A SOUTH-OF-THE-BORDER THEME.

1 TBSP	VEGETABLE OIL	15 ML
1 CUP	FINELY CHOPPED ONION	250 ML
1 TBSP	MINCED GARLIC	15 ML
1 TSP	GROUND CUMIN	5 ML
2 CUPS	DICED COOKED POTATOES	500 ML
1	PACKAGE (10 OZ/300 G) FROZEN CHOPPED SPINACH, INCLUDING LIQUID, THAWED (OR ONE 10-OZ/300 G BAG SPINACH, STEMS REMOVED, COARSELY CHOPPED)	1
1	CAN (14 OZ/398 ML) REFRIED BEANS	1
3 CUPS	SHREDDED MONTEREY JACK CHEESE OR MEXICAN CHEESE MIX, DIVIDED	750 ML
3 CUPS	SALSA VERDE (SEE TIP, OPPOSITE), DIVIDED	750 ML
16	6-INCH (15 CM) TORTILLAS, PREFERABLY CORN	16

PREHEAT OVEN TO 350°F (180°C). IN A SKILLET, HEAT OIL
OVER MEDIUM HEAT. ADD ONION AND COOK, STIRRING,
UNTIL SOFTENED, ABOUT 3 MINUTES. ADD GARLIC AND
CUMIN AND COOK, STIRRING, FOR 1 MINUTE. ADD POTATOES
AND SPINACH AND COOK, STIRRING, UNTIL SPINACH IS
INCORPORATED, ABOUT 3 MINUTES. STIR IN REFRIED
BEANS AND BRING TO A BOIL. ADD 1¾ CUPS (425 ML)
CHEESE AND COOK, STIRRING, UNTIL CHEESE MELTS,
ABOUT 2 MINUTES. REMOVE FROM HEAT. POUR 1 CUP

(250 ML) SALSA VERDE INTO A BOWL. ONE AT A TIME, DIP TORTILLAS INTO SAUCE, TURNING TO ENSURE ALL PARTS ARE MOISTENED. LAY 1 TORTILLA ON A PLATE AND SPREAD WITH A GENEROUS $\frac{1}{4}$ CUP (60 ML) BEAN MIXTURE. ROLL UP AND PLACE, SEAM SIDE DOWN, IN A 13- BY 9-INCH (33 BY 23 CM) BAKING DISH. REPEAT WITH THE REMAINING TORTILLAS UNTIL ALL THE FILLING IS USED. POUR THE REMAINING SALSA VERDE OVER TORTILLAS AND SPRINKLE WITH THE REMAINING CHEESE. COVER AND BAKE UNTIL HOT AND BUBBLING, ABOUT 30 MINUTES. SERVES 4 TO 6.

TIP: SALSA VERDE IS AVAILABLE IN THE MEXICAN FOODS SECTION OF MANY SUPERMARKETS OR IN SPECIALTY FOOD STORES.

TIP: CORN TORTILLAS HAVE A MORE AUTHENTIC MEXICAN FLAVOR THAN THOSE MADE WITH FLOUR.

TIP: ADD GARNISHES SUCH AS FINELY CHOPPED RED OR GREEN ONION, FINELY CHOPPED CORIANDER, SHREDDED LETTUCE OR SOUR CREAM.

VARIATION: IF YOU ARE A HEAT SEEKER, ADD 1 FINELY CHOPPED JALAPEÑO PEPPER WITH THE GARLIC.

NEVER TRUST AN ATOM.
THEY MAKE UP EVERYTHING.

PEAS AND GREENS

SLOW COOKER RECIPE

THIS DELICIOUS COMBINATION OF BLACK-EYED PEAS AND GREENS IS A GREAT DISH FOR BUSY WEEKNIGHTS. JUST ADD SOME WHOLE-GRAIN BREAD.

I TBSP	VEGETABLE OIL	15 ML
2	ONIONS, FINELY CHOPPED	2
I	BULB FENNEL, TRIMMED, CORED AND THINLY SLICED ON THE VERTICAL (SEE TIP, OPPOSITE)	I
4	CLOVES GARLIC, MINCED	4
1/2 TSP	SALT (OR TO TASTE)	2 ML
1/2 TSP	CRACKED BLACK PEPPERCORNS	2 ML
1/4 TSP	FENNEL SEEDS, TOASTED AND GROUND (SEE TIP, OPPOSITE)	I ML
I	CAN (14 OZ/398 ML) DICED TOMATOES, WITH JUICE	I
2 CUPS	DRAINED COOKED BLACK-EYED PEAS (SEE TIP, OPPOSITE)	500 ML
I TSP	PAPRIKA, (SEE TIP, OPPOSITE) DISSOLVED IN 2 TBSP (30 ML) FRESHLY SQUEEZED LEMON JUICE	5 ML
4 CUPS	CHOPPED SPINACH OR SWISS CHARD (ABOUT I BUNCH), STEMS REMOVED	I L

IN A SKILLET, HEAT OIL OVER MEDIUM HEAT. ADD ONIONS AND FENNEL AND COOK, STIRRING, UNTIL FENNEL IS SOFTENED, ABOUT 5 MINUTES. ADD GARLIC, SALT, PEPPERCORNS AND FENNEL SEEDS AND COOK, STIRRING, FOR I MINUTE. ADD TOMATOES AND BRING TO A BOIL. TRANSFER TO A MEDIUM TO LARGE (3$\frac{1}{2}$- TO 5-QUART) SLOW COOKER. (MIXTURE CAN BE COOLED, COVERED AND REFRIGERATED FOR UP TO 2 DAYS AT THIS POINT.)

STIR IN PEAS. COVER AND COOK ON LOW FOR 8 HOURS OR ON HIGH FOR 4 HOURS, UNTIL PEAS ARE TENDER. STIR IN PAPRIKA SOLUTION. ADD SPINACH, IN BATCHES, STIRRING AFTER EACH TO SUBMERGE THE LEAVES IN THE LIQUID. COVER AND COOK ON HIGH FOR 20 MINUTES, UNTIL SPINACH IS TENDER. SERVES 4.

TIP: TO PREPARE FENNEL, BEFORE REMOVING THE CORE, CHOP OFF THE TOP SHOOTS (WHICH RESEMBLE CELERY) AND DISCARD. IF DESIRED, SAVE THE FEATHERY GREEN FRONDS TO USE AS A GARNISH. IF THE OUTER SECTIONS OF THE BULB SEEM OLD AND DRY, PEEL THEM WITH A VEGETABLE PEELER BEFORE USING.

TIP: TOASTING FENNEL SEEDS INTENSIFIES THEIR FLAVOR. TO TOAST FENNEL SEEDS: PLACE IN A DRY SKILLET OVER MEDIUM HEAT AND STIR UNTIL FRAGRANT, ABOUT 3 MINUTES. IMMEDIATELY TRANSFER TO A MORTAR OR SPICE GRINDER AND GRIND.

TIP: FOR THIS QUANTITY OF PEAS, USE 1 CAN (14 TO 19 OZ/398 TO 540 ML) DRAINED AND RINSED BLACK-EYED PEAS, OR COOK 1 CUP (250 ML) DRIED PEAS.

TIP: YOU CAN USE ANY KIND OF PAPRIKA IN THIS RECIPE: REGULAR; HOT, WHICH PRODUCES A NICELY PEPPERY VERSION; OR SMOKED, WHICH ADDS A DELICIOUS NOTE OF SMOKINESS. IF YOU HAVE REGULAR PAPRIKA AND WOULD LIKE A BIT A HEAT, DISSOLVE $1/4$ TSP (1 ML) CAYENNE PEPPER IN THE LEMON JUICE ALONG WITH THE PAPRIKA.

TIP: IF YOU CHOOSE TO HALVE THIS RECIPE, USE A SMALL ($1^1/_2$- TO $3^1/_2$-QUART) SLOW COOKER.

INDIAN PEAS AND BEANS

SLOW COOKER RECIPE

SIMPLE YET DELICIOUS SERVED WITH INDIAN BREAD AND A CUCUMBER SALAD, THIS DISH MAKES A GREAT WEEKNIGHT DINNER. IT ALSO MAKES A NICE ADDITION TO A MULTI-DISH INDIAN MEAL.

1 CUP	YELLOW SPLIT PEAS, RINSED	250 ML
1 TBSP	VEGETABLE OIL (SEE TIP, OPPOSITE)	15 ML
2	ONIONS, FINELY CHOPPED	2
4	CLOVES GARLIC, MINCED	4
1 TBSP	MINCED GINGERROOT	15 ML
1 TBSP	GROUND CUMIN	15 ML
2 TSP	GROUND CORIANDER	10 ML
1 TSP	GROUND TURMERIC	5 ML
1 TSP	CRACKED BLACK PEPPERCORNS	5 ML
2	BAY LEAVES	2
1	CAN (14 OZ/398 ML) DICED TOMATOES, WITH JUICE (SEE TIP, OPPOSITE)	1
2 CUPS	READY-TO-USE VEGETABLE BROTH	500 ML
2 CUPS	FROZEN SLICED GREEN BEANS	500 ML
1/4 TSP	CAYENNE PEPPER, DISSOLVED IN 1 TBSP (15 ML) FRESHLY SQUEEZED LEMON JUICE	1 ML
1 CUP	COCONUT MILK (OPTIONAL)	250 ML
1/2 CUP	FINELY CHOPPED CILANTRO	125 ML

IN A LARGE SAUCEPAN, COMBINE PEAS WITH 6 CUPS (1.5 L) COLD WATER. BRING TO A BOIL AND BOIL RAPIDLY FOR 3 MINUTES. REMOVE FROM HEAT AND SET ASIDE FOR 1 HOUR. RINSE THOROUGHLY UNDER COLD WATER, DRAIN AND SET ASIDE.

IN A LARGE SKILLET, HEAT OIL OVER MEDIUM HEAT. ADD ONIONS AND COOK, STIRRING, UNTIL SOFTENED, ABOUT 3 MINUTES. ADD GARLIC, GINGER, CUMIN, CORIANDER, TURMERIC, PEPPERCORNS AND BAY LEAVES AND COOK, STIRRING, FOR 1 MINUTE. ADD TOMATOES AND RESERVED SPLIT PEAS AND BRING TO A BOIL. TRANSFER TO A MEDIUM TO LARGE ($3\frac{1}{2}$- TO 5-QUART) SLOW COOKER. (MIXTURE CAN BE COOLED, COVERED AND REFRIGERATED FOR UP TO 2 DAYS AT THIS POINT.)

ADD BROTH AND GREEN BEANS AND STIR WELL. COVER AND COOK ON LOW FOR 8 TO 10 HOURS OR ON HIGH FOR 4 TO 5 HOURS, UNTIL PEAS ARE TENDER. STIR IN CAYENNE SOLUTION, AND COCONUT MILK (IF USING). ADD CILANTRO AND STIR WELL. COVER AND COOK ON HIGH FOR 20 MINUTES, UNTIL HEATED THROUGH. DISCARD BAY LEAVES. SERVES 6.

TIP: IF YOU PREFER, USE COCONUT OIL INSTEAD OF VEGETABLE OIL FOR SOFTENING THE VEGETABLES. IT WILL ADD A PLEASANT NUTTY FLAVOR TO THE DISH.

TIP: CAN SIZES VARY FROM LOCATION TO LOCATION. IF YOUR SUPERMARKET CARRIES 19-OZ (540 ML) CANS OF DICED TOMATOES, BY ALL MEANS SUBSTITUTE FOR THE 14-OZ (398 ML) CALLED FOR IN THE RECIPE.

TIP: IF YOU CHOOSE TO HALVE THIS RECIPE, USE A SMALL ($1\frac{1}{2}$- TO $3\frac{1}{2}$-QUART) SLOW COOKER.

MIDDLE EASTERN COUSCOUS WITH CHICKPEAS

THIS IMPRESSIVE ONE-POT PARTY DISH FEATURES EASY-TO-USE COUSCOUS AND CANNED CHICKPEAS WITH RICH FLAVORS OF CUMIN, CORIANDER AND ZESTY ORANGE. REFRIGERATE ANY EXTRAS AND SERVE HOT OR COLD FOR NEXT DAY'S LUNCH.

1½ CUPS	READY-TO-USE VEGETABLE BROTH	375 ML
1½ CUPS	COUSCOUS	375 ML
2 CUPS	SLICED PEELED CARROTS (CUT ON THE DIAGONAL)	500 ML
1	LARGE RED BELL PEPPER, FINELY CHOPPED	1
1	CAN (19 OZ/540 ML) CHICKPEAS, DRAINED AND RINSED	1
1 TBSP	OLIVE OIL	15 ML
1	LARGE ONION, CHOPPED	1
3	CLOVES GARLIC, FINELY CHOPPED	3
2 TBSP	MINCED GINGERROOT	30 ML
2 TSP	GROUND CUMIN	10 ML
1 TSP	GROUND CORIANDER	5 ML
¾ TSP	SALT	3 ML
¼ TSP	CAYENNE PEPPER	1 ML
1 TBSP	GRATED ORANGE ZEST	15 ML
1 CUP	ORANGE JUICE	250 ML
½ CUP	RAISINS OR DRIED CRANBERRIES	125 ML
½ CUP	CHOPPED FRESH CILANTRO OR PARSLEY	125 ML

GREASE A 10-CUP (2.5 L) CASSEROLE DISH. IN A SAUCEPAN, BRING BROTH TO A BOIL. ADD COUSCOUS AND REMOVE FROM HEAT. COVER AND LET STAND FOR 5 MINUTES.

FLUFF WITH FORK. TRANSFER TO PREPARED CASSEROLE DISH. IN A SMALL SAUCEPAN OF BOILING SALTED WATER, COOK CARROTS FOR 3 MINUTES OR UNTIL TENDER-CRISP. RINSE IN COLD WATER; DRAIN. ADD CARROTS, RED PEPPER AND CHICKPEAS TO COUSCOUS IN CASSEROLE AND MIX WELL. IN A LARGE NONSTICK SKILLET, HEAT OIL OVER MEDIUM-HIGH HEAT. COOK ONION, GARLIC, GINGERROOT, CUMIN, CORIANDER, SALT AND CAYENNE, STIRRING, FOR 2 MINUTES. STIR IN ORANGE JUICE. BRING TO A BOIL. ADD RAISINS AND ORANGE ZEST. REMOVE FROM HEAT. STIR INTO COUSCOUS MIXTURE UNTIL WELL COMBINED. (CASSEROLE CAN BE PREPARED UP TO THIS POINT, COVERED AND REFRIGERATED FOR 1 DAY.)

COVER AND MICROWAVE ON HIGH FOR 7 TO 9 MINUTES (10 TO 12 MINUTES IF REFRIGERATED), STIRRING ONCE, OR UNTIL MIXTURE IS STEAMING. OR COVER AND BAKE IN PREHEATED 350°F (180°C) OVEN FOR 45 TO 50 MINUTES (10 MINUTES LONGER IF REFRIGERATED) OR UNTIL MIXTURE IS STEAMING. STIR IN CILANTRO. SERVES 4.

TIP: FRESH CILANTRO, ALSO CALLED CORIANDER AND CHINESE PARSLEY, LASTS ONLY A FEW DAYS IN THE FRIDGE BEFORE IT DETERIORATES AND TURNS TASTELESS. WASH CILANTRO WELL, SPIN DRY AND WRAP IN PAPER TOWELS; STORE IN PLASTIC BAG IN THE FRIDGE. LEAVE THE ROOTS ON — THEY KEEP THE LEAVES FRESH.

CHANA MASALA

1 TBSP	VEGETABLE OIL	15 ML
1 TBSP	BUTTER	15 ML
1	ONION, FINELY CHOPPED	1
1	JALAPEÑO PEPPER, SEEDED AND FINELY CHOPPED	1
2	CLOVES GARLIC, FINELY CHOPPED OR CRUSHED	2
2 TSP	GRATED GINGERROOT	10 ML
1 TBSP	GROUND CUMIN	15 ML
1 TSP	CHILI POWDER	5 ML
1	CAN (19 OZ/540 ML) CHICKPEAS, DRAINED AND RINSED	1
1	CAN (14 OZ/398 ML) DICED TOMATOES, WITH JUICE	1
1/3 CUP	CHOPPED FRESH CILANTRO	75 ML
1/2 CUP	COCONUT MILK OR HEAVY OR WHIPPING (35%) CREAM	125 ML
2 TBSP	FRESHLY SQUEEZED LEMON JUICE	30 ML
	SALT AND FRESHLY GROUND BLACK PEPPER	

IN A LARGE SKILLET, HEAT OIL AND BUTTER OVER MEDIUM-HIGH HEAT. ADD ONION AND JALAPEÑO; COOK, STIRRING, UNTIL SOFTENED. ADD GARLIC, GINGER, CUMIN AND CHILI POWDER; COOK, STIRRING, FOR 1 MINUTE. STIR IN CHICKPEAS, TOMATOES AND CILANTRO; BRING TO A SIMMER. REDUCE HEAT TO MEDIUM-LOW AND SIMMER, STIRRING OFTEN, UNTIL THICKENED. STIR IN COCONUT MILK AND LEMON JUICE. SEASON TO TASTE WITH SALT AND PEPPER. SIMMER UNTIL THICKENED TO YOUR LIKING; ADD EXTRA COCONUT MILK IF IT'S TOO THICK. SERVES 4.

ITALIAN-STYLE POACHED EGGS

FAST-AND-EASY RECIPE

FOR THOSE TIMES WHEN PLAIN POACHED EGGS JUST WON'T DO, HERE'S AN ITALIAN-INSPIRED VERSION THAT IS FLAVORFUL AND DELIGHTFULLY DIFFERENT. ENJOY IT AS A LIGHT DINNER OR FOR BRUNCH.

1	CAN (19 OZ/540 ML) CHUNKY TOMATOES WITH ROASTED GARLIC AND BASIL (SEE TIP, BELOW)	1
	SALT AND FRESHLY GROUND BLACK PEPPER	
4	LARGE EGGS	4
2	SLICES COUNTRY-STYLE BREAD, TOASTED	2

IN A SMALL SKILLET OVER MEDIUM HEAT, BRING TOMATOES TO A BOIL. TASTE AND SEASON WITH SALT AND BLACK PEPPER. REDUCE HEAT TO LOW. BREAK EGGS INTO PAN. COVER AND COOK UNTIL WHITES ARE SET AND YOLKS ARE STILL SOFT, 3 TO 4 MINUTES. SERVE OVER TOASTED BREAD. SERVES 2.

TIP: IF YOU DON'T HAVE A CAN OF SEASONED TOMATOES ON HAND, HERE'S HOW TO MAKE YOUR OWN. IN A SMALL SKILLET, HEAT 1 TBSP (15 ML) OLIVE OIL OVER MEDIUM HEAT. ADD 2 TBSP (30 ML) DICED ONION AND COOK, STIRRING, UNTIL SOFTENED, ABOUT 3 MINUTES. STIR IN 1 TSP (5 ML) MINCED GARLIC AND $\frac{1}{2}$ TSP (2 ML) DRIED ITALIAN SEASONING. COARSELY CHOP 2 CUPS (500 ML) TOMATOES OR USE 1 CAN (19 OZ/540 ML) TOMATOES, WITH JUICE, AND ADD TO PAN. BRING TO A BOIL. TASTE AND ADJUST SEASONING. REDUCE HEAT TO LOW AND CONTINUE WITH THE RECIPE.

POACHED EGGS ON SPICY LENTILS

SLOW COOKER RECIPE

THIS DELICIOUS COMBINATION IS A GREAT
COLD-WEATHER DISH. ADD THE CHILES IF YOU PREFER
A LITTLE SPICE AND ACCOMPANY WITH WARM INDIAN
BREAD, SUCH AS NAAN, AND HOT RICE.

1 TBSP	VEGETABLE OIL	15 ML
2	ONIONS, FINELY CHOPPED	2
1 TBSP	MINCED GARLIC	15 ML
1 TBSP	MINCED GINGERROOT	15 ML
1 TSP	GROUND CORIANDER	5 ML
1 TSP	GROUND CUMIN	5 ML
1 TSP	CRACKED BLACK PEPPERCORNS	5 ML
1 CUP	DRIED RED LENTILS, RINSED	250 ML
1	CAN (28 OZ/796 ML) TOMATOES, WITH JUICE, COARSELY CHOPPED	1
2 CUPS	READY-TO-USE VEGETABLE BROTH	500 ML
1 CUP	COCONUT MILK	250 ML
	SALT	
1	LONG GREEN CHILE PEPPER (OR 2 THAI BIRD'S-EYE CHILES), FINELY CHOPPED (OPTIONAL)	1
4	LARGE EGGS, POACHED (SEE TIPS, OPPOSITE)	4
	FINELY CHOPPED FRESH PARSLEY (OPTIONAL)	

IN A LARGE SKILLET, HEAT OIL OVER MEDIUM HEAT. ADD
ONIONS AND COOK, STIRRING, UNTIL SOFTENED, ABOUT
3 MINUTES. ADD GARLIC, GINGER, CORIANDER, CUMIN AND
PEPPERCORNS AND COOK, STIRRING, FOR 1 MINUTE. ADD
LENTILS, TOMATOES AND BROTH AND BRING TO A BOIL.

TRANSFER TO A MEDIUM (ABOUT 4-QUART) SLOW COOKER. (MIXTURE CAN BE COOLED, COVERED AND REFRIGERATED FOR UP TO 2 DAYS AT THIS POINT.)

COVER AND COOK ON LOW FOR 6 HOURS OR ON HIGH FOR 3 HOURS, UNTIL LENTILS ARE TENDER AND MIXTURE IS BUBBLY. STIR IN COCONUT MILK, SALT TO TASTE, AND CHILE PEPPER (IF USING). COVER AND COOK FOR 20 TO 30 MINUTES UNTIL HEATED THROUGH. WHEN READY TO SERVE, LADLE INTO SOUP BOWLS AND TOP EACH SERVING WITH A POACHED EGG. GARNISH WITH PARSLEY (IF USING). SERVES 4.

TIP: TO MAKE A VISUALLY PERFECT POACHED EGG, BUY EGG-POACHING RINGS AT A KITCHEN STORE OR USE THE RINGS FROM CANNING JARS.

TIP: TO POACH EGGS: IN A SAUCEPAN, BRING ABOUT 2 INCHES (5 CM) LIGHTLY SALTED WATER TO A BOIL OVER MEDIUM HEAT. REDUCE HEAT TO LOW AND DROP POACHING RINGS INTO WATER. BREAK EGGS, ONE AT A TIME, INTO A MEASURING CUP AND POUR ONE EGG INTO EACH RING. COOK UNTIL WHITES ARE SET AND CENTERS ARE STILL SOFT, 3 TO 4 MINUTES. REMOVE FROM WATER USING A SLOTTED SPOON.

TIP: IF YOU CHOOSE TO HALVE THIS RECIPE, USE A SMALL (1½- TO 3½-QUART) SLOW COOKER.

EGGS RANCHEROS WITH BLACK BEAN SAUCE

FAST-AND-EASY RECIPE

HERE IS AN ABSOLUTELY DELICIOUS AND NUTRITIOUS DINNER. USE LEFTOVER BEAN SAUCE AS A DIP FOR TORTILLA CHIPS; JUST REHEAT UNTIL IT IS HOT AND BUBBLING.

I TBSP	VEGETABLE OIL	15 ML
½ CUP	FINELY CHOPPED ONION	125 ML
I TSP	MINCED GARLIC	5 ML
I TSP	CUMIN SEEDS, TOASTED AND GROUND (SEE TIP, PAGE 55)	5 ML
½ TSP	SALT	2 ML
¼ TSP	FRESHLY GROUND BLACK PEPPER	I ML
I	CAN (19 OZ/540 ML) BLACK BEANS, DRAINED AND RINSED	I
½ CUP	TOMATO SALSA	125 ML
I CUP	SHREDDED MONTEREY JACK CHEESE	250 ML
8	TORTILLAS, WARMED	8
8	LARGE EGGS, POACHED (SEE TIPS, PAGE 223)	8

IN A SKILLET, HEAT OIL OVER MEDIUM HEAT. ADD ONION AND COOK, STIRRING, UNTIL SOFTENED, ABOUT 3 MINUTES. ADD GARLIC, CUMIN, SALT AND BLACK PEPPER AND COOK, STIRRING, FOR I MINUTE. ADD BEANS AND SALSA AND BRING TO A BOIL. ADD CHEESE AND STIR UNTIL MELTED, ABOUT I MINUTE. PLACE 4 TORTILLAS ON SERVING PLATES AND SPREAD WITH BEAN MIXTURE. PLACE 2 POACHED EGGS ON EACH BEAN-TOPPED TORTILLA. SERVE THE OTHER TORTILLA ON THE SIDE. SERVES 4.

6	LARGE EGGS	6
I TBSP	VEGETABLE OIL	15 ML
1/2 CUP	FINELY CHOPPED ONION	125 ML
I TSP	DRIED ITALIAN SEASONING	5 ML
1/2 TSP	SALT	2 ML
	FRESHLY GROUND BLACK PEPPER	
I	PACKAGE (10 OZ/300 G) FROZEN CHOPPED SPINACH, THAWED AND SQUEEZED DRY (OR ONE 10-OZ/300 G BAG SPINACH, STEMS REMOVED, CHOPPED)	I
1/4 CUP	FRESHLY GRATED PARMESAN CHEESE	60 ML
2 TBSP	SUN-DRIED TOMATO PESTO	30 ML

PREHEAT OVEN TO 425°F (220°C). IN A BOWL, LIGHTLY BEAT EGGS. SET ASIDE. IN AN OVENPROOF SKILLET, HEAT OIL OVER MEDIUM HEAT. ADD ONION AND COOK, STIRRING, UNTIL SOFTENED, ABOUT 3 MINUTES. STIR IN ITALIAN SEASONING, SALT, AND BLACK PEPPER TO TASTE. ADD SPINACH AND STIR WELL. REDUCE HEAT TO LOW. COVER AND COOK UNTIL SPINACH IS WILTED, ABOUT 5 MINUTES. SLOWLY POUR EGGS OVER SPINACH. INCREASE HEAT TO MEDIUM. COVER AND COOK UNTIL MIXTURE BEGINS TO FORM A CRUST ON THE BOTTOM, 2 TO 3 MINUTES. SPRINKLE WITH PARMESAN CHEESE AND TRANSFER PAN TO OVEN. BAKE, UNCOVERED, UNTIL EGGS ARE SET BUT FRITTATA IS STILL SOFT IN THE CENTER, ABOUT 3 MINUTES. CUT INTO WEDGES AND SERVE TOPPED WITH A DOLLOP OF PESTO. SERVES 2.

TIP: IF THE HANDLE OF YOUR SKILLET IS NOT OVENPROOF, WRAP IT IN FOIL.

CHEESE AND HASH BROWN OMELET

FAST-AND-EASY RECIPE

HERE'S A HEARTY, NO-NONSENSE DISH THAT IS A PARTICULAR FAVORITE WITH TEENAGERS, ALTHOUGH ADULTS ENJOY IT, TOO.

6	LARGE EGGS	6
1/4 TSP	SALT	1 ML
2 TBSP	VEGETABLE OIL, DIVIDED	30 ML
1 CUP	FROZEN HASH BROWN POTATOES	250 ML
	FRESHLY GROUND BLACK PEPPER	
1 CUP	SHREDDED CHEDDAR OR SWISS CHEESE	250 ML

PREHEAT OVEN TO 425°F (220°C). IN A BOWL, LIGHTLY BEAT EGGS AND SALT. SET ASIDE. IN AN OVENPROOF SKILLET, HEAT 1 TBSP (15 ML) OIL OVER MEDIUM HEAT. ADD POTATOES AND SEASON TO TASTE WITH BLACK PEPPER. COOK, STIRRING, UNTIL POTATOES ARE CRISP AND BROWNED, 7 TO 8 MINUTES. TRANSFER TO A PAPER TOWEL-LINED PLATE TO DRAIN AND WIPE SKILLET CLEAN. ADD THE REMAINING OIL TO SKILLET AND RETURN TO HEAT. ADD EGG MIXTURE AND COOK UNTIL MIXTURE BEGINS TO FORM A CRUST ON THE BOTTOM, ABOUT 2 MINUTES. SPRINKLE CHEESE EVENLY OVER TOP AND ARRANGE POTATOES EVENLY OVER CHEESE. BAKE UNTIL EGGS ARE SET AND CHEESE IS MELTED, 2 TO 3 MINUTES. SERVES 2.

TIP: IF THE HANDLE OF YOUR SKILLET IS NOT OVENPROOF, WRAP IT IN FOIL.

EGG FOO YUNG WITH CHINESE VEGETABLES

IN ADDITION TO BEING VERY TASTY, THIS DISH HAS A HEALTHY SERVING OF VEGETABLES.

6	LARGE EGGS, BEATEN	6
3 TBSP	FINELY CHOPPED GREEN ONIONS	45 ML
1/4 TSP	SALT	1 ML
	FRESHLY GROUND BLACK PEPPER	
1 TBSP	VEGETABLE OIL	15 ML
2 CUPS	FROZEN MIXED CHINESE VEGETABLES FOR STIR-FRY	500 ML
2 TBSP	SOY SAUCE	30 ML

PREHEAT OVEN TO 350°F (180°C). IN A BOWL, WHISK TOGETHER EGGS, GREEN ONIONS, SALT, AND BLACK PEPPER TO TASTE. SET ASIDE. IN AN OVENPROOF SKILLET, HEAT OIL OVER MEDIUM HEAT. ADD VEGETABLES AND STIR-FRY UNTIL TENDER, ABOUT 6 MINUTES. STIR IN SOY SAUCE. POUR EGG MIXTURE OVER VEGETABLES. BAKE UNTIL EGG IS FIRMLY SET, ABOUT 15 MINUTES. CUT INTO WEDGES AND SERVE. SERVES 4.

TIP: IF THE HANDLE OF YOUR SKILLET IS NOT OVENPROOF, WRAP IT IN FOIL.

VARIATION
CRAB FOO YUNG: STIR IN A 4-OZ (125 G) CAN OF CRABMEAT, DRAINED, WITH THE SOY SAUCE.

VARIATION
SHRIMP FOO YUNG: STIR IN A 3³⁄₄-OZ (106 G) CAN OF SHRIMP, DRAINED, OR 1/2 CUP (125 ML) COOKED SALAD SHRIMP WITH THE SOY SAUCE.

SOY-BRAISED TOFU

SLOW COOKER RECIPE

IT'S AMAZING HOW TOFU SOAKS UP THE MOUTH-WATERING ASIAN FLAVORS IN THIS RECIPE. USE THIS BRAISED TOFU AS A CENTERPIECE TO A MEAL OF VEGETARIAN DISHES.

1 LB	FIRM TOFU, DRAINED AND CUT INTO 1-INCH (2.5 CM) CUBES (SEE TIP, BELOW)	500 G
1/4 CUP	LIGHT SOY SAUCE	60 ML
1 TBSP	PURÉED GINGERROOT	15 ML
1 TBSP	PURE MAPLE SYRUP	15 ML
1 TBSP	TOASTED SESAME OIL	15 ML
1 TBSP	FRESHLY SQUEEZED LEMON JUICE	15 ML
1 TSP	PURÉED GARLIC	5 ML
1/2 TSP	CRACKED BLACK PEPPERCORNS	2 ML

IN A SMALL TO MEDIUM (1 1/2- TO 3 1/2-QUART) SLOW COOKER, COMBINE SOY SAUCE, GINGER, MAPLE SYRUP, TOASTED SESAME OIL, LEMON JUICE, GARLIC AND PEPPERCORNS. ADD TOFU AND TOSS GENTLY UNTIL COATED ON ALL SIDES. COVER AND REFRIGERATE FOR 1 HOUR.

TOSS WELL. COVER AND COOK ON LOW FOR 5 HOURS OR ON HIGH FOR 2 1/2 HOURS, UNTIL TOFU IS HOT AND HAS ABSORBED THE FLAVOR. MAKES ABOUT 3 CUPS (750 ML).

TIP: TO DRAIN TOFU: PLACE A LAYER OF PAPER TOWELS ON A PLATE. SET TOFU IN THE MIDDLE. COVER WITH ANOTHER LAYER OF PAPER TOWEL AND A HEAVY PLATE. SET ASIDE FOR 30 MINUTES. PEEL OFF PAPER AND CUT INTO CUBES.

FISH & SEAFOOD

EASY ROASTED SALMON

FAST-AND-EASY RECIPE

A FRESH FILLET OF SALMON TAKES ABOUT
10 MINUTES TO COOK — THAT'S REAL FOOD, FAST.

1	SALMON FILLET (ABOUT 1 LB/500 G)	1
1 TBSP	OLIVE OIL	15 ML
	SALT AND FRESHLY GROUND BLACK PEPPER	
1	LEMON, THINLY SLICED	1

PREHEAT OVEN TO 425°F (220°C). LINE A RIMMED BAKING SHEET WITH PARCHMENT PAPER OR FOIL. PLACE SALMON SKIN SIDE DOWN ON PREPARED BAKING SHEET. DRIZZLE WITH OIL AND SPRINKLE WITH SALT AND PEPPER. LAY LEMON SLICES ON TOP. BAKE FOR 10 MINUTES OR UNTIL THE EDGES FLAKE WITH A FORK BUT THE FISH IS STILL MOIST IN THE MIDDLE. SERVES 4.

VARIATION: SPREAD PESTO OVER THE SALMON IN PLACE OF THE OIL AND LEMON.

VARIATION: STIR TOGETHER 2 TBSP (30 ML) EACH BROWN SUGAR, BALSAMIC VINEGAR AND GRAINY MUSTARD. SPREAD OVER THE SALMON IN PLACE OF THE OIL AND LEMON.

VARIATION: STIR TOGETHER 1 CRUSHED GARLIC CLOVE, 1 TSP (5 ML) GRATED GINGERROOT AND 2 TBSP (30 ML) EACH BROWN SUGAR, SOY SAUCE AND RICE VINEGAR OR LIME JUICE. SPREAD OVER THE SALMON IN PLACE OF THE OIL AND LEMON.

THAI-STYLE SALMON CURRY

FAST-AND-EASY RECIPE

IF YOU'RE FOND OF THAI FOOD, HERE'S AN EASY WAY TO TASTE ITS UNIQUE FLAVORS.

1	CAN (14 OZ/398 ML) COCONUT MILK	1
1 to 2	FRESH CHILI PEPPERS, MINCED, OR 3 WHOLE DRIED RED CHILI PEPPERS	1 to 2
1	CAN (7½ OZ/213 G) SALMON, DRAINED	1
1 CUP	COOKED GREEN PEAS (SEE TIP, BELOW)	250 ML
2 TBSP	FISH SAUCE	25 ML
2 TBSP	LEMON JUICE	25 ML
1 TBSP	LIME JUICE	15 ML
1 TSP	PACKED BROWN SUGAR	5 ML
	FINELY CHOPPED FRESH CILANTRO (OPTIONAL)	
	HOT WHITE RICE OR NOODLES	

IN A SAUCEPAN OVER MEDIUM HEAT, COMBINE COCONUT MILK AND CHILI PEPPERS. BRING TO A SIMMER. ADD SALMON AND PEAS AND COOK, STIRRING, BEING CAREFUL NOT TO LET THE MIXTURE BOIL, FOR ABOUT 3 MINUTES. ADD FISH SAUCE, LEMON JUICE, LIME JUICE AND BROWN SUGAR AND COOK, STIRRING, FOR 1 MINUTE. TASTE FOR SEASONING, ADDING MORE FISH SAUCE, LEMON OR LIME JUICE, OR BROWN SUGAR, IF DESIRED. REMOVE DRIED PEPPERS, IF USING. POUR OVER RICE OR NOODLES. GARNISH WITH CILANTRO, IF USING. SERVE IMMEDIATELY. SERVES 2.

TIP: CANNED OR FROZEN PEAS WORK WELL IN THIS CURRY. IF USING CANNED PEAS, BE SURE TO DRAIN THEM BEFORE ADDING TO THE RECIPE. COOK FROZEN PEAS ACCORDING TO PACKAGE INSTRUCTIONS.

SALMON QUICHE

HERE'S A DELIGHTFULLY DIFFERENT
WEEKDAY DINNER OR A GREAT DISH FOR A BRUNCH OR
A BUFFET. ALTHOUGH IT COOKS FOR QUITE A WHILE,
IT DOESN'T TAKE LONG TO PREPARE.

CRUST

30	CHEESE-FLAVORED CRACKERS, SUCH AS RITZ (ABOUT HALF AN 8-OZ/250 G BOX)	30
1/4 CUP	BUTTER, MELTED	60 ML

FILLING

3 OZ	CREAM CHEESE, CUT INTO CUBES AND SOFTENED	90 G
3	LARGE EGGS	3
1 CUP	MILK	250 ML
1/2 TSP	SALT	2 ML
	FRESHLY GROUND BLACK PEPPER	
1	CAN (7 1/2 OZ/213 G) SALMON, INCLUDING JUICE AND BONES, SKIN REMOVED	1
1/4 CUP	CHOPPED GREEN ONION, PARSLEY OR DILL	60 ML
1	ROASTED RED BELL PEPPER (SEE TIPS, PAGE 149), COARSELY CHOPPED	1

CRUST: PREHEAT OVEN TO 400°F (200°C). IN A FOOD
PROCESSOR (SEE TIP, OPPOSITE), PULSE CRACKERS
UNTIL THEY RESEMBLE COARSE CRUMBS. IN A BOWL,
COMBINE CRACKER CRUMBS AND BUTTER. PRESS INTO A
9-INCH (23 CM) PIE PLATE. BAKE UNTIL GOLDEN, ABOUT
8 MINUTES. REDUCE HEAT TO 375°F (190°C).

FILLING: IN A FOOD PROCESSOR, COMBINE CREAM CHEESE
AND EGGS. PROCESS UNTIL SMOOTH. ADD MILK, SALT, AND

BLACK PEPPER TO TASTE AND PROCESS UNTIL BLENDED. ADD SALMON, GREEN ONION AND ROASTED PEPPER AND PULSE TWO OR THREE TIMES UNTIL COMBINED. POUR SALMON MIXTURE INTO WARM CRUST. BAKE UNTIL FILLING IS SET, 40 TO 45 MINUTES. SERVES 4.

TIP: THE QUICHE WILL BAKE MORE QUICKLY IF YOU USE A GLASS PIE PLATE.

TIP: YOU CAN MAKE THIS RECIPE USING A BLENDER INSTEAD OF A FOOD PROCESSOR. TO MAKE THE CRACKER CRUMBS, ADD THE CRACKERS TO THE BLENDER IN TWO OR THREE BATCHES AND PROCESS. TO MAKE THE BATTER, COMBINE THE CREAM CHEESE, EGGS, MILK AND SEASONINGS IN THE BLENDER JUG AND PROCESS UNTIL INTEGRATED. (STOP THE MACHINE AND SCRAPE DOWN THE SIDES ONCE OR TWICE.) GENTLY STIR THE SALMON, ONION AND ROASTED PEPPER INTO THE MIXTURE UNTIL COMBINED. CONTINUE WITH THE RECIPE.

VARIATION: ADD $1/4$ CUP (60 ML) FINELY CHOPPED CELERY WITH THE SALMON.

CRISPY ALMOND BAKED FISH

THIS EASY OVEN METHOD IS A PRACTICAL
WAY TO COOK WHITE FISH FILLETS, SUCH AS
SOLE, HADDOCK OR TURBOT.

1/2 CUP	SOFT FRESH BREAD CRUMBS	125 ML
1/3 CUP	SLICED BLANCHED ALMONDS	75 ML
1/2 TSP	DRIED TARRAGON OR BASIL	2 ML
1/2 TSP	GRATED ORANGE OR LEMON ZEST	2 ML
1 LB	FISH FILLETS, SUCH AS SOLE, HADDOCK OR TURBOT	500 G
2 TBSP	BUTTER, MELTED	30 ML
	SALT AND FRESHLY GROUND BLACK PEPPER	
	LEMON WEDGES	

PREHEAT OVEN TO 425°F (220°C). IN A FOOD PROCESSOR,
COMBINE BREAD CRUMBS, ALMONDS, TARRAGON AND
ORANGE ZEST. PROCESS, USING ON-OFF TURNS, UNTIL
ALMONDS ARE FINELY CHOPPED. WRAP FISH IN PAPER
TOWELS TO ABSORB EXCESS MOISTURE. BRUSH A RIMMED
BAKING SHEET WITH SOME OF THE MELTED BUTTER.
ARRANGE FILLETS ON SHEET IN SINGLE LAYER. BRUSH
TOPS WITH THE REMAINING BUTTER; SEASON WITH SALT
AND PEPPER. SPRINKLE CRUMB MIXTURE OVER FISH AND
PAT LIGHTLY. BAKE FOR 8 TO 10 MINUTES OR UNTIL FISH
FLAKES WHEN TESTED WITH A FORK. (TIME DEPENDS ON
THICKNESS OF FISH; INCREASE TIME ACCORDINGLY.) SERVE
WITH LEMON WEDGES. SERVES 3 TO 4.

SOLE FLORENTINE

IMPRESS YOUR GUESTS WITH THIS ELEGANT DISH, WHICH TAKES JUST MINUTES TO MAKE USING PREPARED ALFREDO SAUCE. SERVE WITH HOT WHITE RICE AND BABY CARROTS FOR A GREAT-TASTING MEAL.

I LB	SOLE FILLETS, THAWED IF FROZEN AND CUT IN HALF LENGTHWISE IF NECESSARY (SEE TIP, BELOW)	500 G
2 TBSP	FRESHLY SQUEEZED LEMON JUICE	30 ML
I TSP	PAPRIKA	5 ML
1/2 TSP	SALT	2 ML
	FRESHLY GROUND BLACK PEPPER	
I CUP	CHOPPED BABY SPINACH	250 ML
1/4 CUP	FINELY CHOPPED GREEN ONION	60 ML
I CUP	ALFREDO SAUCE	250 ML

PREHEAT OVEN TO 425°F (220°C). LIGHTLY GREASE A 6-CUP (1.5 L) SHALLOW BAKING DISH. SPRINKLE SOLE FILLETS EVENLY WITH LEMON JUICE, PAPRIKA, SALT AND BLACK PEPPER. SPRINKLE CHOPPED BABY SPINACH AND GREEN ONION EVENLY OVER EACH FILLET. STARTING AT NARROW END, ROLL UP, JELLY ROLL-STYLE, AND SECURE WITH A TOOTHPICK. PLACE FISH, SEAM SIDE DOWN, IN PREPARED BAKING DISH. COVER WITH ALFREDO SAUCE. BAKE UNTIL FISH FLAKES EASILY WITH A FORK, ABOUT 15 MINUTES. REMOVE TOOTHPICKS AND SERVE IMMEDIATELY. SERVES 4.

TIP: IF FILLETS ARE TOO WIDE TO ROLL EASILY OR TO FIT ATTRACTIVELY ON A PLATE, YOU WILL NEED TO CUT THEM IN HALF LENGTHWISE BEFORE PROCEEDING WITH THE RECIPE. ALSO, BEAR IN MIND THAT YOU WILL NEED 4 STRIPS OF SOLE TO PRODUCE 4 ROLL-UPS.

PAN-FRIED HALIBUT IN SPICY LEMON SAUCE

FAST-AND-EASY RECIPE

SERVE WITH STEAMED BROCCOLI AND PARSLEYED POTATOES FOR A TRADITIONAL FISH DINNER WITH A DIFFERENCE.

I LB	HALIBUT FILLETS OR OTHER FIRM WHITE FISH, SUCH AS SNAPPER OR SOLE, CUT INTO 4 PIECES	500 G
1/2 CUP	ALL-PURPOSE FLOUR	125 ML
2 TBSP	VEGETABLE OIL	30 ML
I TBSP	MINCED GARLIC	15 ML
I CUP	WHITE WINE	250 ML
1/2 CUP	FRESHLY SQUEEZED LEMON JUICE	125 ML
I TBSP	MINCED PICKLED BANANA PEPPER	15 ML
1/2 TSP	SALT	2 ML
	FRESHLY GROUND BLACK PEPPER	

PREHEAT OVEN TO 250°F (120°C). DIP FISH IN FLOUR TO COAT. SHAKE OFF AND DISCARD EXCESS. IN A SKILLET, HEAT OIL OVER MEDIUM HEAT. ADD FISH AND COOK, TURNING ONCE, UNTIL COOKED THROUGH AND OUTSIDE IS CRISP AND GOLDEN, ABOUT 4 MINUTES PER SIDE, DEPENDING UPON THE THICKNESS OF THE FISH. TRANSFER TO A WARM PLATTER AND KEEP WARM IN PREHEATED OVEN. RETURN PAN TO ELEMENT. ADD GARLIC TO PAN AND COOK, STIRRING, FOR I MINUTE. ADD WHITE WINE AND LEMON JUICE AND COOK, STIRRING, UNTIL REDUCED BY HALF, ABOUT 3 MINUTES. STIR IN MINCED BANANA PEPPER, SALT, AND BLACK PEPPER TO TASTE. POUR OVER FISH AND SERVE. SERVES 4.

PARMESAN-CRUSTED SNAPPER WITH TOMATO OLIVE SAUCE

FAST-AND-EASY RECIPE

HERE'S A QUICK AND EASY DISH THAT TAKES ADVANTAGE OF THE RICH MEDITERRANEAN FLAVORS OF BOTTLED ANTIPASTO SAUCE.

1 CUP	COARSE DRY BREAD CRUMBS, SUCH AS PANKO	250 ML
1/2 CUP	FRESHLY GRATED PARMESAN CHEESE	125 ML
1/2 TSP	SALT	2 ML
	FRESHLY GROUND BLACK PEPPER	
1 LB	SNAPPER OR OTHER FIRM WHITE FISH FILLETS, PATTED DRY, CUT INTO 4 PIECES	500 G
2 TBSP	MAYONNAISE	30 ML
1 TBSP	VEGETABLE OIL	15 ML
1/2 CUP	BOTTLED ANTIPASTO SAUCE (SEE TIP, BELOW)	125 ML

IN A BOWL, COMBINE BREAD CRUMBS, PARMESAN, SALT, AND BLACK PEPPER TO TASTE. SPREAD MIXTURE ON A PLATE. BRUSH FISH EVENLY WITH MAYONNAISE, THEN DIP IN CRUMB MIXTURE. IN A SKILLET, HEAT OIL OVER MEDIUM HEAT. ADD FISH AND COOK, TURNING ONCE, UNTIL IT FLAKES EASILY WHEN TESTED WITH A KNIFE AND OUTSIDE IS CRISP AND GOLDEN, ABOUT 3 MINUTES PER SIDE. SERVE IMMEDIATELY TOPPED WITH ANTIPASTO SAUCE. SERVES 4.

TIP: THERE ARE MANY KINDS OF ANTIPASTO SAUCE ON THE MARKET. WHEN MAKING THIS RECIPE, CHECK THE LABEL TO ENSURE THAT IT CONTAINS TOMATO AND BLACK OLIVES.

TILAPIA WITH LEMON CAPER SAUCE

THIS GARLICKY LEMON SAUCE IS THE PERFECT FOIL FOR QUICK-COOKING FISH FILLETS, AS WELL AS PORK OR CHICKEN CUTLETS. SERVE WITH ROASTED POTATO WEDGES AND STEAMED GREEN BEANS OR BROCCOLI.

1/3 CUP	DRY WHITE WINE	75 ML
1/3 CUP	CHICKEN STOCK (PAGE 42) OR READY-TO-USE CHICKEN BROTH	75 ML
1 TSP	GRATED LEMON ZEST	5 ML
1 TBSP	FRESHLY SQUEEZED LEMON JUICE	15 ML
1 TSP	DRIED FINES HERBES OR OREGANO	5 ML
1 TBSP	SMALL CAPERS, RINSED	15 ML
1	CLOVE GARLIC, FINELY CHOPPED	1
1/4 CUP	ALL-PURPOSE FLOUR	60 ML
1/2 TSP	SALT	2 ML
1/4 TSP	FRESHLY GROUND BLACK PEPPER	1 ML
1 1/4 LBS	TILAPIA FILLETS	625 G
1 TBSP	OLIVE OIL (APPROX.)	15 ML
1 TBSP	BUTTER (APPROX.)	15 ML

IN A GLASS MEASURE, COMBINE WINE, STOCK, LEMON ZEST AND JUICE, FINES HERBES, CAPERS AND GARLIC. ON A LARGE PLATE, COMBINE FLOUR, SALT AND PEPPER. PAT FISH DRY WITH PAPER TOWELS. LIGHTLY DREDGE IN SEASONED FLOUR, SHAKING OFF EXCESS. DISCARD EXCESS FLOUR MIXTURE. IN A LARGE NONSTICK SKILLET, HEAT 1 1/2 TSP (7 ML) EACH OIL AND BUTTER OVER MEDIUM-HIGH HEAT UNTIL FOAMY. COOK FISH, IN TWO BATCHES, FOR 1 TO 2 MINUTES PER SIDE OR UNTIL LIGHTLY BROWNED AND FISH FLAKES WHEN TESTED WITH A FORK, ADDING

MORE OIL AND BUTTER AS NEEDED BETWEEN BATCHES. TRANSFER FISH TO A SERVING PLATE AND KEEP WARM. REDUCE HEAT TO MEDIUM AND ADD WINE MIXTURE TO SKILLET. COOK, STIRRING, FOR ABOUT 2 MINUTES OR UNTIL SAUCE IS REDUCED AND SLIGHTLY THICKENED. POUR OVER FISH AND SERVE IMMEDIATELY. SERVES 4.

I NEVER GET TIRED OF HOUSEWORK.
I DON'T DO ANY!

GARLIC CHILI SHRIMP

FAST-AND-EASY RECIPE

WITH A BAG OF SHRIMP IN THE FREEZER AND TWO BASIC BOTTLED ASIAN SAUCES, YOU CAN MAKE THIS ZESTY CHINESE-INSPIRED DISH AT A MOMENT'S NOTICE. SERVE THIS ON A SMALL WHITE OVAL PLATTER TO EMPHASIZE ITS SIMPLICITY OR, FOR A MORE COLORFUL PRESENTATION, SPREAD OVER A BED OF LETTUCE LEAVES OR SLICED CUCUMBER SPIKED WITH HOT PEPPER FLAKES. ACCOMPANY WITH HOT WHITE RICE.

1 TBSP	VEGETABLE OIL	15 ML
1 LB	PEELED AND DEVEINED SHRIMP, THAWED IF FROZEN	500 G
1 TBSP	MINCED GARLIC	15 ML
2 TBSP	SWEET SHERRY, SAKE OR VODKA	30 ML
2 TBSP	SOY SAUCE	30 ML
1 to 2 TSP	ASIAN CHILI SAUCE	5 to 10 ML
2 TBSP	CHOPPED GREEN ONION	30 ML

IN A SKILLET, HEAT OIL OVER MEDIUM-HIGH HEAT. ADD SHRIMP AND COOK, STIRRING, UNTIL THEY FIRM UP AND TURN PINK, 3 TO 5 MINUTES. USING A SLOTTED SPOON, TRANSFER TO A PLATTER OR SERVING PLATE. ADD GARLIC TO PAN AND COOK, STIRRING, FOR 30 SECONDS. ADD SHERRY, SOY SAUCE AND ASIAN CHILI SAUCE AND STIR UNTIL MIXTURE BOILS, ABOUT 30 SECONDS. POUR OVER SHRIMP. GARNISH WITH GREEN ONION AND SERVE IMMEDIATELY. SERVES 4.

VARIATION: ADD 1 TSP (5 ML) CRACKED BLACK PEPPERCORNS ALONG WITH THE GARLIC.

SHRIMP IN TOMATO SAUCE WITH FETA

FAST-AND-EASY RECIPE

WITH ITS BOLD COMBINATION OF FLAVORS, THIS GREEK SPECIALTY WILL CATAPULT TO THE TOP OF YOUR LIST OF FAVORITES. SERVE OVER HOT WHITE RICE.

2 TBSP	VEGETABLE OIL	30 ML
I LB	PEELED AND DEVEINED SHRIMP, THAWED IF FROZEN	500 G
2 TBSP	MINCED GARLIC	30 ML
	FRESHLY GROUND BLACK PEPPER	
1/4 CUP	FRESHLY SQUEEZED LEMON JUICE	60 ML
I CUP	TOMATO SAUCE	250 ML
4 OZ	CRUMBLED FETA CHEESE (ABOUT I CUP/250 ML)	125 G

PREHEAT BROILER. IN A SKILLET, HEAT OIL OVER MEDIUM-HIGH HEAT. ADD SHRIMP AND COOK, STIRRING, UNTIL THEY FIRM UP AND TURN PINK, 3 TO 5 MINUTES. USING A SLOTTED SPOON, TRANSFER TO A 6-CUP (1.5 L) SHALLOW BAKING OR GRATIN DISH. REDUCE HEAT TO MEDIUM-LOW AND RETURN PAN TO ELEMENT. ADD GARLIC, AND BLACK PEPPER TO TASTE. COOK, STIRRING, FOR I MINUTE. ADD LEMON JUICE AND STIR. ADD TOMATO SAUCE AND BRING TO A SIMMER. POUR MIXTURE OVER SHRIMP. SPRINKLE WITH CHEESE. PLACE UNDER PREHEATED BROILER UNTIL CHEESE BEGINS TO MELT AND TURN BROWN, ABOUT 3 MINUTES. SERVES 4.

TIP: IF YOU LIKE THE FLAVOR OF LEMON, ADD I TSP (5 ML) GRATED LEMON ZEST ALONG WITH THE LEMON JUICE.

LOUISIANA SHRIMP

THIS SIGNATURE DISH OF NEW ORLEANS RELIES
ON A BASE OF GARLIC, CELERY AND GREEN PEPPER
IN A FRESH TOMATO SAUCE AND, OF COURSE,
HOT PEPPER SAUCE TO SPICE IT UP A NOTCH
OR TWO. SERVE OVER STEAMED RICE.

1 TBSP	BUTTER	15 ML
1	SMALL ONION, CHOPPED	1
4	GREEN ONIONS, CHOPPED	4
1	GREEN BELL PEPPER, FINELY CHOPPED	1
1/2 CUP	DICED CELERY	125 ML
2	CLOVES GARLIC, FINELY CHOPPED	2
1	BAY LEAF	1
1 TSP	CHOPPED FRESH THYME (OR 1/4 TSP/ 1 ML DRIED THYME)	5 ML
1/4 TSP	SALT	1 ML
	FRESHLY GROUND BLACK PEPPER	
1 1/2 CUPS	PEELED, SEEDED AND CHOPPED TOMATOES (SEE TIP, OPPOSITE)	375 ML
3 TBSP	ALL-PURPOSE FLOUR	45 ML
1 1/2 CUPS	FISH STOCK OR READY-TO-USE VEGETABLE BROTH	375 ML
1 LB	LARGE RAW SHRIMP, PEELED AND DEVEINED, WITH TAILS LEFT ON	500 G
2 TBSP	CHOPPED FRESH PARSLEY	30 ML
1/2 TSP	HOT PEPPER SAUCE (OR TO TASTE)	2 ML
2 TBSP	FRESHLY SQUEEZED LEMON JUICE	30 ML

IN A LARGE SAUCEPAN, MELT BUTTER OVER MEDIUM
HEAT. COOK ONION, GREEN ONIONS, GREEN PEPPER,
CELERY, GARLIC, BAY LEAF, THYME, SALT AND PEPPER,

STIRRING OFTEN, FOR 5 MINUTES OR UNTIL VEGETABLES ARE SOFTENED. ADD TOMATOES; COOK, STIRRING, FOR 5 MINUTES OR UNTIL SAUCE-LIKE. PLACE FLOUR IN A SMALL BOWL AND BLEND IN $1/3$ CUP (75 ML) STOCK UNTIL SMOOTH. ADD TO PAN ALONG WITH THE REMAINING STOCK. BRING TO A BOIL, STIRRING, UNTIL SLIGHTLY THICKENED. REDUCE HEAT, COVER AND SIMMER, STIRRING OCCASIONALLY, FOR 15 MINUTES. ADD SHRIMP, PARSLEY AND HOT PEPPER SAUCE. SIMMER FOR 3 TO 4 MINUTES OR UNTIL SHRIMP TURN PINK. REMOVE BAY LEAF; ADD LEMON JUICE AND SEASON TO TASTE WITH SALT AND PEPPER. SERVES 4.

TIP: USE ONLY RED RIPE TOMATOES, SUCH AS VINE-RIPENED, IN THIS ROBUST SHRIMP STEW. IF GOOD FRESH TOMATOES ARE UNAVAILABLE, SUBSTITUTE A 28-OZ (796 ML) CAN OF TOMATOES, DRAINED AND CHOPPED.

WE'VE BEEN THROUGH THICK AND THIN TOGETHER. YOU DO REMEMBER THIN, DON'T YOU?

COCONUT SHRIMP CURRY

FAST-AND-EASY RECIPE

THIS IS A VERSION OF THE BASIC COCONUT MILK CURRY SERVED ALL OVER THAILAND, BUT PARTICULARLY IN THE SOUTH, WHERE COCONUTS AND SHRIMP ARE ABUNDANT.

1 TBSP	VEGETABLE OIL	15 ML
1 LB	PEELED AND DEVEINED SHRIMP, THAWED IF FROZEN	500 G
	FRESHLY GROUND BLACK PEPPER	
1 TBSP	RED CURRY PASTE	15 ML
1 CUP	COCONUT MILK	250 ML
2 TBSP	FISH SAUCE (NAM PLA)	30 ML
2 TBSP	FRESHLY SQUEEZED LIME JUICE	30 ML
1 TBSP	GRANULATED SUGAR	15 ML

IN A SKILLET, HEAT OIL OVER MEDIUM-HIGH HEAT. ADD SHRIMP AND COOK, STIRRING, UNTIL FIRM AND PINK, 3 TO 5 MINUTES. SEASON WITH PEPPER. USING A SLOTTED SPOON, TRANSFER TO A DEEP PLATTER AND KEEP WARM. RETURN PAN TO ELEMENT. ADD RED CURRY PASTE AND COOK, STIRRING, UNTIL FRAGRANT, 1 TO 2 MINUTES. STIR IN COCONUT MILK, FISH SAUCE, LIME JUICE AND SUGAR. BRING TO A BOIL. SIMMER FOR 1 TO 2 MINUTES TO COMBINE FLAVORS. POUR OVER SHRIMP. SERVES 4.

TIP: FOR A SPICIER VERSION, INCREASE THE AMOUNT OF CURRY PASTE. BUT BE CAREFUL — A LITTLE GOES A LONG WAY.

TIP: GARNISH WITH CILANTRO SPRIGS AND/OR RED BELL PEPPER STRIPS.

CHICKEN & TURKEY

ONE-HOUR ROAST CHICKEN WITH SAGE AND GARLIC

WHO HAS TIME TO WAIT AROUND FOR A CHICKEN TO ROAST? TAKE AN HOUR OFF THE ROASTING TIME BY CUTTING THE BIRD OPEN ALONG THE BACKBONE, PLACING IT FLAT ON THE BROILER PAN AND BOOSTING THE OVEN TEMPERATURE. THE RESULT? A GOLDEN, SUCCULENT BIRD IN HALF THE TIME.

I	WHOLE CHICKEN (ABOUT 3½ LBS/1.75 KG)	I
I TBSP	BUTTER, SOFTENED	15 ML
2	CLOVES GARLIC, MINCED	2
I TBSP	MINCED FRESH SAGE (OR I TSP/5 ML DRIED SAGE)	15 ML
1½ TSP	GRATED LEMON ZEST	7 ML
½ TSP	SALT	2 ML
½ TSP	FRESHLY GROUND BLACK PEPPER	2 ML
2 TSP	OLIVE OIL	10 ML
¼ TSP	PAPRIKA	I ML

PREHEAT OVEN TO 400°F (200°C). GREASE A BROILER PAN. REMOVE GIBLETS AND NECK FROM CHICKEN. RINSE AND PAT CHICKEN DRY INSIDE AND OUT WITH PAPER TOWELS. USING HEAVY-DUTY KITCHEN SCISSORS, CUT CHICKEN OPEN ALONG BACKBONE; PRESS DOWN ON BREAST BONE TO FLATTEN SLIGHTLY AND ARRANGE SKIN SIDE UP ON RACK OF BROILER PAN. IN A BOWL, BLEND BUTTER WITH GARLIC, SAGE, LEMON ZEST, SALT AND PEPPER. GENTLY LIFT BREAST SKIN; USING A KNIFE OR SPATULA, SPREAD BUTTER MIXTURE UNDER SKIN TO COAT BREASTS AND PART OF LEGS. PRESS DOWN ON OUTSIDE SKIN TO SMOOTH AND SPREAD BUTTER MIXTURE. IN A SMALL

BOWL, COMBINE OLIVE OIL AND PAPRIKA; BRUSH OVER CHICKEN. ROAST CHICKEN FOR I HOUR OR UNTIL JUICES RUN CLEAR AND A MEAT THERMOMETER INSERTED IN THE THICKEST PART OF THE THIGH REGISTERS 165°F (74°C). TRANSFER CHICKEN TO A PLATTER. TENT WITH FOIL; LET REST 5 MINUTES BEFORE CARVING. SERVES 4.

TIP: IF YOU DON'T HAVE A RASP GRATER, SUCH AS A MICROPLANE, USE A ZESTER TO REMOVE LEMON ZEST IN THIN SHREDS, THEN FINELY CHOP WITH A KNIFE.

TIP: WHEN LEMONS ARE BARGAIN-PRICED, STOCK UP FOR THE FUTURE. GRATE THE ZEST AND SQUEEZE THE JUICE; PLACE IN SEPARATE CONTAINERS AND FREEZE.

IF YOU CAN'T PRONOUNCE IT,
IT'S REALLY GOOD FOR YOU.

BEST-EVER BAKED CHICKEN

REQUIRING ONLY ABOUT 5 MINUTES OF PREPARATION TIME, THIS CRISPY BAKED CHICKEN IS SO EASY AND DELICIOUS YOU'LL NEVER USE A PACKAGED MIX AGAIN. PANKO CREATES A PARTICULARLY CRUNCHY CRUST, BUT REGULAR BREAD CRUMBS WORK WELL, TOO.

1/4 CUP	MAYONNAISE	60 ML
2 TBSP	PREPARED SUN-DRIED TOMATO PESTO	30 ML
1/2 CUP	BREAD OR CRACKER CRUMBS	125 ML
1/4 CUP	FRESHLY GRATED PARMESAN CHEESE	60 ML
4	BONELESS SKINLESS CHICKEN BREASTS (ABOUT I LB/500 G)	4

PREHEAT OVEN TO 375°F (190°C). IN A SMALL BOWL, COMBINE MAYONNAISE AND PESTO. ON A PLATE, COMBINE BREAD CRUMBS AND CHEESE. BRUSH CHICKEN WITH MAYONNAISE MIXTURE ON ALL SIDES, THEN DIP INTO CRUMBS TO COAT THOROUGHLY. ARRANGE CHICKEN IN A SINGLE LAYER IN A SHALLOW BAKING DISH. BAKE IN PREHEATED OVEN UNTIL NO LONGER PINK INSIDE, ABOUT 30 MINUTES. SERVES 4.

VARIATION: ADD 2 TBSP (30 ML) FINELY CHOPPED FRESH PARSLEY TO THE BREAD CRUMB MIXTURE.

EVEN CLASSIER CHICKEN

A BRIDGE CLASSIC, MADE EVEN CLASSIER.

	BUTTER	
3	BONELESS SKINLESS CHICKEN BREASTS, CUT INTO BITE-SIZE PIECES	3
	FRESHLY GROUND BLACK PEPPER	
2 TBSP	VEGETABLE OIL	30 ML
1	HEAD BROCCOLI OR BUNCH ASPARAGUS	1
1	CAN (10 OZ/284 ML) CAN CREAM OF MUSHROOM OR ASPARAGUS SOUP	1
1/3 CUP	MAYONNAISE OR PLAIN YOGURT	75 ML
1 TBSP	FRESHLY SQUEEZED LEMON JUICE	15 ML
2 TSP	CURRY POWDER OR PASTE	10 ML
1 CUP	SHREDDED SHARP (OLD) CHEDDAR CHEESE	250 ML

PREHEAT OVEN TO 350°F (180°C). BUTTER AN 8-CUP (2 L) CASSEROLE DISH. SPRINKLE CHICKEN WITH PEPPER. IN A SKILLET, HEAT OIL OVER MEDIUM HEAT. ADD CHICKEN AND COOK, STIRRING, UNTIL WHITE ON ALL SIDES. REMOVE FROM HEAT AND SET ASIDE.

SEPARATE BROCCOLI INTO FLORETS, PEELING AND CHOPPING THE STALK, OR CUT ASPARAGUS INTO 1-INCH (2.5 CM) LENGTHS. IN A STEAMER BASKET SET OVER A POT OF SIMMERING WATER, STEAM UNTIL TENDER-CRISP.

ARRANGE BROCCOLI OR ASPARAGUS IN BOTTOM OF PREPARED CASSEROLE DISH. ARRANGE CHICKEN ON TOP. IN A MEDIUM BOWL, COMBINE SOUP, MAYONNAISE, LEMON JUICE AND CURRY POWDER. POUR OVER CHICKEN. SPRINKLE WITH CHEESE. BAKE FOR 30 TO 35 MINUTES OR UNTIL BUBBLY AND GOLDEN. SERVES 6.

OUR FAVORITE CHICKEN DISH

EVERYONE NEEDS AN ALL-PURPOSE CHICKEN DISH TO WHIP UP ON THE SPUR OF THE MOMENT. THIS ONE IS A BREEZE TO COOK AND ALWAYS A HIT. SERVE ALONGSIDE NOODLES OR RICE. ADD A SALAD AND YOU'VE GOT DINNER READY IN 30 MINUTES.

4	BONELESS SKINLESS CHICKEN BREASTS	4
2 TBSP	ALL-PURPOSE FLOUR	30 ML
1/2 TSP	SALT	2 ML
1/2 TSP	FRESHLY GROUND BLACK PEPPER	2 ML
I TBSP	BUTTER	15 ML
1/2 CUP	CHICKEN STOCK (PAGE 42) OR READY-TO-USE CHICKEN BROTH	125 ML
1/2 CUP	ORANGE JUICE OR MIXTURE OF JUICE AND DRY WHITE WINE	125 ML
I	LARGE CLOVE GARLIC, FINELY CHOPPED	I
1/2 TSP	DRIED ITALIAN HERBS OR BASIL	2 ML
1/4 TSP	GRANULATED SUGAR	I ML
I TBSP	CHOPPED FRESH PARSLEY OR CHIVES	15 ML

ON A CUTTING BOARD, USING A SHARP KNIFE, CUT EACH BREAST LENGTHWISE INTO TWO THIN PIECES. PLACE FLOUR IN A SHALLOW BOWL; SEASON WITH SALT AND PEPPER. COAT CHICKEN IN FLOUR MIXTURE, SHAKING OFF EXCESS. HEAT A LARGE NONSTICK SKILLET OVER MEDIUM-HIGH HEAT. ADD BUTTER; WHEN FOAMY, ADD CHICKEN PIECES. COOK 2 MINUTES PER SIDE OR UNTIL LIGHTLY BROWNED. TRANSFER TO A PLATE. REDUCE HEAT TO MEDIUM; ADD STOCK, ORANGE JUICE, GARLIC, ITALIAN HERBS AND SUGAR TO SKILLET. BRING TO A BOIL; COOK FOR I MINUTE OR UNTIL SLIGHTLY REDUCED. SEASON TO

TASTE WITH SALT AND PEPPER. RETURN CHICKEN TO SKILLET; REDUCE HEAT, COVER AND SIMMER FOR 5 MINUTES OR UNTIL NO LONGER PINK INSIDE AND SAUCE IS SLIGHTLY THICKENED. SERVE SPRINKLED WITH PARSLEY. SERVES 4.

TIP: VARY THE FLAVORS BY USING DIFFERENT HERBS, SUCH AS TARRAGON OR HERBES DE PROVENCE.

A FOOL AND HIS MONEY IS MY KIND OF GUY.

TUSCAN CHICKEN WITH SAGE

SLOW COOKER RECIPE

SERVE WITH A BASIC RISOTTO, A GREEN VEGETABLE, SUCH AS BROCCOLI OR SAUTÉED RAPINI, AND HOT CRUSTY BREAD TO SOAK UP THE SAUCE.

2 TBSP	OLIVE OIL	30 ML
2	ONIONS, FINELY CHOPPED	2
2	CLOVES GARLIC, MINCED	2
1 TSP	SALT	5 ML
1/2 TSP	CRACKED BLACK PEPPERCORNS	2 ML
1/2 CUP	FRESH SAGE LEAVES	125 ML
2 CUPS	DRY ROBUST RED WINE (SUCH AS CHIANTI)	500 ML
3 LBS	SKINLESS BONE-IN CHICKEN THIGHS (ABOUT 12 THIGHS)	1.5 KG

IN A SKILLET, HEAT OIL OVER MEDIUM HEAT. ADD ONIONS AND COOK, STIRRING, UNTIL SOFTENED, ABOUT 3 MINUTES. ADD GARLIC, SALT, PEPPERCORNS AND SAGE AND COOK, STIRRING, FOR 1 MINUTE. ADD WINE, BRING TO A BOIL AND COOK, STIRRING, UNTIL SAUCE IS REDUCED BY ONE-THIRD, ABOUT 5 MINUTES. (MIXTURE CAN BE COOLED, COVERED AND REFRIGERATED FOR UP TO 2 DAYS AT THIS POINT.)

ARRANGE CHICKEN EVENLY OVER BOTTOM OF A MEDIUM TO LARGE (3 1/2- TO 5-QUART) SLOW COOKER AND COVER WITH SAUCE. COVER AND COOK ON LOW FOR 6 HOURS OR ON HIGH FOR 3 HOURS, UNTIL JUICES RUN CLEAR WHEN CHICKEN IS PIERCED WITH A FORK. SERVE IMMEDIATELY. SERVES 6.

Indian-Spiced Chicken and Barley (page 258)

Just Peachy Pork (page 270)

Easy Pot Roast with Rich Tomato Gravy (page 274)

Spiced Roasted Cauliflower (page 297)

CHICKEN CURRY WITH RED PEPPERS

IN THE TIME IT TAKES TO COOK RICE OR PASTA, THIS STREAMLINED DISH IS READY TO SERVE.

I CUP	CHICKEN STOCK (PAGE 42) OR READY-TO-USE CHICKEN BROTH	250 ML
2 TSP	CORNSTARCH	10 ML
1/4 TSP	SALT	I ML
4 TSP	VEGETABLE OIL, DIVIDED	20 ML
I LB	BONELESS SKINLESS CHICKEN BREASTS, CUT INTO THIN STRIPS	500 G
2	CLOVES GARLIC, FINELY CHOPPED	2
I TBSP	MINCED GINGERROOT	15 ML
2 TSP	MILD CURRY PASTE (OR TO TASTE)	10 ML
2	LARGE RED BELL PEPPERS, CUT INTO THIN STRIPS	2
3	GREEN ONIONS, SLICED	3

IN A LIQUID GLASS MEASURE, COMBINE STOCK, CORNSTARCH AND SALT; SET ASIDE. IN A LARGE NONSTICK SKILLET, HEAT 2 TSP (10 ML) OIL OVER MEDIUM-HIGH HEAT; COOK CHICKEN, STIRRING OFTEN, FOR 5 MINUTES OR UNTIL NO LONGER PINK INSIDE. TRANSFER TO A PLATE. REDUCE HEAT TO MEDIUM; ADD THE REMAINING OIL; COOK GARLIC, GINGER AND CURRY PASTE, STIRRING, FOR I MINUTE. ADD PEPPERS; COOK, STIRRING, FOR 2 MINUTES. STIR RESERVED STOCK MIXTURE AND POUR INTO SKILLET; BRING TO A BOIL. COOK, STIRRING, UNTIL THICKENED. ADD CHICKEN AND GREEN ONIONS; COOK, STIRRING, FOR 2 MINUTES OR UNTIL HEATED THROUGH. SERVES 4.

CHICKEN PROVENÇAL

HERE'S A QUICK VERSION OF AN OLD CLASSIC, USING BONELESS SKINLESS CHICKEN BREASTS TO SPEED UP THE COOKING TIME. SERVE WITH FLUFFY WHITE RICE AND STEAMED BROCCOLI.

1 LB	BONELESS SKINLESS CHICKEN BREASTS, CUT INTO 1/2-INCH (1 CM) THICK SLICES	500 G
2 TBSP	FRESHLY SQUEEZED LEMON JUICE	30 ML
1/2 CUP	ALL-PURPOSE FLOUR	125 ML
2 TBSP	VEGETABLE OIL	30 ML
4	ANCHOVIES, CHOPPED (SEE TIP, OPPOSITE)	4
1 TBSP	MINCED GARLIC	15 ML
1 TSP	DRIED ITALIAN SEASONING	5 ML
1	CAN (28 OZ/796 ML) DICED TOMATOES, DRAINED	1
1/2 CUP	SLICED PITTED BLACK OLIVES	125 ML
	SALT AND FRESHLY GROUND BLACK PEPPER	
	FINELY CHOPPED FRESH PARSLEY	

PREHEAT OVEN TO 250°F (120°C). COMBINE CHICKEN AND LEMON JUICE IN A BOWL. PLACE FLOUR IN A SEALABLE PLASTIC BAG. ADD CHICKEN MIXTURE AND TOSS UNTIL THOROUGHLY AND EVENLY COATED WITH FLOUR. IN A SKILLET, HEAT OIL OVER MEDIUM HEAT. COOK CHICKEN, IN BATCHES, TURNING ONCE, UNTIL GOLDEN OUTSIDE AND NO LONGER PINK INSIDE, ABOUT 2 MINUTES PER SIDE. TRANSFER TO HEATPROOF DISH AND KEEP WARM IN PREHEATED OVEN. ADD ANCHOVIES TO SKILLET AND COOK, STIRRING, UNTIL DISSOLVED. ADD GARLIC AND ITALIAN

SEASONING AND COOK, STIRRING, FOR 1 MINUTE. ADD
TOMATOES AND BRING TO A BOIL. REDUCE HEAT TO LOW
AND SIMMER UNTIL SAUCE BEGINS TO THICKEN, ABOUT
5 MINUTES. STIR IN OLIVES AND HEAT THROUGH. SEASON
TO TASTE WITH SALT AND BLACK PEPPER. GARNISH WITH
PARSLEY. TO SERVE, POUR SAUCE INTO A DEEP PLATTER
OR SERVING BOWL. LAY CHICKEN OVER TOP. SERVES 4.

TIP: YOU CAN USE 4 TSP (20 ML) ANCHOVY PASTE IN
PLACE OF THE ANCHOVIES; STIR IN AFTER YOU HAVE
COOKED THE GARLIC.

VARIATION: ADD $\frac{1}{2}$ CUP (125 ML) RED OR WHITE WINE TO
THE PAN AFTER THE GARLIC AND ITALIAN SEASONING ARE
COOKED. COOK, STIRRING, UNTIL REDUCED BY HALF, ABOUT
3 MINUTES, THEN ADD THE TOMATOES.

CHICKEN PAPRIKA WITH NOODLES

ECONOMICAL GROUND MEATS PROVIDE VERSATILE OPTIONS FOR THE HARRIED COOK. SERVE THIS TASTY GROUND CHICKEN DISH WITH A SALAD OR GREEN VEGETABLE, SUCH AS BROCCOLI. DINNER IS READY IN ABOUT 30 MINUTES.

1 LB	LEAN GROUND CHICKEN OR TURKEY	500 G
1 TBSP	BUTTER	15 ML
1	ONION, CHOPPED	1
8 OZ	MUSHROOMS, SLICED	250 G
1 TBSP	PAPRIKA	15 ML
2 TBSP	ALL-PURPOSE FLOUR	30 ML
1 1/3 CUPS	CHICKEN STOCK (PAGE 42) OR READY-TO-USE CHICKEN BROTH	325 ML
1/2 CUP	SOUR CREAM	125 ML
2 TBSP	CHOPPED FRESH DILL OR PARSLEY	30 ML
	SALT AND FRESHLY GROUND BLACK PEPPER	
8 OZ	FETTUCCINE OR BROAD EGG NOODLES	250 G

IN A LARGE NONSTICK SKILLET OVER MEDIUM-HIGH HEAT, COOK CHICKEN, BREAKING UP WITH A WOODEN SPOON, FOR 5 MINUTES OR UNTIL NO LONGER PINK. TRANSFER TO A BOWL. MELT BUTTER IN SKILLET. ADD ONION, MUSHROOMS AND PAPRIKA; COOK, STIRRING OFTEN, FOR 3 MINUTES OR UNTIL VEGETABLES ARE SOFTENED. SPRINKLE WITH FLOUR; STIR IN STOCK AND RETURN CHICKEN TO SKILLET. BRING TO A BOIL; COOK, STIRRING, UNTIL THICKENED. REDUCE HEAT, COVER AND SIMMER FOR 5 MINUTES. REMOVE FROM HEAT AND STIR IN SOUR CREAM (IT MAY CURDLE

IF ADDED OVER THE HEAT) AND DILL; SEASON TO TASTE WITH SALT AND PEPPER.

MEANWHILE, COOK PASTA IN A LARGE POT OF BOILING SALTED WATER UNTIL TENDER BUT FIRM. DRAIN WELL. RETURN TO POT AND TOSS WITH CHICKEN MIXTURE. SERVE IMMEDIATELY. SERVES 4.

TIP: WHEN GROUND CHICKEN OR TURKEY IS BROWNED IN A SKILLET, IT DOESN'T TURN INTO A FINE CRUMBLE LIKE OTHER GROUND MEATS. OVERCOME THE PROBLEM BY PLACING THE COOKED CHICKEN IN A FOOD PROCESSOR AND CHOPPING IT USING ON-OFF TURNS TO BREAK UP MEAT LUMPS.

TIP: TO WASH OR NOT WASH MUSHROOMS? YOU CAN WIPE THEM WITH A DAMP CLOTH, IF YOU WISH. HOWEVER, I FEEL IT'S IMPORTANT TO WASH ALL PRODUCE THAT COMES INTO MY KITCHEN. I QUICKLY RINSE MUSHROOMS UNDER COLD WATER AND IMMEDIATELY WRAP IN A CLEAN, DRY KITCHEN TOWEL OR PAPER TOWELS TO ABSORB EXCESS MOISTURE.

INDIAN-SPICED CHICKEN AND BARLEY

SLOW COOKER RECIPE

*THIS IS A GREAT DISH FOR SUNDAY DINNER.
IT IS QUITE EASY TO MAKE, AND THE LIGHTLY
SPICED SAUCE IS DELECTABLE.*

3 LBS	SKINLESS BONE-IN CHICKEN THIGHS (ABOUT 12 THIGHS)	1.5 KG
3 TBSP	FRESHLY SQUEEZED LEMON JUICE	45 ML
1 TSP	GROUND TURMERIC	5 ML
1 TBSP	VEGETABLE OIL	15 ML
2	ONIONS, FINELY CHOPPED	2
4	STALKS CELERY, DICED	4
4	CLOVES GARLIC, MINCED	4
1 TBSP	MINCED GINGERROOT	15 ML
1 TBSP	GROUND CUMIN	15 ML
2 TSP	GROUND CORIANDER	10 ML
2	CARDAMOM PODS, SPLIT	2
$\frac{1}{2}$ TSP	SALT	2 ML
1 CUP	BARLEY, DRAINED AND RINSED (SEE TIP, OPPOSITE)	250 ML
1 CUP	CHICKEN STOCK (PAGE 42) OR READY-TO-USE CHICKEN BROTH	250 ML
1	CAN (28 OZ/796 ML) DICED TOMATOES, WITH JUICE	1
1	LONG RED OR GREEN CHILE PEPPER, FINELY CHOPPED (OR $\frac{1}{2}$ TSP/2 ML CAYENNE PEPPER)	1
1 CUP	FULL-FAT PLAIN YOGURT	250 ML
	FRESH CILANTRO SPRIGS (OPTIONAL)	

SPRINKLE CHICKEN EVENLY WITH LEMON JUICE AND TURMERIC AND ARRANGE OVER BOTTOM OF A MEDIUM TO LARGE (3$\frac{1}{2}$- TO 5-QUART) SLOW COOKER. IN A SKILLET, HEAT OIL OVER MEDIUM HEAT. ADD ONIONS AND CELERY AND COOK, STIRRING, UNTIL CELERY IS SOFTENED, ABOUT 5 MINUTES. ADD GARLIC AND GINGER AND COOK, STIRRING, FOR 1 MINUTE. ADD CUMIN, CORIANDER, CARDAMOM AND SALT AND COOK, STIRRING, FOR 1 MINUTE. ADD BARLEY AND TOSS TO COAT. ADD STOCK AND TOMATOES AND BRING TO A RAPID BOIL. (CHICKEN AND COOLED VEGETABLE MIXTURE CAN BE REFRIGERATED SEPARATELY FOR UP TO 2 DAYS AT THIS POINT.)

TRANSFER VEGETABLE MIXTURE TO SLOW COOKER. COVER AND COOK ON LOW FOR 6 HOURS OR ON HIGH FOR 3 HOURS, UNTIL JUICES RUN CLEAR WHEN CHICKEN IS PIERCED WITH A FORK. IN A SMALL BOWL, COMBINE CHILE PEPPER AND YOGURT. STIR INTO SLOW COOKER. COVER AND COOK ON HIGH FOR 20 MINUTES, UNTIL FLAVORS MELD. TO SERVE, LADLE INTO WARM BOWLS AND GARNISH WITH CILANTRO SPRIGS (IF USING). SERVES 6.

TIP: USE THE VARIETY OF BARLEY YOU PREFER — PEARLED, POT OR WHOLE. WHOLE (ALSO KNOWN AS HULLED) BARLEY IS THE MOST NUTRITIOUS FORM OF THE GRAIN. YOU COULD ALSO MAKE THIS DISH USING AN EQUAL QUANTITY OF WHEAT, SPELT OR KAMUT BERRIES.

TIP: IF YOU CHOOSE TO HALVE THIS RECIPE, USE A SMALL (2- TO 3-QUART) SLOW COOKER.

STIR-FRIED CHICKEN WITH VEGETABLES

THIS TASTY STIR-FRY TAKES ADVANTAGE OF QUICK-COOKING BONELESS SKINLESS CHICKEN AND FROZEN PRECUT CHINESE VEGETABLES TO MINIMIZE DINNER PREPARATION. SERVE WITH HOT WHITE RICE.

1 LB	BONELESS SKINLESS CHICKEN (BREASTS OR THIGHS), CUT INTO 1/2-INCH (1 CM) SLICES	500 G
2 TBSP	SOY SAUCE	30 ML
2 TBSP	SHERRY OR WHITE WINE	30 ML
	FRESHLY GROUND BLACK PEPPER	
2 TBSP	VEGETABLE OIL, DIVIDED	30 ML
1 TBSP	MINCED GARLIC	15 ML
1 LB	FROZEN PRECUT VEGETABLES FOR STIR-FRY	500 G
2 TBSP	HOISIN SAUCE	30 ML

IN A BOWL, COMBINE CHICKEN SLICES, SOY SAUCE, SHERRY, AND BLACK PEPPER TO TASTE. SET ASIDE. IN A SKILLET, HEAT 1 TBSP (15 ML) OIL OVER MEDIUM HEAT. COOK GARLIC AND VEGETABLES, STIRRING, UNTIL TENDER, ABOUT 6 MINUTES. TRANSFER TO A BOWL AND KEEP WARM. RETURN SKILLET TO MEDIUM HEAT AND ADD THE REMAINING OIL. ADD RESERVED CHICKEN MIXTURE. COOK, STIRRING, UNTIL CHICKEN IS NO LONGER PINK INSIDE, ABOUT 6 MINUTES. ADD HOISIN SAUCE AND STIR WELL TO COAT CHICKEN. ADD RESERVED VEGETABLES AND COOK, STIRRING, UNTIL MIXTURE IS HOT AND STEAMING, ABOUT 2 MINUTES. SERVES 4.

SPICY PEANUT CHICKEN

SURPRISE YOUR FAMILY WITH THIS EXOTIC STEW, WHICH IS EASILY MADE WITH PANTRY INGREDIENTS. SERVE OVER HOT WHITE RICE.

1 TBSP	VEGETABLE OIL	15 ML
1 LB	BONELESS SKINLESS CHICKEN, CUT INTO 1-INCH (2.5 CM) CUBES	500 G
1 CUP	FINELY CHOPPED ONION	250 ML
1 TBSP	MINCED GARLIC	15 ML
2 TSP	CURRY POWDER	10 ML
1 TSP	SALT	5 ML
	FRESHLY GROUND BLACK PEPPER	
1 CUP	CHOPPED RED OR GREEN BELL PEPPER	250 ML
1 TBSP	ALL-PURPOSE FLOUR	15 ML
2 CUPS	TOMATO JUICE	500 ML
1/4 CUP	PEANUT BUTTER	60 ML

IN A SKILLET, HEAT OIL OVER MEDIUM HEAT. ADD CHICKEN AND ONION AND COOK, STIRRING, UNTIL ONIONS ARE SOFTENED AND CHICKEN IS NO LONGER PINK INSIDE, ABOUT 8 MINUTES. ADD GARLIC, CURRY POWDER, SALT, AND BLACK PEPPER TO TASTE. COOK, STIRRING, FOR 1 MINUTE. ADD BELL PEPPER AND COOK, STIRRING, FOR 1 MINUTE. ADD FLOUR AND COOK, STIRRING, FOR 1 MINUTE. ADD TOMATO JUICE. BRING TO A BOIL. COOK, STIRRING, UNTIL THICKENED, ABOUT 5 MINUTES. ADD PEANUT BUTTER AND STIR UNTIL BLENDED. SERVES 4.

VARIATION: IF YOU PREFER A SPICIER RESULT, ADD 1 TSP (5 ML) ASIAN CHILI SAUCE ALONG WITH THE PEANUT BUTTER.

ORANGE AND ONION CHICKEN

FAST-AND-EASY RECIPE

USE THIS RECIPE TO DRESS UP A ROTISSERIE CHICKEN OR IF YOU HAVE LEFTOVER GRILLED OR BARBECUED CHICKEN. IF YOU'RE COOKING CHICKEN, COOK EXTRA AND REFRIGERATE LEFTOVERS TO MAKE THIS TASTY DISH FOR DINNER THE FOLLOWING DAY. THIS IS GREAT WITH HOT NOODLES OR FLUFFY WHITE RICE.

2	SMALL ROTISSERIE CHICKENS, QUARTERED (OR I LB/500 G SLICED COOKED CHICKEN BREASTS OR 4 GRILLED CHICKEN BREASTS)	2
I TBSP	VEGETABLE OIL	15 ML
I	RED ONION, SLICED ON THE VERTICAL (SEE TIP, OPPOSITE)	I
I CUP	ORANGE JUICE	250 ML
1/2 CUP	ORANGE MARMALADE	125 ML
I TSP	SOY SAUCE	5 ML
I TBSP	CORNSTARCH, DISSOLVED IN 2 TBSP (30 ML) WATER	15 ML

IN A BAKING DISH OR MICROWAVE-SAFE DISH, HEAT CHICKEN UNTIL WARM (SEE TIP, OPPOSITE). IN A SKILLET, HEAT OIL OVER MEDIUM HEAT. ADD ONION AND COOK, STIRRING, UNTIL IT BEGINS TO GLAZE, ABOUT 3 MINUTES. ADD ORANGE JUICE, ORANGE MARMALADE AND SOY SAUCE. COOK, STIRRING, UNTIL MARMALADE DISSOLVES AND MIXTURE REACHES A SIMMER, ABOUT 3 MINUTES. ADD CORNSTARCH MIXTURE AND STIR JUST UNTIL IT THICKENS (THIS WILL HAPPEN VERY QUICKLY). REMOVE FROM HEAT, POUR OVER WARM CHICKEN AND SERVE IMMEDIATELY. SERVES 4.

TIP: SLICING THE ONION ON THE VERTICAL PRODUCES NICELY SIZED SLICES THAT LOOK VERY ATTRACTIVE IN THIS SAUCE. PEEL THE ONION AND SLICE IT IN HALF VERTICALLY. LAY THE FLAT SIDE DOWN ON A CUTTING BOARD AND CUT THIN CRESCENT-SHAPED SLICES.

TIP: LIKELY YOUR SUPERMARKET HAS A ROTISSERIE OVEN THAT COOKS SUCCULENT CHICKENS FOR YOU TO TAKE HOME. HOW YOU REHEAT A SUPERMARKET CHICKEN IS A MATTER OF CHOICE. YOU CAN PLACE THE CHICKEN IN AN OVEN-TO-TABLE BAKING DISH AND WARM IN A PREHEATED 350°F (180°C) OVEN FOR 15 MINUTES. ALTERNATIVELY, MICROWAVE, COVERED, IN A MICROWAVE-SAFE DISH ON HIGH FOR ABOUT 5 MINUTES OR UNTIL CHICKEN IS HEATED THROUGH.

I NAMED MY DOG FIVE MILES. NOW, I CAN TELL PEOPLE I WALK FIVE MILES EVERY DAY.

YUMMY PARMESAN CHICKEN FINGERS

WHAT A RELIEF, WHEN YOU COME HOME FROM WORK, TO KNOW YOU CAN COUNT ON THESE TASTY CHICKEN FINGERS STASHED IN YOUR FREEZER. ROUND OUT THE MEAL WITH RICE AND A STEAMED VEGETABLE, SUCH AS BROCCOLI, FOR A DINNER THAT'S ON THE TABLE IN 30 MINUTES.

1/2 CUP	FINELY CRUSHED SODA CRACKER CRUMBS (ABOUT 16 CRACKERS)	125 ML
1/3 CUP	FRESHLY GRATED PARMESAN CHEESE	75 ML
1/2 TSP	DRIED BASIL	2 ML
1/2 TSP	DRIED MARJORAM	2 ML
1/2 TSP	PAPRIKA	2 ML
1/2 TSP	SALT	2 ML
1/4 TSP	FRESHLY GROUND BLACK PEPPER	1 ML
4	SMALL BONELESS SKINLESS CHICKEN BREASTS	4
1	LARGE EGG	1
2 TBSP	BUTTER	30 ML
1	CLOVE GARLIC, MINCED	1

PREHEAT OVEN TO 400°F (200°C). GREASE THE RACK OF A RIMMED BAKING SHEET. IN A FOOD PROCESSOR, COMBINE CRACKER CRUMBS, PARMESAN CHEESE, BASIL, MARJORAM, PAPRIKA, SALT AND PEPPER. PROCESS TO MAKE FINE CRUMBS. PLACE IN A SHALLOW BOWL. CUT CHICKEN BREASTS INTO 4 STRIPS EACH. IN A BOWL, BEAT EGG; ADD CHICKEN STRIPS. USING A FORK, DIP CHICKEN STRIPS IN CRUMB MIXTURE UNTIL EVENLY COATED. DISCARD ANY EXCESS EGG AND CRUMB MIXTURE. ARRANGE

ON GREASED RACK SET ON BAKING SHEET. IN SMALL BOWL, MICROWAVE BUTTER AND GARLIC AT HIGH FOR 45 SECONDS OR UNTIL MELTED. BRUSH CHICKEN STRIPS WITH MELTED BUTTER MIXTURE. BAKE FOR 15 MINUTES OR UNTIL NO LONGER PINK IN CENTER. (IF FROZEN, BAKE FOR UP TO 25 MINUTES.) SERVES 4.

TIP: YOU CAN ALSO MAKE EXTRA BATCHES OF THE CRUMB MIXTURE AND STORE IN THE FREEZER.

TIP: INSTEAD OF BONELESS CHICKEN BREASTS, PREPARE SKINLESS CHICKEN DRUMSTICKS IN THE SAME WAY, BUT BAKE IN A 375°F (190°C) OVEN FOR 40 TO 45 MINUTES OR UNTIL TENDER.

ITALIAN-STYLE CHICKEN CUTLETS

FAST-AND-EASY RECIPE

CHICKEN CUTLETS ARE A GREAT MEALTIME SOLUTION.

I LB	CHICKEN BREAST CUTLETS	500 G
1/4 CUP	FRESHLY SQUEEZED LEMON JUICE	60 ML
1/4 CUP	ALL-PURPOSE FLOUR	60 ML
I TSP	DRIED ITALIAN SEASONING	5 ML
1/2 TSP	FRESHLY GROUND BLACK PEPPER	2 ML
2 TBSP	VEGETABLE OIL, DIVIDED	30 ML
2 CUPS	WASHED BABY SPINACH	500 ML
I CUP	TOMATO SAUCE	250 ML
2 TBSP	FRESHLY GRATED PARMESAN CHEESE	30 ML

PREHEAT OVEN TO 250°F (120°C). DIP EACH CUTLET IN LEMON JUICE UNTIL COATED. ON A PLATE, COMBINE FLOUR, ITALIAN SEASONING, AND BLACK PEPPER. DIP CHICKEN INTO FLOUR MIXTURE TO COAT EVENLY ON BOTH SIDES, SHAKING OFF AND DISCARDING EXCESS. IN A SKILLET, HEAT I TBSP (15 ML) OIL OVER MEDIUM-HIGH HEAT. SAUTÉ CHICKEN, IN BATCHES IF NECESSARY, UNTIL BROWNED OUTSIDE AND NO LONGER PINK INSIDE, 2 TO 3 MINUTES PER SIDE. TRANSFER TO A PLATTER AND KEEP WARM IN PREHEATED OVEN WHILE MAKING THE SAUCE. REDUCE HEAT TO MEDIUM-LOW AND ADD THE REMAINING OIL TO PAN, IF NECESSARY. ADD SPINACH AND COOK, STIRRING, UNTIL WILTED. ADD TOMATO SAUCE. BRING TO A BOIL AND COOK, STIRRING, FOR I MINUTE. ADD PARMESAN AND STIR UNTIL CHEESE MELTS. POUR SAUCE OVER CHICKEN AND SERVE IMMEDIATELY. SERVES 4.

CHICKEN MEATLOAF

*THIS ITALIAN-INSPIRED MEATLOAF IS SURE
TO BECOME A FAMILY FAVORITE.*

1 LB	LEAN GROUND CHICKEN, TURKEY OR BEEF	500 G
8 OZ	MILD ITALIAN PORK, BEEF OR CHICKEN SAUSAGE (BULK OR CASINGS REMOVED)	250 G
1 CUP	SHREDDED MOZZARELLA OR PROVOLONE CHEESE	250 ML
1 CUP	SOFT FRESH ITALIAN BREAD CRUMBS	250 ML
1	LARGE EGG	1
1 CUP	TOMATO PASTA SAUCE, DIVIDED	250 ML
2 TBSP	BASIL PESTO	30 ML
1	SMALL ONION, FINELY CHOPPED	1
1	CLOVE GARLIC, FINELY CHOPPED	1
1/2 TSP	SALT	2 ML
1/2 TSP	FRESHLY GROUND BLACK PEPPER	2 ML

PREHEAT OVEN TO 375°F (190°C). GREASE A 9- BY 5-INCH (23 BY 12.5 CM) LOAF PAN. IN A BOWL, COMBINE CHICKEN, SAUSAGE MEAT, CHEESE AND BREAD CRUMBS. IN ANOTHER BOWL, BEAT EGG. STIR IN 1/2 CUP (125 ML) PASTA SAUCE, PESTO, ONION, GARLIC, SALT AND PEPPER. POUR OVER CHICKEN MIXTURE AND GENTLY MIX UNTIL EVENLY COMBINED. PRESS MEAT MIXTURE INTO PREPARED LOAF PAN. SPREAD THE REMAINING PASTA SAUCE OVER TOP. BAKE FOR 55 TO 60 MINUTES OR UNTIL A MEAT THERMOMETER INSERTED IN CENTER REGISTERS 165°F (74°C). LET STAND FOR 5 MINUTES. DRAIN PAN JUICES; TURN OUT ONTO A PLATE AND CUT INTO THICK SLICES.

SERVES 6.

QUICK TURKEY CURRY

THIS RECIPE WILL MAKE YOU WANT TO ROAST A TURKEY JUST SO YOU HAVE SOME LEFTOVERS ON HAND. BUT IF TIME DOES NOT PERMIT, BUY A ROASTED CHICKEN FROM THE DELI SECTION OF THE SUPERMARKET AND USE THE DICED MEAT IN THIS NO-FUSS DISH.

2 TSP	VEGETABLE OIL	10 ML
1	SMALL ONION, CHOPPED	1
1	LARGE CLOVE GARLIC, FINELY CHOPPED	1
2 TSP	MINCED GINGERROOT	10 ML
1	APPLE, PEELED AND CHOPPED	1
1/2 CUP	FINELY DICED CELERY	125 ML
2 TSP	MILD CURRY PASTE (OR TO TASTE)	10 ML
1 TBSP	ALL-PURPOSE FLOUR	15 ML
1 1/3 CUPS	CHICKEN STOCK (PAGE 42) OR READY-TO-USE CHICKEN BROTH	325 ML
3 TBSP	MANGO CHUTNEY	45 ML
2 CUPS	DICED COOKED TURKEY OR CHICKEN	500 ML
1/4 CUP	RAISINS	60 ML
	SALT AND FRESHLY GROUND BLACK PEPPER	

IN A LARGE NONSTICK SKILLET, HEAT OIL OVER MEDIUM HEAT. ADD ONION, GARLIC, GINGER, APPLE, CELERY AND CURRY PASTE; COOK, STIRRING, FOR 5 MINUTES OR UNTIL SOFTENED. BLEND IN FLOUR; ADD CHICKEN STOCK AND CHUTNEY. COOK, STIRRING, UNTIL SAUCE COMES TO A BOIL AND THICKENS. STIR IN TURKEY AND RAISINS; SEASON TO TASTE WITH SALT AND PEPPER. COOK FOR 3 MINUTES OR UNTIL HEATED THROUGH. SERVES 4.

TIP: SERVE OVER BASMATI RICE AND SPRINKLE WITH CHOPPED CILANTRO, IF DESIRED.

PORK, LAMB & BEEF

JUST PEACHY PORK

LOADED WITH PEACHES, THIS SWEET AND TANGY SAUCE IS A GREAT ACCOMPANIMENT FOR PORK. SERVE OVER HOT WHITE RICE AND ADD AN ASSORTMENT OF STEAMED VEGETABLES FOR A DELIGHTFULLY DIFFERENT MEAL.

1	CAN (14 OZ/398 ML) SLICED PEACHES, DRAINED, 1/4 CUP (60 ML) SYRUP RESERVED	1
1 CUP	FINELY CHOPPED GREEN BELL PEPPER (OR 1 1/2 CUPS/375 ML FROZEN MIXED BELL PEPPER STRIPS)	250 ML
1/2 CUP	BARBECUE SAUCE	125 ML
1 TBSP	DIJON MUSTARD	15 ML
1 LB	PORK TENDERLOIN, CUT INTO 1/2-INCH (1 CM) THICK SLICES	500 G

PREHEAT OVEN TO 350°F (180°C). IN A SAUCEPAN OVER MEDIUM HEAT, COMBINE PEACHES, RESERVED SYRUP, GREEN PEPPER, BARBECUE SAUCE AND MUSTARD. BRING TO A BOIL. REDUCE HEAT TO LOW AND SIMMER FOR 3 MINUTES. PLACE PORK SLICES IN A SINGLE LAYER IN AN 8-CUP (2 L) BAKING OR GRATIN DISH. POUR SAUCE OVER MEAT. BAKE UNTIL JUST A HINT OF PINK REMAINS, ABOUT 30 MINUTES. SERVES 4.

ORANGE HOISIN PORK

2 TSP	GRATED ORANGE ZEST	10 ML
1/3 CUP	FRESHLY SQUEEZED ORANGE JUICE	75 ML
3 TBSP	HOISIN SAUCE	45 ML
2 TBSP	RICE VINEGAR	30 ML
1 TBSP	SOY SAUCE	15 ML
1 TBSP	LIQUID HONEY	15 ML
2 TSP	CORNSTARCH	10 ML
2 TBSP	VEGETABLE OIL, DIVIDED	30 ML
1 LB	LEAN BONELESS PORK, CUT INTO VERY THIN STRIPS	500 G
1 TBSP	MINCED GINGERROOT	15 ML
2	CLOVES GARLIC, FINELY CHOPPED	2
2	SMALL ZUCCHINI, HALVED LENGTHWISE, THEN SLICED CROSSWISE	2
1	RED BELL PEPPER, CUT INTO THIN 2-INCH (5 CM) STRIPS	1

IN A GLASS MEASURE, STIR TOGETHER ORANGE ZEST AND JUICE, HOISIN SAUCE, VINEGAR, SOY SAUCE, HONEY AND CORNSTARCH UNTIL SMOOTH. IN A LARGE NONSTICK SKILLET OR WOK, HEAT 1 TBSP (15 ML) OIL OVER MEDIUM-HIGH HEAT. COOK PORK, STIRRING, FOR 2 MINUTES OR UNTIL LIGHTLY COLORED. TRANSFER TO A PLATE. ADD THE REMAINING OIL TO SKILLET. COOK GINGER AND GARLIC, STIRRING, FOR 30 SECONDS OR UNTIL FRAGRANT. ADD ZUCCHINI AND RED PEPPER; COOK, STIRRING, FOR 2 MINUTES OR UNTIL VEGETABLES ARE TENDER-CRISP. RETURN PORK TO SKILLET AND STIR IN ORANGE JUICE MIXTURE. COOK, STIRRING, FOR 1 TO 2 MINUTES OR UNTIL SAUCE THICKENS. SERVE IMMEDIATELY. SERVES 4.

LAMB SHANKS BRAISED IN GUINNESS

SLOW COOKER RECIPE

THIS IRISH-INSPIRED COMBINATION IS A CLASSIC. ADD A GREEN VEGETABLE AND MOUNDS OF MASHED POTATOES, SPRINKLED WITH FINELY CHOPPED GREEN ONION, TO SOAK UP THE DELICIOUS SAUCE.

1/4 CUP	ALL-PURPOSE FLOUR	60 ML
I TSP	SALT	5 ML
1/2 TSP	CRACKED BLACK PEPPERCORNS	2 ML
4 LBS	LAMB SHANKS, WHOLE OR SLICED (SEE TIP, OPPOSITE)	2 KG
2 TBSP	VEGETABLE OIL	30 ML
4	ONIONS, FINELY CHOPPED	4
4	CLOVES GARLIC, MINCED	4
I TSP	DRIED THYME	5 ML
2 TBSP	TOMATO PASTE	30 ML
1 1/2 CUPS	GUINNESS OR OTHER DARK BEER	375 ML
I CUP	HEARTY BEEF STOCK (PAGE 43) OR READY-TO-USE BEEF BROTH	250 ML

ON A PLATE, COMBINE FLOUR, SALT AND PEPPERCORNS. LIGHTLY COAT LAMB SHANKS WITH MIXTURE, SHAKING OFF THE EXCESS. SET ANY REMAINING FLOUR MIXTURE ASIDE. IN A SKILLET, HEAT OIL OVER MEDIUM-HIGH HEAT. ADD LAMB, IN BATCHES, AND COOK, TURNING, UNTIL LIGHTLY BROWNED, ABOUT 6 MINUTES PER BATCH. TRANSFER TO A LARGE (ABOUT 5-QUART) SLOW COOKER. REDUCE STOVETOP HEAT TO MEDIUM. ADD ONIONS TO PAN AND COOK, STIRRING, UNTIL SOFTENED, ABOUT 3 MINUTES. ADD GARLIC, THYME AND RESERVED FLOUR MIXTURE AND

COOK, STIRRING, FOR 1 MINUTE. STIR IN TOMATO PASTE, BEER AND STOCK AND COOK, STIRRING, UNTIL MIXTURE IS THICKENED. POUR OVER MEAT. COVER AND COOK ON LOW FOR 10 HOURS OR ON HIGH FOR 5 HOURS, UNTIL MEAT IS FALLING OFF THE BONE. SERVES 4 TO 6.

TIP: WHETHER YOU COOK THE LAMB SHANKS WHOLE OR HAVE THEM CUT INTO PIECES IS A MATTER OF PREFERENCE. HOWEVER, IF THE SHANKS ARE LEFT WHOLE, YOU WILL BE ABLE TO SERVE ONLY FOUR PEOPLE — EACH WILL RECEIVE ONE LARGE SHANK.

TIP: IF YOU CHOOSE TO HALVE THIS RECIPE, USE A SMALL (2- TO $3\frac{1}{2}$-QUART) SLOW COOKER.

THIS BEER IS MAKING ME AWESOME.

EASY POT ROAST WITH RICH TOMATO GRAVY

SLOW COOKER RECIPE

THERE'S NO SUBSTITUTE FOR AN OLD-FASHIONED POT ROAST. ITS APPETIZING AROMAS, WAFTING THROUGH THE HOUSE, ARE EVERY BIT AS GOOD AS THE MEAL ITSELF. THIS EASY-TO-MAKE VERSION USES A CAN OF TOMATO SOUP TO CREATE A SUMPTUOUS GRAVY. SERVE WITH PLENTY OF MASHED POTATOES TO SOAK UP THE SAUCE.

I	BONELESS BEEF POT ROAST, CHUCK, BLADE OR CROSS RIB (3 TO 4 LBS/ 1.5 TO 2 KG)	I
I TBSP	VEGETABLE OIL	15 ML
2	ONIONS, THINLY SLICED	2
3	STALKS CELERY, THINLY SLICED	3
3	LARGE CARROTS, CUT INTO CHUNKS	3
2	CLOVES GARLIC, MINCED	2
I TSP	DRY MUSTARD	5 ML
1/2 TSP	DRIED THYME	2 ML
1/2 TSP	CRACKED BLACK PEPPERCORNS	2 ML
2 TBSP	ALL-PURPOSE FLOUR	30 ML
I	CAN (10 OZ/284 ML) CONDENSED TOMATO SOUP	I
1/2 CUP	HEARTY BEEF STOCK (PAGE 43) OR READY-TO-USE BEEF BROTH	125 ML
2 TBSP	PACKED BROWN SUGAR (OPTIONAL)	30 ML
2 TBSP	BALSAMIC OR RED WINE VINEGAR (OPTIONAL)	30 ML
I TBSP	WORCESTERSHIRE SAUCE	15 ML

PAT ROAST DRY WITH PAPER TOWEL. IN A SKILLET, HEAT OIL OVER MEDIUM-HIGH HEAT. ADD ROAST AND COOK, TURNING, UNTIL BROWN ON ALL SIDES, ABOUT 10 MINUTES. TRANSFER TO A LARGE (MINIMUM 5-QUART) SLOW COOKER. REDUCE STOVETOP HEAT TO MEDIUM. ADD ONIONS, CELERY AND CARROTS TO PAN AND COOK, STIRRING, UNTIL VEGETABLES ARE SOFTENED, ABOUT 7 MINUTES. ADD GARLIC, MUSTARD, THYME AND PEPPERCORNS AND COOK, STIRRING, FOR 1 MINUTE. SPRINKLE WITH FLOUR AND STIR. ADD TOMATO SOUP AND BROTH AND COOK, STIRRING, UNTIL THICKENED. POUR MIXTURE OVER ROAST, COVER AND COOK ON LOW FOR 8 HOURS OR ON HIGH FOR 4 HOURS, UNTIL MEAT IS VERY TENDER. REMOVE ROAST FROM SLOW COOKER AND PLACE ON SERVING PLATTER. STIR BROWN SUGAR (IF USING), VINEGAR (IF USING) AND WORCESTERSHIRE SAUCE INTO PAN JUICES. POUR SAUCE OVER ROAST OR SERVE IN A SEPARATE SAUCEBOAT. SERVE PIPING HOT. SERVES 6 TO 8.

TIP: THERE IS NO ADDED SALT IN THIS RECIPE BECAUSE THE TOMATO SOUP IS FAIRLY HIGH IN SODIUM. TASTE THE SAUCE ONCE IT IS ASSEMBLED AND ADJUST THE SEASONING TO SUIT YOUR TASTE.

SALISBURY STEAK WITH MUSHROOM GRAVY

SALISBURY STEAK IS A FLAVORED MEAT PATTY THAT IS SMOTHERED IN PAN GRAVY. SERVE IT WITH MOUNDS OF FLUFFY MASHED POTATOES TO SOAK UP THE FLAVORFUL SAUCE.

1/2 CUP	DRY BREAD CRUMBS	125 ML
2 TSP	DRIED ITALIAN SEASONING	10 ML
	FRESHLY GROUND BLACK PEPPER	
4	FROZEN BEEF PATTIES (EACH 4 OZ/125 G)	4
1 TBSP	VEGETABLE OIL	15 ML
8 OZ	SLICED MUSHROOMS	250 G
1/2 CUP	SHERRY, WHITE WINE OR WATER	125 ML
1/2 CUP	WATER	125 ML
1	CAN (10 OZ/284 ML) CONDENSED CREAM OF MUSHROOM SOUP	1
1 TBSP	WORCESTERSHIRE SAUCE	15 ML

ON A PLATE, MIX TOGETHER BREAD CRUMBS, ITALIAN SEASONING, AND BLACK PEPPER TO TASTE. DIP EACH PATTY INTO CRUMB MIXTURE, COATING EVENLY ON BOTH SIDES (SEE TIP, OPPOSITE). IN A SKILLET, HEAT OIL OVER MEDIUM-HIGH HEAT. ADD PATTIES AND COOK UNTIL NO LONGER PINK INSIDE, 4 TO 7 MINUTES PER SIDE, DEPENDING UPON THICKNESS. TRANSFER TO A DEEP PLATTER AND KEEP WARM WHILE MAKING THE GRAVY. DRAIN OFF ALL BUT 1 TBSP (15 ML) FAT FROM PAN. ADD MUSHROOMS AND COOK, STIRRING, UNTIL THEY BEGIN TO BROWN AND LOSE THEIR LIQUID, ABOUT 7 MINUTES. ADD

SHERRY AND WATER AND COOK, STIRRING, FOR I MINUTE, SCRAPING UP ANY BROWN BITS FROM BOTTOM OF PAN. ADD MUSHROOM SOUP AND STIR WELL TO REMOVE LUMPS. BRING TO A BOIL. REDUCE HEAT TO LOW AND SIMMER FOR 2 MINUTES. STIR IN WORCESTERSHIRE SAUCE. TASTE AND ADJUST SEASONING. POUR OVER COOKED PATTIES AND SERVE. SERVES 4.

TIP: TO MAKE YOUR OWN BEEF PATTIES: IN A BOWL, COMBINE I LB (500 G) LEAN GROUND BEEF, I CUP (250 ML) FINELY CHOPPED ONION, $\frac{1}{2}$ CUP (125 ML) DRY BREAD CRUMBS, 2 TSP (10 ML) DRIED ITALIAN SEASONING, $\frac{1}{2}$ TSP (2 ML) SALT AND $\frac{1}{4}$ TSP (I ML) FRESHLY GROUND BLACK PEPPER. MIX WELL AND FORM INTO 4 PATTIES OF UNIFORM SIZE, ABOUT $\frac{1}{2}$ INCH (I CM) THICK. PLACE $\frac{1}{2}$ CUP (125 ML) BREAD CRUMBS ON A PLATE. DIP PATTIES IN CRUMBS TO COAT EVENLY AND CONTINUE WITH THE RECIPE.

TIP: IF YOU HAVE TROUBLE GETTING THE CRUMB MIXTURE TO ADHERE TO THE MEAT, DIP THE PATTIES IN BEATEN EGG BEFORE COATING WITH CRUMBS.

IT'S A FINE LINE BETWEEN AN OUTFIT AND A GETUP.

BISTRO STEAK

DRESSED UP WITH WINE, GARLIC AND HERBS,
THIS STEAK RECIPE BECOMES A SPECIAL DISH.

4	BONELESS STRIPLOIN STEAKS	4
1/2 TSP	COARSELY GROUND BLACK PEPPER	2 ML
2 TSP	OLIVE OIL	10 ML
2 TSP	BUTTER	10 ML
	SALT	
1/4 CUP	FINELY CHOPPED SHALLOTS	60 ML
1	LARGE CLOVE GARLIC, FINELY CHOPPED	1
1/4 TSP	DRIED HERBES DE PROVENCE	1 ML
1/3 CUP	RED WINE OR ADDITIONAL BEEF STOCK	75 ML
1/2 CUP	HEARTY BEEF STOCK (PAGE 43) OR READY-TO-USE BEEF BROTH	125 ML
1 TBSP	DIJON MUSTARD	15 ML
2 TBSP	CHOPPED FRESH PARSLEY	30 ML

PAT STEAKS DRY WITH PAPER TOWELS. SEASON WITH
PEPPER. HEAT A LARGE HEAVY SKILLET OVER MEDIUM
HEAT UNTIL HOT; ADD OIL AND BUTTER. INCREASE HEAT
TO HIGH; BROWN STEAKS ABOUT 1 MINUTE ON EACH SIDE.
REDUCE HEAT TO MEDIUM; COOK TO DESIRED DEGREE OF
DONENESS. TRANSFER TO A HEATED SERVING PLATTER;
SEASON WITH SALT AND KEEP WARM. ADD SHALLOTS,
GARLIC AND HERBES TO SKILLET; COOK, STIRRING, FOR
1 MINUTE. STIR IN RED WINE; COOK, SCRAPING UP ANY
BROWN BITS FROM BOTTOM OF PAN, UNTIL LIQUID HAS
ALMOST EVAPORATED. STIR IN STOCK, MUSTARD AND
PARSLEY; SEASON TO TASTE WITH SALT AND PEPPER.
COOK, STIRRING, UNTIL SLIGHTLY REDUCED. SPOON SAUCE
OVER STEAKS. SERVE IMMEDIATELY. SERVES 4.

EASY ASIAN FLANK STEAK

FLANK STEAK IS ECONOMICAL AND EASY
TO MARINATE AHEAD, AND LEFTOVERS MAKE
GREAT-TASTING SANDWICHES.

1/4 CUP	HOISIN SAUCE	60 ML
2 TBSP	SOY SAUCE	30 ML
2 TBSP	FRESHLY SQUEEZED LIME JUICE	30 ML
I TBSP	VEGETABLE OIL	15 ML
4	CLOVES GARLIC, FINELY CHOPPED	4
2 TSP	ASIAN CHILI SAUCE OR I TSP (5 ML) HOT PEPPER FLAKES	10 ML
1 1/2 LBS	FLANK STEAK	750 G

IN A SHALLOW GLASS DISH, WHISK TOGETHER HOISIN
SAUCE, SOY SAUCE, LIME JUICE, OIL, GARLIC AND CHILI
SAUCE; ADD STEAK, TURNING TO COAT BOTH SIDES
WITH MARINADE. REFRIGERATE, COVERED, FOR AT LEAST
8 HOURS OR UP TO 24 HOURS. REMOVE MEAT FROM
REFRIGERATOR 15 MINUTES BEFORE COOKING.

PREHEAT GREASED BARBECUE GRILL TO MEDIUM-HIGH
(OR PREHEAT BROILER). REMOVE STEAK FROM MARINADE,
DISCARDING MARINADE. GRILL STEAK FOR 7 TO 8 MINUTES
PER SIDE OR UNTIL MEDIUM-RARE. (OR PLACE STEAK ON A
FOIL-LINED BAKING SHEET; BROIL 4 INCHES (10 CM) BELOW
PREHEATED BROILER FOR 7 TO 8 MINUTES ON EACH SIDE.)
TRANSFER TO CUTTING BOARD AND COVER LOOSELY WITH
FOIL; LET STAND FOR 5 MINUTES. THINLY SLICE AT RIGHT
ANGLES TO THE GRAIN OF MEAT. SERVES 6.

TIP: FLANK STEAK BECOMES MORE TENDER THE LONGER
IT'S MARINATED.

SAUCY SWISS STEAK

SLOW COOKER RECIPE

HERE'S A RETRO DISH THAT CHANNELS THE 1950S. BACK THEN IT REQUIRED A FAIR BIT OF MUSCLE TO POUND THE STEAK WITH A MALLET. TODAY, YOU CAN AVOID ALL THAT DREARY WORK BY USING THE SLOW COOKER. THIS IS SO GOOD YOU'LL WANT SECONDS. SERVE WITH GARLIC MASHED POTATOES AND A PLAIN GREEN VEGETABLE.

2 TBSP	VEGETABLE OIL, DIVIDED	30 ML
2 LBS	ROUND STEAK OR "SIMMERING" STEAK (SEE TIP, OPPOSITE)	I KG
2	ONIONS, FINELY CHOPPED	2
I	SMALL CARROT, THINLY SLICED (ABOUT $1/4$ CUP/60 ML)	I
I	SMALL STALK CELERY, THINLY SLICED (ABOUT $1/4$ CUP/60 ML)	I
$1/2$ TSP	SALT	2 ML
$1/2$ TSP	CRACKED BLACK PEPPERCORNS	2 ML
I	BAY LEAF	I
2 TBSP	ALL-PURPOSE FLOUR	30 ML
I	CAN (28 OZ/796 ML) DICED TOMATOES, DRAINED, AND $1/2$ CUP (125 ML) JUICE RESERVED	I
I TBSP	WORCESTERSHIRE SAUCE	15 ML

IN A SKILLET, HEAT I TBSP (15 ML) OIL OVER MEDIUM-HIGH HEAT. ADD STEAK, IN PIECES IF NECESSARY, AND BROWN ON BOTH SIDES. TRANSFER TO A MEDIUM (ABOUT $3\frac{1}{2}$-QUART) SLOW COOKER. REDUCE STOVETOP HEAT TO MEDIUM AND ADD THE REMAINING OIL TO PAN. ADD ONIONS, CARROT AND CELERY TO PAN AND COOK, STIRRING, UNTIL SOFTENED, ABOUT 5 MINUTES. STIR

IN SALT, PEPPERCORNS AND BAY LEAF. SPRINKLE FLOUR OVER VEGETABLES AND COOK, STIRRING, FOR 1 MINUTE. ADD TOMATOES AND RESERVED JUICE. BRING TO A BOIL, STIRRING, UNTIL SLIGHTLY THICKENED. POUR TOMATO MIXTURE OVER STEAK AND COOK ON LOW FOR 8 HOURS OR ON FOR HIGH 4 HOURS, UNTIL MEAT IS TENDER. STIR IN WORCESTERSHIRE SAUCE. DISCARD BAY LEAF AND SERVE. SERVES 6.

TIP: WHILE ROUND STEAK IS TRADITIONALLY USED FOR THIS DISH, AN EQUALLY SUCCESSFUL VERSION CAN BE MADE WITH "SIMMERING STEAK," WHICH IS CUT FROM THE BLADE OR CROSS RIB.

TIP: IF YOU CHOOSE TO HALVE THIS RECIPE, USE A SMALL (ABOUT 2-QUART) SLOW COOKER.

I TRY TO AVOID THINGS THAT MAKE ME FAT, LIKE SCALES, MIRRORS AND PHOTOGRAPHS.

CHINESE PEPPER STEAK

FAST-AND-EASY RECIPE

THIS RECIPE TAKES ADVANTAGE OF BOTTLED ASIAN
SAUCES TO CREATE A GREAT-TASTING DINNER.

1 TBSP	VEGETABLE OIL	15 ML
1 LB	THINLY SLICED BEEF SIRLOIN OR STIR-FRY STRIPS	500 G
1 TBSP	MINCED GARLIC	15 ML
1 TBSP	MINCED GINGERROOT	15 ML
1/2 TSP	CRACKED BLACK PEPPERCORNS	2 ML
1 CUP	FINELY CHOPPED RED OR GREEN BELL PEPPER	250 ML
1/2 CUP	HEARTY BEEF STOCK (PAGE 43) OR READY-TO-USE BEEF BROTH	125 ML
2 TBSP	SOY SAUCE	30 ML
1 TBSP	HOISIN SAUCE	15 ML
1 TBSP	CORNSTARCH, DISSOLVED IN 2 TBSP (30 ML) WATER	15 ML
2 TBSP	FINELY CHOPPED GREEN ONION	30 ML

IN A SKILLET, HEAT OIL OVER MEDIUM-HIGH HEAT.
ADD STEAK AND COOK, STIRRING, UNTIL IT BEGINS TO
BROWN AND THERE IS NO HINT OF RED, 2 TO 3 MINUTES.
TRANSFER TO A WARM PLATTER AND KEEP WARM. REDUCE
HEAT TO MEDIUM. ADD GARLIC, GINGER AND PEPPERCORNS
AND COOK, STIRRING, FOR 1 MINUTE. ADD BELL PEPPER AND
COOK, STIRRING, FOR 1 MINUTE. ADD STOCK, SOY SAUCE
AND HOISIN SAUCE. BRING TO A BOIL. ADD CORNSTARCH
MIXTURE AND COOK, STIRRING, UNTIL THICKENED, ABOUT
2 MINUTES. POUR OVER BEEF. GARNISH WITH GREEN
ONION AND SERVE IMMEDIATELY. SERVES 4.

BEEF AND POTATO CURRY

SERVE THIS ONE-POT FAMILY FAVORITE WITH WARM
PITA BREAD AND A CUCUMBER AND TOMATO SALAD.

I LB	LEAN GROUND BEEF	500 G
I	ONION, CHOPPED	I
2	LARGE CLOVES GARLIC, FINELY CHOPPED	2
2 TBSP	TOMATO PASTE	30 ML
I TBSP	MILD CURRY PASTE (OR TO TASTE)	15 ML
I TBSP	MINCED GINGERROOT	15 ML
1/4 TSP	SALT	I ML
4	POTATOES, PEELED AND DICED (ABOUT 1 1/2 LBS/750 G)	4
2 CUPS	HEARTY BEEF STOCK (PAGE 43) OR READY-TO-USE BEEF BROTH	500 ML
1 1/2 CUPS	FROZEN PEAS	375 ML
1/4 CUP	CHOPPED FRESH CILANTRO OR PARSLEY (OPTIONAL)	60 ML

IN A DUTCH OVEN OR LARGE SAUCEPAN OVER MEDIUM-
HIGH HEAT, COOK BEEF, BREAKING UP WITH A WOODEN
SPOON, FOR 5 MINUTES OR UNTIL NO LONGER PINK.
DRAIN OFF ANY FAT. ADD ONION, GARLIC, TOMATO PASTE,
CURRY PASTE, GINGER AND SALT; COOK, STIRRING, FOR
5 MINUTES OR UNTIL ONION IS SOFTENED. ADD POTATOES
AND STOCK; BRING TO BOIL. REDUCE HEAT, COVER AND
SIMMER FOR 15 MINUTES. STIR IN PEAS; COOK, COVERED,
FOR 5 MINUTES OR UNTIL POTATOES AND PEAS ARE
TENDER. STIR IN CILANTRO (IF USING). SERVES 4.

BEEF STROGANOFF

HERE'S A DISH THAT IS QUICK TO MAKE
YET ELEGANT ENOUGH FOR SPECIAL OCCASIONS.
THE SAUCE IS DELICIOUS OVER HOT BUTTERED
EGG NOODLES. JUST ADD A BOTTLE OF ROBUST
RED WINE AND A CRISP GREEN SALAD.

1 TBSP	VEGETABLE OIL	15 ML
2 TBSP	BUTTER, DIVIDED	30 ML
8 OZ	SLICED MUSHROOMS	250 G
1 LB	SIRLOIN STEAK, CUT INTO 1/2-INCH (1 CM) SLICES	500 G
1/4 TSP	SALT	1 ML
	FRESHLY GROUND BLACK PEPPER	
2 TBSP	MINCED SHALLOTS OR FINELY CHOPPED GREEN ONION (WHITE PART ONLY)	30 ML
1 TBSP	ALL-PURPOSE FLOUR	15 ML
1 CUP	HEARTY BEEF STOCK (PAGE 43) OR READY-TO-USE BEEF BROTH	250 ML
1 TBSP	DIJON MUSTARD	15 ML
1/2 CUP	SOUR CREAM	125 ML
1	DILL PICKLE, FINELY CHOPPED	1

PREHEAT OVEN TO 250°F (120°C). IN A SKILLET, HEAT OIL
AND 1 TBSP (15 ML) BUTTER OVER MEDIUM-HIGH HEAT.
ADD MUSHROOMS AND COOK, STIRRING, UNTIL THEY
BEGIN TO LOSE THEIR LIQUID, ABOUT 7 MINUTES. USING
A SLOTTED SPOON, TRANSFER TO A PLATE AND KEEP
WARM IN PREHEATED OVEN. ADD THE REMAINING BUTTER
TO PAN. ADD STEAK SLICES AND SAUTÉ UNTIL DESIRED
DEGREE OF DONENESS, ABOUT 1 1/2 MINUTES PER SIDE
FOR MEDIUM. SEASON WITH SALT, AND BLACK PEPPER
TO TASTE. TRANSFER TO A WARM PLATTER AND KEEP

WARM IN OVEN. REDUCE HEAT TO MEDIUM. ADD SHALLOTS TO PAN AND COOK, STIRRING, FOR I MINUTE. ADD FLOUR AND COOK, STIRRING, FOR I MINUTE. ADD STOCK. BRING TO A BOIL. COOK, STIRRING, UNTIL THICKENED, ABOUT 3 MINUTES. STIR IN MUSTARD. RETURN MUSHROOMS TO PAN. ADD SOUR CREAM AND CHOPPED DILL PICKLE AND COOK, STIRRING, JUST UNTIL CREAM IS HEATED THROUGH, ABOUT I MINUTE. (DO NOT LET MIXTURE BOIL OR IT WILL CURDLE.) POUR OVER STEAK. SERVES 4.

VARIATION: ADD 1/4 CUP (60 ML) VODKA TO PAN BEFORE ADDING THE FLOUR AND COOK, STIRRING, FOR I MINUTE.

VARIATION: ADD I TSP (5 ML) PAPRIKA WITH THE FLOUR.

VARIATION: GARNISH WITH FINELY CHOPPED DILL OR DILL SPRIGS.

ADULT: A PERSON WHO HAS STOPPED GROWING AT BOTH ENDS AND IS NOW GROWING IN THE MIDDLE.

BEEF AND BROCCOLI STIR-FRY

HERE'S A FAST STIR-FRY THAT DOESN'T REQUIRE A LOT OF CHOPPING.

1 LB	LEAN BONELESS SIRLOIN STEAK, CUT INTO THIN STRIPS	500 G
2 TBSP	HOISIN SAUCE	30 ML
2	CLOVES GARLIC, FINELY CHOPPED	2
1 TBSP	MINCED GINGERROOT	15 ML
1 TSP	GRATED ORANGE ZEST	5 ML
1/2 CUP	FRESHLY SQUEEZED ORANGE JUICE	125 ML
3 TBSP	SOY SAUCE	45 ML
2 TSP	CORNSTARCH	10 ML
1/4 TSP	HOT PEPPER FLAKES	1 ML
1 TBSP	VEGETABLE OIL	15 ML
6 CUPS	SMALL BROCCOLI FLORETS AND PEELED CHOPPED STEMS (ABOUT 1 LARGE BUNCH)	1.5 L
3	GREEN ONIONS, SLICED	3

IN A BOWL, TOSS BEEF STRIPS WITH HOISIN SAUCE, GARLIC AND GINGER. LET MARINATE AT ROOM TEMPERATURE FOR 15 MINUTES. IN A GLASS MEASURING CUP, COMBINE ORANGE ZEST AND JUICE, SOY SAUCE, CORNSTARCH AND HOT PEPPER FLAKES. IN A LARGE NONSTICK SKILLET, HEAT OIL OVER HIGH HEAT; COOK BEEF, STIRRING, FOR 2 MINUTES OR UNTIL NO LONGER PINK. TRANSFER TO A PLATE. ADD BROCCOLI AND SOY SAUCE MIXTURE TO SKILLET; REDUCE HEAT TO MEDIUM, COVER AND COOK FOR 2 TO 3 MINUTES OR UNTIL BROCCOLI IS TENDER-CRISP. ADD BEEF STRIPS WITH ANY ACCUMULATED JUICES AND GREEN ONIONS; COOK, STIRRING, FOR 1 MINUTE OR UNTIL HEATED THROUGH. SERVES 4.

CRISPY SHEPHERD'S PIE

2 TBSP	VEGETABLE OIL, DIVIDED	30 ML
2 CUPS	FROZEN HASH BROWN POTATOES	500 ML
1 LB	LEAN GROUND BEEF	500 G
1 CUP	FINELY CHOPPED ONION	250 ML
1 TBSP	MINCED GARLIC	15 ML
1/4 TSP	SALT	1 ML
	FRESHLY GROUND BLACK PEPPER	
2 TBSP	ALL-PURPOSE FLOUR	30 ML
1 CUP	HEARTY BEEF STOCK (PAGE 43) OR READY-TO-USE BEEF BROTH	250 ML
1/2 CUP	KETCHUP	125 ML
1 TBSP	WORCESTERSHIRE SAUCE	15 ML

PREHEAT OVEN TO 375°F (190°C). IN A SKILLET, HEAT
1 TBSP (15 ML) OIL OVER MEDIUM-HIGH HEAT. ADD
POTATOES AND COOK, STIRRING, UNTIL CRISP, ABOUT
7 MINUTES. USING A SLOTTED SPOON, TRANSFER TO A
PLATE LINED WITH PAPER TOWELS TO DRAIN. ADD THE
REMAINING OIL TO PAN. ADD BEEF AND ONION AND COOK,
BREAKING UP MEAT, UNTIL BEEF IS NO LONGER PINK
INSIDE, ABOUT 5 MINUTES. DRAIN OFF FAT. ADD GARLIC,
SALT, AND BLACK PEPPER TO TASTE TO THE PAN AND
COOK, STIRRING, FOR 1 MINUTE. ADD FLOUR AND COOK,
STIRRING, FOR 1 MINUTE. ADD STOCK AND BRING TO A
BOIL. COOK, STIRRING, UNTIL MIXTURE THICKENS, ABOUT
3 MINUTES. STIR IN KETCHUP AND WORCESTERSHIRE
SAUCE AND RETURN TO A BOIL. POUR MIXTURE INTO A
9-INCH (23 CM) PIE PLATE. SPRINKLE POTATOES OVER
TOP. BAKE UNTIL MIXTURE IS HOT AND BUBBLING, ABOUT
10 MINUTES. SERVES 4.

MEATBALL GOULASH

SLOW COOKER RECIPE

*SERVED OVER HOT BUTTERED NOODLES,
THIS DISH IS POSITIVELY AMBROSIAL.*

1/2 CUP	FINE BULGUR (SEE TIP, OPPOSITE)	125 ML
1/2 CUP	COLD WATER	125 ML
1	ONION, QUARTERED	1
2	CLOVES GARLIC, CHOPPED	2
1/2 CUP	FRESH FLAT-LEAF (ITALIAN) PARSLEY LEAVES	125 ML
1 TSP	SALT	5 ML
	FRESHLY GROUND BLACK PEPPER	
1 LB	LEAN GROUND BEEF	500 G
1 LB	LEAN GROUND PORK	500 G
1	LARGE EGG, BEATEN	1
2 TBSP	OLIVE OIL (APPROX.), DIVIDED	30 ML
2	ONIONS, FINELY CHOPPED	2
4	CLOVES GARLIC, MINCED	4
1 TSP	CARAWAY SEEDS	5 ML
1/2 TSP	SALT	2 ML
1/2 TSP	CRACKED BLACK PEPPERCORNS	2 ML
1	CAN (28 OZ/796 ML) TOMATOES, WITH JUICE, COARSELY CHOPPED	1
1 CUP	HEARTY BEEF STOCK (PAGE 43) OR READY-TO-USE BEEF BROTH	250 ML
2	RED BELL PEPPERS, FINELY CHOPPED	2
1 TBSP	PAPRIKA (SWEET OR HOT), DISSOLVED IN 2 TBSP (30 ML) LEMON JUICE	15 ML
1/2 CUP	FINELY CHOPPED FRESH DILL	125 ML
	SOUR CREAM (OPTIONAL)	

IN A BOWL, COMBINE BULGUR AND WATER. STIR WELL AND SET ASIDE UNTIL LIQUID IS ABSORBED, ABOUT 10 MINUTES. IN A FOOD PROCESSOR, PULSE QUARTERED ONION, CHOPPED GARLIC, PARSLEY, 1 TSP (5 ML) SALT, AND PEPPER TO TASTE UNTIL ONION IS FINELY CHOPPED. ADD BEEF, PORK, EGG AND BULGUR, IN BATCHES, AND PULSE TO COMBINE. SHAPE MIXTURE INTO 12 EQUAL BALLS. IN A SKILLET, HEAT 1 TBSP (15 ML) OIL OVER MEDIUM-HIGH HEAT. ADD MEATBALLS, IN BATCHES, AND BROWN WELL, ABOUT 5 MINUTES PER BATCH, ADDING MORE OIL AS NECESSARY. TRANSFER TO A MEDIUM TO LARGE (3½- TO 5-QUART) SLOW COOKER. REDUCE STOVETOP HEAT TO MEDIUM. ADD THE REMAINING OIL TO PAN. ADD CHOPPED ONIONS AND COOK, STIRRING, UNTIL SOFTENED, ABOUT 3 MINUTES. ADD MINCED GARLIC, CARAWAY, ½ TSP (2 ML) SALT AND PEPPERCORNS AND COOK, STIRRING, FOR 1 MINUTE. ADD TOMATOES AND STOCK AND BRING TO A BOIL. POUR OVER MEATBALLS. COVER AND COOK ON LOW FOR 6 HOURS OR ON HIGH FOR 3 HOURS. STIR IN BELL PEPPERS AND PAPRIKA SOLUTION. COVER AND COOK ON HIGH FOR 30 MINUTES, UNTIL PEPPERS ARE TENDER AND FLAVORS MELD. GARNISH WITH DILL AND A DOLLOP OF SOUR CREAM (IF USING). SERVES 6 TO 8.

TIP: IF USING COARSE BULGUR, INCREASE THE SOAKING TIME TO 30 MINUTES.

TIP: IF YOU CHOOSE TO HALVE THIS RECIPE, USE A SMALL (ABOUT 2-QUART) SLOW COOKER.

BEST-EVER MEATLOAF

1 TBSP	VEGETABLE OIL	15 ML
1	ONION, CHOPPED	1
2	CLOVES GARLIC, FINELY CHOPPED	2
1 TSP	DRIED BASIL	5 ML
1 TSP	DRIED MARJORAM	5 ML
3/4 TSP	SALT	3 ML
1/4 TSP	FRESHLY GROUND BLACK PEPPER	1 ML
1	LARGE EGG	1
1/4 CUP	CHILI SAUCE OR KETCHUP	60 ML
1 TBSP	WORCESTERSHIRE SAUCE	15 ML
2 TBSP	CHOPPED FRESH PARSLEY	30 ML
1 1/2 LBS	LEAN GROUND BEEF	750 G
3/4 CUP	QUICK-COOKING ROLLED OATS (OR 1/2 CUP/125 ML DRY BREAD CRUMBS)	175 ML

PREHEAT OVEN TO 350°F (180°C). GREASE A 9- BY 5-INCH (23 BY 12.5 CM) LOAF PAN. IN A LARGE NONSTICK SKILLET, HEAT OIL OVER MEDIUM HEAT. ADD ONION, GARLIC, BASIL, MARJORAM, SALT AND PEPPER; COOK, STIRRING, FOR 3 MINUTES OR UNTIL SOFTENED. (OR PLACE IN MICROWAVE-SAFE BOWL; MICROWAVE, COVERED, ON HIGH FOR 3 MINUTES.) LET COOL SLIGHTLY. IN A LARGE BOWL, BEAT EGG; STIR IN ONION MIXTURE, CHILI SAUCE, WORCESTERSHIRE SAUCE AND PARSLEY. CRUMBLE BEEF OVER MIXTURE AND SPRINKLE WITH ROLLED OATS. USING A WOODEN SPOON, GENTLY MIX UNTIL EVENLY COMBINED. PRESS MIXTURE LIGHTLY INTO LOAF PAN. BAKE FOR 1 HOUR OR UNTIL MEAT THERMOMETER REGISTERS 160°F (71°C). LET STAND FOR 5 MINUTES. DRAIN PAN JUICES; TURN OUT ONTO A PLATE AND CUT INTO THICK SLICES. SERVES 6.

SIDE DISHES

MARINATED ASPARAGUS

A SIMPLE WAY TO PREPARE ASPARAGUS — AND IT CAN BE DONE IN ADVANCE.

1	BUNCH ASPARAGUS	1
1	CLOVE GARLIC, MINCED	1
2 TSP	GRATED GINGERROOT	10 ML
1/4 CUP	ORANGE JUICE	60 ML
2 TBSP	RICE VINEGAR	30 ML
1 TBSP	SOY SAUCE	15 ML
1 TBSP	SESAME OIL	15 ML
1 TBSP	SESAME SEEDS, TOASTED (SEE TIP, BELOW)	15 ML

IN A LARGE SAUCEPAN, BRING 1 INCH (2.5 CM) OF WATER TO A SIMMER. ADD ASPARAGUS AND SIMMER FOR 3 TO 4 MINUTES OR UNTIL TENDER-CRISP. DRAIN AND RUN UNDER COLD WATER TO COOL. PLACE ASPARAGUS IN A SHALLOW DISH. IN A SMALL BOWL, COMBINE GARLIC, GINGER, ORANGE JUICE, VINEGAR, SOY SAUCE AND OIL. POUR OVER ASPARAGUS. COVER AND REFRIGERATE FOR A FEW HOURS OR OVERNIGHT. SPRINKLE WITH SESAME SEEDS BEFORE SERVING. SERVES 4.

TIP: TO TOAST SESAME SEEDS, PUT THEM IN A SMALL DRY SKILLET SET OVER MEDIUM-LOW HEAT. TOAST, SHAKING THE PAN OFTEN, FOR A FEW MINUTES, OR UNTIL PALE GOLDEN AND FRAGRANT.

ROASTED ASPARAGUS WITH LEMON BROWN BUTTER

FAST-AND-EASY RECIPE

SOUND FANCY? NOT AT ALL — THIS DELICIOUS SIDE DISH CAN BE PUT TOGETHER IN 10 MINUTES!

1	BUNCH ASPARAGUS	1
1 TBSP	OLIVE OIL	15 ML
1 TSP	SALT	5 ML
	FRESHLY GROUND BLACK PEPPER	
3 TBSP	BUTTER	45 ML
1 TBSP	FRESHLY SQUEEZED LEMON JUICE	15 ML

PREHEAT OVEN TO 450°F (230°C). LINE A BAKING SHEET WITH PARCHMENT PAPER. SNAP OFF THE TOUGH ENDS OF THE ASPARAGUS WHERE THEY NATURALLY BREAK. TOSS ASPARAGUS WITH OIL AND SPREAD IN A SINGLE LAYER ON PREPARED BAKING SHEET. SEASON WITH SALT AND PEPPER TO TASTE. ROAST FOR 5 TO 10 MINUTES, DEPENDING ON THE THICKNESS OF THE ASPARAGUS, UNTIL JUST TENDER.

MEANWHILE, IN A SMALL SKILLET, MELT BUTTER OVER MEDIUM HEAT. COOK, STIRRING FREQUENTLY, UNTIL IT FOAMS AND BEGINS TO TURN DEEP GOLDEN, ABOUT 3 MINUTES. REMOVE FROM HEAT AND STIR IN LEMON JUICE. SERVE ASPARAGUS TOPPED WITH BROWNED BUTTER. SERVES 4 TO 6.

ROASTED BRUSSELS SPROUTS

THESE WILL BRING OUT THE SPROUT LOVER IN YOU.

4 CUPS	BRUSSELS SPROUTS, ENDS TRIMMED	1 L
1 TBSP	VEGETABLE OIL	15 ML
	SALT AND FRESHLY GROUND BLACK PEPPER	
3 TBSP	MAPLE SYRUP OR LIQUID HONEY	45 ML
2 TBSP	BALSAMIC VINEGAR	30 ML

PREHEAT OVEN TO 450°F (230°C). CUT ANY LARGE BRUSSELS SPROUTS IN HALF. TOSS WITH OIL AND SPRINKLE WITH SALT AND PEPPER. SPREAD OUT ON A RIMMED BAKING SHEET AND ROAST FOR 20 MINUTES OR UNTIL TENDER AND CHARRED ON THE EDGES. TOSS WITH MAPLE SYRUP AND VINEGAR WHILE STILL WARM. SERVES 4.

PLEASE HELP ME TO ACCEPT THE THINGS THE SALON CANNOT CHANGE.

LEMON-GLAZED BABY CARROTS

*THIS IS A GREAT CHOICE TO ACCOMPANY
A HOLIDAY ROAST OR TURKEY.*

1 LB	PEELED BABY CARROTS	500 G
1/4 CUP	CHICKEN STOCK (PAGE 42) OR READY-TO-USE CHICKEN OR VEGETABLE BROTH	60 ML
1 TBSP	BUTTER	15 ML
1 TBSP	PACKED BROWN SUGAR	15 ML
1/2 TSP	GRATED LEMON ZEST	2 ML
1 TBSP	FRESHLY SQUEEZED LEMON JUICE	15 ML
	SALT AND FRESHLY GROUND BLACK PEPPER	
1 TBSP	FINELY CHOPPED FRESH PARSLEY OR CHIVES	15 ML

IN A MEDIUM SAUCEPAN, COOK CARROTS IN BOILING SALTED WATER FOR 5 TO 7 MINUTES (START TIMING WHEN WATER RETURNS TO A BOIL) OR UNTIL JUST TENDER-CRISP; DRAIN AND RETURN TO SAUCEPAN. ADD STOCK, BUTTER, BROWN SUGAR, LEMON ZEST AND JUICE, AND SALT AND PEPPER TO TASTE. COOK, STIRRING OFTEN, FOR 3 TO 5 MINUTES OR UNTIL LIQUID HAS EVAPORATED AND CARROTS ARE NICELY GLAZED. SPRINKLE WITH PARSLEY AND SERVE. SERVES 4.

TIP: IF DOUBLING THE RECIPE, GLAZE CARROTS IN A LARGE NONSTICK SKILLET TO EVAPORATE THE STOCK QUICKLY.

VARIATION: TRY THIS TASTY TREATMENT WITH A COMBINATION OF BLANCHED CARROTS, RUTABAGA AND PARSNIP STRIPS, TOO.

CAULIFLOWER WITH HAZELNUT CRUMB TOPPING

SNOWY CAULIFLOWER TOPPED WITH CHEESE AND NUTS MAKES THE PERFECT SIDE DISH FOR A SUNDAY ROAST. FOR VEGETARIANS, IT BECOMES A MAIN-COURSE DISH WHEN SERVED ALONG WITH GRAINS OR A BOWL OF PASTA.

2 TBSP	BUTTER	30 ML
1/4 CUP	HAZELNUTS OR WALNUTS, FINELY CHOPPED	60 ML
1/2 CUP	SOFT FRESH BREAD CRUMBS	125 ML
1	LARGE CLOVE GARLIC, MINCED	1
1/2 CUP	FINELY SHREDDED GRUYÈRE OR SHARP (OLD) CHEDDAR CHEESE	125 ML
2 TBSP	CHOPPED FRESH PARSLEY	30 ML
1	CAULIFLOWER, BROKEN INTO FLORETS	1

PREHEAT BROILER. LIGHTLY GREASE A 10-CUP (2.5 L) SHALLOW BAKING DISH. IN A MEDIUM SKILLET, MELT BUTTER OVER MEDIUM HEAT. ADD HAZELNUTS AND COOK, STIRRING, FOR 1 MINUTE OR UNTIL LIGHTLY TOASTED. ADD BREAD CRUMBS AND GARLIC; COOK, STIRRING, FOR 1 MINUTE MORE OR UNTIL CRUMBS ARE LIGHTLY COLORED. REMOVE FROM HEAT; LET COOL. IN A BOWL, COMBINE CRUMB MIXTURE, CHEESE AND PARSLEY. IN A LARGE SAUCEPAN OF BOILING SALTED WATER, COOK CAULIFLOWER FOR 3 TO 5 MINUTES OR UNTIL TENDER-CRISP. DRAIN WELL. PLACE IN PREPARED BAKING DISH; SPRINKLE WITH CRUMB MIXTURE. PLACE UNDER PREHEATED BROILER FOR 1 TO 2 MINUTES OR UNTIL TOPPING IS LIGHTLY BROWNED. SERVES 6.

TIP: SPRINKLE THE GARLIC-CRUMB MIXTURE OVER OTHER VEGETABLES, SUCH AS BROCCOLI, BRUSSELS SPROUTS OR SPINACH.

VARIATION: UNBLANCHED ALMONDS, PECANS OR WALNUTS CAN REPLACE THE HAZELNUTS.

SPICED ROASTED CAULIFLOWER

TIRED OF STEAMED CAULIFLOWER? TRY ROASTING IT!

1	HEAD CAULIFLOWER	1
2 TBSP	VEGETABLE OIL	30 ML
2 TSP	CHILI POWDER	10 ML
1 TSP	GROUND CUMIN	5 ML
1/2 TSP	SALT	2 ML
1/4 TSP	FRESHLY GROUND BLACK PEPPER	1 ML

PREHEAT OVEN TO 425°F (220°C). SEPARATE CAULIFLOWER INTO FLORETS. TOSS WITH OIL AND SPREAD OUT ON A BAKING SHEET. SPRINKLE WITH CHILI POWDER, CUMIN, SALT AND PEPPER, THEN TOSS TO COAT. ROAST FOR 20 TO 30 MINUTES, STIRRING ONCE OR TWICE, UNTIL TENDER AND GOLDEN. SERVES 4 TO 6.

GREEN BEANS STEWED WITH TOMATOES

THIS IS A FAVORITE DISH TO MAKE IN LATE SUMMER WHEN YOUNG BEANS AND RIPE TOMATOES ARE AT THEIR BEST. BUT EVEN IN WINTER, WITH VINE-RIPENED GREENHOUSE TOMATOES AND IMPORTED FRESH BEANS, THIS RECIPE IS STILL GOOD.

I LB	GREEN BEANS	500 G
I TBSP	OLIVE OIL	15 ML
I	SMALL RED ONION, HALVED LENGTHWISE, THINLY SLICED	I
2	CLOVES GARLIC, THINLY SLICED	2
2	RIPE TOMATOES, DICED	2
I TBSP	BALSAMIC VINEGAR	15 ML
2 TBSP	WATER (APPROX.)	30 ML
1/4 TSP	SALT	I ML
1/4 TSP	FRESHLY GROUND BLACK PEPPER	I ML
2 TBSP	CHOPPED FRESH BASIL	30 ML

TRIM ENDS OF BEANS; CUT INTO 1 1/2-INCH (4 CM) LENGTHS. IN A SAUCEPAN, COOK BEANS IN LIGHTLY SALTED BOILING WATER FOR 3 MINUTES (START TIMING WHEN WATER RETURNS TO A BOIL) OR UNTIL STILL CRISP. DRAIN WELL; RESERVE. IN A LARGE NONSTICK SKILLET, HEAT OIL OVER MEDIUM HEAT. ADD ONION AND GARLIC; COOK, STIRRING, FOR 2 MINUTES OR UNTIL SOFTENED. STIR IN TOMATOES, VINEGAR, WATER, SALT AND PEPPER; COOK, STIRRING OFTEN, FOR 3 MINUTES OR UNTIL SAUCE-LIKE. ADD BEANS; COVER AND SIMMER FOR 8 TO 10 MINUTES, STIRRING OCCASIONALLY, UNTIL TENDER.

ADD MORE WATER, IF NECESSARY, TO KEEP MIXTURE MOIST. SPRINKLE WITH BASIL AND SERVE WARM OR AT ROOM TEMPERATURE. SERVES 4.

TIP: IF BITS OF TOMATO SKIN IN THE SAUCE BOTHER YOU, PEEL THE TOMATOES BEFORE DICING.

VARIATION: FOR A QUICK SUPPER, TOSS VEGETABLE SAUCE WITH 8 OZ (250 G) COOKED PASTA, SUCH AS PENNE, AND SPRINKLE GENEROUSLY WITH PARMESAN CHEESE.

VARIATION: SUBSTITUTE OTHER VEGETABLES, SUCH AS FENNEL, ASPARAGUS OR BROCCOLI, FOR THE BEANS.

I'VE NEVER BEEN A MILLIONAIRE,
BUT I KNOW I'LL JUST BE DARLING AT IT.

SZECHUAN GREEN BEANS

THESE EASY, SPICY GREEN BEANS ARE ADDICTIVE!

2 TSP	VEGETABLE OIL	10 ML
1 TSP	SESAME OIL	5 ML
8 OZ	GREEN BEANS, STEM ENDS TRIMMED	250 G
4	CLOVES GARLIC, THINLY SLICED	4
2	GREEN ONIONS, CHOPPED	2
2 TSP	GRATED GINGERROOT	10 ML
1 TSP	GRANULATED SUGAR	5 ML
1 TBSP	SOY SAUCE	15 ML
1 TSP	SRIRACHA SAUCE OR CHILI PASTE	5 ML
2 TBSP	SESAME SEEDS, TOASTED (SEE TIP, PAGE 292)	30 ML

IN A LARGE SKILLET, HEAT VEGETABLE AND SESAME OILS OVER MEDIUM-HIGH HEAT. ADD BEANS AND COOK, TOSSING, UNTIL GOLDEN IN SPOTS. ADD GARLIC, GREEN ONIONS, GINGER, SUGAR, SOY SAUCE AND SRIRACHA; COOK, TOSSING, FOR 2 TO 3 MINUTES OR UNTIL GARLIC IS GOLDEN AND BEANS ARE DARK AND STICKY. SPRINKLE WITH SESAME SEEDS. SERVES 4.

TOMATO AND ZUCCHINI SAUTÉ

FAST-AND-EASY RECIPE

*THIS COLORFUL VEGETABLE MEDLEY IS
A GREAT SUMMER SIDE DISH.*

1 TBSP	OLIVE OIL	15 ML
3	SMALL ZUCCHINI, HALVED LENGTHWISE AND THINLY SLICED	3
2 CUPS	CHERRY TOMATOES, HALVED	500 ML
1/2 TSP	GROUND CUMIN (OPTIONAL)	2 ML
2	GREEN ONIONS, SLICED	2
2 TSP	BALSAMIC VINEGAR	10 ML
	SALT AND FRESHLY GROUND BLACK PEPPER	
2 TBSP	CHOPPED FRESH BASIL OR MINT	30 ML
2 TBSP	LIGHTLY TOASTED PINE NUTS (OPTIONAL) (SEE TIP, BELOW)	30 ML

IN A LARGE NONSTICK SKILLET, HEAT OIL OVER MEDIUM-HIGH HEAT. ADD ZUCCHINI AND COOK, STIRRING, FOR 1 MINUTE. ADD CHERRY TOMATOES, CUMIN (IF USING), GREEN ONIONS AND BALSAMIC VINEGAR. COOK, STIRRING, FOR 1 TO 2 MINUTES OR UNTIL ZUCCHINI IS TENDER-CRISP AND TOMATOES ARE HEATED THROUGH. SEASON TO TASTE WITH SALT AND PEPPER. SPRINKLE WITH BASIL AND PINE NUTS (IF USING) AND SERVE IMMEDIATELY. SERVES 4.

TIP: TO TOAST PINE NUTS, PLACE NUTS IN DRY SKILLET OVER MEDIUM HEAT. TOAST, STIRRING, FOR 3 TO 4 MINUTES OR UNTIL LIGHTLY BROWNED AND FRAGRANT.

SAUTÉED GREENS WITH DOUBLE-SMOKED BACON

COOKING DARK GREENS, SUCH AS COLLARD, KALE OR RAPINI, WITH SMOKY BACON AND HOT PEPPER FLAKES MELLOWS THE MILD BITTERNESS OF THESE HEALTHY VEGETABLES.

8 CUPS	PREPARED GREENS, SUCH AS KALE, COLLARD, RAPINI OR SWISS CHARD (SEE TIPS, OPPOSITE)	2 L
6	SLICES DOUBLE-SMOKED OR REGULAR BACON, CHOPPED	6
1 TBSP	OLIVE OIL	15 ML
1	SMALL ONION, FINELY CHOPPED	1
3	CLOVES GARLIC, FINELY CHOPPED	3
1/4 TSP	HOT PEPPER FLAKES	1 ML
	SALT AND FRESHLY GROUND BLACK PEPPER	

IN A LARGE POT OF BOILING SALTED WATER, BLANCH GREENS FOR 2 MINUTES. POUR INTO A LARGE SIEVE TO DRAIN, USING THE BACK OF A WOODEN SPOON TO PRESS OUT AS MUCH LIQUID AS POSSIBLE. IN A LARGE NONSTICK SKILLET OVER MEDIUM-HIGH HEAT, COOK BACON, STIRRING OFTEN, FOR 5 MINUTES OR UNTIL CRISP. TRANSFER TO A PLATE LINED WITH PAPER TOWELS. DRAIN ANY FAT FROM SKILLET. REDUCE HEAT TO MEDIUM AND ADD OIL TO SKILLET. COOK ONION, GARLIC AND HOT PEPPER FLAKES, STIRRING, FOR 1 MINUTE OR UNTIL ONION IS LIGHTLY COLORED. ADD GREENS AND COOK, STIRRING OFTEN, FOR 2 TO 5 MINUTES OR UNTIL JUST TENDER. SPRINKLE WITH BACON BITS AND SEASON TO TASTE WITH SALT AND PEPPER. SERVES 4.

TIP: TO PREPARE GREENS, REMOVE TOUGH STEM ENDS. CUT TENDER STEMS INTO 2-INCH (5 CM) LENGTHS AND COARSELY CHOP LEAVES. WASH WELL IN A SINKFUL OF COOL WATER TO REMOVE ANY DIRT; DRAIN.

TIP: FOR A SIMPLE PASTA DISH, TOSS THE COOKED GREENS WITH HOT COOKED PASTA, SUCH AS SPAGHETTI OR LINGUINI, AND SPRINKLE WITH PARMESAN CHEESE.

I LOVE YOU THE WAY YOU ARE.
BUT DON'T GET ANY WORSE!

ROASTED ROOT VEGETABLES

STURDY ROOT VEGETABLES STAND UP TO THE HEAT OF THE OVEN, WITH DELICIOUS RESULTS!

2 to 3	CARROTS, CUT INTO 1-INCH (2.5 CM) CHUNKS	2 to 3
2	PARSNIPS, CUT INTO 1-INCH (2.5 CM) CHUNKS	2
2	BEETS, PEELED AND CUT INTO WEDGES	2
1	SWEET POTATO, PEELED AND CUT INTO 1-INCH (2.5 CM) CHUNKS	1
1	SMALL RED ONION, CUT INTO WEDGES	1
1	HEAD GARLIC, SEPARATED INTO CLOVES	1
3 TBSP	VEGETABLE OIL	45 ML
2 TBSP	CHOPPED FRESH ROSEMARY OR THYME	30 ML
	SALT AND FRESHLY GROUND BLACK PEPPER	

PREHEAT OVEN TO 425°F (220°C). LINE A RIMMED BAKING SHEET WITH FOIL. SPREAD CARROTS, PARSNIPS, BEETS, SWEET POTATO, RED ONION AND GARLIC OUT ON PREPARED BAKING SHEET, KEEPING BEETS TO ONE SIDE SO THEY DON'T STAIN THE OTHER VEGGIES. DRIZZLE WITH OIL AND TOSS WITH YOUR HANDS TO COAT. SPREAD OUT IN A SINGLE LAYER AND SPRINKLE WITH ROSEMARY. SEASON TO TASTE WITH SALT AND PEPPER. ROAST FOR 30 MINUTES, STIRRING ONCE OR TWICE, UNTIL VEGETABLES ARE TENDER AND GOLDEN ON THE EDGES. SERVE IMMEDIATELY. SERVES 8.

BUTTERNUT SQUASH WITH SNOW PEAS AND RED PEPPER

IF THE SOFT TEXTURE OF A SQUASH PURÉE DOESN'T APPEAL TO YOU, TRY THIS EASY STIR-FRY INSTEAD.

I TBSP	VEGETABLE OIL	15 ML
5 CUPS	PREPARED BUTTERNUT SQUASH (SEE TIP, BELOW)	1.25 L
4 OZ	SNOW PEAS, ENDS TRIMMED	125 G
I	RED BELL PEPPER, CUT INTO THIN STRIPS	I
I TBSP	PACKED BROWN SUGAR	15 ML
1½ TSP	GRATED GINGERROOT	7 ML
	SALT AND FRESHLY GROUND BLACK PEPPER	

IN A LARGE NONSTICK SKILLET, HEAT OIL OVER MEDIUM-HIGH HEAT. COOK SQUASH, STIRRING, FOR 3 TO 4 MINUTES OR UNTIL ALMOST TENDER. ADD SNOW PEAS, RED PEPPER, BROWN SUGAR AND GINGER. COOK, STIRRING OFTEN, FOR 2 MINUTES OR UNTIL VEGETABLES ARE TENDER-CRISP. SEASON TO TASTE WITH SALT AND PEPPER. SERVES 4.

TIP: TO PREPARE SQUASH, PEEL IT WITH A VEGETABLE PEELER OR PARING KNIFE. CUT INTO LENGTHWISE QUARTERS AND SEED. CUT INTO THIN 1½- BY ¼-INCH (4 BY 0.5 CM) PIECES.

SWEET POTATO OVEN FRIES

THE KEY TO GREAT OVEN FRIES IS TO CUT THE
SWEET POTATOES INTO THIN STRIPS AND ROAST THEM
AT A HIGH TEMPERATURE IN A SINGLE LAYER ON THE
BAKING SHEET. IF THICKLY CUT, THE FRIES DON'T
CRISP PROPERLY — THEY STEAM INSTEAD.

3	SWEET POTATOES (2 LBS/1 KG)	3
2 TBSP	OLIVE OIL	30 ML
1 TSP	PACKED BROWN SUGAR	5 ML
$\frac{1}{2}$ TSP	CHILI POWDER	2 ML
$\frac{1}{4}$ TSP	SALT	1 ML
$\frac{1}{4}$ TSP	FRESHLY GROUND BLACK PEPPER	1 ML
$\frac{1}{4}$ TSP	GROUND CUMIN	1 ML
$\frac{1}{4}$ TSP	PAPRIKA	1 ML

PREHEAT OVEN TO 425°F (220°C), WITH RACK POSITIONED
IN UPPER THIRD OF OVEN. LINE A LARGE RIMMED BAKING
SHEET WITH FOIL. PEEL SWEET POTATOES AND CUT
LENGTHWISE INTO $\frac{1}{2}$-INCH (1 CM) SLICES. CUT SLICES
INTO $\frac{1}{2}$-INCH (1 CM) THICK STRIPS. PLACE IN A BOWL.
POUR IN OLIVE OIL AND TOSS TO COAT EVENLY. IN A
SMALL BOWL, COMBINE BROWN SUGAR, CHILI POWDER,
SALT, PEPPER, CUMIN AND PAPRIKA. SPRINKLE EVENLY
OVER SWEET POTATOES AND TOSS TO COAT. ARRANGE
SEASONED POTATOES IN A SINGLE LAYER ON PREPARED
BAKING SHEET. ROAST IN UPPER THIRD OF OVEN, USING
A SPATULA TO TURN FRIES OVER A FEW TIMES DURING
ROASTING, FOR ABOUT 30 MINUTES OR UNTIL GOLDEN
AND CRISP. SERVE IMMEDIATELY. SERVES 4.

Fudge Drops (page 321)

Apple Blondies with Brown Sugar Frosting (page 324)

Two-Tone Dream Bars (page 330)

Blackberry Peach Cobbler (page 338)

OVEN FRENCH FRIES

IF YOU LOVE FRENCH FRIES (AND WHO DOESN'T?), BUT YOU'RE CONCERNED ABOUT CALORIES, HERE'S THE NEXT BEST THING TO DEEP FRYING.

4	LARGE (OR 6 MEDIUM) RUSSET POTATOES (ABOUT 2 LBS/1 KG)	4
2 TBSP	OLIVE OR VEGETABLE OIL	30 ML
	SALT	

PREHEAT OVEN TO 450°F (230°C). GREASE 2 RIMMED BAKING SHEETS. PEEL POTATOES AND CUT INTO LONG STRIPS, 1/2-INCH (1 CM) IN DIAMETER. RINSE IN SEVERAL CHANGES OF COLD WATER TO REMOVE STARCH. COVER WITH COLD WATER UNTIL READY TO COOK. DRAIN WELL; WRAP IN A CLEAN, DRY KITCHEN TOWEL TO DRY POTATOES THOROUGHLY. PLACE POTATOES ON PREPARED BAKING SHEETS; DRIZZLE WITH OIL, SPRINKLE WITH SALT AND TOSS TO COAT EVENLY. ARRANGE IN A SINGLE LAYER. ROAST FOR 25 TO 30 MINUTES, STIRRING OCCASIONALLY, UNTIL TENDER AND GOLDEN BROWN. SERVES 4.

TIP: DARK RIMMED BAKING SHEETS ATTRACT THE OVEN HEAT AND WILL ROAST THE POTATOES FASTER AND GIVE THEM A MORE INTENSE COLOR THAN SHINY ALUMINUM ONES.

FLUFFY GARLIC MASHED POTATOES

THE SECRET TO THESE CREAMY MASHED POTATOES IS BUTTERMILK. IT ADDS A TANGY FLAVOR AND KEEPS THE POTATOES MOIST SO THEY REHEAT BEAUTIFULLY THE NEXT DAY.

6	LARGE RUSSET OR YUKON GOLD POTATOES (ABOUT 3 LBS/1.5 KG)	6
2 TBSP	BUTTER OR OLIVE OIL	30 ML
2	CLOVES GARLIC, FINELY CHOPPED (OR TO TASTE)	2
1/2 CUP	MILK	125 ML
3/4 CUP	BUTTERMILK OR SOUR CREAM (APPROX.)	175 ML
	SALT AND FRESHLY GROUND BLACK PEPPER OR FRESHLY GRATED NUTMEG	

PEEL POTATOES AND CUT INTO 3-INCH (7.5 CM) CHUNKS. IN A LARGE SAUCEPAN, COOK POTATOES IN BOILING SALTED WATER UNTIL TENDER, ABOUT 20 MINUTES OR UNTIL FORK-TENDER. (YUKON GOLD POTATOES TAKE A FEW MINUTES LONGER.) DRAIN WELL AND RETURN TO SAUCEPAN. PLACE OVER LOW HEAT AND DRY FOR 1 TO 2 MINUTES. PRESS POTATOES THROUGH A FOOD MILL OR RICER, MASH WITH POTATO MASHER OR USE AN ELECTRIC MIXER AT LOW SPEED UNTIL VERY SMOOTH. (DO NOT USE A FOOD PROCESSOR OR THE POTATOES WILL TURN INTO GLUE.) IN A SMALL SAUCEPAN, HEAT BUTTER AND GARLIC OVER MEDIUM-LOW HEAT FOR 1 TO 2 MINUTES; DO NOT LET GARLIC BROWN. ADD MILK AND HEAT UNTIL PIPING HOT. BEAT GARLIC MIXTURE INTO POTATOES ALONG WITH ENOUGH BUTTERMILK OR SOUR CREAM TO MAKE

A SMOOTH PURÉE. ADJUST SEASONING WITH SALT AND PEPPER OR NUTMEG TO TASTE. PLACE OVER MEDIUM HEAT, STIRRING OCCASIONALLY, UNTIL POTATOES ARE PIPING HOT. CAN BE MADE A FEW HOURS AHEAD AND REHEATED. BEAT IN ADDITIONAL MILK OR BUTTERMILK TO MAKE POTATOES CREAMY, IF NECESSARY. SERVES 6.

VARIATION
ROASTED GARLIC MASHED POTATOES: BEAT IN A WHOLE BULB OF ROASTED GARLIC (INSTEAD OF FRESH GARLIC). IT MAY SEEM LIKE A LOT, BUT ONCE ROASTED, GARLIC LOSES ITS HARSH TASTE AND BECOMES VERY MILD AND BUTTERY.

I'M NOT 50. I'M 18 WITH 32 YEARS OF EXPERIENCE.

CREAMY MASHED POTATO CASSEROLE

EVERYONE'S FAVORITE DO-AHEAD MASHED POTATO CASSEROLE — PERFECT FOR A ROAST TURKEY OR ROAST BEEF FAMILY DINNER. FOR LUMP-FREE MASHED POTATOES, USE A FOOD MILL OR RICER INSTEAD OF A POTATO MASHER.

6	LARGE RUSSET POTATOES (ABOUT 3 LBS/1.5 KG) (SEE TIPS, OPPOSITE)	6
4 OZ	LIGHT CREAM CHEESE, SOFTENED, CUBED	125 G
3/4 CUP	HOT MILK (APPROX.)	175 ML
	SALT AND FRESHLY GRATED NUTMEG	
1/2 CUP	SHREDDED CHEDDAR CHEESE	125 ML
1/4 CUP	FINE DRY BREAD CRUMBS	60 ML
1/2 TSP	PAPRIKA	2 ML

PREHEAT OVEN TO 350°F (180°C). GREASE AN 8-CUP (2 L) CASSEROLE DISH. PEEL POTATOES AND CUT INTO 3-INCH (7.5 CM) CHUNKS. IN A LARGE SAUCEPAN OF BOILING SALTED WATER, COOK POTATOES FOR 20 TO 25 MINUTES OR UNTIL FORK-TENDER. DRAIN WELL AND RETURN TO SAUCEPAN. PLACE OVER LOW HEAT AND DRY FOR 1 TO 2 MINUTES. PRESS POTATOES THROUGH A FOOD MILL OR RICER, MASH WITH POTATO MASHER OR USE AN ELECTRIC MIXER AT LOW SPEED UNTIL VERY SMOOTH. (DO NOT USE A FOOD PROCESSOR OR THE POTATOES WILL TURN INTO GLUE.) BEAT IN CREAM CHEESE AND MILK UNTIL SMOOTH; SEASON TO TASTE WITH SALT AND NUTMEG. SPREAD EVENLY IN PREPARED CASSEROLE DISH. (CASSEROLE CAN BE COOLED, COVERED AND REFRIGERATED FOR UP

TO 2 DAYS AT THIS POINT; INCREASE BAKING TIME BY
IO MINUTES.)

IN A SMALL BOWL, COMBINE CHEDDAR CHEESE, BREAD
CRUMBS AND PAPRIKA. SPRINKLE EVENLY OVER POTATOES.
BAKE, UNCOVERED, FOR 40 TO 50 MINUTES OR UNTIL TOP
IS GOLDEN AND A KNIFE INSERTED IN CENTER IS HOT TO
THE TOUCH. SERVES 6.

TIP: THE TYPE OF POTATOES USED DETERMINES HOW
FLUFFY YOUR MASHED POTATOES WILL BE. THE STARCHY
RUSSET, OR BAKING, VARIETY PRODUCES FLUFFY MASHED
POTATOES. YELLOW-FLESHED POTATOES, SUCH AS YUKON
GOLD, HAVE A SLIGHTLY BUTTERY TASTE AND MAKE
DELICIOUS MASHED POTATOES WITH A CREAMIER TEXTURE.
REGULAR WHITE POTATOES ALSO MAKE A CREAMY PURÉE,
ALTHOUGH NOT AS FLAVORFUL. NEW POTATOES ARE
NOT SUITABLE FOR MASHING AS THEY DON'T HAVE THE
STARCH CONTENT OF STORAGE POTATOES.

BASMATI RICE WITH GINGER

GINGER AND AROMATIC SPICES ADD WONDERFUL FLAVOR TO BASMATI RICE. SERVE THIS ALONGSIDE A CURRY DISH MADE WITH CHICKEN, LAMB OR LENTILS.

1½ CUPS	BASMATI RICE	375 ML
1 TBSP	BUTTER OR OIL	15 ML
1	SMALL ONION, FINELY CHOPPED	1
1 TBSP	MINCED GINGERROOT	15 ML
1	STICK CINNAMON, BROKEN IN HALF	1
1	LARGE BAY LEAF, BROKEN IN HALF	1
1 TSP	SALT	5 ML
¼ CUP	CHOPPED FRESH CILANTRO (OR 2 TBSP/30 ML CHIVES OR GREEN ONIONS)	60 ML

PLACE RICE IN SIEVE AND RINSE. TRANSFER TO A BOWL AND ADD WATER TO COVER. LET SOAK FOR 15 MINUTES. DRAIN. IN A MEDIUM SAUCEPAN, MELT BUTTER OVER MEDIUM HEAT. COOK ONION, GINGER, CINNAMON AND BAY LEAF, STIRRING, FOR 2 MINUTES OR UNTIL ONION IS SOFTENED. ADD RICE, 2¼ CUPS (550 ML) WATER AND SALT; BRING TO A BOIL. REDUCE HEAT TO LOW, COVER AND SIMMER FOR 10 MINUTES OR UNTIL WATER IS ABSORBED. LET STAND, UNCOVERED, FOR 5 MINUTES. FLUFF RICE WITH A FORK AND REMOVE AND DISCARD CINNAMON STICK AND BAY LEAF. TRANSFER TO SERVING DISH AND SPRINKLE WITH CILANTRO. SERVES 6.

TIP: ALWAYS RINSE AND SOAK BASMATI RICE TO REMOVE EXCESS STARCH. THIS RESULTS IN A LESS STICKY, MORE FLUFFY RICE WHEN COOKED.

HERB RICE PILAF

THIS HERB-INFUSED RICE MAKES THE PERFECT ACCOMPANIMENT TO A WIDE RANGE OF DISHES. TRY IT WITH FISH, CHICKEN, BEEF, LAMB OR PORK.

2 TBSP	BUTTER	30 ML
1	SMALL ONION, FINELY CHOPPED	1
1	CLOVE GARLIC, MINCED	1
1/2 TSP	DRIED THYME	2 ML
	FRESHLY GROUND BLACK PEPPER	
1 1/2 CUPS	LONG-GRAIN WHITE RICE	375 ML
3 CUPS	HEARTY BEEF STOCK (PAGE 43) OR READY-TO-USE BEEF BROTH	750 ML
1	SMALL RED BELL PEPPER, FINELY CHOPPED	1
1/4 CUP	CHOPPED FRESH PARSLEY	60 ML

IN A LARGE SAUCEPAN, MELT BUTTER OVER MEDIUM HEAT. ADD ONION, GARLIC, THYME AND PEPPER; COOK, STIRRING OFTEN, FOR 3 MINUTES OR UNTIL SOFTENED. ADD RICE AND STOCK; BRING TO A BOIL. REDUCE HEAT TO LOW; COVER AND SIMMER FOR 15 MINUTES OR UNTIL MOST OF STOCK IS ABSORBED. STIR IN RED PEPPER; COVER AND COOK FOR 7 TO 9 MINUTES OR UNTIL RICE IS TENDER. STIR IN PARSLEY; LET STAND, UNCOVERED, FOR 5 MINUTES. SERVES 6 TO 8.

VARIATION

SAFFRON RICE PILAF: SUBSTITUTE 1/4 TSP (1 ML) CRUSHED SAFFRON THREADS FOR THE THYME.

WILD AND BROWN RICE PILAF

1/2 CUP	WILD RICE	125 ML
3 CUPS	CHICKEN STOCK (PAGE 42) OR READY-TO-USE CHICKEN BROTH, DIVIDED	750 ML
2 TBSP	BUTTER	30 ML
1	ONION, FINELY CHOPPED	1
1 1/2 TSP	CHOPPED FRESH THYME (OR 1/2 TSP/2 ML DRIED)	7 ML
1 CUP	LONG-GRAIN BROWN RICE	250 ML
1	RED BELL PEPPER, FINELY DICED	1
1/3 CUP	COARSELY CHOPPED PECANS (OPTIONAL)	75 ML
1/4 CUP	CHOPPED FRESH PARSLEY	60 ML
	SALT AND FRESHLY GROUND BLACK PEPPER	

RINSE WILD RICE UNDER COLD WATER. PLACE IN SMALL SAUCEPAN WITH 1 CUP (250 ML) OF STOCK. BRING TO A BOIL, REDUCE HEAT AND SIMMER, COVERED, FOR 15 MINUTES OR UNTIL MOST OF STOCK IS ABSORBED. IN A MEDIUM SAUCEPAN, HEAT BUTTER OVER MEDIUM-HIGH HEAT. ADD ONION AND THYME AND COOK, STIRRING OFTEN, FOR 2 MINUTES OR UNTIL ONION IS SOFTENED. ADD PARTIALLY COOKED WILD RICE, BROWN RICE AND THE REMAINING STOCK; BRING TO A BOIL. REDUCE HEAT TO LOW, COVER AND SIMMER FOR 20 MINUTES OR UNTIL RICE IS ALMOST TENDER. STIR IN RED PEPPER AND COOK FOR 5 MINUTES OR UNTIL LIQUID IS ABSORBED. LET STAND, UNCOVERED, FOR 5 MINUTES. FLUFF RICE WITH A FORK AND STIR IN PECANS (IF USING) AND PARSLEY. SEASON TO TASTE WITH SALT AND PEPPER. SERVES 6.

DESSERTS & SWEET TREATS

CHOCOLATE CHIP REFRIGERATOR COOKIES

ONCE YOU'VE TRIED THESE, YOU'LL NEVER BUY ANOTHER ROLL OF SLICE 'N' BAKE CHOCOLATE CHIP COOKIES. THEY ARE DELICIOUS AND VERY EASY TO MAKE.

2 3/4 CUPS	ALL-PURPOSE FLOUR	675 ML
I TSP	BAKING SODA	5 ML
1/4 TSP	BAKING POWDER	I ML
1/4 TSP	SALT	I ML
I CUP	BUTTER, SOFTENED	250 ML
I CUP	PACKED BROWN SUGAR	250 ML
1/2 CUP	GRANULATED SUGAR	125 ML
2	LARGE EGGS	2
I TSP	VANILLA EXTRACT	5 ML
I CUP	SEMISWEET CHOCOLATE CHIPS	250 ML
1/2 CUP	FINELY CHOPPED PECANS	125 ML

ON A SHEET OF WAXED PAPER OR IN A BOWL, COMBINE FLOUR, BAKING SODA, BAKING POWDER AND SALT. SET ASIDE. IN A LARGE BOWL, USING AN ELECTRIC MIXER ON MEDIUM SPEED, BEAT BUTTER AND BROWN AND GRANULATED SUGARS UNTIL LIGHT AND CREAMY, ABOUT 3 MINUTES. ADD EGGS, ONE AT A TIME, BEATING WELL AFTER EACH ADDITION. ADD VANILLA. ON LOW SPEED, GRADUALLY ADD FLOUR MIXTURE, BEATING UNTIL BLENDED. WITH A WOODEN SPOON, STIR IN CHOCOLATE CHIPS AND PECANS. DIVIDE DOUGH INTO HALVES. SHAPE EACH INTO A ROLL 12 INCHES (30 CM) LONG. WRAP AND CHILL UNTIL FIRM, AT LEAST 4 HOURS.

FIFTEEN MINUTES BEFORE YOU'RE READY TO BAKE, PREHEAT OVEN TO 350°F (180°C). CUT ROLLS INTO $\frac{1}{4}$-INCH (0.5 CM) SLICES. PLACE ABOUT 2 INCHES (5 CM) APART ON A BAKING SHEET. BAKE FOR 8 TO 12 MINUTES OR UNTIL LIGHT GOLDEN. LET COOL FOR 5 MINUTES ON SHEET; TRANSFER TO A WIRE RACK AND LET COOL COMPLETELY. MAKES ABOUT 8 DOZEN COOKIES.

TIP: WHEN CHILLING, WRAP DOUGH IN WAXED PAPER OR PLASTIC WRAP.

TIP: THE CHOCOLATE CHIPS MAKE CUTTING A BIT DIFFICULT, BUT NOT TO WORRY. IF THE ROUNDS AREN'T EVEN, RESHAPE THEM ON THE BAKING SHEET WITH YOUR FINGERS. THE COOKIES WILL LOOK GREAT WHEN BAKED AND TASTE EVEN BETTER.

TIP: ROLLS OF COOKIE DOUGH CAN ALSO BE FROZEN. THAW FOR ABOUT AN HOUR AT ROOM TEMPERATURE OR IN THE REFRIGERATOR OVERNIGHT, UNTIL THE DOUGH CAN BE SLICED EASILY.

VARIATION: USE MILK CHOCOLATE CHIPS OR MINIATURE SEMISWEET CHOCOLATE CHIPS.

VARIATION: OMIT NUTS OR REPLACE PECANS WITH YOUR FAVORITE NUT.

SCRUMPTIOUS OATMEAL COOKIES

³⁄₄ CUP	BUTTER, SOFTENED	175 ML
1¹⁄₄ CUPS	PACKED BROWN SUGAR	300 ML
2	LARGE EGGS	2
1 TSP	VANILLA EXTRACT	5 ML
1¹⁄₄ CUPS	ALL-PURPOSE FLOUR	300 ML
¹⁄₂ TSP	BAKING SODA	2 ML
¹⁄₄ TSP	SALT	1 ML
1¹⁄₂ CUPS	LARGE-FLAKE (OLD-FASHIONED) ROLLED OATS	375 ML
³⁄₄ CUP	SLICED ALMONDS OR CHOPPED PECANS	175 ML
³⁄₄ CUP	DRIED CHERRIES, DRIED CRANBERRIES, RAISINS OR CHOCOLATE CHIPS	175 ML

PREHEAT OVEN TO 350°F (180°C). GREASE BAKING SHEETS OR LINE WITH PARCHMENT PAPER. IN A LARGE BOWL, USING AN ELECTRIC MIXER, CREAM BUTTER AND BROWN SUGAR UNTIL FLUFFY; BEAT IN EGGS AND VANILLA UNTIL INCORPORATED. IN ANOTHER BOWL, STIR TOGETHER FLOUR, BAKING SODA AND SALT. STIR INTO BUTTER MIXTURE, MIXING WELL. STIR IN ROLLED OATS, ALMONDS AND DRIED CHERRIES. DROP BY HEAPING TABLESPOONFULS (15 ML) ABOUT 2 INCHES (5 CM) APART ONTO PREPARED BAKING SHEETS AND FLATTEN WITH A FORK. BAKE ONE SHEET AT A TIME ON MIDDLE RACK FOR 12 TO 14 MINUTES OR UNTIL EDGES ARE GOLDEN. LET COOL FOR 5 MINUTES ON SHEET; TRANSFER TO A WIRE RACK AND LET COOL COMPLETELY. MAKES 36 COOKIES.

PEANUT BUTTER COOKIES

THESE CRISP COOKIES ARE SURE TO SATISFY A CRAVING FOR SOMETHING SWEET AND INDULGENT.

1/2 CUP	BUTTER, SOFTENED	125 ML
2/3 CUP	SMOOTH PEANUT BUTTER	150 ML
1 CUP	PACKED BROWN SUGAR	250 ML
1	LARGE EGG	1
1 TSP	VANILLA EXTRACT	5 ML
1 3/4 CUPS	ALL-PURPOSE FLOUR	425 ML
1/2 TSP	BAKING SODA	2 ML
1/4 TSP	SALT	1 ML

PREHEAT OVEN TO 375°F (190°C). LIGHTLY GREASE BAKING SHEETS. IN A LARGE BOWL, USING AN ELECTRIC MIXER, CREAM BUTTER, PEANUT BUTTER AND BROWN SUGAR UNTIL FLUFFY. BEAT IN EGG AND VANILLA UNTIL INCORPORATED. IN ANOTHER BOWL, STIR TOGETHER FLOUR, BAKING SODA AND SALT. STIR INTO CREAMED MIXTURE UNTIL COMBINED. FORM INTO 1-INCH (2.5 CM) BALLS AND PLACE 2 INCHES (5 CM) APART ON PREPARED BAKING SHEETS. USING THE TINES OF A FORK, FLATTEN BY MAKING CRISSCROSS PATTERNS ON TOPS. BAKE ONE SHEET AT A TIME ON MIDDLE RACK FOR 11 TO 13 MINUTES OR UNTIL LIGHT GOLDEN. TRANSFER TO A WIRE RACK TO COOL. MAKES 40 COOKIES.

TIP: THE BROWN SUGAR YOU USE IN RECIPES IS TOTALLY YOUR PREFERENCE. BROWN SUGAR COMES IN BOTH LIGHT AND DARK BROWN. DARK BROWN SUGAR IS NOTICEABLY DARKER IN COLOR AND HAS A STRONGER MOLASSES TASTE.

CHUNKY CHOCOLATE SHORTBREAD

THIS CRISP SHORTBREAD COOKIE HAS LOTS OF CRUNCH FROM THE NUTS AND A GREAT CHOCOLATE FLAVOR FROM THE CHOPPED CHOCOLATE.

1 CUP	BUTTER, SOFTENED	250 ML
1/2 CUP	SUPERFINE GRANULATED SUGAR (SEE TIP, BELOW)	125 ML
1 3/4 CUPS	ALL-PURPOSE FLOUR	425 ML
1/4 CUP	CORNSTARCH	60 ML
4	SQUARES (1 OZ/28 G EACH) BITTERSWEET CHOCOLATE, COARSELY CHOPPED	4
2/3 CUP	COARSELY CHOPPED PECANS, TOASTED	150 ML

PREHEAT OVEN TO 350°F (180°C). IN A BOWL, BEAT BUTTER AND SUGAR UNTIL LIGHT AND CREAMY. COMBINE FLOUR AND CORNSTARCH. STIR INTO BUTTER MIXTURE, MIXING WELL. STIR IN CHOCOLATE AND PECANS. PRESS EVENLY INTO A 13- BY 9-INCH (33 BY 23 CM) CAKE PAN. BAKE UNTIL LIGHTLY BROWNED AROUND EDGES, 30 TO 35 MINUTES. LET COOL COMPLETELY IN PAN ON A WIRE RACK. CUT INTO BARS OR SQUARES. MAKES 20 TO 54 BARS OR 24 SQUARES.

TIP: IF YOU DON'T HAVE SUPERFINE SUGAR, WHIRL REGULAR GRANULATED SUGAR IN A BLENDER OR FOOD PROCESSOR UNTIL FINE.

FUDGE DROPS

THESE YUMMY DROPS ARE CRISP ON THE OUTSIDE WITH A CHEWY MIDDLE. THEY HAVE LOTS OF CHOCOLATE, NUTS AND COCONUT THROUGHOUT.

I CUP	SEMISWEET CHOCOLATE CHIPS	250 ML
2	LARGE EGG WHITES	2
PINCH	SALT	PINCH
1/2 TSP	WHITE VINEGAR	2 ML
1/2 TSP	VANILLA EXTRACT	2 ML
1/2 CUP	GRANULATED SUGAR	125 ML
1/2 CUP	UNSWEETENED FLAKED COCONUT	125 ML
1/2 CUP	CHOPPED PECANS	125 ML

PREHEAT OVEN TO 350°F (180°C). GREASE A BAKING SHEET OR LINE IT WITH PARCHMENT PAPER. IN A SMALL SAUCEPAN OVER LOW HEAT, MELT CHOCOLATE CHIPS, STIRRING UNTIL SMOOTH. SET ASIDE TO COOL. IN A SMALL BOWL, USING AN ELECTRIC MIXER ON HIGH SPEED, BEAT EGG WHITES, SALT, VINEGAR AND VANILLA UNTIL FROTHY. GRADUALLY ADD SUGAR, 2 TBSP (30 ML) AT A TIME, BEATING UNTIL STIFF, SHINY PEAKS FORM. WITH A SPATULA, FOLD IN COCONUT AND NUTS GENTLY BUT THOROUGHLY. FOLD IN MELTED CHOCOLATE JUST UNTIL MIXTURE IS LIGHTLY MARBLED. DROP MIXTURE BY TABLESPOONFULS (15 ML) ABOUT 2 INCHES (5 CM) APART ON PREPARED BAKING SHEET. BAKE FOR 12 TO 16 MINUTES OR UNTIL DRY ON TOP. LET COOL COMPLETELY ON SHEET. MAKES ABOUT 2 1/2 DOZEN COOKIES.

BROWNIE OVERLOAD

THIS IS THE ULTIMATE BROWNIE. IT'S A REAL HIT AT BAKE SALES. YOU COULDN'T STIR ANY MORE INGREDIENTS INTO THE BATTER IF YOU TRIED.

1 CUP	BUTTER	250 ML
2½ CUPS	COARSELY CHOPPED BITTERSWEET CHOCOLATE, DIVIDED	625 ML
2 CUPS	ALL-PURPOSE FLOUR	500 ML
½ CUP	UNSWEETENED COCOA POWDER, SIFTED	125 ML
1 TSP	BAKING SODA	5 ML
½ TSP	SALT	2 ML
4	LARGE EGGS	4
1 CUP	GRANULATED SUGAR	250 ML
1 CUP	PACKED BROWN SUGAR	250 ML
2 TSP	VANILLA EXTRACT	10 ML
2 CUPS	COARSELY CHOPPED DELUXE MIXED NUTS (ABOUT 8 OZ/250 G)	500 ML
1 CUP	DRIED CRANBERRIES	250 ML

PREHEAT OVEN TO 350°F (180°C). GREASE A 13- BY 9-INCH (33 BY 23 CM) BAKING PAN. IN A SAUCEPAN OVER LOW HEAT, MELT BUTTER AND 1½ CUPS (375 ML) CHOCOLATE, STIRRING CONSTANTLY, UNTIL SMOOTH. REMOVE FROM HEAT. LET COOL FOR 10 MINUTES. COMBINE FLOUR, COCOA, BAKING SODA AND SALT. MIX WELL. IN A BOWL, USING AN ELECTRIC MIXER ON MEDIUM SPEED, BEAT EGGS, GRANULATED AND BROWN SUGARS AND VANILLA UNTIL THICK AND CREAMY, ABOUT 2 MINUTES. ADD MELTED CHOCOLATE MIXTURE AND MIX ON LOW SPEED UNTIL BLENDED. STIR IN FLOUR MIXTURE, MIXING JUST TO

COMBINE. STIR IN NUTS, THE REMAINING CHOCOLATE AND CRANBERRIES AND MIX WELL (THE BATTER WILL BE VERY THICK). SPREAD EVENLY IN PREPARED PAN. BAKE UNTIL SET, 30 TO 35 MINUTES. LET COOL COMPLETELY IN PAN ON A WIRE RACK. CUT INTO BARS OR SQUARES. MAKES 20 TO 54 BARS OR SQUARES.

TIP: TO EASE CLEANUP, RATHER THAN COMBINING THE DRY INGREDIENTS IN A BOWL, PLACE A LARGE PIECE OF WAXED PAPER ON THE COUNTER. SPREAD THE FLOUR ON THE PAPER. FILL A FINE SIEVE WITH THE COCOA POWDER, BAKING SODA AND SALT AND TAP UNTIL ALL HAVE SIFTED THROUGH TO THE FLOUR. USING THE PAPER AS A FUNNEL, TRANSFER THE DRY INGREDIENTS TO THE CHOCOLATE MIXTURE. THAT WAY, THERE'S ONE LESS BOWL TO WASH.

TIP: WHEN BAKING, ALWAYS USE EGGS AT ROOM TEMPERATURE TO OBTAIN THE BEST VOLUME.

TIP: THIS METHOD DIFFERS FROM SOME BROWNIES IN THAT THE EGGS ARE BEATEN THOROUGHLY, RESULTING IN A BEAUTIFUL, SHINY TOP.

TIP: ALWAYS SIFT COCOA BEFORE USING TO GET RID OF ANY LUMPS THAT HAVE FORMED DURING STORAGE.

VARIATION: REPLACE THE DRIED CRANBERRIES WITH DRIED CHERRIES OR RAISINS.

VARIATION: SUBSTITUTE AN EQUAL QUANTITY OF GOOD-QUALITY CHOCOLATE CHIPS FOR THE CHOPPED CHOCOLATE.

APPLE BLONDIES WITH BROWN SUGAR FROSTING

BOTH THE FROSTING AND THE BLONDIE ARE SCRUMPTIOUS. YOU'LL HAVE A TOUGH TIME DECIDING WHICH YOU LIKE BEST.

BLONDIE

2/3 CUP	BUTTER, SOFTENED	150 ML
2 CUPS	PACKED BROWN SUGAR	500 ML
2	LARGE EGGS	2
1 TSP	VANILLA EXTRACT	5 ML
2 CUPS	ALL-PURPOSE FLOUR	500 ML
2 TSP	BAKING POWDER	10 ML
1/4 TSP	SALT	1 ML
1 CUP	CHOPPED PEELED APPLES	250 ML
3/4 CUP	CHOPPED WALNUTS	175 ML

BROWN SUGAR FROSTING

1/2 CUP	BUTTER	125 ML
1 CUP	PACKED BROWN SUGAR	250 ML
1/4 CUP	MILK OR CREAM	60 ML
2 CUPS	CONFECTIONERS' (ICING) SUGAR, SIFTED	500 ML

BLONDIE: PREHEAT OVEN TO 350°F (180°C). GREASE A 13- BY 9-INCH (33 BY 23 CM) BAKING PAN. IN A LARGE BOWL, USING AN ELECTRIC MIXER ON MEDIUM SPEED, BEAT BUTTER, BROWN SUGAR, EGGS AND VANILLA UNTIL THICK AND SMOOTH, ABOUT 3 MINUTES. COMBINE FLOUR, BAKING POWDER AND SALT. ADD TO BUTTER MIXTURE ON LOW SPEED, MIXING UNTIL BLENDED. STIR IN APPLES AND NUTS, MIXING WELL. SPREAD EVENLY IN PREPARED PAN. BAKE

UNTIL SET AND GOLDEN, 25 TO 30 MINUTES. LET COOL COMPLETELY IN PAN ON A WIRE RACK.

BROWN SUGAR FROSTING: IN A SMALL SAUCEPAN OVER LOW HEAT, MELT BUTTER. STIR IN BROWN SUGAR AND MILK. BRING MIXTURE JUST TO A BOIL THEN REMOVE FROM HEAT AND LET COOL TO LUKEWARM. STIR IN CONFECTIONERS' SUGAR, MIXING UNTIL SMOOTH. SPREAD EVENLY OVER BAR. LET STAND UNTIL FROSTING IS FIRM ENOUGH TO CUT. CUT INTO BARS OR SQUARES. MAKES 20 TO 54 BARS OR SQUARES.

TIP: THIS FROSTING IS VERY SOFT WHEN FIRST MIXED, WHICH MAKES IT VERY NICE TO SPREAD. IT FIRMS UP ON COOLING.

TIP: CHOOSE APPLES THAT ARE CRISP, TART AND NOT TOO MOIST. GRANNY SMITH, GOLDEN DELICIOUS AND SPARTANS ARE GOOD CHOICES FOR THIS RECIPE.

VARIATION: OMIT THE FROSTING IF YOU PREFER A PLAIN APPLE WALNUT BLONDIE.

VARIATION: IF YOU'RE NOT A FAN OF NUTS, OMIT THE WALNUTS.

IT DOESN'T MATTER IF THE
GLASS IS HALF EMPTY OR HALF FULL.
THERE IS CLEARLY ROOM FOR MORE WINE.

MILK CHOCOLATE PECAN BROWNIES

THIS PAIRING OF CHUNKS OF MILK CHOCOLATE AND PECANS IN A DARK CHOCOLATE BROWNIE IS A PERENNIAL FAVORITE.

7	SQUARES (1 OZ/28 G EACH) UNSWEETENED CHOCOLATE, CHOPPED	7
3	SQUARES (1 OZ/28 G EACH) SEMISWEET CHOCOLATE, CHOPPED	3
1 CUP	BUTTER	250 ML
2 CUPS	PACKED BROWN SUGAR	500 ML
4	LARGE EGGS	4
1 CUP	ALL-PURPOSE FLOUR	250 ML
3/4 TSP	BAKING POWDER	3 ML
1/2 TSP	SALT	2 ML
1 CUP	MILK CHOCOLATE CHIPS	250 ML
1 1/4 CUPS	COARSELY CHOPPED PECANS	300 ML

PREHEAT OVEN TO 350°F (180°C). GREASE A 13- BY 9-INCH (33 BY 23 CM) BAKING PAN. IN A SAUCEPAN OVER LOW HEAT, MELT UNSWEETENED AND SEMISWEET CHOCOLATE AND BUTTER, STIRRING CONSTANTLY, UNTIL SMOOTH. REMOVE FROM HEAT. WHISK IN BROWN SUGAR UNTIL SMOOTH. ADD EGGS, ONE AT A TIME, WHISKING LIGHTLY AFTER EACH ADDITION. COMBINE FLOUR, BAKING POWDER AND SALT. STIR INTO CHOCOLATE MIXTURE, MIXING WELL. STIR IN MILK CHOCOLATE CHIPS AND PECANS. SPREAD EVENLY IN PREPARED PAN. BAKE JUST UNTIL SET, 25 TO 30 MINUTES. LET COOL COMPLETELY IN PAN ON A WIRE RACK. CUT INTO BARS OR SQUARES. MAKES 20 TO 54 BARS OR SQUARES.

LUSCIOUS LEMON SQUARES

THESE CLASSY LEMON TREATS WITH A SHORTBREAD
CRUST ARE ALWAYS APPRECIATED WHEN FRIENDS ARE
INVITED FOR A FRESH-BREWED CUP OF TEA OR COFFEE.

I CUP	ALL-PURPOSE FLOUR	250 ML
1/4 CUP	GRANULATED SUGAR	60 ML
1/2 CUP	BUTTER, CUT INTO PIECES	125 ML

FILLING

2	LARGE EGGS	2
I CUP	GRANULATED SUGAR	250 ML
2 TBSP	ALL-PURPOSE FLOUR	30 ML
1/2 TSP	BAKING POWDER	2 ML
PINCH	SALT	PINCH
I TBSP	GRATED LEMON ZEST	15 ML
1/4 CUP	FRESHLY SQUEEZED LEMON JUICE	60 ML
	CONFECTIONERS' (ICING) SUGAR	

PREHEAT OVEN TO 350°F (180°C). LINE AN 8-INCH (20 CM)
SQUARE BAKING PAN WITH PARCHMENT PAPER OR GREASED
FOIL (SEE TIP, PAGE 329). IN A BOWL, COMBINE FLOUR AND
SUGAR; CUT IN BUTTER WITH A PASTRY BLENDER TO MAKE
COARSE CRUMBS. PRESS INTO BOTTOM OF BAKING PAN.
BAKE FOR 15 MINUTES OR UNTIL LIGHT GOLDEN. LET COOL
ON RACK.

FILLING: IN A BOWL, BEAT EGGS WITH SUGAR; STIR IN
FLOUR, BAKING POWDER, SALT, LEMON ZEST AND JUICE.
POUR OVER BASE. BAKE FOR 25 TO 30 MINUTES OR UNTIL
FILLING IS SET AND LIGHT GOLDEN. PLACE PAN ON A WIRE
RACK TO COOL. DUST WITH CONFECTIONERS' SUGAR; CUT
INTO SMALL SQUARES. MAKES 36 SQUARES.

FABULOUS DATE SQUARES

THIS VERSION OF DATE SQUARES HAS A
BURST OF LEMON IN THE FILLING, WHICH ONLY
ENHANCES ITS TRADITIONAL APPEAL.

FILLING

3 CUPS	CHOPPED PITTED DATES (ABOUT 12 OZ/375 G)	750 ML
1 CUP	WATER	250 ML
1/4 CUP	PACKED BROWN SUGAR	60 ML
1 TSP	GRATED LEMON ZEST	5 ML

CRUMB LAYER

1 1/2 CUPS	QUICK-COOKING ROLLED OATS	375 ML
1 CUP	ALL-PURPOSE FLOUR	250 ML
3/4 CUP	PACKED BROWN SUGAR	175 ML
1/2 TSP	BAKING POWDER	2 ML
1/4 TSP	SALT	1 ML
3/4 CUP	COLD BUTTER, CUT INTO PIECES	175 ML

FILLING: PREHEAT OVEN TO 350°F (180°C). LINE AN 8-INCH
(20 CM) SQUARE BAKING PAN WITH PARCHMENT PAPER
OR GREASED FOIL (SEE TIP, OPPOSITE). IN A SAUCEPAN,
COMBINE DATES, WATER, BROWN SUGAR AND LEMON
ZEST. PLACE OVER MEDIUM HEAT; COOK, STIRRING, FOR
8 TO 10 MINUTES OR UNTIL DATES FORM A SMOOTH
PASTE. LET COOL.

CRUMB LAYER: IN A BOWL, COMBINE ROLLED OATS, FLOUR,
BROWN SUGAR, BAKING POWDER AND SALT. CUT IN BUTTER
WITH A PASTRY CUTTER OR FORK TO MAKE COARSE
CRUMBS. PRESS TWO-THIRDS OF CRUMB MIXTURE IN
BOTTOM OF PREPARED PAN. SPREAD EVENLY WITH DATE

FILLING. SPRINKLE WITH THE REMAINING CRUMB MIXTURE, PRESSING DOWN LIGHTLY. BAKE FOR 25 TO 30 MINUTES OR UNTIL GOLDEN. LET COOL ON A WIRE RACK; CUT INTO SQUARES. MAKES 16 SQUARES.

TIP: RATHER THAN USING A KNIFE TO CUT STICKY DRIED FRUITS LIKE DATES AND APRICOTS, YOU'LL FIND THAT KITCHEN SCISSORS DO A BETTER JOB.

TIP: TO REMOVE BARS EASILY, LINE THE BAKING PAN WITH PARCHMENT PAPER OR HEAVY-DUTY FOIL. CUT THE SHEET OF PARCHMENT PAPER OR FOIL THE SAME WIDTH AS THE PAN, WITH LENGTH TO OVERHANG. FIT INTO THE PAN WITH THE ENDS OVERHANGING THE EDGES.

WE INTERRUPT THIS MARRIAGE
TO BRING YOU THE HOCKEY SEASON.

TWO-TONE DREAM BARS

ALTHOUGH THESE LOOK AND SOUND QUITE DECADENT, THEY'RE ACTUALLY FAIRLY LIGHT IN TEXTURE — THE PERFECT SOLUTION FOR MIDNIGHT CRAVINGS.

CRUST

1 CUP	ALL-PURPOSE FLOUR	250 ML
1/3 CUP	GRANULATED SUGAR	75 ML
1/3 CUP	BUTTER, SOFTENED	75 ML

FILLING

1 CUP	GRAHAM WAFER CRUMBS	250 ML
1 CUP	SEMISWEET CHOCOLATE CHIPS	250 ML
2/3 CUP	COARSELY CHOPPED WALNUTS	150 ML
1	CAN (14 OZ OR 300 ML) SWEETENED CONDENSED MILK	1

TOPPING

8	SQUARES (1 OZ/28 G EACH) WHITE CHOCOLATE, CHOPPED	8
2 TBSP	BUTTER	30 ML

CRUST: PREHEAT OVEN TO 350°F (180°C). GREASE A 13- BY 9-INCH (33 BY 23 CM) BAKING PAN. IN A BOWL, COMBINE FLOUR, SUGAR AND BUTTER. USING AN ELECTRIC MIXER ON LOW SPEED, BEAT UNTIL CRUMBLY. PRESS EVENLY INTO PREPARED PAN. BAKE UNTIL GOLDEN AROUND THE EDGES, 10 TO 12 MINUTES.

FILLING: IN A BOWL, COMBINE GRAHAM WAFER CRUMBS, CHOCOLATE CHIPS, WALNUTS AND CONDENSED MILK, MIXING UNTIL WELL BLENDED. DROP MIXTURE BY SPOONFULS OVER WARM BASE. SPREAD EVENLY. BAKE

UNTIL TOP IS LIGHTLY BROWNED, ABOUT 20 MINUTES. LET COOL COMPLETELY IN PAN ON A WIRE RACK.

TOPPING: IN A SAUCEPAN OVER LOW HEAT, MELT WHITE CHOCOLATE AND BUTTER, STIRRING CONSTANTLY, UNTIL SMOOTH. SPREAD EVENLY OVER BARS. CHILL UNTIL CHOCOLATE SETS, ABOUT 10 MINUTES. CUT INTO BARS. MAKES 20 TO 54 BARS.

TIP: A SMALL OFFSET SPATULA MAKES SPREADING EASY, ESPECIALLY ON SMALL AREAS SUCH AS THE TOP OF BARS. IT'S ALSO GOOD AT GETTING INTO CORNERS.

TIP: IF YOU PLAN TO FREEZE BARS, WRAP THEM TIGHTLY IN PLASTIC WRAP AND FREEZE FOR UP TO 3 MONTHS. CUT THEM INTO BARS BEFORE FREEZING SO YOU CAN REMOVE THE REQUIRED NUMBER WHENEVER YOU NEED THEM, RATHER THAN HAVING TO THAW OR CUT THE ENTIRE PIECE.

VARIATION: USE YOUR FAVORITE KIND OF CHOCOLATE CHIP FOR THE FILLING IN THIS RECIPE. WHITE AND MILK CHOCOLATE CHIPS ARE ESPECIALLY NICE.

VARIATION: REPLACE THE GRAHAM WAFER CRUMBS WITH VANILLA WAFER CRUMBS.

CARAMEL HONEY PECAN BARS

CRUST

1/2 CUP	PECAN HALVES	125 ML
2 1/2 CUPS	ALL-PURPOSE FLOUR	625 ML
1 CUP	COLD BUTTER, CUBED	250 ML
1/3 CUP	GRANULATED SUGAR	75 ML
1	LARGE EGG, BEATEN	1

FILLING

3 1/2 CUPS	PECAN HALVES	875 ML
3/4 CUP	BUTTER	175 ML
1/2 CUP	LIQUID HONEY	125 ML
3/4 CUP	PACKED BROWN SUGAR	175 ML
1/2 TSP	GROUND CINNAMON	2 ML
1/4 CUP	HEAVY OR WHIPPING (35%) CREAM	60 ML

CRUST: PREHEAT OVEN TO 350°F (180°C). GREASE A 15- BY 10- BY 1-INCH (2 L) JELLY ROLL PAN. IN A FOOD PROCESSOR, PROCESS PECANS UNTIL FINE. ADD FLOUR, BUTTER, BROWN SUGAR AND EGG. PROCESS UNTIL MIXTURE RESEMBLES COARSE CRUMBS. PRESS EVENLY INTO PREPARED PAN. BAKE UNTIL EDGES ARE LIGHTLY BROWNED, 12 TO 15 MINUTES.

FILLING: SPRINKLE PECANS EVENLY OVER HOT CRUST. SET ASIDE. IN LARGE HEAVY SAUCEPAN OVER MEDIUM-HIGH HEAT, MELT BUTTER AND HONEY. ADD BROWN SUGAR AND CINNAMON AND BOIL, STIRRING CONSTANTLY, UNTIL MIXTURE IS A RICH CARAMEL COLOR, 5 TO 7 MINUTES. REMOVE FROM HEAT. STIR IN CREAM, MIXING WELL. POUR EVENLY OVER PECANS. BAKE UNTIL TOP IS BUBBLY, ABOUT 15 MINUTES. LET COOL COMPLETELY IN PAN ON A WIRE RACK. CUT INTO BARS. MAKES 40 TO 48 BARS.

GRANDMA WOODALL'S BAKED LEMON PUDDING CAKE

THIS TANGY CAKE MAKES ITS OWN SAUCE — NO FROSTING REQUIRED.

	BUTTER	
1½ CUPS	GRANULATED SUGAR, DIVIDED	375 ML
½ CUP	ALL-PURPOSE FLOUR	125 ML
½ TSP	BAKING POWDER	2 ML
¼ TSP	SALT	1 ML
3	LARGE EGGS, SEPARATED	3
1½ CUPS	MILK	375 ML
	FINELY GRATED ZEST OF 1 LEMON	
¼ CUP	FRESHLY SQUEEZED LEMON JUICE	60 ML
2 TBSP	BUTTER, MELTED	30 ML

PREHEAT OVEN TO 375°F (190°C). BUTTER A 6-CUP (1.5 L) GLASS OR CERAMIC BAKING DISH. IN A LARGE BOWL, STIR TOGETHER 1 CUP (250 ML) SUGAR, FLOUR, BAKING POWDER AND SALT. IN A SMALL BOWL, STIR TOGETHER EGG YOLKS, MILK, LEMON ZEST, LEMON JUICE AND BUTTER. STIR THE EGG YOLK MIXTURE INTO THE SUGAR MIXTURE UNTIL JUST COMBINED.

IN A CLEAN GLASS OR STAINLESS STEEL BOWL, BEAT EGG WHITES UNTIL SOFT PEAKS FORM. GRADUALLY BEAT IN THE REMAINING SUGAR UNTIL STIFF PEAKS FORM. GENTLY FOLD INTO BATTER. SCRAPE INTO PREPARED BAKING DISH. SET THE DISH IN A ROASTING PAN AND FILL THE PAN HALFWAY WITH WATER. BAKE FOR 45 MINUTES OR UNTIL GOLDEN AND SPRINGY TO THE TOUCH. SERVES 8.

PINEAPPLE UPSIDE-DOWN CAKE

THE UPSIDE-DOWN CAKE — SO POPULAR IN THE 1950S
AND '60S — HAS BEEN MAKING A COMEBACK. THIS IS THE
TRADITIONAL VERSION, BUT OTHER FRUITS, SUCH AS
SLICED PEACHES AND PLUMS, CAN ALSO BE USED.

2 TBSP	BUTTER, MELTED	30 ML
1/3 CUP	PACKED BROWN SUGAR	75 ML
1	CAN (14 OZ/398 ML) PINEAPPLE RINGS	1
1/4 CUP	DRIED CRANBERRIES	60 ML
1 1/3 CUPS	ALL-PURPOSE FLOUR	325 ML
1 1/2 TSP	BAKING POWDER	7 ML
1/4 TSP	SALT	1 ML
6 TBSP	BUTTER, SOFTENED	90 ML
2/3 CUP	GRANULATED SUGAR	150 ML
1	LARGE EGG	1
1 1/2 TSP	GRATED ORANGE ZEST	7 ML
1/2 CUP	MILK	125 ML

PREHEAT OVEN TO 350°F (180°C). GREASE A 9-INCH (23 CM)
ROUND OR SQUARE BAKING DISH OR SPRINGFORM PAN
AND LINE THE BOTTOM WITH PARCHMENT PAPER. DRIZZLE
MELTED BUTTER IN BOTTOM OF PREPARED DISH; SPRINKLE
EVENLY WITH BROWN SUGAR. DRAIN PINEAPPLE AND
RESERVE JUICE FOR ANOTHER USE. ARRANGE PINEAPPLE
RINGS TO FIT SNUGLY IN BOTTOM OF PAN (THERE MAY
BE ONE RING LEFT OVER). PLACE DRIED CRANBERRIES
IN CENTER OF EACH RING. IN A BOWL, STIR TOGETHER
FLOUR, BAKING POWDER AND SALT. IN ANOTHER BOWL,
USING AN ELECTRIC MIXER, CREAM SOFTENED BUTTER
WITH GRANULATED SUGAR UNTIL SMOOTH. BEAT IN EGG

AND ORANGE ZEST UNTIL INCORPORATED. BEAT IN FLOUR MIXTURE ALTERNATELY WITH MILK TO MAKE A SMOOTH BATTER. SPOON OVER PINEAPPLE, SPREADING EVENLY. BAKE ON MIDDLE RACK FOR 30 TO 35 MINUTES OR UNTIL A TESTER INSERTED IN THE CENTER COMES OUT CLEAN. LET COOL IN PAN FOR 5 MINUTES. INVERT ONTO SERVING PLATE. SERVE WARM OR AT ROOM TEMPERATURE. SERVES 6.

TIP: THE BROWN SUGAR YOU USE IN RECIPES IS TOTALLY YOUR PREFERENCE. BROWN SUGAR COMES IN BOTH LIGHT AND DARK BROWN. DARK BROWN SUGAR IS NOTICEABLY DARKER IN COLOR AND HAS A STRONGER MOLASSES TASTE.

WOULDN'T IT BE GREAT IF WE COULD PUT OURSELVES IN THE DRYER FOR 10 MINUTES AND COME OUT WRINKLE-FREE AND TWO SIZES SMALLER?

DELECTABLE APPLE-CRANBERRY COCONUT CRISP

SLOW COOKER RECIPE

4 CUPS	SLICED PEELED APPLES	1 L
2 CUPS	CRANBERRIES, THAWED IF FROZEN	500 ML
1/2 CUP	GRANULATED SUGAR	125 ML
1 TBSP	CORNSTARCH	15 ML
1/2 TSP	GROUND CINNAMON	2 ML
2 TBSP	FRESHLY SQUEEZED LEMON JUICE OR PORT WINE	30 ML

COCONUT TOPPING

1/2 CUP	PACKED BROWN SUGAR	125 ML
1/2 CUP	QUICK-COOKING ROLLED OATS	125 ML
1/4 CUP	SWEETENED FLAKED COCONUT	60 ML
1/4 CUP	BUTTER	60 ML

LIGHTLY GREASE THE STONEWARE OF A MEDIUM (ABOUT 3 1/2-QUART) SLOW COOKER. IN A BOWL, COMBINE APPLES, CRANBERRIES, SUGAR, CORNSTARCH, CINNAMON AND LEMON JUICE OR PORT. MIX WELL AND TRANSFER TO PREPARED STONEWARE.

COCONUT TOPPING: IN A SEPARATE BOWL, COMBINE BROWN SUGAR, ROLLED OATS, COCONUT AND BUTTER. USING TWO FORKS OR YOUR FINGERS, COMBINE UNTIL CRUMBLY. SPREAD OVER APPLE MIXTURE. PLACE A CLEAN TEA TOWEL, FOLDED IN HALF (SO YOU HAVE TWO LAYERS), OVER TOP OF STONEWARE. COVER AND COOK ON HIGH FOR 3 TO 4 HOURS, UNTIL CRISP IS HOT AND BUBBLY. SERVE WITH WHIPPED CREAM OR ICE CREAM, IF DESIRED. SERVES 6 TO 8.

BLUEBERRY PEACH TOFFEE CRISP

NOT ONLY ARE PEACHES AND BLUEBERRIES
A DELICIOUS COMBINATION, THEY CREATE FRESH
INTEREST IN GRANDMA'S CRISP, TRADITIONALLY
MADE WITH CHERRIES OR APPLES. THE ADDITION OF
TOFFEE BITS ADDS FLAVOR AND CRUNCH TO THE
OLD-FASHIONED TOPPING. SERVE WITH VANILLA
ICE CREAM OR A BIG DOLLOP OF WHIPPED CREAM.

1	CAN (14 OZ/398 ML) SLICED PEACHES, DRAINED (OR 2 CUPS/500 ML SLICED PEACHES, THAWED IF FROZEN)	1
1	PACKAGE (10 OZ/300 G) FROZEN BLUEBERRIES, THAWED (OR 1 1/2 CUPS/ 375 ML BLUEBERRIES)	1
1/2 CUP	QUICK-COOKING ROLLED OATS	125 ML
1/2 CUP	PACKED BROWN SUGAR	125 ML
1/2 CUP	TOFFEE BITS	125 ML
2 TBSP	COLD BUTTER, CUT INTO BITS	30 ML
1/2 TSP	GROUND CINNAMON	2 ML

PREHEAT OVEN TO 400°F (200°C). GREASE A 6-CUP (1.5 L)
BAKING DISH. ARRANGE PEACHES AND BLUEBERRIES
EVENLY OVER BOTTOM OF PREPARED DISH. IN A BOWL,
COMBINE OATS, BROWN SUGAR, TOFFEE BITS, BUTTER
AND CINNAMON. USING TWO FORKS OR YOUR FINGERS,
COMBINE UNTIL CRUMBLY. SPREAD OVER FRUIT. BAKE
UNTIL TOP IS BROWNED AND FRUIT IS BUBBLING, ABOUT
20 MINUTES. SERVES 6.

VARIATION
RASPBERRY PEACH TOFFEE CRISP: SUBSTITUTE
RASPBERRIES FOR THE BLUEBERRIES.

BLACKBERRY PEACH COBBLER

SLOW COOKER RECIPE

4	PEACHES, PEELED AND SLICED	4
3 CUPS	BLACKBERRIES	750 ML
3/4 CUP	GRANULATED SUGAR	175 ML
1 TBSP	CORNSTARCH	15 ML
1 TBSP	FRESHLY SQUEEZED LEMON JUICE	15 ML

TOPPING

1 1/2 CUPS	ALL-PURPOSE FLOUR	375 ML
2 TSP	BAKING POWDER	10 ML
1 TSP	GRATED LEMON ZEST	5 ML
1/2 TSP	SALT	2 ML
1/2 CUP	COLD BUTTER, CUT INTO 1-INCH (2.5 CM) CUBES	125 ML
1/2 CUP	MILK	125 ML

LIGHTLY GREASE THE STONEWARE OF A MEDIUM (ABOUT 3 1/2-QUART) SLOW COOKER. IN PREPARED STONEWARE, COMBINE PEACHES, BLACKBERRIES, SUGAR, CORNSTARCH AND LEMON JUICE. STIR WELL. COVER AND COOK ON LOW FOR 4 HOURS OR ON HIGH FOR 2 HOURS.

TOPPING: IN A BOWL, COMBINE FLOUR, BAKING POWDER, LEMON ZEST AND SALT. USING YOUR FINGERS OR A PASTRY BLENDER, CUT IN BUTTER UNTIL MIXTURE RESEMBLES COARSE CRUMBS. DRIZZLE WITH MILK AND STIR WITH A FORK UNTIL A BATTER FORMS. DROP BATTER BY SPOONFULS OVER HOT FRUIT. COVER AND COOK ON HIGH FOR 1 HOUR, UNTIL A TESTER INSERTED IN THE CENTER COMES OUT CLEAN. SERVES 6.

RHUBARB BETTY

SLOW COOKER RECIPE

THERE ARE MANY VARIATIONS ON THIS TRADITIONAL DESSERT, WHICH IS BASICALLY BAKED FRUIT WITH A SEASONED TOPPING. THIS VERSION IS PARTICULARLY SIMPLE AND GOOD. SERVE WITH SWEETENED WHIPPED CREAM OR SOY CREAMER.

1/3 CUP	MELTED BUTTER OR MARGARINE	75 ML
2 CUPS	FRESH BREAD CRUMBS (ABOUT HALF A LARGE LOAF)	500 ML
4 CUPS	CHOPPED RHUBARB (1-INCH/2.5 CM CHUNKS)	1 L
1 CUP	GRANULATED SUGAR	250 ML
1 TBSP	ALL-PURPOSE FLOUR	15 ML
1 TSP	GROUND CINNAMON	5 ML
	GRATED ZEST AND JUICE OF 1 ORANGE	

LIGHTLY GREASE THE STONEWARE OF A MEDIUM (ABOUT 3-QUART) SLOW COOKER. IN A BOWL, COMBINE BUTTER AND BREAD CRUMBS. SET ASIDE. IN ANOTHER BOWL, COMBINE RHUBARB, SUGAR, FLOUR AND CINNAMON. IN PREPARED SLOW COOKER STONEWARE, LAYER ONE-THIRD OF THE BREAD CRUMB MIXTURE, THEN HALF THE RHUBARB MIXTURE. REPEAT LAYERS OF BREAD CRUMBS AND FRUIT, THEN FINISH WITH A LAYER OF BREAD CRUMBS ON TOP. POUR ORANGE ZEST AND JUICE OVER TOP. PLACE A CLEAN TEA TOWEL, FOLDED IN HALF (SO YOU HAVE TWO LAYERS), OVER TOP OF STONEWARE TO ABSORB MOISTURE. COVER AND COOK ON HIGH FOR 3 HOURS, UNTIL BUBBLY AND BROWN. SERVES 6.

CHERRY CLAFOUTI

CLAFOUTI IS BASICALLY A FRUIT PANCAKE THAT IS OFTEN SERVED AS A DESSERT IN FRENCH BISTROS. EATEN WARM, IT IS COMFORTING AND DELICIOUS.

1	CAN (14 OZ/398 ML) PITTED CHERRIES IN SYRUP, DRAINED (ABOUT 1⅓ CUPS/325 ML)	1
2	LARGE EGGS	2
½ CUP	MILK	125 ML
¼ CUP	GRANULATED SUGAR	60 ML
3 TBSP	ALL-PURPOSE FLOUR	45 ML
2 TBSP	BUTTER, MELTED	30 ML
1 TSP	GRATED LEMON ZEST	5 ML
1 TSP	ALMOND EXTRACT	5 ML
PINCH	SALT	PINCH
	CONFECTIONERS' (ICING) SUGAR	

PREHEAT OVEN TO 375°F (190°C). GREASE A 9-INCH (23 CM) SQUARE BAKING OR GRATIN DISH (ABOUT 2 INCHES/5 CM DEEP) OR A SMALL GLASS PIE PLATE. SPREAD CHERRIES OVER BOTTOM OF PREPARED DISH. IN A BLENDER OR FOOD PROCESSOR, COMBINE EGGS, MILK, SUGAR, FLOUR, BUTTER, LEMON ZEST, ALMOND EXTRACT AND SALT. BLEND UNTIL MIXTURE IS SMOOTH, ABOUT 1 MINUTE. POUR OVER CHERRIES. BAKE UNTIL PUFFED AND GOLDEN, ABOUT 25 MINUTES. SERVE WARM. DUST WITH CONFECTIONERS' SUGAR JUST BEFORE SERVING. SERVES 4.

BAKED APPLES WITH BUTTERED RUM SAUCE

WHAT COULD BE MORE QUINTESSENTIALLY COMFORT FOOD THAN HOMESPUN BAKED APPLES? HERE, THEY TAKE ON AN ENTERTAINING FLAIR WITH A SPLASH OF RUM. THEY'RE TERRIFIC SERVED WARM.

6	APPLES (SUCH AS SPARTAN OR CORTLAND)	6
1/2	LEMON	1/2
1/3 CUP	CHOPPED PECANS	75 ML
1/3 CUP	SULTANA RAISINS OR DRIED CRANBERRIES	75 ML
2 TBSP	BUTTER, CUT INTO PIECES	30 ML
3/4 CUP	PACKED BROWN SUGAR	175 ML
1/4 TSP	FRESHLY GRATED NUTMEG	1 ML
1/4 CUP	DARK RUM OR BRANDY	60 ML

PREHEAT OVEN TO 350°F (180°C). CORE APPLES; PEEL SKINS STARTING AT TOP, LEAVING 1-INCH (2.5 CM) BAND AT THE BOTTOM. RUB APPLES WITH LEMON HALF TO PREVENT BROWNING. ARRANGE IN A SHALLOW BAKING DISH JUST LARGE ENOUGH TO HOLD THEM. IN A BOWL, COMBINE PECANS AND RAISINS; STUFF INTO APPLE CAVITIES AND TOP WITH BUTTER. IN A SMALL SAUCEPAN, COMBINE BROWN SUGAR, 1/3 CUP (75 ML) WATER AND NUTMEG; BRING TO A BOIL OVER MEDIUM HEAT, STIRRING UNTIL SUGAR IS DISSOLVED. STIR IN RUM. POUR OVER APPLES. BAKE, BASTING OCCASIONALLY WITH SAUCE, FOR 45 TO 50 MINUTES OR UNTIL APPLES ARE JUST TENDER WHEN PIERCED WITH A KNIFE. PLACE IN INDIVIDUAL SERVING DISHES AND DRIZZLE WITH SAUCE. SERVE WARM.

SERVES 6.

GINGER STRAWBERRY FOOL

AN OLD ENGLISH DESSERT, FOOLS
ARE DELICIOUS AND VERY EASY TO MAKE.

1	PACKAGE (10 OZ/300 G) FROZEN STRAWBERRIES, THAWED (OR 1½ CUPS/ 375 ML STRAWBERRIES)	1
2 TBSP	FINELY CHOPPED CANDIED GINGER	30 ML
2 TBSP	FROZEN ORANGE JUICE CONCENTRATE OR ORANGE-FLAVORED LIQUEUR (SUCH AS COINTREAU)	30 ML
1 CUP	HEAVY OR WHIPPING (35%) CREAM	250 ML
¼ CUP	CONFECTIONERS' (ICING) SUGAR	60 ML

IN A FOOD PROCESSOR, COMBINE STRAWBERRIES, GINGER AND ORANGE JUICE CONCENTRATE. PROCESS JUST UNTIL MIXTURE IS THE CONSISTENCY OF WELL-MASHED FRUIT. (IT SHOULD NOT BE SMOOTH.) IN A BOWL, USING AN ELECTRIC MIXER, BEAT CREAM WITH SUGAR UNTIL SOFT PEAKS FORM. GENTLY FOLD IN STRAWBERRY MIXTURE. SPOON INTO 4 PARFAIT OR WINE GLASSES AND REFRIGERATE UNTIL WELL CHILLED, ABOUT 1 HOUR. SERVES 4.

TIP: YOU CAN ALSO USE STEM GINGER IN SYRUP, AVAILABLE IN MANY SPECIALTY STORES. USE THE SAME QUANTITY OF GINGER AND SUBSTITUTE 2 TBSP (30 ML) OF THE SYRUP FOR THE FROZEN ORANGE JUICE CONCENTRATE.

TIP: GARNISH WITH A SPRIG OF FRESH MINT, IF AVAILABLE.

VARIATION
STRAWBERRY ORANGE FOOL: SUBSTITUTE 1 TSP (5 ML) GRATED ORANGE ZEST OR 2 TBSP (30 ML) CHOPPED CANDIED ORANGE PEEL FOR THE GINGER.

KIDS' FAVORITE CHOCOLATE PUDDING

FAST-AND-EASY RECIPE

WHY RELY ON EXPENSIVE STORE-BOUGHT PUDDINGS WHEN YOU CAN MAKE NOURISHING HOMEMADE ONES THAT TAKE LITTLE TIME? MILK PUDDINGS ARE ALSO A GREAT WAY TO BOOST CALCIUM.

1/3 CUP	GRANULATED SUGAR	75 ML
1/4 CUP	CORNSTARCH	60 ML
2 1/4 CUPS	WHOLE MILK	550 ML
1/3 CUP	SEMISWEET CHOCOLATE CHIPS	75 ML
1 TSP	VANILLA EXTRACT	5 ML

IN A MEDIUM SAUCEPAN, WHISK TOGETHER SUGAR AND CORNSTARCH; ADD MILK, WHISKING UNTIL SMOOTH. PLACE OVER MEDIUM HEAT; COOK, STIRRING, FOR 5 MINUTES OR UNTIL MIXTURE COMES TO A FULL BOIL; COOK FOR 15 SECONDS. REMOVE FROM HEAT. STIR IN CHOCOLATE CHIPS AND VANILLA; BLEND UNTIL SMOOTH. POUR PUDDING INTO INDIVIDUAL SERVING DISHES. LET COOL SLIGHTLY; COVER SURFACE WITH PLASTIC WRAP TO PREVENT SKINS FROM FORMING ON SURFACE. REFRIGERATE. SERVES 4.

TIP: WHOLE MILK GIVES A CREAMIER CONSISTENCY THAN LOWER-FAT MILK IN THIS EASY DESSERT.

VARIATION
BUTTERSCOTCH PUDDING: SUBSTITUTE 1/2 CUP (125 ML) BUTTERSCOTCH CHIPS FOR THE CHOCOLATE CHIPS AND REDUCE THE SUGAR TO 1/4 CUP (60 ML).

CINNAMON RAISIN BREAD PUDDING

12	SLICES CINNAMON RAISIN BREAD (1 LB/500 G LOAF)	12
6	LARGE EGGS	6
2 CUPS	WHOLE MILK	500 ML
1 CUP	HALF-AND-HALF (10%) CREAM	250 ML
3/4 CUP	GRANULATED SUGAR	175 ML
2 TSP	VANILLA EXTRACT	10 ML

TOPPING

2 TBSP	GRANULATED SUGAR	30 ML
1/2 TSP	GROUND CINNAMON	2 ML

PREHEAT OVEN TO 375°F (190°C). PLACE BREAD SLICES IN A SINGLE LAYER ON RIMMED BAKING SHEETS AND LIGHTLY TOAST IN OVEN FOR 10 TO 12 MINUTES. LET COOL. LEAVE OVEN ON. GENEROUSLY BUTTER A 10-CUP (2.5 L) SHALLOW BAKING DISH. CUT BREAD INTO CUBES AND PLACE IN PREPARED BAKING DISH. IN A BOWL, WHISK TOGETHER EGGS, MILK, CREAM, SUGAR AND VANILLA. POUR OVER BREAD. LET SOAK FOR 10 MINUTES, PRESSING DOWN GENTLY WITH A SPATULA.

TOPPING: IN A SMALL BOWL, COMBINE SUGAR AND CINNAMON. SPRINKLE OVER BREAD MIXTURE. PLACE BAKING DISH IN A LARGE, SHALLOW ROASTING PAN OR A DEEP BROILER PAN; ADD ENOUGH BOILING WATER TO COME HALFWAY UP SIDES OF DISH. BAKE FOR 45 TO 50 MINUTES OR UNTIL TOP IS PUFFED AND CUSTARD IS SET IN CENTER. REMOVE FROM WATER BATH; PLACE ON A WIRE RACK TO COOL. SERVE WARM OR AT ROOM TEMPERATURE.

SERVES 8.

OLD-FASHIONED RICE PUDDING

SLOW COOKER RECIPE

THIS RECIPE IS ADAPTED FROM A 19TH-CENTURY ENGLISH RECIPE THAT DESCRIBES THE SECRET TO A DELICIOUSLY CREAMY PUDDING AS "VERY SLOW AND PROLONGED BAKING ON THE OUTER EDGES OF THE FIRE." TODAY, THE SLOW COOKER TAKES ALL THE GUESSWORK OUT OF THE TASK. IT'S ALSO REMARKABLY EASY. JUST MIX THE INGREDIENTS TOGETHER AND TURN THE COOKER ON — YOU DON'T EVEN HAVE TO PRECOOK THE RICE!

3/4 CUP	LONG-GRAIN RICE	175 ML
3 CUPS	MILK OR SOY MILK	750 ML
3/4 CUP	GRANULATED SUGAR	175 ML
3/4 TSP	GROUND CINNAMON	3 ML
PINCH	SALT	PINCH
1/3 CUP	MELTED BUTTER OR MARGARINE	75 ML
	VANILLA-FLAVORED WHIPPED CREAM OR SOY CREAMER (OPTIONAL)	

IN A COLANDER, RINSE RICE THOROUGHLY UNDER COLD WATER. PLACE IN A SMALL (MAXIMUM 3 1/2-QUART) SLOW COOKER. ADD MILK, SUGAR, CINNAMON AND SALT. STIR TO COMBINE. POUR BUTTER OVER RICE MIXTURE. COVER AND COOK ON HIGH FOR 4 HOURS, UNTIL RICE IS TENDER AND PUDDING IS CREAMY. WHEN READY TO SERVE, SPOON INTO INDIVIDUAL DESSERT BOWLS AND TOP WITH WHIPPED CREAM (IF USING). SERVES 6.

TIP: IF YOU CHOOSE TO HALVE THIS RECIPE, USE A SMALL (1 1/2- TO 3-QUART) SLOW COOKER.

SIMPLE HOT FUDGE SAUCE

WHO KNEW SUCH DECADENCE COULD BE SO EASY!

1 CUP	HEAVY OR WHIPPING (35%) CREAM	250 ML
1/2 CUP	CHOPPED DARK OR SEMISWEET CHOCOLATE	125 ML

IN A SMALL SAUCEPAN, HEAT CREAM OVER MEDIUM HEAT JUST UNTIL STEAMING. PLACE CHOCOLATE IN A BOWL AND POUR HOT CREAM OVERTOP. LET STAND FOR 1 MINUTE, THEN WHISK UNTIL SMOOTH. MAKES 1 CUP (250 ML).

TIP: EXTRA SAUCE CAN BE STORED IN AN AIRTIGHT CONTAINER IN THE REFRIGERATOR FOR UP TO 1 WEEK. REHEAT IN THE MICROWAVE OR OVER LOW HEAT ON THE STOVETOP.

VARIATION

MOCHA SAUCE: ADD 1 TSP (5 ML) INSTANT COFFEE GRANULES.

VARIATION

CHOCOLATE MINT SAUCE: ADD 1 TSP (5 ML) PEPPERMINT EXTRACT.

EASY CARAMEL SAUCE

CARAMEL SAUCE IS EASIER THAN IT SOUNDS — JUST HEAT, STIR AND POUR OVER YOUR FAVORITE CAKE OR ICE CREAM. IT'S ALSO ACCEPTABLE TO EAT IT STRAIGHT FROM THE JAR, WITH A SPOON!

1/2 CUP	PACKED BROWN SUGAR	125 ML
1/2 CUP	HEAVY OR WHIPPING (35%) CREAM	125 ML
1/4 CUP	BUTTER	60 ML
PINCH	SALT	PINCH
1 TSP	VANILLA EXTRACT	5 ML

IN A SMALL SAUCEPAN, COMBINE BROWN SUGAR, CREAM, BUTTER AND SALT; BRING TO A SIMMER. SIMMER, STIRRING OCCASIONALLY, FOR 5 MINUTES. REMOVE FROM HEAT AND STIR IN VANILLA. MAKES 1 CUP (250 ML).

TIP: CARAMEL SAUCE STORES WELL IN A JAR OR AIRTIGHT CONTAINER IN THE REFRIGERATOR FOR UP TO 2 WEEKS. WARM IT IN THE MICROWAVE OR OVER LOW HEAT ON THE STOVETOP.

VARIATION: DURING THE HOLIDAYS, SWAP EGGNOG FOR THE CREAM, FOR A FESTIVE FLAVOR.

TRIPLE-BERRY SUNDAE SAUCE

USE THIS QUICK SAUCE TO FANCY UP A BOWL OF
VANILLA ICE CREAM, OR ON YOGURT OR PANCAKES.

2 CUPS	FROZEN MIXED BERRIES (OR BLUEBERRIES, STRAWBERRIES AND RASPBERRIES)	500 ML
2 TBSP	GRANULATED SUGAR	30 ML
2 TSP	CORNSTARCH	10 ML
1 TBSP	FRESHLY SQUEEZED LEMON JUICE	15 ML
1 TBSP	WATER	15 ML

PLACE BERRIES IN A MEDIUM SAUCEPAN. MIX TOGETHER
SUGAR AND CORNSTARCH, POUR OVER BERRIES AND TOSS
TO COMBINE. ADD LEMON JUICE AND WATER. COOK OVER
MEDIUM-HIGH HEAT, STIRRING OFTEN, UNTIL BERRIES ARE
THAWED. BRING TO A BOIL, THEN REMOVE FROM HEAT AND
LET COOL COMPLETELY. MAKES 2 CUPS (500 ML).

TIP: EXTRA SAUCE CAN BE STORED IN AN AIRTIGHT
CONTAINER IN THE REFRIGERATOR FOR UP TO 1 WEEK OR
IN THE FREEZER FOR UP TO 4 MONTHS.

Johanna Burkhard
500 Best Comfort Food Recipes
Recipes from this book are found on pages 9,
11–22, 31, 34, 35, 38, 42, 48, 60, 64, 68, 72, 74,
77, 78, 81, 84, 90, 94, 96, 97, 100, 102, 103,
109, 110, 113, 114, 116, 119, 120–22, 128, 129,
143, 144, 150–52, 156, 160–64, 168–71, 176,
180, 182, 186, 188, 191–93, 198, 200, 206, 210,
218, 234, 238, 242, 246, 250, 253, 256, 264,
267, 268, 271, 276–79, 283, 286, 290, 295, 296,
298, 301–3, 305–14, 318, 319, 327–29, 334,
341, 343 and 344.

Judith Finlayson
150 Best Slow Cooker Recipes
Recipes from this book are found on pages 7,
8, 36, 52, 104–7, 130, 134–37, 140, 154, 184,
194–97, 252, 258, 272–75, 280, 288, 336, 338,
339 and 345.

Judith Finlayson
175 Essential Slow Cooker Classics
Recipes from this book are found on pages 33,
50, 54–58 and 66.

Judith Finlayson
The Complete Whole Grains Cookbook
Recipes from this book are found on pages 70,
88 and 91.

Judith Finlayson
The Convenience Cook
Recipes from this book are found on pages 32,
40, 44, 45, 80, 82, 83, 87, 93, 98, 99, 101, 108,
111, 115, 118, 123, 126, 138, 139, 142, 146–49,
165, 172–74, 178, 179, 181, 187, 190, 204,
211–13, 221, 224–27, 231, 232, 235–37, 240,
241, 244, 248, 254, 260–63, 266, 270, 282, 284,
287, 337, 340 and 342.

Judith Finlayson
The Healthy Slow Cooker
A recipe from this book is found on page 43.

Judith Finlayson
The Vegetarian Slow Cooker
Recipes from this book are found on pages 37,
46, 62, 124, 158, 208, 214–17, 222 and 228.

Jill Snider
Bars & Squares
Recipes from this book are found on pages 24,
28–30, 320, 322–26 and 330–32.

Jill Snider
Cookies
Recipes from this book are found on pages 316
and 321.

Julie Van Rosendaal
Recipes by this author, developed for this book,
are found on pages 6, 10, 26, 27, 75, 76, 86,
92, 112, 132, 153, 166, 167, 199, 202, 205,
220, 230, 249, 292–94, 297, 300, 304, 333 and
346–48.

Library and Archives Canada Cataloguing in Publication

Best of Bridge home cooking : 250 easy & delicious recipes.

Includes index.
ISBN 978-0-7788-0514-4 (wire-o hardcover binding)

1. Cooking. 2. Cookbooks. I. Best of Bridge Publishing Ltd., author

TX714.B465 2015   641.5   C2015-903324-1

INDEX